DREAM TREASURE

DREAM TREASURE

Learning the Language of Heaven

I will give you the treasures of darkness, and hidden wealth of secret places, in order that you may know that it is I, the Lord...(Is. 45:3).

Judith A. Doctor, MSW, RN
Gerald R. Doctor, MSEE

Judith Doctor Resources LLC

Published in the United States by

Judith Doctor Resources LLC
6753 Vintage Drive
Hudsonville, MI 49426-9211
www.judithdoctor.com
www.dreamtreasure.us

Dream Treasure
Judith A. Doctor & Gerald R. Doctor

Copyright © 2011 by Gerald R. & Judith A. Doctor
All rights reserved. No duplication allowed without permission from the publisher.

Unless otherwise specified, Scripture taken from the New American Standard Bible Copyright © 1960, 1962, 1963, 1968, 1971, 1972, 1973, 1975, 1977 by The Lockman Foundation. Used by permission.

ISBN: 978-0-9837917-0-6
1. Dreams—Religious aspects—Christianity. 2. Dream interpretation—Symbolic language. 3. Dreams—Holy Spirit—Spiritual life. 4. Dreams—Counseling, Christian.
I. Doctor, Judith A. II. Title.

Printed in the United States of America

Judith Doctor Resources LLC provides educational and inspirational publications and other resources that nurture Christian spiritual maturity and transformative growth through the Holy Spirit.

Cover design: Stanley Doctor
The concept for the cover illustration is based on the renowned biblical dream commonly known as *Jacob's Ladder*. Stanley Doctor is an artist and illustrator living in Boulder Colorado.

To our sons…

Jeff, who has witnessed and validated the odyssey of our lives.
Tim, who has encouraged us to dream big and write this book.
May you also follow your dreams.

Jacob's Ladder

Dreams—and their day-time spiritual partners, visions—are of colossal importance in the story of God relating to His people. Not very long into the narrative of origins and beginnings, the book of Genesis records the visionary experience used by the Creator to jolt Jacob out of daily existence and into prominence on the Middle Eastern stage.

Jacob is a vital character in the history of God's dealings with the Israelites. Most of the Old Testament is about this wandering tribe of people whose behavior is remarkably similar to many of us today—afraid to hear from the Almighty directly, preferring to let our priest or pastor trudge up Mt. Sinai on Sunday mornings to fetch the Word on our behalf.

So how does God get through to this guy running from Esau out in the Luz/Bethel wilderness? A dream. Catch him while his wily mind is quiet. Probably the most famous dream in history is Jacob's dream of a ladder between earth and heaven:

> *(Jacob) took one of the stones of the place and put it under his head, and lay down in that place. And he had a dream, and behold a ladder was set on the earth with its top reaching to heaven; and behold, the angels of God were ascending and descending on it.*
>
> *And behold, the Lord stood above it and said, "I am the Lord, the God of your father Abraham and the God of Isaac; the land on which you lie, I will give it to you and to your descendants…I am with you, and will keep you wherever you go, and will bring you back to this land; for I will not leave you until I have done what I have promised you."*
>
> *Then Jacob awoke from his sleep and said, "Surely the Lord is in this place, and I did not know it" (Genesis 28:11-16).*

Awakening from his nighttime vision, Jacob recognizes that God was speaking to him. He builds an altar using his stone pillow, and there begins his transformation from birthright-stealing rebel into patriarch of a worldwide community of people.

Contents

Foreword xi
Preface xiii
Acknowledgments xvii

Part One Why Consider Dreams? 1

Chapter 1 Authors' Awakening 3
    Dreams offer wise counsel and guidance
    Dreams, God's neglected gift
    Dreams have a divine purpose
    The Holy Spirit is key to understanding dreams

Chapter 2 God Wants Us To Hear His Voice 13
    The cornerstone of Christian dream work
    Discovering ways God speaks to us
    The visual word of God
    Hearing God's voice brings blessings

Chapter 3 Dreams, A Way To Hear God's Voice 25
    God promises to speak through dreams
    Dreams carry blessings from God
    Dreams contain hidden treasure
    The dream is like a bucket

Chapter 4 Dream Robbers 37
    Rogue's gallery of dream robbers
    Modern legacy of dream thievery
    The Holy Spirit brings renewed awareness of dreams
    Dreams are a neglected part of our spiritual heritage
    Reengaging our historical roots

Part Two The Christian Basis Of Dreams 49

Chapter 5 Biblical Record 51
    Biblical attitude values dreams/visions
    God spoke through dreams in the Old Testament
    God spoke through dreams in the New Testament
    God to continue using dreams in the last days
    The scriptural basis for listening to dreams

Chapter 6 Church Fathers 65
    Apostolic Fathers valued dreams as a way to hear God
    Early Church Fathers validated the biblical attitude towards dreams
    Church Doctors embraced dreams
    The Church continued to value dreams for hundreds of years

Chapter 7 Historical Evidence 73
    Dreams influenced music, literature, science, and inventions
    Dreams changed history
    People today are receiving dreams from God
    God still uses dreams to reveal things He wants to give us

Chapter 8 Christian Worldview 83
    Christian orthodoxy validates importance of the spiritual realm
    Rational Christianity denies relevance of supernatural phenomena
    The scriptural perspective recognizes the inner man
    Dreams are essential in the Christian worldview

PART THREE Christian Approach To Dreams 97

Chapter 9 A God-Centered Lens 99
    God speaks to people through dreams
    The Holy Spirit brings the dreams
    Dreams offer relationship with our Creator
    Dreams give us divine revelation
    Dreams carry divine purpose
    Dreams originate from an unseen realm within us
    Dreams contain hidden treasure
    Dreams use a language of pictures and symbols
    Dream interpretation belongs to God
    Dreams contain divine energy
    Dreams require a response
    Dreams are a gift from God

Chapter 10 Biblical Purposes of Dreams 113
    Dreams make God known
    Dreams make God's words known
    Dreams provide divine counsel
    Dreams give godly instruction
    Dreams open our ears, get our attention
    Dreams adjust attitudes, keep us from pride
    Dreams change conduct, behavior
    Dreams keep our soul from death
    Dreams enlighten us with the light of life
    Dreams reveal divine mysteries
    Dreams foretell the future
    Dreams reveal our inner thoughts

Chapter 11 Scriptural Guidelines 133
    Take dreams seriously
    Most dreams cannot be taken literally
    Interpreting dreams requires effort
    Dream work requires applying the heart
    Dreams convey messages important to the heart
    Pay attention to dreams when seeking God on an issue

    Repetitive themes indicate importance
    Share your dreams with friends
    You are the decision-maker
    Recognize the witness of the Holy Spirit
    Dreams require action

Chapter 12   *Spiritual Discernment* 147
    Ignorance of dreams breeds fear
    Dreams help us wage spiritual warfare
    Testing accuracy of interpretations using biblical principles
    Dream work requires trained spiritual senses

PART FOUR   The World Of Dreaming 161

Chapter 13   *Science of Dreaming* 163
    The nature of dreams
    Dreaming essential to mental health
    Dreams are concerned with fundamental life issues
    Sources of dream images
    Structure of the personality
    Four-part dream structure

Chapter 14   *Classifying Dreams* 177
    Common dream categories
    Special types of dreams
    Nightmares
    Death and dying dreams
    Balancing dreams

Chapter 15   *The Language of Dreams* 189
    Symbolism 101
    Ruling categories of symbolism
    Symbolic communication in the Bible
    Why God uses symbolic language
    Symbols touch the heart of man

Chapter 16   *Dream Dynamics* 205
    Figurative expressions
    Personification in dreams
    Role of projection in dreams
    Common dream characters
    Objective or subjective dreams

PART FIVE   Unlocking The Meaning Of Dreams 225

Chapter 17   *Cardinal Rules* 227
    Most dreams are about you
    Dreams reveal something you do not know
    All dreams are not equally valid
    Repetitive themes indicate importance
    Take responsibility for your dream images

    Most dream images come out of your own life
    Pay attention to details
    Begin by assuming dream is symbolic
    Pay attention to intensity of a dream image
    Make personal associations
    Be alert to word plays and puns
    Recognize archetypal figures
    Dreams may carry meaning for different levels of life
    Meaning must come from dreamer

Chapter 18 First Steps 243
    Basic steps of dream work
    Recalling dreams
    Writing down dreams
    TTAQ technique
    Dream journal format

Chapter 19 Exploring The Dream 255
    Five steps for exploring a dream
    Identifying dream elements/images
    Amplifying elements/images
    Making personal associations
    Connecting the elements to your inner life
    Summarizing meaning of dream

Chapter 20 Strategies & Interpretation Techniques 263
    Eleven non-interpretive dream work strategies
    Five imaginative dream interpretation techniques
    Seven symbolic dream interpretation techniques

APPENDIX A Survey Of Attitudes & Beliefs About Dreams 277

APPENDIX B What Is Your Life Situation? 279

APPENDIX C The Holy Spirit 281

APPENDIX D New Testament Words For Dream & Vision 283

APPENDIX E Biblical Blessings Of Dreams 285

APPENDIX F Intuitive & Imaginative Faculties 287

APPENDIX G Dream Exploration Guide 289

Endnotes *297*

Bibliography *305*

Index *309*

About The Authors *319*

Dream Resources *320*

Foreword

Years ago we visited a salt mine beneath the city of Detroit, with tunnels going in every direction and salt all around us, beautiful, white as snow, glistening like ice. To the men working in the maze of tunnels, the salt appeared as a single 30-foot thick mineral layer, waiting to be brought to the surface where it could be used—they were unconcerned with subdivisions and property boundaries on the surface above. Similarly, the core truths that God has for us in dreams acknowledge no religious boundaries. Everyone dreams and everyone benefits.

Many years ago, when I and my dear wife, Lillie, discovered the core truth about dreams, we received invitations from people around the world hungry to hear about the reality of dreams. In *Dream Treasure*, Gerald and Judith Doctor have struck this same vein of truth. As I read this full book on dreams, I realized it contains the elements of all that I had learned about dreams and dream interpretation over the years.

Gerald & Judith, whom we have known for a long time, have gathered all the information needed to understand dreams. Their book is rich and thorough, with a historical background of dreams both in the Scriptures and the Early Church, as well as scriptural principles, personal experiences, and recent research. Much emphasis is given to the role of the Holy Spirit in dream interpretation.

After 45 years of working with dreams, I realize the importance of learning material such as presented in this book. Although there is no limit to what we can learn about dreams, to interpret the dream we must ask God, the author, "What are you saying to me through this picture that you have given me?" This approach reflects the theme of this helpful book—discovering the hidden treasure that God has for us in our dreams.

Herman Riffel

Editor's note:

Originally from a Mennonite background, Herman Riffel served many years as a Baptist pastor, before the Lord called him to travel and lecture on hearing the voice of God. After much intensive studying about how God communicates through dreams, Herman and Lillie worked with people's dreams in fifty countries, teaching in churches across all denominations. Their audiences varied from analysts, psychologists and psychiatrists in Sydney, Australia, to priests, nuns and Gregorian University professors in Rome.

Herman authored several books on hearing the voice of God in dreams. Not long after he wrote this foreword, Herman died in July, 2009, on the eve of his 93rd birthday. His books and other media materials (available at www.cgllcmedia.com) continue to provide insight and encouragement to many people around the world on their spiritual odysseys.

Preface

Back in the 1960s when God's death was reported in the news, the Holy Spirit was being poured out on people around the world. The dynamic presence of God brought a divine touch to millions of people in all faith traditions.[1] This fire of the Spirit created a whole new aliveness in many people, prompting a renewed interest in hearing from God. People aglow with the Spirit began to share dreams and visions they were receiving from God.

Today people are dreaming valuable dreams. As a hospice nurse, I (Judith) heard how families of dying loved ones find comfort from God in their dreams. Working in addiction treatment, I (Judith) listened to dreams of addicts revealing the traumatic roots underlying their addictions. As a counselor, I continue to see how dreams reveal hidden problems and offer solutions to troubled souls.

However, inside the walls of institutional religion, few people are talking about dreams. Why not? Why are God's people afraid to go there? The New Age goes there. Secular humanists go there. Muslims go there. Why do *we* not value dreams as a valid way to hear from God?

Dreams, a vital way to hear from God

Two millennia ago St. Peter boldly asserted at Pentecost that when the Holy Spirit comes, visions, prophecies, and *dreams* will follow. The apostolic church continued this belief, and the writings of the Church Fathers showed their strong conviction in the value of dreams as a vehicle for God to speak to people.

Tertullian believed we get much knowledge from God through dreams; Clement felt that dreams reveal spiritual reality; Origen said dreams give us knowledge of the spiritual world through symbolic awareness; John Chrysostom believed we can depend upon dreams to hear from God.

Now God's people are rediscovering the dream is one way He uses to offer His counsel and wisdom. Listening to dreams brings wholeness and transformative spiritual growth in people's lives. Personally, we have become more spiritually alive and whole. We have encountered the love of our Heavenly Father, received revelation of spiritual truths, seen more clearly who God has made us to be, received healing and comfort, and realized God's divine purpose for us.

The topic of hearing from God through our dreams is a sadly neglected aspect of religious experience today. As a result, God's people are missing out on this vital part of their heritage. The world desperately needs us to reclaim our leadership role in bringing divine counsel and wisdom to our society through people's dreams.

Our voice of personal experience

Since 1991 we have been teaching on how dreams offer us a way to hear God's voice, and this book is an outgrowth of our seminars on this theme. Dream experts, erudite interpreters, or scholarly theologians we are not. Instead, we are ordinary people who have learned to respond to God's voice in our dreams. Between us we enjoy more than 60 years of listening to our dreams and benefiting from God's divine counsel and wisdom in them. What we are sharing with you is not just theory, it's biblical truth we have *experienced*—the things we write about have been tested and they are real in our lives.

Who is this book on dreams for?

We offer our book on dreams to people longing to know the voice of God on a deeply personal level. To troubled souls who cry out for healing and wholeness. To fellow pilgrims who are searching for personal meaning and purpose in life. To spiritual adventurers who are on a quest to *know* the reality of a loving God for themselves. Our book is a gold mine for people moving toward personal wholeness and transformation.

Healing ministries, counselors and clergy

Since a dream may reveal what is wrong in our lives or where we are stuck, it is a great resource for healing ministries, counselors, and clergy. Working with the dreams of troubled or conflicted people may help you discover the roots of their problems and how to guide them to healing and resolution. After attending our dream seminar, a pastor said, "I did not realize how important the dream is to help heal the wounds of our people."

Anybody can do it

Be encouraged; by relying upon the Holy Spirit, we do not need a lot of training to benefit from listening to our dreams—a little understanding, support and encouragement go a long way! You'll find this tour of the world of dreams lively, encouraging and supportive. As you read, ponder and interact with the material in our book, we encourage you to plunge in with abandon. Trust the Lord to reveal what He wants you to know about your dream life.

What this book offers

Our purpose is to provide people with a comprehensive resource manual on how to listen for God's guidance and counsel in dreams. We call our book a *comprehensive resource* because of its prodigious amount of descriptive material, explanatory information, and footnoted references.

Our search into dreams explored a wide variety of sources, primarily Judeo-Christian authors, but also some key works by dream experts, sleep researchers, and depth psychologists, as well as professional journals.

In this book we distill our understanding of these writings and cite authors from a broad perspective of Christian faith traditions, identifying our sources in the End Notes. Through our prolific use of Scriptures, we offer a thorough documentation of the concepts, principles, and practices we offer you.

It is also a manual, a *guide* to experience, because we include strategies and skills, along with techniques and methods to help you unlock the meaning of your dreams. We do not offer a fixed approach to the meaning of specific symbols. Instead we give you practical tools, so *you* can safely uncover the hidden treasure in your own dreams.

Throughout its pages, we include illustrative dream examples from our own experience and explain how they influenced our lives. A great deal can be learned about understanding dreams simply by listening to the dreams of other people.

Our core concepts, principles, and practices are often repeated throughout the book, in the hope that you will remember them and thereby avoid mistakes we made. Truths are retained through repetition—only by reviewing them will they be truly learned. In the appendices, we offer a more in-depth understanding of concepts relevant to the Judeo-Christian use of dreams.

Using the book

We have divided the book into the following five parts, enabling you to quickly identify your areas of interest.

Part One—Introduction: Why Consider Dreams?

In Part One we offer reasons why you need to consider dreams. We describe how we came to pay attention to our dreams as a way to hear from God. Viewed favorably in early Christianity, dreams became devalued over time. Supported by Scripture, the Church Fathers, and historical evidence, we assert that God uses dreams to speak to modern man just as in days of old. We encourage an awakening to the value of dreams in our daily experience.

Part Two—The Christian Basis of Dreams

In Part Two we describe the four foundational pillars that provide the basis for God's people to embrace the dream as a valid way to hear from Him. First is to recognize that the entire scriptural narrative supports belief that God speaks through dreams and visions. The Church Fathers, influential thinkers who developed the basis of our faith tradition, established a strong foundation for valuing our dreams. Down through the ages beneficial dreams have come to people of all religions. The historic Judeo-Christian faith perspective says that valid knowledge can be gained from supernatural phenomena, including dreams and visions.

Part Three—The Christian Approach to Dreams

In Part Three we lay out a framework in which God's people can safely evaluate their dreams, and identify twelve divine purposes of dreams. After identifying core beliefs that are central to a religious approach to dreams, we highlight what the Scriptures tell us about how to break open the dream and discern its message for our lives. Included is a discussion of common fears about dreams and some key principles to enable you to determine the validity of your dream interpretations.

Part Four—The Wonderful World of Dreaming

In Part Four we try to get a handle on the nature of dreaming, origins of symbols appearing in dreams, and how to categorize the myriad types of dreams we experience. We present findings from dream and sleep lab research, and look at how dreams influence our well-being. Included here is a comprehensive study of the symbolic language of dreams—how the imaginative and pictorial language of symbols works. You will learn how to decide if a dream is to be taken objectively or subjectively, and then begin organizing your exploration of dream understanding.

Part Five—Unlocking The Meaning of Dreams

In Part Five, we highlight the cardinal principles, strategies and interpretation techniques for working confidently with your dreams. A step-by-step guide shows how to explore a dream, draw out its meaning, and connect with God's divine purpose in it. Some imaginative and non-interpretive methods are offered to discover the hidden treasure buried in dream images. We continue to stress the importance of following biblical principles and engaging your heart.

Special features

Each chapter is enriched with special features to help you learn, interact, and apply the concepts, principles, practices, and skills essential to unlocking the meaning of your dreams.

Core Concepts: Identifies important concepts and principles to be presented.

Learning Objectives: Establishes desired outcomes as you study the material.

Interactive Learning: Offers exercises to help you interact with the ideas throughout each chapter.

Tips: Highlights ideas vital to understanding dreams.

Your Response: Provides end-of-chapter activities to help you reflect on and evaluate what the material means to you.

Dream Work Skills: Introduces new strategies or techniques to use with dreams.

Dream Work Terminology: Lists new terms introduced in a chapter.

Our invitation

We encourage you to use our book as a springboard to enable you to enter more deeply into the mysterious world of dreams. As you read, ask God to identify the ideas He wants you to reflect on. Underline those that capture your attention. Write in the margins your comments, disagreements, or questions. Check off the boxes to mark the progress of your journey into the exciting field of dreams.

Once you begin unearthing that hidden treasure, you'll never be the same again. May God guide you as you discover the value of dreams as a way to receive His counsel and wisdom for your lives.

Dream on!

Acknowledgments

We acknowledge the many men and women who have influenced our spiritual development and personal growth. Thank you for your insight and revelation you have shared through your teaching and the living example of your lives. From you we learned about the reality of an inner world within us, where Christ dwells.

We give credit to the many authors and teachers whose ideas and wisdom on dreams are woven into the fabric of our lives. We have experienced deeply your truths, and found them to be reliable and trustworthy. Thank you for encouraging us to listen for the voice of our Creator in our dreams. What we learned from you has become part of us. Although it is sometimes extremely difficult to separate our own thoughts and ideas from what we have learned from others, wherever possible we have acknowledged the sources of information we used.

Valerie Dwyer and Dee Beasley offered indispensable assistance with editing our writing. Their careful analysis of the organization, structure, presentation and layout of the material was a tremendous help in getting our thoughts and ideas into readable form. Thank you, friends, for your kind and patient help.

We thank our friends, Frank and Margaret Tagliente, who as fellow pilgrims have witnessed our journey, listened to our dreams, and shared their intuitive knowings with us throughout the years. Thank you, Margaret, for proofreading the manuscript, checking and rechecking its many references.

Special appreciation goes to Ralph Nault, our dear friend and spiritual mentor for over 30 years. Ralph and his wife, Pauline, have traveled with us through the major crises of our lives, supporting us and encouraging us to put our complete trust in the power of God and to be led by the Holy Spirit. Himself a great dreamer, Ralph demonstrates in his own life the relevance of dreams to our experience with God.

PART ONE
Why Consider Dreams?

Why you will find this part helpful

This part helps you discover the amazing truth that dreams are one way God promises to make His words known to us. You will read testimonies of contemporary people who are hearing from God through their dreams.

You will recognize that dreams contain God's counsel and wisdom for our lives—hidden treasure. Also you'll learn the sad truth about how dreams, once highly valued, have been virtually ignored in modern times due largely to scientific reason and rationalism.

PART ONE chapters:
- Authors' Awakening (Chapter 1)
- God Wants Us To Hear His Voice (Chapter 2)
- Dreams, A Way To Hear God's Voice (Chapter 3)
- Dream Robbers (Chapter 4)

PART ONE Why Consider Dreams?

Authors' Awakening   1

I will bless the Lord who has counseled me; Indeed, my mind instructs me in the night (Ps. 16:7).

Core Concepts
- Dreams offer wise counsel and guidance.
- Dreams, God's neglected gift.
- Dreams have a divine purpose.
- The Holy Spirit is key to understanding dreams.

Learning Objectives
At the completion of this chapter, you will be able to:
- ☐ Explain why the dream is called "an invaluable counselor."
- ☐ Discuss the relationship of your current concerns to your dreams.
- ☐ Reflect on the relationship of the Holy Spirit to dreams.
- ☐ Recognize the difference between clear dreams and symbolic dreams.
- ☐ Update your beliefs and attitudes about dreams.

Our journey into the world of dreams

Powerful nighttime visions exploding across our pillows have transformed our lives forever. Based upon our study of the word of God, early church history, the testimony of many people down through the ages, and our own experience, we are absolutely convinced the dream is relevant to our experience with God. The power of the images coming to us in our sleep have enabled us to do things—if you'll pardon the expression—we never dreamed we could do.

Dreams changed our lives

Without discovering the "hidden treasure"[i] in the dream, we would have been far less fruitful in our personal lives and in the kingdom of God. Without God's guidance in the dream, we would not have discovered our gifts and calling. We would probably still be trapped in depression and despair. We would not have been healed and transformed from within.

Without dreams, our marriage would likely have been broken beyond repair. We would not have had the courage to respond to a call from God on our lives, estab-

---
i The term "*hidden treasure*" refers to God's divine guidance, counsel, wisdom, instruction, and knowledge embedded in dreams.

lish Kairos Ministries, Inc., and sell most of our belongings to live and minister in Europe for a year.

Gerald leaves his career

I (Gerald) could never have summoned the courage to leave my high-tech career and find a new way to make a living; I would not understand God's purposes for my life; I would lack the courage to vault my walls of self-defense to keep moving forward in my own personal growth; I never would have been transformed in my attitudes, in my self image. Here is a dream God used to help set me free.

Bluebird of Happiness

Back in the early 1980s, I was in depression, stalled in my high-tech career, and unhappy with my life. When God decided to redirect my life, He knew how to get past the argumentative, educated brain box resting on my shoulders. Catching me while my conscious mind slept, He sent me this dream:

On the 8th floor of a high-tech building, I enter the office of a man named Mr. Sadd. On his desk is a placard which says, "Forecasting." I look out the window at a dull, gray day and notice a bluebird on a limb. I feel delighted.

> ▶ *Dream Work Tip:*
> One of the first steps in understanding our dreams is to start a dream journal where we write down—and sometimes sketch—what we experienced. As Gerald's illustration demonstrates, artistic skills are not necessary. Better to focus on feeling and re-experiencing the dream instead of drawing it perfectly.

Although I knew very little then about symbolic language, one thing stood out clearly: "happiness" for me would require me to step outside the corporate walls. The initial vision I had for my life—to be an engineer—was completed, and no longer worked for me. In a few short months I left my faltering 23-year high-tech career and found a more satisfying way of life: a free lance writer about high-tech.

Judith goes to college

I (Judith) would never have started my first small groups; I would not have discovered my gifts and talents; I would not have ministered in Germany; I would not have a radio program in Germany; I would not have been healed of destructive attitudes; I would not have gone to college and grad school, nor become a Christian counselor.

Without a Degree
I was restless, searching for God's purpose and direction for my life. As a teen, I had a yearning to go to college, but lacking role models, I didn't know how. Plus, I was the oldest of six children, a girl, and "who was I to go to college"? So I went to nursing school, married young, raised children. However, the longing lingered. In the late 1980s, I dreamed:

A voice speaks directly to me, saying, "Without a degree, certain doors will not open for you."

The dream gave me courage to enroll in the university, graduating at age 55. Seven years later I returned for my Masters. Because of these degrees, many new doors opened for me. For example, I was given an hour program on Radio Horeb (Germany), teaching live on inner healing and spiritual growth every month since 2002.

Divine purpose of authors' dreams

Gerald's dream is concerned with his current situation—what's happening in his daily life. Its purpose is to give him divine counsel and wisdom about his work. It also warns him what will happen if he doesn't change his career. It uses symbolic imagery to convey its message.

Judith's dream is also related to her current concerns—what is God's purpose for her life. Its purpose is to give her specific instruction, very clear information, about something she needs to do. It also warns her she will not be able to go through some doors unless she has academic credentials. Classified as a clear dream; it doesn't use any symbolic imagery. It is an auditory vision, occurring while she is asleep.

> **Dream Work Tip:**
> Dreams often come in the context of what is going on in our lives. To understand our dreams, we must first consider our current concerns—prayers, heart issues, recent significant situations, experiences & events.

1. Interactive learning
☐ Do you think the authors' dreams were from God? Yes/No. Explain?
☐ Did their dreams contain *divine* counsel and wisdom? Yes/No. Explain?

Deciphering the wacky images

Our beginning dream exploration felt really awkward. Having never heard a sermon on dreams, those bizarre incidences related over coffee in the morning sure sounded strange sometimes. Images, symbols, and mystical themes spun their yarns for us in the night hours while our minds rested, uninhibited by conscious ego control.

> *Most dreams communicate their messages using images, pictures, and metaphors in a figurative and imaginative way, thus they must not be taken literally (Herman Riffel).*

 Dream Treasure

Dreams, God's forgotten language

On our quest to understand our dreams, we looked to Christian authors Morton Kelsey, John A. Sanford, and Herman Riffel. Sanford's and Kelsey's books established the groundwork for serious consideration of dreams in the Christian community. Sanford's enormously helpful book, *Dreams, God's Forgotten Language*[1], brought home to us the relevance of dreams to our daily experience. He expanded our understanding of the origin and nature of the dream and the types of symbolic figures we might encounter in our dream world.

Dreams, God's neglected gift

Kelsey's scholarly work on the historical validity of dreams in Christianity, *Dreams, The Dark Speech Of The Spirit: A Christian Interpretation*,[2] gave us an understanding of the richness of our faith tradition and why the dream fell into disrepute in the Church. His thorough review of Judeo-Christian attitudes from Old and New Testament times, and also his examination of the beliefs of the Church Fathers regarding dreams, gave us a strong foundation upon which to approach our dreams and their meaning.

We are grateful to the late Herman Riffel for the example of his life and teaching—he helped make it safe for us to listen for the Father's voice while asleep. In his book, *Your Dreams: God's Neglected Gift,* he tells his story of how God awakened him to pay attention to his dreams. A former pastor, he was led by the Spirit of God to adventure beyond the limitations of his rational theology. He dreamed.

In some ways that's not so unusual. Everyone dreams—so the researchers assert, and anecdotal evidence from story and history affirms. But Riffel took his dreams seriously, even suggesting some of them were direct messages from God.

Dreams, God's wise counsel

Through listening to his dreams, Riffel found treasure buried in the vast ocean of his unseen inner world—hidden away from his natural mind. Asserting the dream is an invaluable counselor, he says, "It is with us every night, charges no fee, and makes no demand except that we listen to it and learn to detect God's voice in symbolic language…there is no better way to get to heart of our problem."[3]

> *The dream is an invaluable counselor…and makes no demand except that we…learn to detect God's voice in symbolic language.*

This idea presented us with a challenge: could those chaotic images playing across our sleeping minds actually have some meaning for our lives? This fascinating possibility bears serious investigation! But then the doubts and questioning begin. Is it biblical? Are dreams from God? Can we trust dreams? What are they telling us?

As you begin to examine the topic of dreams, you'll probably have similar questions. A key goal in writing this book is to share what we have discovered and experienced, hopefully making it easier for you to value your dreams and uncover God's counsel and wisdom in them.

2. Interactive learning
- ☐ To clarify your needs, see Appendix B, *"What Is Your Life Situation?"*
- ☐ In what areas do you currently feel the need for His counsel and wisdom?

A Christian approach

In our search to understand dreams, we read extensively the works of Christian authors, sleep researchers, and depth psychologists—books, research papers, and professional journals. In this book, we distill our understanding of these writings and cite authors from a broad perspective of Judeo-Christian faith traditions, footnoting our sources. Catholic psychologist Charles Zeiders notes that taking a broad approach allows us to accept the truth and efficacy in social/psychological methods to understand God's grace exhibited in dreams.[4]

Acknowledging all truth belongs to God, we can—without fear—examine the understanding gained from sleep lab and dream research to help us more fully realize how God blesses us night after night in our dreams. As we began our exploration of the realm of dreams, we made a *decision* we would trust the Holy Spirit to guide us to all truth.

Although we had been believers since childhood, when we experienced the fullness of the Holy Spirit, we began looking to the Spirit of God for guidance and direction in our lives. We came to understand that God sent the Holy Spirit so He could make God's words known to us (Prov. 1:23), and dreams are one of the ways He uses (Acts 2:14-17). (For more about the Holy Spirit, see Appendix C, *"The Holy Spirit"*.)

God sent the Holy Spirit so He can make God's words known to us.

Holy Spirit is key to understanding dreams

As with any other attempt to understand the spiritual realm, we must learn to discern what is/what is not from God. We should reject any teaching on dreams that does not follow biblical guidelines. Christian authors on dreams concur that any interpretation contradicting principles in the Holy Scriptures is not valid.

We study, we learn, we meditate, we pray, but our spiritual growth and transformation depends on God revealing to us what He wants us to know—the Holy Spirit is vital. Although God can use spiritually-attuned men and women to help a dreamer draw out the meaning of a dream, *reliance upon the Holy Spirit is central in our approach to dream work and interpretation.*

Look to our Heavenly Father

If you are uncomfortable with anything we say, please don't put the book down, but instead ask our Heavenly Father to reveal what is His truth for you. You don't have to receive everything we say as absolute truth; we are simply trying to share with you what has helped us on our journey. We can only give you the biblical record, what we have learned from our studies, and our personal experiences, but

Dream Treasure

ultimately it depends upon the Holy Spirit to witness to you what is important for *your* life.

We hope we have written with humility about the wonderful, loving gift of God in dreams. Perhaps we overstate some things in our enthusiasm, or make a caricature of a subject to make a point. I (Gerald) tend to use satire in my writing to encourage you to think about something. I do not mean to offend—just get your attention. Agree or disagree, either way, as a friend once encouraged us, "eat the chicken, and spit out the bones."

> *3. Interactive learning*
> ☐ Take the *Survey of Attitudes & Beliefs about Dreams* (see Appendix A*)*.
> ☐ Write a prayer to God telling Him of your concerns and questions about dreams.
> ☐ Using a scale of 0 to 10 (*none at all to great*), how much can you trust the Holy Spirit to lead you and guide you? Your response:

Nocturnal grace

Our testimony is that God has often used dreams as a way to speak to us. With conscious heads comfortably quiet on our pillows, we have been able to receive God's *living* word for us deep in our hearts. Upon many occasions God has graced our lives with dreams that brought us His wisdom and knowledge for our lives.

In one sense, our lives are similar to those of people in the Bible. In the stories from both the Old and New Testaments, dreams and visions are spoken of as actual events, something concrete and real that happens to people and makes a difference in their lives. This is also our experience.

We're not talking about ephemeral events and whimsical discussions about nice little spiritual principles. We have experienced directly the communication from our Creator in nighttime dreams that have changed our lives. We'll never be the same again.

> *Lord, I acknowledge that I can trust You to lead me and guide me as I study this book on dreams. I do need Your divine guidance and counsel in my life. Please confirm Your truth about dreams for me.*

Musings on Joseph, the dreamer

Joseph is a dreamer, led while sleeping, can't seem to function with his head. I'm sure he'll not amount to much significance; the world will soon forget him when he's dead. A lowly carpenter knows nothing but his hands, the rough-hewn pieces that he fashions from the trees. How could he hear or see beyond tomorrow, his vision blurred by dirt beneath his nails?

Perhaps he imagines that the son assigned to him will somehow leave his imprint while He's here. But then, of course, he will, too, soon be forgotten, the quiet, steady son of a quadruple dreamer, who moves his family across the rugged wasteland multiple times because he fancies that his dreams come straight from God.

A scribe named Matthew wrote upon the pages that a humble carpenter made note of nighttime visions, logged in the journal of his heart the word from God, and carried young Jesus Messiah to safety. But that was then, and we live now, and our God's surely different from his.

In days of old He sent them dreams, visions, prophesies, spoke to them directly. Prepared their hearts for what's ahead, or simply how to live today. He played His magic on the land; directly intervened in man's affairs; spoke strongly by His Spirit to the inner spirit of man. Some so strongly that they were called prophets, seers, wise men (where'd they ever get such names?).

With such a sea of inspiration for the soul of man in those far bygone days, too bad He only left us a book; so we could read about how it used to be when God could save the life of His chosen Messiah by speaking to his earthly father with the angel of a dream.[i]

---

[i] Gerald Doctor, personal journal entry (1987).

Applied Learning

✎ *Your response*

- ☐ Underline the most significant point for you in this chapter.
- ☐ Are the authors' experiences with dreams believable? Explain?
- ☐ Describe how the authors' dreams relate to their Christian experience.
- ☐ Write out what Psalms 16:7 means to you.
- ☐ Have you ever received counsel from God in the night?
- ☐ Affirm aloud: "God wants to give me His counsel and wisdom for my life. I like that!"

✲ *Dream work strategies, skills & techniques*

- ☐ Note how the authors' RECORDED their dreams. (#1)
- ☐ Underline their CURRENT CONCERNS (CC). (#2)
- ☐ How did Gerald TITLE (T) his dream? *(#3)*
- ☐ How did the authors' dreams relate to their CURRENT CONCERNS (CC)? (#4)
- ☐ How did Judith's dream differ from Gerald's dream?
- ☐ Did their dreams contain DIVINE COUNSEL for their lives? (#5)

> ▶ *Dream Work Tip:*
> Recording your dreams signals God that you are listening.

Explaining new strategies, skills & techniques

#1 RECORD A DREAM, including the date you received it.

#2 When you record a dream, log your CURRENT CONCERNS (CC)— current prayers, heart issues/concerns, desires, recent significant situations, and experiences.

#3 Give the dream a TITLE (T). What title does the dream want to have?

#4 Consider how the dream might relate to your CURRENT CONCERNS (CC).

#5 Can you discern any DIVINE COUNSEL in your dream? DIVINE COUNSEL means God's wisdom, knowledge, counsel, or instruction for your life?

✎ *Practicing your skills*

- ☐ Select a dream to work with.
- ☐ RECORD your dream and *date it*. (#1)
- ☐ Log your CURRENT CONCERNS (CC). (#2)
- ☐ TITLE (T) your dream. (#3)
- ☐ Decide if your dream a symbolic dream or a clear dream.
- ☐ Consider how the dream relates to your CURRENT CONCERNS (CC). (#4)
- ☐ Ask, "God, does my dream contain DIVINE COUNSEL?" Can you discern any counsel or instruction in your dream? (#5)

> ➤ *Dream Work Tip:*
> Always pray, asking God to reveal His divine counsel.

> **Dream Work Terminology**
> Can you explain the following terms?
> - Hidden Treasure
> - Divine counsel
> - Current Concerns (CC)
> - Counsel and instruction dreams
> - Symbolic dreams
> - Clear dreams
> - Your life situation
> - Dream Title (T)

Dream Treasure

PART ONE Why Consider Dreams?

God Wants Us To Hear His Voice

2

He awakens my ear, morning by morning…He awakens My ear to listen as a disciple (Is. 50:4).

Core Concepts
- The cornerstone of Christian dream work.
- Discovering ways God speaks to us.
- The visual word of God.
- Hearing God's voice brings blessings.

Learning Objectives
At the completion of this chapter, you will be able to:
- ☐ Describe the *cornerstone* of listening to our dreams.
- ☐ Enlarge your understanding of the "word of God."
- ☐ Acknowledge that people are receiving helpful dreams from God.
- ☐ Discuss the difference between the direct and indirect voice of God in dreams.
- ☐ Explain the concept, "hearing the voice of God."

God wants to communicate with us

Mother Theresa received direction and energy for her ministry through a dream. When Dr. A. J. Gordon (founder of Gordon College) dreamed that Jesus attended his church, his ministry, indeed his entire life, was deeply affected. St. Therese of Lisieux, canonized in 1925, experienced a powerful dream that established the certainty of her belief and brought her inner serenity.

What is the common thread in these stories? In each case our Creator, the Lord God Almighty, spoke personally to them through their dreams. Why should we consider dreams? This is the *cornerstone* of our approach to dream work: God wants to communicate with us! Woven through the Holy Scriptures is the story of how our Creator has actively revealed Himself to mankind throughout the ages.

Restoration of garden fellowship

Incredible as it may seem, God longs for *relationship* with us. Originally, in the pristine paradise of Eden's Garden, early man was intimately linked to His Creator. According to Scripture, Adam recognized God's voice as he strolled the garden at dusk.

   Dream Treasure

In those warm evening chats, Adam likely received counsel and instruction on how to manage the earth and tend his lush new garden. Here in this unimaginably delightful place of love and beauty, free of guilt and shame, Adam and God enjoyed fellowship together. But then something broke, seemingly irreparably.

Sin entered the Garden, and mankind lost this precious gift of relationship with our Creator. The human race became separated from God by an insurmountable spiritual space. Adam was certainly the great loser—we all are—but God also must have missed the fellowship. Because He loved His creation so deeply, He made a plan to redeem it from its lost condition.

In the new covenant God gave the world a New Adam, Jesus Christ, *"...the only Son of God, eternally begotten of the Father, God from God, Light from Light, true God from true God...,"* so fellowship could be restored between our Heavenly Father and us. At the cross Jesus dealt with the sin issue, removing every barrier separating us from God and preventing us from knowing His voice.

We can be a friend of God

Abraham was called "the friend of God" because he communed with God (James 2:23). Abraham recognized God's voice, believed His words, and obeyed His instructions. The Lord God appeared to him in a vision and a dream, assuring him of a great future (Gen. 15:1-21). God gave promises to Abraham and his descendents, establishing a covenant with them. Abraham *experienced* God speaking to him, and it changed his life—and history.

So did the psalmist and the prophet Isaiah

Notice how the psalmist and the prophet Isaiah described their experiences in hearing God speak to them:

> *I will bless the Lord who has counseled me;...my mind instructs me the night (Ps. 16:7).*
>
> *He awakens my ear, morning by morning...He awakens My ear to listen as a disciple (Is. 50:4).*

Invited to hear His voice

The Bible makes it clear God longs for communion with us and seeks those who will listen to His voice and do what He says. We see portrayed there a God who wanted so keenly to communicate with His people that, when they failed to listen, He used a *donkey* to reach them (Num. 22:22-31). This supposedly dumb animal not only saw a vision from God, but also *spoke the word of life* to Balaam.

Over and over, we are invited to hear what the Lord wants to say to us. Here are a few Scriptures revealing God's longing for us to hear His voice.

> *Call to me, and I will answer you, and I will tell you great and mighty things, which you do not know (Jer. 33:3).*
>
> *Ho, everyone who thirsts...Listen carefully to me, and eat what is good, and delight yourself in abundance; incline your ear and come to me, listen that you may live (Is 55: 1-9).*

 Dream Treasure

He who listens to me shall live securely, and shall be at ease from the dread of evil (Pro. 1:33).

Behold I stand at the door and knock, if anyone hears my voice and opens the door, I will come in to him and will dine with him, and he with Me (Rev. 3:20).

1. Interactive learning
- ☐ Read aloud the above Scriptures; *listen in your heart to the longing of God.*
- ☐ Reflect on Revelation 3:20. Using your imaginative capability, envision a door to your heart with Jesus knocking on it. Is the door open or closed?
- ☐ Examine & express any feelings of resistance to hearing the voice of God.

Discovering the ways God speaks to us

Many of God's people do not know how to hear His voice. Some are ignorant of the ways God may speak to us today. Here is a brief review of what the Holy Scripture says about how God speaks—in Old Testament times, in the New Testament era, and in contemporary life today.

Ways God spoke in Old Testament times

God used many ways to get His message across to His people in the Old Testament, as varied as angels, pillar of cloud, Urim and Thummim, tablets of stone, still small voice, signs and fleeces, thunder, visions—and *dreams*.

- *Angels (Gen. 16:7; Ex. 14:19; Judges 6:11-22)*
- *Pillar of cloud (Ex. 14:19; Num. 12:5)*
- *Urim & Thummim (Ex. 28:30; I Sam. 28:6; Num. 27:21)*
- *The midst of darkness & blazing fire (Deut. 5:23,24)*
- *Tablets of stone (Deut. 5:22; II Cor. 3:3)*
- *Still, small voice (I Kings 19-11-13)*
- *Signs & fleeces (Gen. 9:12-15; Ex. 8:20-25; Joshua 10:12-14; Judges 6:37-40; Jer. 32:6-8)*
- *External audible voice (I Sam. 3:1-21)*
- *Thunder, hailstones, coals of fire, lightning (Ps. 18:11-13, 19:1-6)*
- *Prophets (Num. 12:6; Hab. 1:1)*
- *Dreams & visions (Gen. 15:1,12; 28:10,12; Num. 12:6; I Sam. 3:15; 28:6,15; I Kings 3:5-15; Job 33:14-17; Judges 7:13; Jer. 1:11-19; Dan. 1:17; 10:7; Hab. 1:1)*

Ways God spoke in New Testament era

Likewise, in the New Testament God reached the hearts of His people in virtually unlimited ways—from the life and words of Jesus to the inner witness of the Spirit, from the sacraments to spiritual perception and intuition, from the evidence of creation to the gifts of the Holy Spirit, from visions—to *dreams*. According to the New Testament writers, here are just some of the ways God communicated:

- *God's son, Jesus Christ (Heb. 1-4; John 1:1-4; Col. 1:15-16)*
- *Signs (Luke 1:19-20)*
- *Healing & miraculous acts (Mt. 5:23-25; 10:1,8; Acts 4:30-33; 13:11; 16:16-18)*
- *Angels (Mt. 1:20; Luke 1:26; 2:9-14; Acts 12:7-15, 23; Heb. 1:14, 13:2)*
- *Audible voice (Acts 22:6-16; 26:13-16)*
- *The Holy Spirit (Mt. 4:4; Luke 2:25-27; 1:67; Rom. 8:14; Gal. 5:18)*
- *Prophecy (Luke 1:67; 2:25-35; Acts 2:17-18; 21:11)*
- *Prophets (Luke 2:36-38; 1:13-17)*
- *Open & closed doors (Acts 14:27; I Cor. 16:5-9)*
- *Drawing lots & prayer (Acts 1:24-26)*
- *Through His creation (Rom. 1:19, 20)*
- *Circumstances; divine interruptions (Acts 22:6-16)*
- *Dreams (Mt. 1:20; 2:12-13, 19, 22; Acts 2:17)*
- *Visions (Luke 1:11-22; Acts 2:17; 9:10; 10:3, 19; 16:9; 22:17-21)*

Ways God may speak today

People living in the 21st century are also privileged to hear from God in numerous ways. Although Larry Kreider discusses 30 ways to hear God in everyday life, he emphasizes we cannot limit how God may decide to communicate with us.[1] As believers with the presence of the indwelling Christ and the Holy Spirit, we can expect to hear from God through spiritual practices such as prayer, sacred writings, liturgy, Eucharist, praise, worship, and meditation—and in dreams and visions.

According to the Scriptures, here are some ways God uses to speak to us today:

- *Circumstances; divine interruptions (Acts 22:6-16)*
- *Holy Scriptures (Heb. 4:12; John 6:63; Acts 17:10-11; I Tim. 4:6,13; Prov. 4:4,5)*
- *The Church (Mt 18:17; Heb 13:7; I Thes 5:12-13)*
- *Teachers, evangelists, pastors, apostles, prophets (Rom 10:14-15; I Thes 5:12; Eph 4:11-12)*
- *Other people (Heb 3:13; Mt18:19-20; II Cor 13:1; Rom 10:14; Prov 11:14; 15:22)*
- *Gifts of the Holy Spirit (I Cor. 12:4-11; Rom. 1:11-12)*
- *Prophecy (Rev. 19:10; I Cor. 14:1-3; 13:9; I Tim. 1:18; I Thes. 5:19-22)*
- *Holy Spirit through our spirit (Mt. 10:20; Rom. 8:14,16; II Cor. 3:3; Gal. 5:18; Eph.1:18; Heb. 8:10; Prov. 20:27)*
- *Tablets of the human heart (II Cor. 3:3; Heb. 8:10)*
- *Peace in the heart (John 14:27; Col. 3:15; Phil. 4:7)*
- *Spiritual thoughts in the mind (Heb. 8:10)*
- *Dreams & visions (see Acts 2:17; Joel 2:28-32; Job 33:14-17).*

God to continue using dreams in the future

From this review of Scripture, we see that God spoke through dreams in both the Old and New Testament eras—and He plans to continue using dreams in the last days.

 Dream Treasure

It shall be in the last days, God says, I will pour out my Spirit on all people. Your sons and daughters will prophesy, your young men will see visions, your old men will dream dreams (Acts 2:16)

2. Interactive learning
- ☐ Underline the ways God has used to speak to you.
- ☐ Are these ways sufficient for you? Yes/No Explain?

The visual word of God

The messages God brings us in the Holy Scriptures are presented in part as rational propositional truth and part as story, vision, symbol and narrative—that is, *image, picture*. Both of these are necessary to God's revelation, and most of the time they are integrated with each other. However, Brian Godawa estimates conservatively that 30 percent of it is rational propositional truth and laws, while 70 percent is presented as image.[2]

> *"God's Word" is not an exclusively word-oriented concept.*

When we look at how God communicated with His prophets, we see that the very concept of "God's Word" is not an exclusively word-oriented concept. As Godawa says so colorfully, "God did not float Hebrew words in the air like ancient sky-writing."[3] God defines image-based *visions* as His *Word*.

- Isaiah reported his visionary experiences this way: "the *word* which Isaiah the son of Amoz *saw*" (Is 2:1; also see Is 1:1 & 13:1).
- Jeremiah described what he *saw* as the *word* of the Lord (Jer 1:11, 13; 24:3).
- Micah said "the *word* of the Lord which came to Micah…which he *saw*" (Micah 1:1).
- Ezekiel informs us the *visions* of God he saw are "the *word* of the Lord" (Ez 1:1-3).
- Zechariah says the "*Word* of the Lord" came to him, and then he recounts the *vision* he had (Zech 1:7-8).
- Amos says of God's revelation to him in several places, "the Lord God *showed* me" (Amos 7:1,4,7; 8:1).

Apparently God doesn't regard imagery as an inferior method for communicating truth as compared with words, or He would not have used so much imagery described *as His word*. So, are dreams and visions really all that different from words?

3. Interactive learning
- ☐ How do you explain the concept of the "visual word of God?"
- ☐ Have you ever had a visionary experience from God? Yes/No
- ☐ Describe one such visual experience and what it meant to you.

Dream Treasure

PART ONE Why Consider Dreams?

Hearing God's voice brings blessings

In the sacred Scriptures we are promised blessings if we hear and respond to God speaking to us. "All these blessings shall come on thee, and overtake thee, if thou shalt hearken unto the voice of the Lord thy God" (Deuteronomy 28:1-2).

Jesus said the person who hears Him and does what He says is *like* a wise man who built his house on a rock—when the storms of life hit, he does not fall apart, but stands firm (Mt. 7:24-27). The Psalmist explains that the one who delights in the law of God will be *like* a tree which yields its fruit in season…and will prosper in whatever he does (Ps. 1:2-4).

> **About blessings**
>
> The Scriptures reveal the existence of two spiritual dynamics called blessings and curses. These invisible forces influence our lives, either for good or for evil. According to Derek Prince, the intent of a blessing is for it to release positive, godly, spiritual power on the person being blessed; the intent of a curse is for it to release negative spiritual power against someone. The blessings of God bring about good and beneficial results, whereas curses produce bad and harmful results.[4]

Listen carefully to me, and eat what is good, and delight yourself in abundance; incline your ear and come to me, listen that you may live (Is 55:1-9).

He who listens to me shall live securely, and shall be at ease from the dread of evil (Prov. 1:33).

My sheep hear My voice and I know them, and they follow Me (John 10:27).

When He the spirit of truth, comes…He will disclose to you what is to come (John 16:13).

Hearing God's voice brings wholeness and transformation

German psychiatrist Walther Lechler told us he found that, if a person did not have "a healthy dialogue with a loving Heavenly Father," he or she could not get better.[i] Knowing what God is saying to us is essential to our well-being, because it directly relates to the restoration of our souls. It is through hearing God's voice we are transformed and made wholly alive.

Revive me according to Thy Word [refers to a deposit delivered in a visitation from God] (Ps. 119:25b).

He sent His Word and healed them, and delivered them from their destructions (Ps. 107:20).

4. Interactive learning
☐ List five blessings which come from hearing the voice of God.
☐ Do you currently *need* these blessings in your life? Yes/No

Muslim woman hears Jesus in her dream

Friends hosted an Iranian Christian couple in their home. The woman shared the following story of the blessing she received from God in a dream.

Come, My Daughter
Shayda, who came from a militant Islamic background, was married to a man who had formerly been associated with Hezbollah. Now a Christian, he urged her to attend a women's Bible study group. When she heard the women

---

i   Walther Lechler, *Personal communication*, Bad Herrenalb Klinik, Germany (1988).

 Dream Treasure

talking about God speaking to them, in her heart she mocked them, "God never answers my prayer. He doesn't speak to women." She cried out to God, "Talk to me, if you are there." That night she dreamed this dream:

I am under a beautiful blue sky walking through tall green grass with three other women and Jesus. Suddenly Jesus and two of the women are far ahead, with a cliff and valley separating us. Jesus calls to me, "Come, my daughter, do not be afraid." But I answer, "It is a valley, master." When He repeats, "Do not be afraid," I and the other woman step out, holding hands like innocent children. We walk forward on level, beautiful ground.

In the morning she awoke feeling very happy, and excitedly told her husband that Jesus had talked to her in her dream. At the next women's meeting, Shayda also had something to share: God speaks to her, too.[ii]

Divine purpose of Shayda's dream

Shayda had a divine encounter with Jesus in human form in her dream. This type of dream may be associated with religious conversion. Its divine purpose is to bring Shayda spiritual revelation, to reveal Christ, and to let her know that God wants to speak to her too.

5. Interactive learning
☐ Describe the blessing Shayda received from God through her dream.
☐ Why do you think God answered Shayda's prayer through a dream?

The direct or indirect voice of God

According to Numbers 12:6-8, Moses heard God's voice speaking directly to him, face-to-face, while others experienced God's voice indirectly, through dreams and visions. This establishes the idea that God's voice can be encountered either directly or indirectly. However, most dreams seem to belong to the category of the indirect voice of God because they use symbolic language. Therefore, when we accept the premise God speaks to us through dreams, it does not mean we are going to take them as literally being His voice.

> *Accepting the premise that God speaks through dreams does not mean we take them as literally being His voice.*

Never-the-less, there are times when dreams such as Shayda's seem to contain direct messages meant to be taken literally. In these rare dreams, we sense we are encountering the voice of God very directly. We never forget these dreams; they stay alive for us throughout our lives.

---

ii   *Personal communication* (**May 5, 2008**).

Dream Treasure

"Abba, Father, I can hear your voice"

A vital truth of the new covenant is the understanding that God has come to dwell within the hearts of people. Because of the Spirit of Christ in us, we have more than a shadow. As Catholic lay evangelist Ralph Nault says, "We have a reality, a *living word* in us, which is able to make itself known to us. We call it God speaking to us." [iii] God sends His Holy Spirit into our hearts, enabling us to call 'Abba, Father' (Rom. 8:14) and enjoy direct encounters with Him.

> *We have a reality, a living word in us, which is able to make itself known to us. We call it God speaking to us.*

We can know what God is saying to us

God is capable of speaking personal truth into our minds and hearts. Moreover, we are blessed by God with the capacity to *hear with spiritual ears.* Jesus Christ followed the Father's leading by doing and saying only what the Father wanted Him to do (John 8:28). We also can be led by the Spirit to hear and respond to the voice of our heavenly Father (Rom. 8:14).

We have spiritual senses

We are human souls, containing a spirit. When we receive Jesus Christ, our spirit becomes activated through the Spirit of God. Thus, it is not just our spirit anymore, but God's Spirit becomes fused with our spirit, bringing about a new creation.

This new creation in us has spiritual senses. It is not blind or deaf. It can hear; it has ears. It can see; it has eyes. It can speak, it has a voice. We call these senses *intuition, inward voice, inner guidance, inward witness.* We can recognize the witness of the Spirit in our spirit. [iv]

> *For to us God revealed them through the Spirit;...Now we have received,...,but the Spirit who is from God, that we might know the things freely given to us by God...(I Cor. 2:10-12).*
>
> *I pray that the eyes of your heart may be enlightened, so that you may know what is the hope of His calling...(Eph. 1:17-19).*

Do you know the Father's voice?

It is important for us to have more than just a knowledge about God—we need an *experiential* knowing of Him. Yet, most of us talk to God, but do not know if He is talking to us. Henry Blackaby says in *Experiencing God*, "If a Christian does not know when God is speaking, he is in trouble at the heart of his Christian life."[5] God is not dumb, He has no problem communicating, He speaks to people everywhere. So, where's the problem? It must be in the hearing and listening.

[iii] Personal conversation with Ralph Nault, June, 2005.
[iv] We recommend *The Spiritual Man* by Watchman Nee This book has helped many people learn what it means to become a spiritual Christian, able to discern the living word from God that transforms us.

> **About "hearing the voice of God"**
>
> When we refer to "hearing the voice of God," we are not talking about a literal, audible voice—if we seek a literal voice, we will most likely be misled. Although it is possible to literally hear God speak, it is extremely rare. When we talk about hearing God's voice, we mean being aware in our spiritual senses—the eyes and ears of our heart—God is communicating with us. Through pictures, visions, prophetic inspiration, spontaneous thoughts and images sent by God, in the day or night, we can sense what God is communicating to us.

6. Interactive learning

- [ ] Explain what "hearing God's voice" means to you.
- [ ] Recall times when you have heard God speak to you.

Lord, I thank You that You desire to have fellowship with me. I pray that You will give me a hunger to hear Your voice. Awaken me to hear Your voice in the morning; open my spiritual ears to hear Your voice. I want to be taught by You.

Applied Learning

✎ *Your response*
- ☐ Identify the blessings Mother Theresa, Dr. A. J. Gordon, and St. Therese of Lisieux received from God through their dreams?
- ☐ Using a scale of 0 to 10 (*0 not at all; 10 absolutely true*) how true does this statement feel in your heart: "God wants to speak to me personally." Your response ___
- ☐ Write Isaiah 50:4 into a prayer of response to God.
- ☐ When you first awaken, practice listening to see if the Lord is speaking to you.
- ☐ Affirm aloud: "God wants me to hear His voice. I like that!"

☼ *Dream work strategies, skills & techniques*
- ☐ Identify the Current Concerns (CC) on Shayda's heart.
- ☐ What Title (T) would you give Shayda's dream?
- ☐ Describe the overall THEME (T) in Shayda's dream. (#1)
- ☐ Explain how Shayda's dream relates to her Current Concerns (CC).
- ☐ What is God TRYING TO SAY to Shayda through her dream? (#2)
- ☐ What was the divine purpose of Shayda's dream?
- ☐ What divine counsel did Shayda's dream bring her?

Explaining new strategies, skills & techniques

#1 Identify the dream's THEME (T). Dream theme refers to the overall issue, conflict, or problem in the dream. It is usually quite clear. If not, ask "What is this dream mainly about? What is the key issue the dream is addressing?"

#2 Always pray, asking God, WHAT ARE YOU TRYING TO SAY TO ME through my dream?

> ▶ *Dream Work Tip:*
> Praying helps you to position your heart before God in humility.

✎ Practicing your skills

- ☐ Select a dream to work with.
- ☐ Record your dream and the date you received it.
- ☐ Log your Current Concerns (CC).
- ☐ Title (T) your dream.
- ☐ Identify the overall THEME (T) in your dream. (#1)
- ☐ Consider how your dream might relate to your Current Concerns (CC).
- ☐ Does your dream use the direct or indirect voice of God?
- ☐ Ask God, "WHAT ARE YOU TRYING TO SAY TO ME in my dream?" (#2)
- ☐ What do you think might be the divine purpose of your dream?
- ☐ Does your dream contain counsel or instruction from God?

Dream Work Terminology

Can you explain the following terms?
- Hearing the voice of God
- The visual word of God
- Divine encounter dreams
- Divine revelation dreams
- Direct and indirect voice of God in dreams
- What is God trying to say to you?
- Dream Theme (T)

PART ONE Why Consider Dreams?

Dreams, A Way To Hear God's Voice

3

The dream is the voice of God speaking to us in the night while our conscious mind is stilled. (Herman Riffel)[1]

Core Concepts
- God promises to speak through dreams.
- Dreams carry blessings from God.
- Dreams contain hidden treasure.
- The dream is like a bucket.

Learning Objectives
At the completion of this chapter, you will be able to:
☐ Describe the relationship of the Holy Spirit to dreams.
☐ Understand the term, "dream interpretation."
☐ Identify blessings God may bring through dreams.
☐ Discuss the concept "hidden treasure."
☐ Explain the meaning of Proverbs 20:5.
☐ Evaluate whether dreams are a way to hear from God.

History Reveals God Speaks Through Dreams

To begin addressing the question of why it is important to consider dreams, we briefly look back over the scriptural record, the teachings of the Church Fathers, and the promise of the Father that the Holy Spirit will bring dreams in the last days. We will cover these points in greater depth in Part Two.

Scriptural record values dreams

Despite the absolute avoidance of dreams in most studies of the Scripture, stories of dreams and visions pepper the pages from Genesis to Revelation. Beginning with the scriptural record and continuing down through the ages, dreams have played a key role in the story of God's dealings with His people.

Scripture reveals that God chooses to communicate with people through visions, prophecies—and dreams. Abraham Lincoln said, "It seems strange how much there is in the Bible about dreams. There are, I think, some sixteen chapters in the Old

Dream Treasure

25

Testament and four or five in the New in which dreams are mentioned."[2]

Lincoln's estimate was way low—dreams or similar experiences are mentioned in almost every part of the Bible. If we cut out all these references, their surrounding stories and ensuing prophecies, the book ends up about 30% thinner. Worse, we shut out the possibility we might hear the personal word of God in our dreams.

Starting with Jacob's legendary stone pillow dream (see Gen. 28:11-15), many great events in the Old Testament hinged on the lives of Israeli dreamers who heard from God through their night-time images. The New Testament also shows that God speaks through supernatural phenomena such as dreams, visions, prophecies, and appearances of angels. The Gospel of Matthew relates four dreams God gave Joseph to guide the young Messiah from conception to carpenter's assistant.

Dreams help us maintain a vital, vibrant connection with God.

In his quest to discover the validity of dreams as a way to listen to God, Herman Riffel "discovered that references to dreams (that come while we are asleep) and visions (that come while we are awake) were not only in the Old Testament…but they filled the New Testament as well. Once I began to study, I found the references were almost unending."[3]

> *1. Interactive learning*
> ☐ Review the blessings people received through dreams in the Holy Scriptures. (See Appendix E, 40 *Biblical Blessings Of Dreams*).
> ☐ Which blessing do you currently feel the need for in your life?

Church Fathers continue to value dreams

In his seminal work on dreams, Dr. Morton Kelsey—who reviewed extensively the writings of the early Church Fathers—says early leaders regarded dreams, visions, and prophecy as vehicles for communication from the divine.[4] Augustine said dreams are important for understanding our relationship to God. Irenaeus believed we get revelation of the spiritual world in dreams. Cyprian said God used visions to guide and direct the councils of the church. Ambrose taught that dreams were one of God's methods of bringing revelation to man.[5]

If we believe the Bible, we must accept the fact that…God and His angels…made themselves known in dreams.

Dreams help us maintain a vital, vibrant connection with God. This was the common viewpoint for several centuries after the Early Church Fathers. As we will see later, this valuable means of hearing from God was lost from Christianity by some unfortunate events.

Famous dreamers confirm biblical narrative

President Abraham Lincoln possessed an impressive knowledge of the Scriptures, and often quoted biblical passages in his speeches. He said: "If we believe the Bible, we must accept the fact that…God and His angels…made themselves known in dreams."[6] Lincoln followed his own dreams throughout his life, leaving a record of some particularly interesting ones immediately preceding his death.

Stravinsky wrote some of his music in dreams. Isaac Newton often solved problems during dreams. In *Pilgrim's Progress*, John Bunyan wove his narrative from his dreams, visions, and meditations.

2. Interactive learning
☐ List the evidence supporting the contemporary use of dreams.
☐ Can you agree with President Lincoln? Yes/No Explain?

God promises to speak through dreams

Our experience with the Holy Spirit was vital in motivating us to pay attention to our dreams. God sent the Holy Spirit so He can speak to us personally, and one of the methods He uses is dreams.

Holy Spirit to bring dreams in the last days

According to Hebrews 1:1-2, in Old Testament times God spoke to His people through the prophets. In New Testament times God spoke to His people through His son, Jesus Christ of Nazareth. When Jesus returned to the right hand of God, the Father promised to pour out the Holy Spirit (Acts 2:33). The promise of the Father is that He would send the Holy Spirit, who would be in us and would lead and guide us (John 14:16-17).

The language of the Holy Spirit is dreams, visions and prophecies. (Cho)

In the Old Testament, God promised He would pour out His Spirit and make His words known to us (Prov. 1:23). The prophet Joel tells us that a time will come when the Holy Spirit *is* poured forth, and ordinary people will receive dreams, visions and prophecies (Joel 2:28). At Pentecost it happened. St. Peter reminds them that the coming of the Holy Spirit results in God speaking through prophecies, visions, and dreams (Acts 2:14-17).

Dreams, the language of the Holy Spirit

It may startle you, but some writers go so far as to say dreams are "God's language."[7] According to Paul Youngi Cho, the language of the Holy Spirit is dreams, visions and prophecies.[8] Rev. John A. Sanford seems to agree with this—he titled his book, *Dreams: God's Forgotten Language*! If we long to know what God is saying to us, we must become familiar with the language the Holy Spirit uses: our nighttime dreams, visions, and the prophetic flow.

The three-legged stool—prophecy, visions, dreams

Consider the Holy Spirit's language to be like a three-legged stool—prophecy, visions, and dreams. Many people believe prophecy is a way to hear from God. Some even accept visions, great or small. That's two legs of the stool, but might we have missed His word if we're not dreaming?

Dream Treasure

3. Interactive learning
- ☐ What is the role of the Holy Spirit in your life?
- ☐ List 3 ways the Holy Spirit will make God's words, in the last days.
- ☐ Is prophecy more important than visions or dreams? Yes/No. Explain?

A contemporary dreamer

Our friend, Catholic lay evangelist Ralph Nault received a dream from the Lord that helped him in his spiritual journey. [9]

Dancing Skeleton

For several weeks my spirit had been heavy—I didn't seem to have any joy. My Christian walk did not seem exciting any more, it had become a drag. Everything seemed so hard to do—even the ministry work I have always loved had lost its excitement. I knew something was seriously wrong. One morning I awoke with this dream from the Lord:

I am digging in the shell of a building which has no foundation and no floor. As I attempt to build a foundation under the edges of the building, I strike a metallic box. It turns out to be a tiny casket. It makes strange sounds and the casket moves and sways, rising above the surface. Suddenly a voice behind me says, "Here, this is yours," and hands me a tiny skeleton that is kicking and screaming loudly in a shrill voice. Kicking free, the skeleton begins dancing, leaping, somersaulting and shouting joyfully, "I'm free! I'm free! Praise God, I'm free!"

When he doesn't go away, I realize he wants to stay with me. I know the skeleton came from the tiny casket and does not want to go back there. Suddenly I feel as if I am the skeleton, and know what it wants, what it thinks, what it feels; then I am myself again. At this moment I realize we are both one.

I prayed that the Lord would give me the interpretation, and at once I knew the skeleton was my spiritual man. The building is my spiritual house (notice it didn't have a foundation). My digging symbolizes my own efforts to build a spiritual house, and while I am doing this, I run into the casket, which symbolizes the letter of the law, engraved in stone. Even though it was good, it had brought me death and bondage, bound up my spiritual man, robbed me of all my joy and freedom.

My spiritual man had finally become strong enough to break loose from the laws, rules, regulations, and the fleshly practice of religion. The person standing behind me who handed me the skeleton was the Holy Spirit, bringing me into a new place of freedom in Christ Jesus. Now I understand better the vision of the valley of dry bones from the book of Ezekiel 37, where the Lord made the bones come together, to rise up and live.

Dream Treasure

Divine purpose of Ralph's dream
The purpose of Ralph's dream was to give him divine counsel, revealing the root of his problem. The dream enlightened him with the light of life, making him more fully alive.

Notice that he asked the Lord to give him the interpretation of his dream. *Interpretation* refers to the opening up of our understanding as to the meaning of the symbolic images in a dream.

Dream work or dream interpretation?
In working with dreams, some authors use the term *dream interpretation* and others, *dream work*. In our view, the concept of *dream work* offers more ways to interact with the dream—including non-interpretive techniques—whereas *dream interpretation* refers to the process of deciphering the dream's symbols. The interpretation is the end result of your dream work. Nevertheless, in this book we will use both terms interchangeably.

---

4. Interactive learning
- ☐ Does Ralph's dream contain the direct or indirect voice of God?
- ☐ How did Ralph discover the hidden treasure in his dream?
- ☐ Do you think Ralph's dream was from God? Yes/No

What do dreams do for us?
Hearing God communicate with us in our dreams has been one of the most significant discoveries of our lives. Now in the seventh decade of our lives, we continue our adventure with God by listening to His voice in our dreams. Images impressed upon us, themes revealed, issues resolved, all help us become more spiritually alive and whole.

Help open us to the spiritual realm
Dreams open us to the reality of the spiritual dimension—the kingdom of God. Because we have been educated in a worldview that excludes supernatural phenomena, the Holy Spirit uses the dream to help unlock the door to the realm of spiritual reality. Here God can touch us far more directly than in the physical world, enriching our lives with profound religious experiences.

Reveal things the Father has for us
It is the work of the Holy Spirit to reveal the things God has for each one of us, and one way He does this is through prophecies, visions, and dreams.

For to us God revealed them through the Spirit...Now we have received...the Spirit who is from God, that we might know the things freely given to us by God (I Cor. 2:10-12).

Our dreams may *reveal our potential, gifts, calling, and the divine purpose* of our lives. Remember Solomon? It was in his dream that Lord imparted gifts to him (I Kings 3:5-28). It was in a dream that Judith was taught how to release the anointing of God.

Through our dreams we receive God's guidance and direction for our lives, giving us guideposts along the journey that direct us toward the purpose of our lives. Dreams help us discover the things God has in store for us, and enable us to realize our potential.

Nurture healing, wholeness, and transformation

By bringing us revelation about the condition of our own souls, dreams help *improve our psychological, emotional, and mental health*. Herman Riffel said dreams help us realize every part of our potential and bring us into harmony with God, others, and ourselves.[10] Knowing what God is saying to us is essential to our becoming fully alive and transformed.

> **Symbols promote healing**
>
> Helen Luke warns that theoretical changes can create a deeper and more destructive conflict in the soul. She says, "no amount of rational analysis can bring healing. We must connect the theories and emotions aroused with our symbolic life for changes to occur in actual life. We must nourish our inner imagery. Only the images by which we live can bring transformation. Images from the unconscious may convey in a symbol the power of the Spirit.[14]

Dreams give us a practical and safe approach to correcting deep-seated problems. The messages in our dreams offer us a means to solve problems in our relationships, personal life, and work. By enabling us to see deep-seated problems in ourselves, dreams nurture the well-being of our whole person.

Therapeutic function

Christian psychiatrist Len Sperry says that in marital and family work dreams can have a therapeutic effect because they provide access into both the unconscious and the religious realm. Bypassing the client's defense mechanisms, the dream can get to the heart of the client's problem quickly, making them aware of their inner conflicts and unlived emotions. A dream may even point toward a solution.[11]

Social workers sometimes advocate use of dreams in counseling. For example, Sackheim observes "like any other life experience, they admit of interpretation on varying levels." Catalano uses children's dreams in his clinical social work practice, noting that "dreams provide a wealth of useful material about the issues, feelings, and memories most important to the child."

Dream research shows that dreams representing traumatic events convey how the dreamer feels relative to the trauma, including helplessness, terror, and grief. M.P. Hartmann asserts a dream can help the dreamer integrate a traumatic event into consciousness.[12]

Because *God is at the source of the dream energy,* dreams contain healing power, capable of transforming and healing conflicted, divided personalities. Dreams often provide clear directives about what we need to do to restore balance in our lives, to heal our broken heart, to release our pain, guilt, and failures. For someone who has difficulty relating feelings or connecting to internal thoughts, dream work can facilitate the healing process.[13]

> *In dreams...we may find treasures in the sea, suggesting a transformation process in which valuable treasure can come out of disaster or tragedy. (Riffel)*

Deepen our relationship to God

Dream work enables us to develop a deeper, more meaningful relationship to God. It helps us become responsible for our own spiritual development and maturity. Instead of being emotionally dependent upon others, we learn to hear the voice of God for our own lives!

Do you want to hear from God more often? Pay attention to your dreams. Through our dreams we may come to a new awareness of both God and ourselves. Our dreams offer us fulfilling, long-lasting experiences with God that give meaning and purpose to our lives.

An underlying premise is that there is a vast unseen, inner realm within us, containing a storehouse of hidden treasure.

Connect us to our inner heart

Dreams help to connect us to our hearts, where Christ is. They enable us to experience the presence of God in a deeper, more satisfying way. Dream work helps move us downward into our innermost being, quickening our soul at its very center, connecting us to our heart, the center of our lives.

> *Athanasius, bishop of Alexandria, said, "Often when the body is quiet, and at rest and asleep, man moves inwardly...and the soul...imagines and beholds things above the earth, and often even holds converse with the saints and angels who are above earthly and bodily existence."*[15]

By being open to hearing from God through whatever ways He chooses, we can come to know God in a deeper, richer, more satisfying way. Through our dreams we come to an inner awareness of God, and discover the presence of Christ dwelling in the depths of our hearts.

5. Interactive learning
☐ List the blessings from God that dreams bring to us.
☐ What do you consider to be the most significant blessing of dreams?

Dreams convey hidden treasure

In the religious use of dreams, an underlying premise is that there is a vast unseen, inner realm within us, containing a storehouse of hidden treasure. Before depth psychology postulated the existence of a deep substrata (*the unconscious*) just beyond consciousness, the sacred writings had already established that we have a deeply concealed inner part known as the heart.

Dream Treasure

> *This mystery has not been revealed to me for any wisdom residing in me…but for the purpose of making the interpretation known to the king, and that you may know the thoughts of your heart (Dan. 2:30).*
>
> *For the inward part and heart of man are deep (Ps. 64:6b).*
>
> *But let it be the hidden man of the heart… (I Pet. 3:4a).*

Inner riches buried deep within us

According to the Holy Scriptures, God has hidden a secret storehouse of wealth in a place our natural man's understanding cannot reach. This treasure trove, containing divine wisdom and knowledge, lies deep within our hearts, below consciousness.

Notice how these verses refer to treasures of darkness and hidden wealth:

> *I will give you the treasures of darkness, and hidden wealth of secret places, in order that you may know that it is I, the Lord… (Is. 45:3).*
>
> *It is He who reveals the profound and hidden things; he knows what is in the darkness" (Dan. 2: 22)*
>
> *We have this treasure in earthen vessels (II Cor. 4:7).*
>
> *…that is, Christ Himself, in whom are hidden all the treasures of wisdom and knowledge (Col. 2:2b-3).*

The dream comes to reveal the wisdom and knowledge of God hidden away (from the natural man) in an undisclosed place within us. Dream work is about the search for this *great treasure* buried in the depth of our hearts.

Dreams originate in an unseen place

Thousands of years ago, the prophet Daniel recognized the existence of this hidden unseen realm and its relationship to our dreams. He said Nebuchadnezzar's dream came to *reveal the thoughts and intents of his heart—an inner unseen place* (see Dan. 2:30).

Amazing! Deep in our own heart and soul, buried in darkness away from our rational minds, we have a secret storehouse of hidden riches and wealth that is accessible through our dreams.

> *A traditional Christian view of dreams acknowledges the existence of an inner spiritual reality within us which can be known to us directly, intuitively (John Sanford).*[16]

The unseen place

When we mention this "unseen place," we are referring to our vast inner world, what psychology calls "the unconscious," an invisible dimension of which we are not ordinarily aware. In this book we interchangeably use the terms the *unconscious,* the *inner world,* or the *heart* for this unseen realm within us.

Consider the dream to be *like* a bucket

King Solomon, this wisest of all men, himself a famous dreamer (see I Kings 4:29-32), proclaimed that *counsel* in the *heart* of man is like *deep water*, but a man of *understanding* will *draw* it out (Prov. 20:5, KJV).

A quick Hebrew word study reveals the following meanings:

- Counsel— refers to advice or plans.
- Heart— refers to the core or center, the unseen hidden part.
- Deep water—refers to something existing exceedingly deep.
- Understanding—means intelligence; the capacity to separate mentally or to distinguish something.
- Draw—means to dangle, to let down a bucket, in order to bring up something.

> *Counsel in the heart of man is like deep water, but a man of understanding will draw it out (Prov. 20:5, KJV).*

What King Solomon says is that buried very deep within our hearts is some type of *helpful advice or plans*—i.e., hidden treasure. In order to access this treasure, it must be brought up into our awareness.

The dream is *like* a bucket that carries the helpful advice or plans into consciousness; dream work is drawing up the bucket to discover the treasure from our hearts.[17] However, Solomon warns that it requires *understanding*—the capacity to separate, distinguish, and discern—to make known the meaning of the wise counsel contained in the bucket.

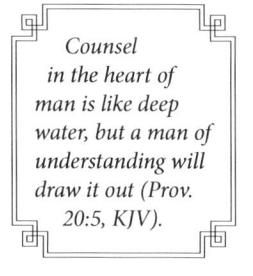

6. Interactive learning

- ☐ How would you explain the meaning of King Solomon's words in Proverbs 20:5?
- ☐ A premise of Judeo-Christian dream work says we contain a storehouse of hidden treasure. Agree/Disagree? Explain?
- ☐ In your own words, describe the treasure we contain.

Knowledge of dreams is ancient

If dreams were a recent invention of dubious worth, valid concerns could be raised about their significance. However, according to the sacred writings, dreams began long ago in the very heart of Father God. In fact, throughout the events conveyed to us in the Bible, dreams are actually one of the most prominent methods God used to speak to people.

So there's nothing new here—knowledge of dreams and their meaning is very ancient. Books such as Daniel are full of dreams, visions, and supernatural understanding of events, both present and future. In both the Old and New Testaments, and throughout much of Church history, dreams play a central role in God's revelation to His people.

> *Lord, give me the courage to listen to my dreams and discover Your treasure buried in them.*

Dream Treasure

PART ONE Why Consider Dreams?

Applied Learning

✎ *Your response*
- ☐ What are the most important ideas for you in this chapter?
- ☐ Can you agree with our understanding of Proverbs 20:5?
- ☐ Ask, "Lord, do my dreams contain treasure for me?" Write out the thoughts that spontaneously flow through your mind.
- ☐ Affirm aloud: "My dreams contain hidden treasure for me. I like that!"

✲ *Dream work strategies, skills & techniques*
- ☐ If the "Dancing Skeleton" dream were yours, what Title (T) would you give it?
- ☐ Identify the overall Theme (T) in Ralph's dream.
- ☐ What was the primary emotion or AFFECT (A) in his dream? (#1)
- ☐ Why did Ralph ask God for the INTERPRETATION of his dream? (#2)
- ☐ How did his dream relate to his Current Concerns (CC)?
- ☐ Describe the HIDDEN TREASURE contained in his dream. (#3)
- ☐ What BLESSINGS from God did his dream bring him? (#4)

Explaining new dream work strategies, skills & techniques

#1 Identify the AFFECT (A), the primary emotion or basic feeling in the dream. Then try to connect the feeling to your everyday life. Where in your life are you experiencing the same feeling?

#2 Ask God to give you the INTERPRETATION of your dream, meaning to open up your understanding, the meaning of its symbolic images.

#3 Value your dream as if it contains HIDDEN TREASURE; i.e., God's wisdom, knowledge, divine counsel, instruction, guidance, or revelation.

#4 Dream BLESSING is something from God that brings about good and beneficial results.

✎ *Practicing your skills*

- ☐ Record a dream and the date you received it.
- ☐ Note your Current Concerns (CC).
- ☐ Give your dream a Title (T).
- ☐ Identify the overall Theme (T) in your dream.
- ☐ Identify the emotional feeling or AFFECT (A) in your dream? (#1)
- ☐ Try to connect the feeling to your everyday life: Where in my life am I experiencing the same feeling AFFECT? (#1)
- ☐ Consider how your dream relates to your Current Concerns (CC).
- ☐ "God, please give me the INTERPRETATION of my dream." (#2)
- ☐ Approach your dream as if it contains HIDDEN TREASURE for you. (#3)
- ☐ What is the HIDDEN TREASURE be in your dream? (#3)
- ☐ What BLESSINGS from God does your dream bring to you? (#4)

Dream Work Terminology

Can you explain the following terms?

- Dream blessing
- Dream interpretation
- Dream work
- The unconscious
- Dream Affect (A)
- Hidden Treasure

Dream Treasure

PART ONE Why Consider Dreams?

Dream Robbers

4

In the last days, God says, I will pour out my Spirit on all people. Your sons and daughters will prophesy, your young men will see visions, your old men will dream dreams (Acts 2:17).

Core Concepts
- Rogue's gallery of dream robbers.
- Modern legacy of dream thievery.
- The Holy Spirit brings renewed awareness of dreams.
- Dreams are a neglected part of our spiritual heritage.
- Reengaging our historical roots.

Learning objectives
At the completion of this chapter, you will be able to:
- ☐ Understand when and why the Church lost touch with dreams.
- ☐ Explore factors contributing to your ignorance of dreams.
- ☐ Update your attitudes and beliefs about dreams.
- ☐ Determine whether you want to wake up and listen to your dreams.

Brief Church History of Dream Thieves

Dreams have played a significant part in helping people down through the ages experience God communicating personally to them in their sleep. Although New Testament writers and early Church Fathers got us started on the right pathway, dreams nearly disappeared from the radar screen in the past few centuries. In this chapter, we will briefly trace our understanding of how this precious heritage was misplaced.

Nearly half of the New Testament involves references to spiritual (non-rational) experiences. Since New Testament times, *spiritual reality* and *personal experience* have been hallmarks of authentic religious experience. People touched spiritual reality via insight, revelation, intuition, visions and dreams.

Lost touch with spiritual reality
Early Church Fathers valued dreams, visions, and prophecy, recognizing them as vehicles for God to communicate to His people. However, for several centuries after the time of the early Church Doctors, little is recorded about dreams and visions. In the medieval period, individual exploration of spirituality—including examination

Dream Treasure

PART ONE Why Consider Dreams?

of dreams—was not encouraged by the Church, so we know little about medieval thinking on dreams.

Rogue's gallery of dream robbers

Aristotle misled us!

The Western world has been heavily influenced by the ancient Greek philosopher, Aristotle, who asserted that we can know truth through only two sources: reason, and our senses. Aristotle and his followers rejected the spiritual realm and supernatural phenomena, recognized by Plato as a way of knowing truth.

Eventually an Aristotelian, humanistic philosophy seeped in, and subsequently nearly everything supernatural was leached out of the Western Church by rationalism. No dreams, no visions, no prophetic words for today.

St. Jerome's mistranslation

> **Warning!**
> *The Christian use of dreams is not about fortune-telling, but listening to God!*

In the 5th century the great scholar and Doctor of the Church, Jerome, gave the church a valuable gift by translating the Bible into the Latin Vulgate. Unfortunately, Jerome did us a huge disfavor by incorrectly adding dreams to the list of prohibited practices (divination, soothsaying, fortune-telling, witchcraft or interpreting omens) in Leviticus 19:26 and Deuteronomy 18:10. With a stroke of the translator's quill, paying attention to your dreams was classified alongside other superstitious practices. Until mid-20th century nearly all translations of the Bible were based on Jerome's Vulgate.

Christians misuse dreams

Jerome's mistranslation wasn't the only problem for sixth century dreamers. As Christianity took root, people forgot about persecution and became preoccupied with daily concerns. Instead of looking to their dreams to draw closer to God and do His will, they used dreams more like divination—to predict the future, get more power, attain better health and wealth.

Double-minded St. Thomas Aquinas

The 13th century theologian St. Thomas Aquinas is the foremost proponent of natural theology—the attempt to find God based on reason and ordinary experience, without supernatural revelation. In his thousand-page *Summa Theologica*, he essentially concluded dreams had no divine significance.[1]

Aquinas recanted his anti-dream position before he died, but by then the Church had embraced the negative story.

Paradoxically, Aquinas indicated that dreams helped him in his own life—he even *dialogued with St. Peter and St. Paul* in a dream about a thorny issue in writing the *Summa*. Although Aquinas recanted his anti-dream position before he died, it was too late—by then the Church had embraced the negative story.

John Calvin denies revelation by dreams

From the Protestant viewpoint, John Calvin's theological views line up pretty much with Aquinas. In his *Institutes,* he disallowed revelation of God through images or

38   Dream Treasure

symbols of any kind. However, in his *Commentaries on the Book of Daniel,* Calvin defended the idea that God speaks through dreams.

Age of reason

Throughout church history, some faithful believers have maintained that God uses dreams and visions to give people guidance, insight and wisdom. However, with the advent of the age of reason in the 18th century, rational thinking crept in, jostling the Church from its position as the "powerful, untamable, Spirit-driven, Mysterious Body of which Paul spoke."[2]

As a rationalistic worldview was embraced, the idea of touching the Divine through dreams, visions, and other supernatural means was dismissed as archaic. A purely rational philosophy insinuated itself deeply into the institutional church, and people were left starving for meaningful relationship with our Creator.

1. Interactive learning

- ☐ Identify the factors contributing to the loss of dreams by the Church.
- ☐ What does it mean to you that Aquinas dialogued with St. Peter & St. Paul in his dream?
- ☐ How does natural theology contribute to the loss of dreams?

Modern legacy of dream thievery

Today much of what we hear intellectualizes our relationship to God—everything is upstairs in our thinkers, not down in our hearts where it can truly affect our lives. With our thinking all trussed up by rationalism, we miss the opportunity to commune with Our Lord in true worship, to experience His presence, and to receive God's guidance through dreams.

Influence of evangelical dispensationalism

Many people raised in an evangelical environment embrace a theology based on the dispensationalist teachings of D.L. Moody, R.A. Torrey, and C.I. Scofield. Dispensationalism claims God divides world history into specific time slices. In ancient times God revealed Himself through miracles, prophecies, visions, and dreams, but this doesn't occur in our time slice—we merely get to read about those spiritual events in the Bible.

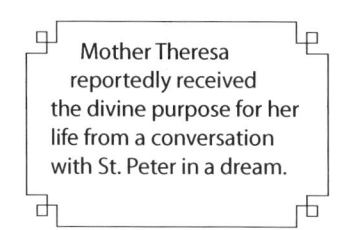

> Mother Theresa reportedly received the divine purpose for her life from a conversation with St. Peter in a dream.

Dreams viewed as insignificant

Even many people who eschew the narrow stance of dispensationalism have too often taken the attitude stated in the *International Standard Bible Encyclopedia*: "Dreams are abnormal, …sleep should be without dreams of any conscious occurrence, …the Bible…attaches relatively little religious significance to dreams."[3] Unfortunately, this type of thinking permeates much of modern Evangelicalism.

Fear of the Holy Spirit

Many people are terrified of spiritual experiences. Rejecting visitations from God, angelic beings, speaking in tongues, and gifts of the Holy Spirit, if it sounds at all spiritual, they run the other way in fear. Cutting from the Bible all passages dealing with supernatural events and the surrounding spiritual activities results in a pretty skinny book. But, isn't this in effect what we do?

Preferring the "safety" of our church pews, we simply ignore the spiritual realm. Yet, our homes are afflicted with marriage breakdowns, addictions, pornography, abortion, sexual aberrations, violence, abuse—all results of the kingdom of darkness. You call that safety?!

Fear of Freud

People admit to being afraid to look at their dreams because of the pop-culture legacy of dream understanding handed down by Sigmund Freud, the father of analytical psychology. Better to keep a lid on those sexual fantasies from dreams—we shouldn't think like that! Unlike what Freud taught, contemporary dream researchers discovered that dreams are not trying to hide information, but instead are expressing it similar to the way we use imaginative language in everyday speech.[4]

> *The dream is trying to reveal the truth to us—what the mind cannot or will not accept—but it never condemns (Riffel).*

New Age spirituality fills the void

Denial of the supernatural has created a spiritual vacuum among people everywhere. A widespread upsurge of spiritual enthusiasm in the 20th century, loosely called the New Age, has attempted to meet the *felt* needs of spiritually hungry people. Largely ignorant of the value of dreams, we have essentially handed over this priceless historical heritage to New Agers, psychologists, and TV talk shows.

Ignorant of dreams, we have yielded this priceless heritage to New Agers, psychologists, and TV talk shows.

Dreams are only for the elite

Afraid to trust the leading of the Holy Spirit in their lives, many people look to priests, pastors, prophets, and famous leaders to tell them what God is saying. They believe dreams are given only to specialists, only for prophetic words for the whole family of God, or only to saints. They fail to realize that God sent the Holy Spirit so *all* people could know His voice. We believe it is possible for every human being to hear from God—including in their dreams.

---

2. Interactive learning

☐ Explain how dispensationalism contributed to the loss of dreams by the Church.

☐ Do you agree with the idea that dreams are abnormal? Yes/No

☐ Which factor(s) contributed most to your own ignorance of dreams?

Lord, Restore The Dream!

The advent of the age of rationalism approximately 300 years ago swept up the institutional church into an age of reason—people "believed" with their heads instead of their hearts. The dream suffered greatly in this context. Thankfully, in recent years some of God's people are starting to consider if God may be speaking to them in their dreams. Books on dreams for believers are beginning to appear, enabling us to begin appreciating this wonderful way God speaks to us in the nighttime.

Recent outpouring of Holy Spirit

When God poured out His Spirit in the latter part of the last century, some people began valuing prophecy and vision (see Appendix C, *"The Holy Spirit"*). Yet, because the dream is suspect, it remains largely outside the Christian domain, a sadly neglected aspect of our spiritual heritage. Very little teaching is offered on hearing from God in dreams.

Most people have never even heard a sermon on dreams, let alone learned how to understand them. According to Kelsey, for approximately three hundred years the Christian community wrote almost nothing about dreams.[5]

> *Not only does the Holy Spirit speak to us in dreams, he is the interpreter* par excellence, *and his help is available to every one of us.*

As author Catherine Marshall wrote, "It is encouraging to recall that our lives are set in the era prophesied by the Old Testament prophet Joel…In Old Testament times only the privileged few ever had the gift of the Spirit…From this elite group the only true dream interpretations had come."[6] In our times, not only does the Holy Spirit speak to us in dreams, "he is the interpreter *par excellence*. And his help is available to every one of us."

Contemporary dreamer

Earlier I (Gerald) described a bluebird dream that convinced me I would never find happiness inside the corporate life. It would be necessary for me to go outside the office walls to find my true life. Okay, now what am I supposed to do? One day God answered my prayer with an extremely powerful dream.

Flood Waters At My Doorstep

Flood waters are swirling at the doorstep of my house. An office colleague says we should all leave immediately. However, I suggest we go to the second floor to wait out the flood. The others leave, but I go upstairs. I am uncomfortable leaving without my favorite leather jacket, which I cannot find. I start feeling quite concerned about the flood waters. Finally a young woman guides me to my jacket, which is in a dresser drawer. Feeling relieved, I put on the jacket and step outside.

I realized this dream meant I was about to be emotionally overwhelmed if I didn't take action immediately. Suddenly I knew I needed to take a leave of absence from my job. My identity was tied to my job. However, I could no longer live in the corporate world that provided me security for many years—I was being forced to leave it.

Divine purpose of Gerald's dream

Without this dream, I would not have been able to summon the courage to sell our house and travel for six months and eventually change my career. Even though I came back to work in high tech for another 18 months, something profound had changed inside as a result of this dream: I began to seriously listen to the voice of God in my dreams.

The divine purpose of my dream was to warn me I needed to make a major change in my direction in life. When dreams call for life-changing direction, it is vital to share them with spiritually-attuned people. Although I was confident I knew what I needed to do, I did not make the decision solely on the dream alone. I shared the dream with a spiritually-attuned friend and with Judith—they both witnessed to the meaning of the dream and my decision.

3. Interactive learning
- ☐ How do you explain why people are receiving helpful dreams?
- ☐ Discuss dreams with your friends; ask them what they think of dreams.
- ☐ Ask your friends if they have ever been helped by a dream.

Wake up and hear the voice of God

Because of the Holy Spirit, we can hear the voice of our Father God speaking into our lives through dreams and visions. Long neglected as a means of communication from the Divine, dreams are being restored to the people of God. Spiritually-attuned people worldwide are beginning to listen to their dreams to discover what God is saying to them individually, to the faith community, and to the world.

Reengaging historical roots

Since the 1980s there has been a movement among evangelicals to look back at the beliefs, spirituality, and practices of the Early Church. Scholarly authors suggest that Protestant Christians, by rejecting many of the traditions of the church, have lost the fullness of our Christian heritage. They suggest that, while remaining true to the biblical limits of the gospel, we "need to learn from other times and movements concerning the whole meaning of that gospel."[7] People hungry for renewed encounters with God are eager to tap all the riches of our historic faith.

Dreams bringing people to Jesus

As we begin to embrace dreams, it is important to realize this realm does not belong exclusively to God's people. Everyone dreams. Jesus said God causes the sun to rise and the rain to fall on both the just and the unjust (Mt. 5:45), and Joel's prophecy said God would pour out His spirit on *all* flesh.

We may be uncomfortable with the idea that non-believers can contact spiritual realities transcending our humanity, but the Christian church does not offer exclusive contact with the spiritual realm. In fact, it is the universal reality of the spiritual world that makes the power of Christ within us so vital to our lives.[8]

God even uses dreams to bring people to Himself today. One woman came out of New Age spirituality and became a believer because a dream brought her revelation of Jesus as Lord. Missionaries working in Israel tell us they hear stories of people seeing Jesus appear in their dreams.

Muslims reportedly are receiving dreams and visions of Christ, and are turning to Him for salvation.[9] While working in the Middle East, Scott Breslin and Mike Jones report that people kept asking for help with dreams because they were seeing Jesus in their dreams.[10]

People longing for more

As a Willow Creek[11] survey showed, churches are realizing that their programs have not met the spiritual hunger of their parishioners nor produced spiritual development. Many people are hungry for an authentic experience with the Living God. For this to happen, we must have our spiritual senses awakened. We must be taught to take responsibility for our own spiritual growth and learn to be led by the Holy Spirit.

We can no longer afford to neglect this tremendous gift God offers us—it is time once again to take our dreams seriously. We encourage people of faith everywhere to wake up and hear the voice of the Lord.

Awake, sleeper…and Christ will shine on you (Eph. 5:14).

In the Bible, God's people were sometimes asked to interpret the dreams of unbelievers, as in the case of Joseph and Daniel. Might God want to use dreams to reach unbelievers today? Perhaps we should become more familiar with understanding our own dreams—and those of others.

4. Interactive learning
☐ Using a scale of 0 (not at all) to 10 (absolutely yes), how willing are you for the Lord to speak to you through your dreams? Your response: _____
☐ Write out your reasons for wanting to wake up and listen to your dreams.

Wake Up, Wake Up

Wake up, wake up, and go down to Egypt,
This is the Word of the Lord.
A Hebrew scribe named Matthew wrote upon the page,
A carpenter made note of night-time visions;
Logged upon the journal of his heart the Word from God
And saved the young Messiah for His mission.
Wake up, wake up, take note of dreams and visions,
And you may hear the word of the Lord.
Wake up, wake up, all you saints of God,
You may have missed His Word if you're not dreaming.
Wake up, wake up, and listen to your heart,
And God will speak to you in dreams and visions.[i]

---
i Gerald Doctor, *Joseph*, ©1985.

Fear not!

We believe dreams are a vehicle of communication from our Heavenly Father. By keeping the cross of Jesus Christ central in our exploration of the world of dreams, we need not be afraid. We have confidence in approaching the spiritual realm because Our Lord has gone before us and made a safe way for us.

The Holy Spirit, the Spirit of truth, has come to lead and guide us into all truth. Long before our modern search for meaning, God was speaking to eager listeners through their nighttime visions. We can trust the Holy Spirit to lead us to the truth.

At Jubilee 2000, Pope John Paul II called the church to prepare for a fresh work of the Holy Spirit. He stood at the doors of the Vatican and said before a listening world, "We welcome you, Spirit of Jesus."

> *Lord God, I confess my fear of the Holy Spirit. I ask You to forgive me for not being open to the Holy Spirit. I need Your power in my life. I ask You to fill me now with the Holy Spirit. Give me the courage to hear what Your Spirit wants to say to me.*

Applied Learning

✎ *Your response*
- ☐ Review the chapter, underline the one most significant idea for you.
- ☐ Prayerfully meditate on Acts 2:17, asking God to give you revelation of its meaning for you.
- ☐ Write a letter to God, telling Him of your decision to wake up and listen for His voice in your dreams.
- ☐ Affirm aloud: "Lord, I want to wake up and consider my dreams!"

✲ *Dream work strategies, skills & techniques*
- ☐ How might you have Titled (T) Gerald's *"Flood Waters Rising"* dream?
- ☐ Describe the overall Theme (T) in Gerald's dream.
- ☐ What do you think the primary emotion or Affect (A) was in Gerald's dream?
- ☐ What QUESTION (Q) might God be asking Gerald in his dream? (#1)
- ☐ Why did Gerald need to SHARE HIS DREAM with someone? (#2)
- ☐ How did his dream relate to his Current Concerns?
- ☐ What was the divine counsel in Gerald's dream?
- ☐ Describe the Treasure embedded in his dream.
- ☐ What Blessing from God did his dream result in?

Explaining new dream work strategies, skills & techniques

#1 QUESTION FROM GOD. Consider your dream as if it brings you a question from God, not an answer. Brainstorm a list of questions the dream might be trying to make you aware of.

#2 SHARE YOUR DREAM. Say to a friend, "I am having some interesting dreams. I want to know what God is saying to me through them. I would appreciate your ideas of what it might be about. What do you see in my dream? What area of my life do you think the dream could be about?"

✎ Practicing your skills

- ☐ Record a dream and the date you received it.
- ☐ Note your Current Concerns (CC).
- ☐ Give your dream a Title (T).
- ☐ Define the overall Theme (T) in your dream.
- ☐ Identify the dream Affect (A) or primary emotion in the dream.
- ☐ Identify a QUESTION (Q) God might be asking you through your dream. (#1)
- ☐ SHARE YOUR DREAM with another person. (#2)
- ☐ Consider how the dream relates to your Current Concerns (CC).
- ☐ "God, please give me the interpretation of my dream."
- ☐ Approach your dream as if it contains Hidden Treasure for you.
- ☐ What Treasure might your dream contain for you?
- ☐ What Blessing from God might your dream result in?

You have just learned the dream work method we find most helpful: the TTAQ technique, which is short for Title, Theme, Affect, Question.[14] The authors of this technique claim—and our experience verifies—that using it provides significant insight into dreams.

Dream Work Terminology
Can you explain the following terms?
- Dream question from God
- Dream sharing
- TTAQ technique

PART TWO
The Christian Basis of Dreams

Why you will find Part Two helpful

To break free from rational, humanistic influence and restore the dream as a valid way to hear from God requires us to diligently examine the evidence about dreams, visions and other supernatural manifestations of God. In this part you will learn that the basis for valuing the dream stands solidly on four foundational pillars:

As we open the Scriptures on this topic, you will recognize that the biblical authors held a reverence for dreams that is reflected throughout the entire narrative of God's dealings with his people. Writings of the Church Fathers continued this emphasis on listening for the voice of the Lord in supernatural encounters that often included visions and dreams. Examples of historical testimony down through the centuries will provide you with evidence that dreams have been an integral part of the human experience of the Divine.

Finally, you will come to value dreams as a way to hear from God today. You will be encouraged, with the help of the Holy Spirit, to update your theological viewpoint. You will learn that the historical Christian worldview affirms the validity of supernatural phenomena.

PART TWO chapters
- Biblical Record (Chapter 5)
- Church Fathers (Chapter 6)
- Historical Evidence (Chapter 7)
- Christian Worldview (Chapter 8)

Part Two The Christian Basis Of Dreams

Biblical Record

5

Hear now My words: If there is a prophet among you, I the Lord, shall make Myself known to him in a vision. I shall speak with him in a dream (Num. 12:6).

Core Concepts
- Biblical attitude values dreams/visions.
- God spoke through dreams in the Old Testament.
- God spoke through dreams in the New Testament.
- God to continue using dreams in the last days.
- The scriptural basis for listening to dreams.

Learning Objectives
At the completion of this chapter, you will be able to:
- ☐ Describe the biblical attitude toward dreams.
- ☐ Understand why Christians continue to receive dreams from God.
- ☐ Evaluate the scriptural basis for listening to your dreams.

In this chapter we examine the first foundational pillar of the Christian use of dreams—the Holy Scriptures. Evidence God spoke through dreams and visions is embedded in the entire scriptural record. An important first step in valuing dreams is to understand our sacred Scriptures. Exploring the biblical attitude enabled us to honor dreams as gifts from God.

We encourage you to look closely at how dreams are treated in the Scriptures, asking God to speak to you as you reflect on their meaning.

Biblical attitude towards dreams

In the sacred Scriptures we see a continuous record of God using dreams and visions to speak to people who would listen. Its books are chock full of supernatural events like visions and dreams, as the authors of these records relate how the Almighty communicated His love and will to His people.

In the Old Testament, Abraham, Jacob, Joseph, Solomon, Isaiah, Jeremiah, Ezekiel, Daniel, Zechariah, and many others saw visions, dreamed dreams, and had discourse with angels. Similarly, key New Testament people experienced personal communication from God through dreams and visions: Joseph & Mary, the disciples, Paul, Cornelius, Peter, and St. John in the apocalyptic revelations.

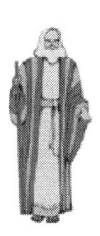

Dream Treasure

51

Visionaries like Daniel could forecast the future in their prophecies; Jeremiah's task was to jar the people into awareness of God's will for the present moment. Either way, the Word of The Lord came to the prophets—as *dreams* in the night while they slept, or as *visions* while they stood, staff in hand, gazing over the mountains.

Dreams prevalent in every biblical era

Dreams and visions were common in every period of the Bible—before the birth of Jesus Christ, in events surrounding His birth, during His lifetime, and in the acts of the Apostles. The scriptural record provides overwhelming evidence that dreams and visions were valued as a vital part of the way God communicates with His people.

A study of both the Old and New Testaments reveals that approximately one-third of the Bible involves dreams and visions.

A study of both the Old and New Testaments reveals that approximately one-third of the Bible involves dreams and visions. Riffel said that his review of *Strong's Concordance* yielded 224 direct references to dreams and visions, with approximately 50 dreams specifically mentioned.[1]

Little distinction between dream and vision

In both the Old and New Testaments, often little distinction is made between the dream and vision. Both "are related to the same prophetic root experience" and are sometimes mentioned together (e.g., Num. 12:6).[2] Sometimes the writers refer to the dream as a *vision in the night*. So when they mention visions, we can't be certain whether they are referring to waking visions or to dreams in the night.

In a dream, a vision of the night... (Job 33:15).

Then the mystery was revealed to Daniel in a night vision (Dan. 2:19).

...a vision appeared to Paul in the night: a certain man of Macedonia was standing and appealing to him, and saying, "Come over to Macedonia and help us" (Acts 16:9).

Old Testament words for dream and vision

In the Old Testament there seems to be little difference between the dream and the vision. The words for *to dream* and *to see* were one and the same. Interestingly, the Hebrew word for dream is linked to the Aramaic and Hebrew verb "to be made healthy or strong." Kelsey suggests *dream* refers to the mode or expression of experience, while *vision* refers to the content of the experience.[3]

Listen to King Nebuchadnezzar's understanding:

I saw a dream and it made me fearful; and these fantasies as I lay on my bed and the visions in my mind (of my head) kept alarming me (Dan. 4:4-5).

I was looking in the visions in my mind (of my head) as I lay on my bed, and behold, an angelic watcher, a holy one, descended from heaven. He shouted out and spoke... (Dan. 4:13).

New Testament words for dream and vision

The same lack of distinction between dream and vision is found in the New Testament. For understanding of the words translated *dream* or *vision* in the New Testament see Appendix D, "*New Testament Words For Dream & Vision.*"

Visions and dreams valued equally

According to historians, the Church Fathers seemed not to distinguish between dreams and visions, valuing them both equally. In the Judeo-Christian worldview, angels, visions, and dreams were all seen as aspects of the same reality—the Kingdom of God, existing beyond sense perception and the material world. Dreams come while we are asleep, and visions while we are awake—but they're essentially of the same nature.[4]

Hebrew people valued dreams as way to hear God

The Scriptures provide overwhelming evidence that dreams and visions were valued as a vital part of the way God communicates with His people. To start with, God Himself said He will speak through dreams.

> *(The Lord) said, Hear now My words: If there is a prophet among you, I the Lord, shall make myself known to him in a vision. I shall speak with him in a dream, not so with My servant Moses...with him I speak mouth to mouth... and not in dark sayings. (Num. 12:6-8)*

In both the Old and New Testaments, little distinction is made between the dream and vision.

In their very culture and way of life, Hebrew people valued the dream as a way for God to speak directly to them, giving them both knowledge and gifts. Dreams were a given fact. The Rabbinical attitude reveals this: "Dreams which are not interpreted are like letters which have not been opened" (*Talmud*). In fact, the *Talmud* mentions dreams 217 times.

---

1. Interactive learning
- ☐ Underline the most important idea for you in this section.
- ☐ Why do you think there is little distinction between dreams and visions?

Even unbelievers have dreams from God

Clearly we can see from Scripture that God's people aren't the only ones who can contact the spiritual realm in dreams. In the Old Testament even idolatrous heathen received dreams from God. Check these out:

- Abimelech, a Canaanite (Gen 20:3)
- Laban, from Ur of the Chaldea (Gen 31:24)
- Pharaoh of Egypt (Gen 41:7)
- The Midianite soldier (Jg 7:13)
- Nebuchadnezzar, the Babylonian (Dan 4:18)
- Pilate's wife, the Roman (Mt 27:19)

As we begin to embrace dreams, it is important to realize that this realm does not belong exclusively to God's chosen people. Everyone dreams. After all, Jesus said that God causes the rain to fall on both the just and the unjust (Mt. 5:45), and Joel's prophecy said God would pour out His spirit on *all* people.

Dream Treasure

2. Interactive learning
- How do you think Pilate's wife knew Jesus was a righteous man?
- Why do you think Pilate's wife took her dream seriously?

About disputed Scriptures

Although people who want to disparage dreams will point to Scripture passages seeming to speak negatively about dreams, the context indicates that warnings are against believing false prophets who attempt to use their dreams to mislead people. The Scriptures seem to deliver no injunction against listening to dreams/visions, but only against failure to correctly distinguish the Word of the Lord.

Zechariah (who wrote his prophetic book inspired by his dreams/visions) warned the people who looked to idols for guidance, instead of their God, that they would be (surprise!) deceived by diviners who lie and tell them false dreams (Zech. 10:2). When Jeremiah, a true prophet, warns God's people against listening to the dreams of false prophets (Jer. 23:25-32), the emphasis is not on devaluing dreams, but rather on the need to speak faithfully the Word of God.

> *The Holy Scripture expresses reverence for dreams, but also offers critical evaluation of them so God's people will not be conned by false religious leaders.*

Dreams were so important that the Holy Scripture not only expresses reverence for dreams, but also offers critical evaluation of them so God's people will not be conned by false religious leaders. Dreams purported to be for the larger group of people must be examined carefully and discerned properly—to prevent charlatans from misleading the populace.

3. Interactive learning
- Using an unabridged concordance, look at the references to dreams, visions and angels in the Holy Bible.
- How many of these references viewed dreams positively? ____
- How many of these references viewed dreams negatively? ____

Prominent characters esteemed dreams

As we examine the Holy Scriptures, we see that God's people believed God speaks through dreams and visions.

- **The teenage Joseph** and **his brothers** recognized Joseph's dreams about sheaves and the sun, moon, and stars were from God (Gen. 37:1-11).
- **Moses** knew this—he heard it firsthand in a divine encounter (Num. 12:6-8).
- **King Saul** knew it—he was scared out of his wits when he could not sense God's guidance in dreams or by the prophets (I Sam. 28:6, 15).
- **Job** understood it too. He made it clear that God opens the ears of men in a dream, a vision of the night, for specific purposes (Job 33:14-16).
- **Daniel** knew that God spoke in dreams when he asked God for the interpretation of Nebuchadnezzar's dreams (see Dan. 2:17-23, 28).

- *Habakkuk* set himself to *look* for God's word coming in dreams/visions (Hab. 2:1-3).
- *Joel,* a prophet of God, prepared ordinary people to expect dreams when the Holy Spirit was poured out (Joel 2:28).
- *Joseph,* the earthly father of Jesus, understood God was speaking to him through his dreams (Matt. 1 & 2)
- *Peter,* called by Jesus to feed *His* sheep, expected the first Christians to receive dreams because the Holy Spirit was being poured out (Acts 2:1-18).

> Peter, called by Jesus to feed His sheep, expected the first Christians to receive dreams because the Holy Spirit was being poured out.

God spoke through dreams in Old Testament

In their very culture and way of life, the Old Testament people valued the dream as a way for God to speak directly to them, giving them both knowledge and gifts. The Old Testament is replete with stories of Hebrew patriarchs whose very approach to life came from the dreams and visions God gave them. Emboldened by their revelations, the exploits of the nation's leaders changed the course of history for the ancient Israeli people.

God spoke through dreams in major events

Here are some examples of history-altering dreams:

- *God established His covenant with Abraham in a dream/vision, assuring him of a great future (Gen. 15:1-21).*

- *Joseph received dreams from God about his destiny. He dreamed of his sheaf standing erect while his brothers' sheaves bowed to his; in a second dream, the sun, moon, stars bowed down to him (Gen. 37:1-11).*

- *Prophet Isaiah received visions from the Lord containing prophetic warnings, encouragement, correction, promises, and the coming kingdom of God (Is. 1:1; 2:1; 6:1; 13:1; 21:2).*

- *Prophet Jeremiah received visions, dreams, and prophecies: his prophecies seemed to come from his visions (Jer. 1:11-19).*

- *God gave Daniel the ability to understand visions and dreams (Dan. 1:17). King Nebuchadnezzar received dreams and visions to reveal the future and the thoughts of his heart. When he forgot a dream, Daniel, faced with losing his head along with his Chaldean colleagues, immediately sought divine help to interpret the dream (Dan. 2:1-46).*

- *Later, Daniel again correctly interpreted the king's dream about a tree in the middle of the world that was cut down (Dan. 4:5-27). Daniel rejoiced that the Lord "reveals the profound and hidden things; he knows what is in the darkness" (Dan. 2: 22)*

- *Daniel had several great dreams and visions of his own (Dan. 7:1-28; 8:1-27; 10:1-19; 12:5-6).*

Dream Treasure

PART TWO The Christian Basis Of Dreams

> *4. Interactive learning*
> ☐ How did these patriarchs know that God might speak to them in dreams/visions?
> ☐ Why did God speak to Solomon in a dream, rather through a prophet?
> ☐ How did the *word of the Lord* come to Daniel, words or pictures (Dan. 7:1-2)?

Jacob's legendary ladder dream

This profound dream of angels traversing a ladder stretched between heaven and earth is perhaps the most famous dream in history, often depicted in art, literature, and song. Jacob's renowned religious experience reveals the dream as a way to receive guidance and direction from God.

> ➤ *Dream Work Tip:*
> Dreams require a response from us, to let God know we heard Him (see I Samuel 3:9). Many dream communications from God are conditioned upon our obedience to them.

(Jacob) took one of the *stones of the place* and put it under his head, and lay down in that place. And he had a dream, and behold a ladder was set on the earth with its top reaching to heaven; and behold, the angels of God were ascending and descending on it. And behold, the Lord stood above it and said, "I am the Lord, the God of your father Abraham and the God of Isaac; the land on which you lie, I will give it to you and to your descendants…I am with you, and will keep you wherever you go, and will bring you back to this land; for I will not leave you until I have done what I have promised you. "Then Jacob awoke from his sleep and said, "Surely the Lord is in this place, and I did not know it" (Genesis. 28:11-16).

Dream Treasure

When he awoke, Jacob, recognizing that it was God speaking to him, built an altar and worshipped God. This dream has influenced the history and culture of many nations for thousands of years.

Divine purpose of Jacob's dream

The Lord God establishes a covenant with Jacob, forming the origin of a chosen people who will bear God's name and banner. All this from a dream!

5. Interactive learning
- ☐ Did Jacob's dream help him come to *know* the Lord for himself (Is. 45:3)?
- ☐ What blessings from God did Jacob receive through his dream?
- ☐ Describe the treasure Jacob's dream contained for him.

Angels and dreams

There seems to be a connection between angels and dreams or visions. In the Old Testament when Daniel asked for understanding of a vision (Dan. 8:16), a voice said, "*Gabriel*, give this man an understanding of the vision" (Talmud refers to the angel Gabriel as the prince of dreams[5]—Judith once dreamed of the angel Gabriel teaching her to fly).

The Talmud refers to the angel Gabriel as the prince of dreams

In the New Testament, an angel appeared in holy dreams to both Mary and Joseph. In one dream the angel tells Joseph that Mary is pregnant with child. In another, the angel warns Joseph in a dream that Jesus is in danger, and Joseph and Mary should flee to Egypt.

God spoke through dreams in everyday circumstances

God not only used the dream and vision to speak in life's major historical events, He also used them to help people in their daily lives:[6]

- Jacob received wisdom in his relationship with Laban via a dream, telling him what to do with the flock (Gen. 31:10-29).
- A dream warned Laban to be careful how he spoke to Jacob (Gen. 31:24).
- Pharaoh's butler and baker in prison experienced dreams revealing their immediate future (Gen. 40:1-23).
- When his brothers came to buy grain, God reminded Joseph of his dreams about them (Gen. 42:9).
- Balaam's donkey saw an angel of the Lord standing before him in a vision. God also opened Balaam's spiritual eyes to see the angel of the Lord (Num. 22:20-31).
- Angel of the Lord spoke to Gideon at the wine press, giving him a vision and purpose for his life (Judges 6:11).
- Midianite soldier dreamed of a bread loaf tumbling into camp, and as Gideon

Dream Treasure

PART TWO   The Christian Basis Of Dreams

eavesdropped, another soldier's interpretation revealed God's protection over Israel (Judges 7:13-15).

Dreams and visions were authentic events experienced by ordinary people that affected their lives concretely. In Gideon's story, nobody flippantly joked that the soldier overate pizza at Dominoes last night. They all treated the soldier's dream as valid and important to act upon—even critical to their lives.

6. Interactive learning
- ☐ Read the dreams concerned with everyday circumstances in the Bible.
- ☐ Identify the divine purpose in each of the dreams.
- ☐ How did the baker's and cupbearer's dreams relate to their current concerns?
- ☐ What was the result of the baker and cupbearer sharing their dreams?
- ☐ What does it mean that Gideon's enemy received a dream from God?

God spoke through dreams in New Testament era

Since Moses was told by God explicitly that he would speak through dreams (see Num. 12:6), they were *commonly* accepted as vehicles for divine communication by the Hebrew people.

In New Testament times, God appeared often to people in supernatural visitations—visions, trances, angels, and dreams. In the brief period of history of the events surrounding the birth of the Messiah, the writers record several dreams used as vehicles for divine communication.

Life of Jesus begins with dreams

According to the scriptural record, the story of the most important birth in history weaves together several supernatural experiences, including angel visitations, divinely-inspired knowledge, visions and dreams.

It's tough to imagine how Joseph could have stayed linked up with an already-pregnant Mary. Knowing he had not touched her, no force of reason could have convinced Joseph that Mary had not been unfaithful.

However, a dream carried *divine power* to persuade the humble carpenter to embrace his destiny.

- Joseph dreams of an angel telling him to not be afraid to take Mary as his wife, even though she is with child (Mt. 1:20).
- The Lord God protects the Christ Child by warning the Magi in a dream, telling them not to return to Herod (Mt. 2:12).
- Angel appears to Joseph in a dream, telling him to flee to Egypt and stay there, awaiting further instruction (Mt. 2:13).

Dream Treasure

- Once again an Angel appears to Joseph in a dream, telling him to go back to Israel (Mt. 2:19,20).
- Joseph receives yet another dream warning him of danger, and he diverts his family to Nazareth (Mt. 2:22-23).

Joseph is an interesting study in dream understanding. He listens to his dream and values it, accepting it as a word from God. Moreover, instead of following Jewish tradition (stone the offending woman for adultery), Joseph exhibits love and forgiveness way beyond the call of duty.

7. Interactive learning

☐ Read "*Musings on Joseph, the dreamer*" (see end of Chapter 1), circling the ideas that arouse feeling in you.

☐ How do you understand the challenge of this prose?

Other New Testament seers

Following are some New Testament dreams, visions and other supernatural visitations that hold authority similar to dreams:

1. **Heathen wife of Pilate** received a dream that warned not to have anything to do with Jesus, that righteous man (Mt. 27:19).
2. **Zacharias** encounters angel in a vision, telling him God will answer their prayer (Luke 1:11-22).
3. **Women at Jesus' tomb** saw a vision of angels, telling them Jesus was alive (Luke 24:4,5,22-24).
4. As he was dying, **Stephen** saw a vision of the heavens open with Jesus standing at the right hand of God (Acts 7:55).
5. **Saul** encounters the Lord in an auditory vision, receiving revelations and direction (Acts 9:1-6).
6. The Lord spoke to **Ananias**, a disciple of God, in a vision, telling him where to go, what to say and do (Acts 9:10-18).
7. Angel of God came to **Cornelius** in a vision, informing him his prayers had been heard and telling him what he is to do—find Peter (Acts 10:1-8).
8. In a trance, **Peter** sees the sky open up and a great sheet lowered to the ground by four corners. The Spirit leads him to Cornelius, who helps Peter understand the radical meaning of this iconoclastic vision (Acts 10:9-20; 11:5-10).
9. **Peter** says of his prison escape that he did not know whether what was being done by the angel was real, but thought he was seeing a vision (Acts 12:9).
10. In a "vision in the night" **Paul** saw a Macedonian man asking him to come to Macedonia and help. Taking action immediately, Paul changed his direction (Acts 16:9, 10).
11. The Lord speaks to **Paul** one "night in a vision," telling him to not be afraid any

longer, but to go on speaking and do not be silent for the Lord was with him (Acts 18:9, 10).

12. **Paul** falls into a trance as he was praying, and sees Jesus telling him that his life is in danger, his testimony won't be received, and to go out of Jerusalem—far away to the Gentiles (Acts 22:17).

13. Experiencing what was apparently an auditory vision, **John** heard behind him a loud voice like the sound of a trumpet, saying, "Write in a book what you see and send it to the 12 churches" (Rev. 1:10,11).

14. In a vision, **John** goes through a door and enters heaven (Rev. 4:1-3; 5:6; 6:8).

8. Interactive learning
☐ What was God's purpose in each of the above spiritual experiences?
☐ What response did St. Paul give to his vision-in-the-night?
☐ How did St. Peter's vision change his theology?

Dreams to continue in the last days

Not only did God speak through dreams and visions in the Old and New Testaments, He also says they are to continue through the Holy Spirit, even in the last days.

> *It will come about after this that I will pour out My Spirit on all mankind; and your sons and daughters will prophesy, your old men will dream dreams, your young men will see visions…(Joel 2:28-29).*

> *It shall be in the last days, God says, I will pour out my Spirit on all people. Your sons and daughters will prophesy, your young men will see visions, your old men will dream dreams (Acts 2:1-18).*

Holy Spirit to abide with us
In the Old Testament promised to send the Holy Spirit so that He could make His words known to us.

> *I will pour out my spirit on you; I will make my words known to you (Prov. 1:23).*

Because the Holy Spirit abides in us, we can continue to hear the voice of God speaking very personally to us through dreams, visions, and prophecy.

> *I will ask the Father, and He will give you another Helper, that He may be with you forever; that is the Spirit of truth (John 14:16-17).*

To answer the question, Are we living in the last days, consider the following Scripture: *"Children, it is the last hour; and just as you heard that the antichrist is coming, even now many antichrists have arisen; from this we know that it is the last hour"* (I John 2:18).

> Dreams are to continue through the Holy Spirit, even in the last days!

9. Interactive learning
- ☐ Does the Holy Spirit bring dreams, visions, and prophecies to ordinary people? Yes/No Explain?
- ☐ How long do the Scriptures say the Holy Spirit will be with us?
- ☐ When did God say He would no longer use dreams to speak to people?

> *We encourage you to pray and ask God to give you revelation concerning the importance and work of the indwelling presence of the Holy Spirit in the life of a believer. See the Kairos Ministries web site for more understanding of the work of the Holy Spirit:*
> http://www.kairosministries.us/The Holy Spirit Will Lead You.pdf

Holy Scriptures authenticate dreams

The notion that God communicates with His creation using dreams and visions is established firmly and authoritatively on the Scriptures. Sacred writings of Old Testament sages—supported by New Testament records—convey a reverence toward dreams and a deep appreciation for their impact on the lives of God's people.

Scriptural basis of dreams

The Christian use of dreams draws its authority from the following Scriptures:

1. Hear now My words: If there is a prophet among you, I the Lord, shall make myself known to him in a vision. I shall speak with him in a dream, not so with My servant Moses…with him I speak mouth to mouth…and not in dark sayings (Num. 12:6-8).

2. Indeed God speaks once, or twice, yet no one notices it. In a dream, in a vision of the night, when sound sleep falls on men, while they slumber in their beds, then He opens the ears of men, and seals their instruction (Job 33:14-16).

3. I will bless the Lord who has counseled me; indeed, my heart [*inner man*] instructs me in the night (*while asleep*) (Ps. 16:7).

4. There is a God in heaven who reveals mysteries…He has made known to King Nebuchadnezzar what will take place in the latter days…this was your dream and the visions in your mind while on the bed (Dan. 2:28).

5. Behold, I will pour out My Spirit on you; I will make my words known to you (Prov. 1:23).

6. I will pour out My Spirit on all mankind; and your sons and daughters will prophesy, your old men will dream dreams, your young men will see visions (Joel 2:28).

7. It shall be in the last days, God says, That I will pour forth of My Spirit upon all mankind; and your sons and your daughters shall prophecy, and your young men shall have visions, and your old men shall dream dreams (Acts 2:16-17).

8. Things which eye has not seen and ear has not heard, and have not entered the heart of man, all that God has prepared for those who love Him. For to us God revealed them through the Spirit… Now we have received, not the spirit of the world, but the Spirit who is from God, that we might know the things freely given to us by God (I Cor. 2:9-10, 12).

There is no scriptural basis for asserting that God no longer speaks through dreams in our time!

Clearly there is no place in the sacred writings stating God will no longer speak through dreams after the New Testament era. Thus, there is no *scriptural basis* for asserting that God no longer speaks through dreams in our time!

Dreamers given special recognition

In ancient times, dreams were considered to be a commonly accepted way to receive wisdom and understanding from the spiritual realm. Virkler & Virkler[7] observe that famous characters who understood and appreciated their divine revelations were afforded special acknowledgment.

Abraham and Solomon were viewed as wise. Daniel and Joseph were revered for their ability to interpret dreams. Ezekiel was a great prophet. St. Paul became a renowned missionary. Powerful things, these dreams and visions.

Scriptures reveal that God chooses to use the Holy Spirit to communicate with people through visions, prophecies—and dreams. However, we failed to take this seriously and lost touch with this vital resource from God. Dreams need to be valued just as much as visions and prophecies if we want to experience more fully the blessings God has for each one of us.

Lord, I ask You to forgive me for ignoring the scriptural evidence on dreams. Throughout the ages You never rescinded Your plan to use the dream as a way to speak to people. Lord, please open my understanding about dreams.

Applied Learning

✎ *Your Response*
- ☐ Review this chapter, marking the most important ideas for you.
- ☐ Meditate on Numbers 12:6-9. What importance will you give to God's own words about dreams?
- ☐ Using a scale of 0 to 10 (0 not at all; 10 maximum), how much will the scriptural record on dreams influence you? Response: ____
- ☐ What evidence do you need to validate the Christian use of dreams?
- ☐ Affirm: "God wants to bless me through my dreams. I like that."

☼ *Dream work strategies, skills & techniques*
- ☐ READ ALOUD "Jacob's Ladder" dream (Gen. 28:11-16). (#1)
- ☐ Use the TTAQ technique with Jacob's dream.
- ☐ Use a MEDITATION technique on Jacob or Solomon's dreams. (#2)
- ☐ How did Jacob's dream relate to his Current Concerns (CC)?
- ☐ What did Jacob do in RESPONSE to his dream? (#3)

Explaining new dream work strategies, skills & techniques

#1 READ YOUR DREAM ALOUD. Simply hearing your self read a dream may help unlock its meaning.

#2 MEDITATING on a dream asks you to quiet yourself, tune into your heart and simply ponder on it, rather than trying to grasp its meaning with your intellect.

#3 What RESPONSE will you give this dream? Dreams require a response from us, to let God know we are listening, we hear Him, and we will take action on it (see I Samuel 3:9). Many dream communications from God are conditioned upon our obedience to them.

> ➤ *Dream Work Tip:*
> Try meditating on your dream as if it were a parable by Jesus or a scriptural passage.

Dream Treasure

PART TWO The Christian Basis Of Dreams

✒ Practicing your skills
- ☐ Select a dream to work with.
- ☐ READ ALOUD your dream. (#1)
- ☐ Use a MEDITATION technique on your dream. (#2)
- ☐ How does your dream relate to your Current Concerns (CC)?
- ☐ What RESPONSE will you give your dream? (#3)
- ☐ What blessing from God does your dream offer you?
- ☐ Do you think your dream might contain hidden treasure for you?

Dream Work Terminology
Can you explain the following terms?
- Vision in the night
- Read dream aloud
- Meditation techniques
- Your Response

Church Fathers

6

Dreams give us revelation of the spiritual world, and they demonstrate that we can be very close to God. (Irenaeus)

Core Concepts
- Apostolic Fathers valued dreams as a way to hear God.
- Early Church Fathers validated the biblical attitude towards dreams.
- Church Doctors embraced dreams.
- The Church continued to value dreams for hundreds of years.

Learning Objectives
At the completion of this chapter, you will be able to:
- ☐ Discuss the beliefs of the Church Fathers.
- ☐ Clarify when the Church lost touch with dreams.
- ☐ Explain the position the Church Fathers took toward dreams.
- ☐ Evaluate whether God planned to stop using dreams to speak to people.

We began this section on the Christian foundation of dreams by showing how the Scriptures report numerous dreams and visions experienced by men and women of faith. Now we will briefly consider the beliefs, actions and writings of the Church Fathers' concerning dreams. These important men of God held to a deep conviction that Our Lord speaks through the dream and vision, and provide us with the second foundational pillar for valuing dreams as a way to hear from God. .

About the Church Fathers
The Church Fathers are influential theologians who wrote during the first few centuries of Christian Church history. The very earliest of the Fathers, called the Apostolic Fathers, are men who apparently had direct contact with the Apostles of Jesus Christ. What they had learned directly from the Master, the Apostles passed on to the Apostolic Fathers, whose writings were highly regarded—sometimes nearly on a level with Scripture.

Long before Luther hammered on the Wittenberg castle church door (1517), before the Catholic Pope and Eastern Patriarch excommunicated each other (1054), before Constantine institutionalized the Church (313), everybody enjoyed the rich, spiritual, biblically-based, theological writings of the Church Fathers. By considering what they wrote, we came to realize that God never stopped using dreams to speak to people. Understanding that dreams were part of orthodoxy from the very early centuries of the Christian Church was a critical factor in enabling us to embrace dreams in our lives.

Early Church Fathers value dreams

Following the New Testament period, the Early Church Fathers continued the Apostolic tradition of valuing visions and dreams as key ways to hear the divine voice. A careful study of what they said about dreams makes it clear the Church Fathers viewed the dream as one of the most important ways in which God revealed His will to people.

> *"Almost the greater part of mankind get their knowledge of God from dreams."*
> Tertullian

Throughout the first few centuries of the Church, dreams continued to hold a central place in the lives of God's people. Dreams gave people access to a spiritual reality difficult to contact any other way.

Rooted deeply in biblical tradition, the Early Church Fathers and later Doctors of the Church lay a rich foundation for the spiritual practice of valuing our dreams. Let's examine the viewpoint of some of the historic giants of the faith on this topic. Kelsey[1] and others develop this in detail; here are just a few examples:

Earliest writings (up to 150 A.D.)

Hermas' inspirational work *Shepherd of Hermas*—highly valued, and even considered as canonical Scripture by many people of the 2nd & 3rd centuries—begins with a dream/vision, and continues with a series of visions over time.

Christian apologists (150 to 325 A.D.)

Justin Martyr, one of the most important Christian apologists of the second century, was a great believer in dreams. He said dreams indicate we live in a spiritual dimension, beyond mere existence in a physical world.

Irenaeus, bishop of Lyons, and another early Church giant, believed dreams give us revelation of the spiritual world, and they demonstrate that we can be very close to God.

> *Dreams give us revelation of the spiritual world, and they demonstrate that we can be very close to God.*

Clement, widely traveled and highly educated, believed that true dreams come from the depth of our ever-active *soul*, and he argued that dreams reveal spiritual reality. During sleep we are especially open to spiritual reality because our soul is not bothered by sense input as it is during waking hours.

Origen—one of the greatest Christian thinkers of the third century—viewed dreams, visions, and divine inspiration as all of a piece. An essential part of the way God reveals things to us, the dream/vision gives us knowledge of the spiritual world through symbolic awareness.

Tertullian, the great Latin apologist, believed dreams and visions are available to people today just as much as they were to the first apostles, and God reveals Himself to people in dreams. He went so far as to say, "almost the greater part of mankind get their knowledge of God from dreams."[2]

Bishop Cyprian, a founder of the Latin Church and a pupil of Tertullian, asserted that God often used noticeable visions to guide and direct the councils of the church. He emphasized personal encounters with God via dreams and visions, which he described in many places.

Early orthodoxy includes dreams

Athanasius, bishop of Alexandria (328–373), was a brilliant thinker whose writings were considered to be authoritative by Catholic, Protestant, and Orthodox theologians. In *Against the Heathen* he said that frequently during sleep, "the soul… imagines and beholds things above the earth, and often even holds converse with the saints and angels who are above earthly and bodily existence."[3]

> *If we are finely tuned to God, we don't need visions and other more dramatic divine revelations—we can depend upon dreams to hear from God (John Chrysostom)*

John Chrysostom, known as John the Golden-mouth, said dreams are a frequent source of revelation from the spiritual realm, and God reveals Himself through dreams. His writings were viewed by the Greek Church as nearly on a par with the Scriptures. According to Kelsey, Chrysostom seemed to say that, if we are finely tuned to God, we don't need visions and other more dramatic divine revelations—we can depend upon dreams to hear from God.[4]

Church Doctors embrace dreams

Doctors in the East

Basil the Great said this about dreams: "The enigmas in dreams have a close affinity to those things which are signified in an allegoric or hidden sense in the Scriptures. Thus both Joseph and Daniel, through the gift of prophecy, used to interpret dreams, since the force of reason by itself is not powerful enough for getting at truth."[5] Way ahead of modern psychology, Basil understood that dreams reveal the inner workings of our unconscious.

> *The force of reason by itself is not powerful enough for getting at truth.*

Synesius of Cyrene in 415 A.D. wrote a highly valued book on dreams, describing the dream as an opening of the self to God and the spiritual world. He laid out sound reasoning for discussing dreams, and detailed the blessings we gain from studying our dreams.[6]

Doctors in the West

Ambrose (340 A.D.) taught that dreams were one of God's methods of bringing revelation to man. He valued his dreams, even going to confront the emperor because of a dream.

Augustine, writing in the 4th century, established the intellectual foundation for Western Christian thinking until Aquinas. A keen thinker with good psychological insight, Augustine believed dreams were important for understanding both human psychology and people's relationship to God.

PART TWO The Christian Basis Of Dreams

Augustine believed dreams were important for understanding both human psychology and people's relationship to God.

Jerome, a great 5th century scholar and Doctor of the Church, claimed that dreams dramatically affected the direction of his life. However, when he later mistranslated key verses of the Bible into the Latin Vulgate, it led to widespread unbelief about dreams in the Western world (see Chapter 4).

1. Interactive learning
☐ Write down a list of beliefs held by the Church Fathers.
☐ In your words, summarize the position of the Church Fathers toward dreams.
☐ Which Church Father do you easily agree with?
☐ Identify the one idea you find most challenging.

Church Fathers confirm scriptural view

Deeply convinced that God speaks through the dream and vision, the Church Fathers in no way suggest God stopped speaking this way at the end of the Apostolic era. Instead, the writings of the Early Church Fathers reveal that they continued the Apostolic tradition of valuing the dream as a way to hear from God. Later, Doctors of the Church continued this belief, and Kelsey notes, "until the year 1200, there were no Christian writers or philosophers who ignored or underestimated the importance of visions or dreams."[7]

Until the year 1200, there were no Christian writers or philosophers who ignored or underestimated the importance of visions or dreams.

Things changed in the 13th century when the highly influential theologian Thomas Aquinas de-emphasized the supernatural dimension in favor of Aristotelian thinking. Writing with great ambivalence about dreams and visions, ironically, Aquinas was helped by his dreams in his own life. He even claimed to have a dialogue with St. Peter and St. Paul in a dream that helped him with a theological issue in writing his *Summa Theologica*. Even though he mellowed his views before he died, by then he had managed to turn much of the Church away from appreciating dreams.

2. Interactive learning
☐ Explain what happened in the 13th century that influenced the devaluing of dreams by the Church.
☐ Did God stop using dreams during the early church era? Yes/No
☐ What do you think replaces dreams in the life of a believer today?

Dream Treasure

Contemporary dreamers

One of the elements contributing to the vibrant spirituality of the early believers was their appreciation for hearing from God in their dreams. Down through the centuries this has been part of the Christian experience—people valued supernatural, non-rational information as an important source of knowledge for living their lives. So, by taking our dreams seriously, far from going against historic tradition, we are embracing it!

> *By taking our dreams seriously, far from going against historic tradition, we are embracing it.*

In the following dream, I (Judith) accepted the message of my dream as direction from God for my work in Europe.

Director of Marketing

After I returned from five months in Germany in 1991, the Lord asked me not to return until he told me. I waited three long years, then I dreamed...

I am looking at a large map of Europe on the wall. Tiny little lights on the map are going on all over Germany, but mostly in a specific northern area. A business man, CEO of his own small company (someone I had known in the past), says to me: "We want to make you director of marketing in Europe. We know you are the one, because the Lord has said so."

It was time to return! I wrote letters to friends in Germany, asking them if they would like to schedule a meeting for me if I came. The Lord opened the doors, and for the next seven years, I traveled to Germany once or twice each year, ministering in homes, clinics, retreat centers, and Christian groups. In 2002, I was offered a live monthly program on Radio Horeb in Germany, which I have been doing ever since. All because of a dream!

Divine purpose of Judith's dream

God used this dream to tell me (Judith) it was time to go back to Europe, and exactly where I was to go—northern part of Germany. Moreover, God also enlarged my understanding of who I am and my purpose for going there.

> *Lord, I thank You for the wealth of biblical and theological treasures inherent in our rich heritage. Give us the courage to once more value our dreams.*

Dream Treasure

Applied Learning

✎ *Your Response*
- ☐ Reflect on the quote by Irenaeus at the beginning of this chapter; decide whether you agree with him.
- ☐ What would have been lost if Judith had not listened to and acted on her dream?
- ☐ How do the beliefs of the Church Fathers about dreams compare with yours?
- ☐ How will this chapter influence your view of dreams?

☼ *Dream work strategies, skills & techniques*
- ☐ Identify the KEY STATEMENT in Judith's "Director of Marketing" dream. (#1)
- ☐ How does the KEY STATEMENT relate to Judith's HEART CONCERNS? (#2)
- ☐ How did Judith respond to her dream?
- ☐ Describe the blessing/s the dream brought Judith.

Explaining new dream work strategies, skills & techniques
#1 KEY STATEMENT—any prominent sentence, words, or thoughts expressed in dream. It offers clues about the meaning of the dream.

#2 How does this KEY STATEMENT relate to your LIFE AT THE MOMENT (your HEART CONCERNS)?

✍ *Practicing your skills*
- ☐ Select a dream to work with.
- ☐ Read your dream aloud.
- ☐ Does your dream contain a KEY STATEMENT? (#1)
- ☐ How might the KEY STATEMENT relate to your LIFE AT THE MOMENT? (#2)
- ☐ Can you identify a blessing from God in your dream?
- ☐ What response will you give your dream?

Dream Work Terminology
Can you explain the following terms?
- Symbolic awareness
- Soul of man
- Personal encounters with God in dreams
- Human psychology
- Dream enigmas
- Key statement

PART TWO The Christian Basis Of Dreams

Historical Evidence

7

Things which eye has not seen and ear has not heard, and which have not entered the heart of man, all that God has prepared for those who love Him. For to us God revealed them through the Spirit…(I Cor. 2:9-10).

Core Concepts
- Dreams influenced music, literature, science, and inventions.
- Dreams changed history.
- People today are receiving dreams from God.
- God still uses dreams to reveal things He wants to give us.

Learning Objectives
At the completion of this chapter, you will be able to:
- ☐ Describe the role of dreams in music, literature and science.
- ☐ Understand the influence dreams have played in history.
- ☐ Explain how dreams have influenced church history.
- ☐ Ponder the historical evidence, in the context of I Corinthians 2:9-10.
- ☐ Recount the blessings dreams have brought humanity.

In this chapter we examine the indisputable historical evidence of how dreams have been valued by all mankind. By considering the testimony of people down through the ages, we conclude that God never stopped using the dream to speak to people. Historical evidence forms the third foundational pillar for valuing dreams as a way to receive God's counsel and wisdom in the night. .

Musical & literary creations

Herman Riffel noted that many inventions, musical compositions, and other artistic and scientific endeavors were the direct result of a dream or a vision, or a dreamy, trancelike state (remember Peter in Acts 10?).[1] Here are a few examples:

- **Stravinsky** wrote some of his music in dreams.
- **Wagner** composed parts of *Die Meister Singer* and *Das Rheingold* in a dream-like condition. About *Tristan und Isolde*, he wrote, "For once you are going to hear a dream, I dreamed all this: never could my poor head have invented such a thing purposely."[2]

- **Tartini's** violin masterpiece, *The Devil's Trill* came to him while he slept.
- **Tchaikovsky, Mozart, Haydn**, and **Brahms** were often close to a dream-state while composing.
- **Handel** claimed that parts of *The Messiah* came to him in a dream.
- **Robert Louis Stevenson** claims that the plots for many of his stories such as *The Strange Case of Dr. Jekyll and Mr. Hyde* came from his dreams.
- Authors such as **Edgar Allan Poe, H.G. Wells**, and **Rudyard Kipling** were inspired by their dreams to write their renowned tales.
- In writing *Pilgrim's Progress*, **John Bunyan** wove his narrative from a series of dreams, visions, and contemplative experiences.
- **Paul McCartney** received the complete melody for *Yesterday* in a dream.

Scientific advancements & inventions

- **Isaac Newton** was reputed to have solved problems during dreams.
- **Elias Howe** is said to have invented the sewing machine as a result of a nightmare/dream.
- **Kekulé** formulated the molecular structure of the benzene ring after he saw a vision of six snakes in a ring chasing each others' tails.
- **Otto Loewi**, 20th century physiologist, had a dream about the design of an experiment that resulted in the (Nobel prize-winning) theory of chemical transmission of nervous impulses.
- **Albert Einstein** experienced an adolescent dream in which he achieved the speed of light and saw stars change into amazing patterns and colors. Reflecting on this dream through the years led to him to propose his famous theory of relativity.
- **Niels Bohr** developed the quantum theory of atomic structure after dreaming about a race track.

We have read fascinating reports about scientists or inventors who, unable to complete a project because of something missing, decide to "sleep on it." In the morning they awaken with the missing piece—sometimes attributed to a dream, other times they just know it when they awaken. Moreover, people are divinely inspired in their dreams and visions to see into other dimensions in ways that advance the whole of mankind on the planet.

Reflecting on an adolescent dream through the years led Einstein to propose his famous theory of relativity.

> *A researcher once commented, "Perhaps we should encourage more scientists to leave the laboratory on occasion, walk in the countryside, be contemplative, or even take their technical problems to bed!"*[3]

1. Interactive learning
- ☐ What blessings would we have been deprived of, if these musical and literary people had not listened to their dreams?
- ☐ What might have been lost, if the scientists and inventors had not valued their dreams?

Famous church figures

Although typical Christian literature says very little about dreams, stalwart believers from every era populate our gallery of dreamers. In addition to renowned Saints and prominent Bishops, some famous Protestants have also given us a glimpse into the world of nighttime receptivity to the Word of the Lord. Following are just a few examples.

Jerome, famous for his translation of the Bible into the Latin Vulgate, had mixed views about dreams. Although he claimed that dreams had a dramatic effect on his life, his mistranslation of verses in Leviticus and Deuteronomy—often cited to discourage divination and fortune-telling—also squelched talk about dreams in most churches for a very long time.

St. Thomas Aquinas is another enigmatic Church writer about dreams, attempting to balance spirituality with natural theology (finding God using reason only). Although he was helped by his dreams, he managed to give dreams a bad rap in his famous tome *Summa Theologica*.

Bishop Bruno, dreaming of a hideously deformed old woman taunting him, made the sign of the cross over her and she was transformed into a lovely woman. The woman represented the deplorable condition of the Church, which was restored to its original beauty during Bruno's pontificate as Pope Leo IX.

John Bunyan wrote Pilgrim's Progress based on his visions, dreams, and meditations. This book—one of the most popular books for many years—is actually the story of the author's own inner life, of his conversion and religious experience.

John Newton, author of *Amazing Grace*, ceased being a slave-trading ship captain and became an Anglican clergyman as the result of a dream.

John Wesley, the founder of Methodism, recognized dreams have a value that cannot be rationally explained. Calling attention to the mysterious nature of dreams in one of his sermons, he noted that God sometimes reveals Himself in dreams and visions of the night.

> David Simpson's work is apparently the last serious religious discussion of dreams until modern times.

David Simpson, a close friend of Wesley, said in his 1791 work, *Discourse on Dreams and Night Visions*, "…and has not the experience that many men have of significant dreams and night visions a more powerful effect on their minds than the most pure and refined concepts?"[4] Simpson's work is apparently the last serious religious discussion of dreams until modern times.

Dream Treasure

Dr. A. J. Gordon (founder of Gordon College) dreamed he saw Jesus sitting in the pew of his church as he was preaching. This dream deeply affected his entire life. Regarding dreams, he said, "Apparently we are most awake to God when we are asleep to the world."[5]

Mother Theresa once had a dream where she encountered St. Peter at the gates of Heaven. He asked her what she was doing there because there are no slums in heaven. She said this dream provided her the direction and energy for her ministry.

St. Thérèse of Lisieux (canonized 1925) dreamed that a famous Carmelite sister lifted her big veil, and an ethereal light surrounded them. Thérèse was elated when the sister assured her God was pleased with her life. As a result of the dream, Thérèse's belief became a certainty and she serenely accepted her approaching death.

> *2. Interactive learning*
> ☐ Describe the blessings that came to the world through the dreams of John Bunyan? John Newton?
> ☐ How did Bishop Bruno's dream affect the Church?
> ☐ When did the last serious consideration of dreams take place?

Dreams that changed history

Many dreams are ignored or forgotten, even when we are trying to remember them. As we will learn in later chapters on dream exploration techniques, most of the dreams in our journals deal with our own personal issues. However, occasionally a dream stands out in the human narrative because of its influence on events in history. Following are a few of these prominent dreams.

Military dreamers

The Midianite soldier, enemy of Gideon, dreamed about a loaf of barley bread tumbling into the camp. As Gideon eavesdropped, the soldier's buddy gave the interpretation, revealing God's protection over Israel. All three military men took their cue for battle from the soldier's dream—nobody doubted its meaning. The outcome of the battle was determined by the direction shown in the dream (Judges 7:13-25).

Constantine, the Roman emperor, in his quest to liberate Rome in 312, was instructed in a dream to paint the sign of a cross on his soldiers' shields, which led to victory against Maxentius in the historic Battle of the Milvian Bridge.[6]

General George Patton reputedly received intuitions for military maneuvers during sleep, presumably from dreams. During the Battle of the Bulge (1944), he awakened with an awareness of an imminent German attack, and a plan to thwart the German advance was formed in his mind as soon as he awoke.

Famous American presidents

Abraham Lincoln is honored in the USA because he was instrumental in abolishing slavery. Far less known is the legacy he left us of belief in the value of dreams. He firmly believed that the scriptural record reveals God made Himself known to people in their dreams. Shortly before his assassination, he reported the following dream:

Who is dead in the White House?
Around the coffin were stationed soldiers who were acting as guards; and there was a throng of people, some gazing mournfully upon the corpse, whose face was covered, others weeping pitifully. 'Who is dead in the White House,' I demanded of one of the soldiers. 'The President,' was his answer; 'he was killed by an assassin!' Then came a loud burst of grief from the crowd, which awoke me from my dream.[7]

George Washington experienced a vision at Valley Forge where he saw three great trials overtake the Union: the Revolutionary War, the Civil War, and a third war fought on U.S. soil, requiring supernatural intervention to achieve victory.[8]

Dr. Benjamin Rush's dream in 1809

Recently we stumbled across a dream given on October 17, 1809, to Dr. Benjamin Rush (a signer of the Declaration of Independence and prominent colonial era physician).[i] This dream was used to reconcile a long-standing feud between John Adams and Thomas Jefferson.

This page relates to Mr. Adams
"What book is that in your hands?" said I to my son Richard [who later became the Secretary of State under President James Monroe] a few nights ago in a dream. "It is the history of the United States," said he. "Shall I read a page of it to you?" "No, no," said I. "I believe in the truth of no history but in that which is contained in the Old and New Testaments." "But, sir," said my son, "this page relates to your friend Mr. Adams." "Let me see it then," said I. I read it with great pleasure and herewith send you a copy of it.

Divine purpose of Dr. Rush's dream

Knowing the heavy burden on Dr. Rush's heart about his two dear friends who had co-labored during the revolution and the birth of the Republic, The Lord sent Rush a dream, which he wrote down and sent to Adams.

In his response Adams wrote: "My friend, there is something very serious in this business. The Holy Ghost carries on the whole Christian system in this earth. Not a baptism, not a marriage, not a sacrament can be administered but by the Holy Ghost, Who is transmitted from age to age by laying the hands of the Bishop on the heads of candidates for the ministry…There is no authority, civil or religious—there

---

i   Read the complete account of Dr. Benjamin Rush's dream and how God used it: http://www.wallbuilders.com/LIBissuesArticles.asp?id=10152

PART TWO The Christian Basis Of Dreams

can be no legitimate government—but what is administered by this Holy Ghost."

"I have no resentment of animosity against the gentleman [Jefferson] and abhor the idea of blackening his character or transmitting him in odious colors to posterity… If I should receive a letter from him…I should not fail to acknowledge and answer it."

The Lord used the dream to give Rush divine wisdom, faith, and courage to reach out to his friends and help them resolve their feud.

3. Interactive learning
☐ How do you explain the vision of George Washington?
☐ Why did Dr. Benjamin Rush believe his dream?
☐ What did Rush do, in response to his dream?
☐ What was the divine purpose of Rush's dream?
☐ Is there credible evidence that dreams have affected history? Yes/No

Contemporary dreamers

Amazing as it may seem to our rational Western minds, people today do indeed experience significant dreams. Maybe a dream at first seems inconsequential; perhaps it lands in our awareness with tremendous energy. Either way, modern folks are capable of receiving divine dreams and visions that affect their lives. Here are just a few examples:

Dr. Morton Kelsey claimed it was his own dreams that launched his serious study of dreams. Admitting to having "an intellectual faith but little experiential knowledge of the Divine," a troubling dream revealed his anxieties. With an analyst's help, Kelsey recognized how to address his problems. His religious hopelessness ceased, and he began to experience "the presence of a loving, caring God." [9]

Rev. Herman Riffel—Baptist minister, author, dream counselor—described the dream that started his study of dreams as a way God speaks to people. While mountain climbing with his family, the stones gave way under his feet and everyone started sliding toward a chasm below. He suddenly awoke, sensing God was trying to get his attention about a certain family situation.

> *I owe my awakening of interest in dreams to God's wonderful working in my life to reveal my inner self to me.* [10]

Catherine Marshall (renowned Christian author) dreamed of the stinking head of a woman on a pedestal-stand in her living room. The dream warned about her over-reliance on her intellect rather than the leading of the Holy Spirit and faith in her heart.[11]

Ralph Nault, founder of The New Life, Inc., relates in his books, *Out of Confusion* and *How Are We Led by the Spirit*, how the Lord brought him dreams and visions to encourage him in his spiritual life and give him wisdom for his ministry.[12]

Native American Indians, an example of whole groups of peoples who valued dreams, enjoyed a culture in which dreams were at the center of a deeply spiritual way of life. Dreams helped them locate better hunting grounds, find direction for their individual lives, and solve community problems. Nes Perce Indian prophet Shohalla said "Wisdom comes to us in dreams." Dreams enable the soul to reach the source of all learning—the knowledge of God.[13]

J. Lee Grady, former editor of *Charisma* magazine, dreamed he was inside the Vatican when a tsunami turned the building upside down. As he walked out on the ceiling, he met a group of priests and nuns with hands raised, singing choruses and praying loudly in tongues. When the dream ended, Grady was praying with them. He felt the dream meant the Lord wants to send another wave of the Spirit that will turn the Church upside down.[14]

House Foundation Is Sick

Educated as an engineer, when I (Gerald) was confronted with a midlife crisis, followed the advice of two spiritual mentors and began listening to my dreams. As I became aware that dreams are one of the ways God uses to help us find a new way to function, I experienced the following dream.

My house was undergoing reconstruction, especially the family room. The house foundation was in very bad condition, in need of major repair.

> **Dream Work Tip:**
> Houses, especially unknown ones, usually represent our inner self. If the house is known, then it probably has a different meaning, perhaps our relationship with people in it at that time or what we learned or experienced in that house.

Because our marriage was in crisis, I understood the dream was about my relationship with Judith. In response to the dream, I knelt before God, with Judith, and surrendered our marriage to God. Later I realized the dream was speaking to me on a spiritual level too—my spiritual foundation needed to be substantially revamped.

Dream Treasure

4. Interactive learning
☐ How would you describe the divine purpose of Gerald's dream?
☐ Do you want to join the ranks of contemporary dreamers? Yes/No

Historical testimony provides clear evidence

So, are dreams just for people of faith? Hardly. Dreaming is a valid experience of both nonbelievers and believers alike. Regardless of our spiritual or psychological persuasion, God visits in the night to offer direction and encouragement for everyone. Dreams have impacted the fields of science, literature, music, ministry, psychotherapy, military planning, and numerous other new discoveries and advancements that provide insights for living shared by people everywhere.

Following the Scriptural record and Apostolic leadership, the early Church Fathers continued the tradition of paying attention to the voice of God in dreams. However, it's pretty obvious we can't say Christianity has a corner on dreams (good thing—most Church people ignore their dreams). No matter who the dreamer is, God is at work bringing human beings to a higher level through their dreams.

Lord, I thank You for the men and women who have had the courage to listen to their dreams. I thank You for their testimony.

Applied Learning

✎ *Your Response*
- ☐ Meditate on I Corinthians 2:9-10, asking God how it relates to dreams.
- ☐ Evaluate how this chapter will influence your position on dreams.
- ☐ Ask, "Lord, why am I not hearing from You like these people?" Write the spontaneous thoughts that flow through your mind in response.
- ☐ Affirm: "God wants me to know the things He has prepared for me. I like that!"

✧ *Dream work strategies, skills & techniques*
- ☐ IMAGINE Gerald's "*House Foundation Is Sick*" is *your* dream—What might it be saying to you? (#1)
- ☐ Try to IMAGINE Jacob's ladder dream is *yours*; what might God say to you in it? (#1)
- ☐ How did Gerald respond to his dream?
- ☐ Reflect on Grady's dream about the Vatican *as if it were a* PARABLE. (#2)

Explaining new dream work strategies, skills & techniques

#1 The act of IMAGINING another's dream as *yours* may help you learn to use your imaginative capacity and to engage your heart.

#2 Reflect on a dream *as if it were a* PARABLE. Parables are not direct statements we can grasp with our conscious ego—they're riddles. This approach engages the heart in an experience that may yield important information.

#3 PRETEND your dream is not *yours*. Consider your dream as if it belongs to someone else. Ask, "If this dream were theirs, what might it be saying to them?" This, too, may take pressure off you, enabling you to use your heart.

Dream Treasure

Practicing your skills

- ☐ Select a dream to work with.
- ☐ Does your dream have a house in it? A house you have lived in or an unknown house? Other kinds of buildings?
- ☐ Practice IMAGINING other people's dreams are yours. (#1)
- ☐ Engage your dream *as if it were a* PARABLE. (#2)
- ☐ PRETEND your dream is not *yours*, but belongs to someone else. Ask, what might it be saying to this person? (#3)
- ☐ What response will you give to your dream?

Dream Work Terminology

Can you explain the following terms?
- Parable
- Intuition (see Appendix F, "*Intuitive & Imaginative Faculties*")
- Imagination (see Appendix F, "*Intuitive & Imaginative Faculties*")
- Pretend your dream is not yours.

Christian Worldview

8

Now we have received, not the spirit of the world, but the Spirit who is from God, that we might know the things freely given to us by God (I Corinthians 2:12).

Core Concepts
- Christian orthodoxy validates importance of the spiritual realm.
- Rational Christianity denies relevance of supernatural phenomena.
- The scriptural perspective recognizes the inner man.
- Dreams are essential in the Christian worldview.

Learning Objectives
At the completion of this chapter, you will be able to:
- ☐ Describe the difference in the worldviews of traditional Christianity and the contemporary faith largely practiced today.
- ☐ Explain the role of the Holy Spirit in your life.
- ☐ Decide if you want to experience the spiritual reality Christianity offers
- ☐ Update your worldview to correspond with the historic Christian worldview.

As we have already established, the scriptural record forms the basis for listening to our dreams. The early Church Fathers upheld this view. The evidence of history—that dreams have been valued by all mankind, and God continues to bring dreams for the good of everyone—strengthens our foundation.

Now we want to discuss dreams from a Christian worldview asserting that a spiritual world exists beyond reason and the physical world—and we can experience it. Because we are more entrenched in a secular worldview than we are with the realm of the spirit, we simply do not appreciate it as the Early Fathers did. We must be willing, with the help of the Holy Spirit, to challenge our theological grid.

Worldview of Christian Orthodoxy

Interpretation of dreams is not some newly-minted theology for the 21st century. Dreams originated in the heart of God long before we ever came to this planet. The historic Christian faith perspective believes we can function both at the level of the natural world around us and also at the spiritual level, in communication with God. A worldview including valid sources of knowledge coming from supernatural phe-

Dream Treasure

83

nomena—including dreams—is solidly based in Christian orthodoxy.

Traditional Christianity, the Old & New Testaments, early Church Fathers, as well as Plato, held to the belief that there are three sources of valid knowledge—five senses, reason, and supernatural phenomena. The secular worldview, the two-source opinion, has its roots in Aristotle, 2200 years ago, when he and his followers departed from Plato: they rejected the spiritual realm and supernatural phenomena as a way of knowing truth.

Importance of spiritual dimension

Lost touch with spiritual reality

Since New Testament times, spiritual reality and personal experience have been distinctive features of Christianity. People have touched spiritual reality via insight, revelation, intuition, visions and dreams. However, along the way we seem to have lost this capacity.

A purely rational philosophy has insinuated itself deeply into the Christian church, leaving us starved for meaningful experience with our Creator. Too often our relationship with God is defined intellectually, instead of in our hearts, where it can actually impact our lives. Full of doctrine and theology, we practice a sterile religion, feeling empty inside, lacking inner reality because we are not in touch with the living Christ within us.

> *A worldview including valid sources of knowledge coming from supernatural phenomena—including dreams—is solidly based in Christian orthodoxy.*

People of the Christian faith are being deceived by other worldviews—humanism, Utopianism, New Age and Eastern Philosophies. These secular, humanistic, atheistic, agnostic and Eastern forms of spirituality are accepted because they are regarded as politically correct; whereas Christianity is increasingly met with hostility.[1]

Rational versus spiritual Christianity

Western civilization has advocated rationalism and reason as the basis for establishing religious truth. Reason alone—independent of other perceptions—is a superior source of knowledge. It leaves us pretty dry and bereft of meaning in our lives, but at least we feel comfortable we are in control.

Or are we? The world we inhabit is awash in spiritual data that we are largely unaware of—information we cannot access via our physical senses (or scientific instruments), nor can the mind grasp it. As St. Paul says, these things can be understood only by spiritual insight (I Cor. 2:14).

Denial of the supernatural

A major difficulty with a rationalistic worldview is that it rejects anything coming from outside our five senses and reason. It denies any communication from the supernatural world, including dreams, miracles, visions, and dialogue with God, as well as the nine gifts of the Holy Spirit. Dogma and formulas substitute for life and experience, robbing us of any spiritual power.

1. Interactive learning
- ☐ How does your worldview differ from rationalism? From humanism?
- ☐ Have you ever received revelation from God? Yes/No
- ☐ How does revelation differ from intellectual understanding?

Inner, unseen realm within us

The Scriptures call the unconscious part of us the inner man, the spiritual man, the man hidden in our heart. When we use the term "the unconscious," we are referring to a vast inner world, an unseen dimension of which we are not ordinarily aware. We interchangeably use the terms, the *unconscious,* the *inner world,* or the *hidden man* of the heart (I Peter 3:4) for this unseen realm within us.

Old Testament refers to inner world

Long before psychology "discovered" the unconscious, poets and prophets were writing about it in the Bible:

> *For the inward thought* [inward part] *and the heart of a man are deep (Ps. 64:6).*
>
> *Behold Thou does desire truth in the innermost being, and in the hidden part Thou wilt make me know wisdom (Ps. 51:6).*
>
> *The spirit of man is the lamp of the Lord, searching all the innermost parts of his being (Prov. 20:27).*

> *The spirit of man is the lamp of the Lord, searching all the innermost parts of his being (Prov. 20:27).*

New Testament refers to inner world

New Testament people knew that the meaning and purpose of the outer world originates in an inner, spiritual world. God speaks and works through this inner world, using non-material media such as dreams, visions, prophecies, appearances of angels, and intuitions of spiritual truth:

> *From his innermost being shall flow rivers of living water (John 7:38).*
>
> *For who among men knows the thoughts of a man except the spirit of the man, which is in him (I Cor. 2:11)?*
>
> *For the word of God is living…and piercing as far as the division of soul and spirit… and able to judge the thoughts and intentions of the heart (Heb. 4:12).*
>
> *But let it be the hidden man of the heart (I Pet. 3:4).*

We meet God in our inner world

According to many Christian writers on this theme, the unconscious is where we have our primary meeting with God. David Benner says that, if properly understood, the unconscious can be seen as the source of spiritual experience—visions, dreams, prophecies, the still small voice, and the sense of the presence of God.[2]

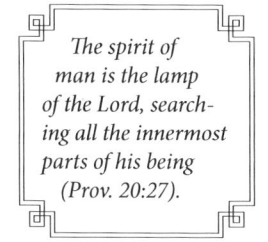

Christian worldview: another realm of reality—a spiritual dimension—exists beyond the material world.

The Kingdom of God is within

When the Pharisees inquired of Jesus Christ when the Kingdom of God was destined to come, Jesus replied that they wouldn't recognize its presence with their natural senses. Instead, he said, "the Kingdom of God is in your midst/within you" (Luke 17:21); i.e., we would have to look within us to find it. The following Scriptures describe a reality condition within us.

> *The Kingdom of God...is righteousness, peace, and joy in the Holy Spirit (Rom 14:17).*
>
> *The Kingdom of God...does not consist in word, but in power (I Cor. 4:20).*

According to St. John, Jesus asserts we can enter the Kingdom only if we have been born from above, born of water and the spirit (John 3:3, 5). Since we hold this Kingdom within our souls, we are able to experience spiritual reality personally—we can achieve a personal relatedness to God.[3]

> *God is far too big for our engagement with Him...to be adequately contained within consciousness. (Benner)*

Faith comes from within—our heart

Aware of the importance of the inner world, *Jesus Christ tried to get people to embrace faith in their hearts*, not just the rationality of their conscious minds. In urging people to get out of their heads and into their hearts, He used metaphors, paradoxes and parables to help them skirt around the conscious mind and directly connect to the unconscious. As Benner says, "God is far too big for our engagement with Him or response to Him to be adequately contained within consciousness."[4]

> *Written not with ink, but with the Spirit of the living God, not on tablets of stone, but on tablets of human hearts (II Cor. 3:3).*

Approach the inner world with confidence

Through the death and resurrection of Jesus Christ, a Spirit of creative power, a new life, is available to mankind and comes from this invisible world to make us fully alive. We need not fear entering the spiritual realm, as long as we engage it in union with the One who has already gone before us—our all-conquering leader and guide, Our Lord, Jesus Christ.

---

2. Interactive learning
- ☐ Identify the types of supernatural phenomenon we might experience.
- ☐ Have you ever experienced any supernatural phenomena? Yes/No
- ☐ Describe one such experience.

Holy Spirit is key

A social gospel wants to change our environment, adjust our behavior by altering the external milieu; a rational approach wants to change our thinking. But we need change that begins from deep inside, from the heart. We can only comprehend spiritual truth by *revelation*, by direct intervention by Something Transcendent from outside ourselves. Only the Holy Spirit can do this.

Jesus told his followers He had to return to the Father in order for them to function well in this world. Master, how are we going to get along with you gone? The answer is a supernatural approach, one that rational thinking cannot grasp. When Jesus ascended to heaven, God deposited the Holy Spirit into His Church—comforter, teacher, guide for living a spiritual life.

> *Now we received, not the spirit of the world, but the Spirit who is from God, that we might know the things freely given to us by God (I Cor. 2:12).*

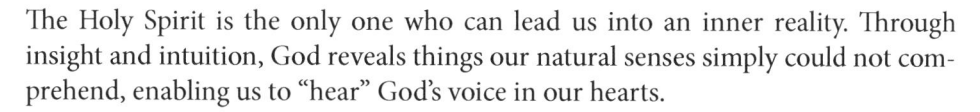

The Holy Spirit is the only one who can lead us into an inner reality. Through insight and intuition, God reveals things our natural senses simply could not comprehend, enabling us to "hear" God's voice in our hearts.

> *All who are being led by the Spirit of God, these are sons of God (Rom. 8:14).*

> *The Spirit searches all things, even the depths of God. For who among men knows the thoughts of a man except the spirit of the man, which is in him (I Cor. 2:9-11).*

> *The Spirit Himself bears witness with our spirit that we are children of God (Romans 8:16).*

The Holy Spirit is the only one who can lead us into an inner reality.

Existence of other spirits

The historic Judeo-Christian worldview recognizes the existence of other spirits who are not from God. Many deceiving spirits are working in this world—in religions, in the media, and throughout our culture.

It is important to understand that people can be spiritually active even before they experience regeneration. People are involved in spiritualism. Mediums call up the dead. People around us practice divination, witchcraft, sorcery. Don't go to them for spiritual knowledge! Go to the Holy Spirit of God.

---

3. Interactive learning
- ☐ Recount moments of spiritual revelation or spiritual insight.
- ☐ Can you recall when you experienced the inner witness of the Holy Spirit? Yes/No
- ☐ Describe one such occurrence.

Dream Treasure

Importance of Dreams to Christian Worldview

Since God chooses to dwell within the human spirit, the height of spirituality is to practice the presence of God—to be attuned to the inner world. The Old Testament records were written by people "who had *known* God in the immediacy of present experience, an intimacy ultimately meant for all."[5]

God reveals Himself to His people—and to the world—through the intimacy of the inner word and dreams. Daniel understood this—he says King Nebuchadnezzar's dream came to reveal the thoughts and intents of his *heart* (Dan. 2:1-49). Justin Martyr, a foremost Christian apologist, felt that dreams have meaning and importance because they suggest mankind participates in a more-than-physical world.[6]

> *God reveals Himself to His people—and to the world—through the intimacy of the inner word and dreams.*

To tap into the power of our dreams, we need a spiritual framework. A historic Christian view of dreams recognizes that spiritual reality can be experienced directly, intuitively from within. This spiritual reality is both within us and external to us—God is transcendent, above and beyond His creation, as well as in it. We must look outside our ego awareness to a Divine Source wiser than ourselves to value the hidden wisdom in our dreams.

> *The Christian worldview allows for—indeed encourages—looking to our dreams for knowledge and understanding beyond our sense experience and reasoning.*

Changing our theological grid

Sometimes it's good to have our comfortable cage rattled a bit. We can get too complacent in our so-called beliefs, which are often just warmed over ideas from childhood that were never challenged by reality. If your theology is still what it was 40 years ago, maybe you need to give it a good shake and see what remains. God will not be offended if you poke around the edges of your thinking just a little to see if maybe you've ignored something important—such as dreams!

Dreams get Judith's attention

I (Judith) formed my theological grid growing up in a baptist church, where I was taught that God divided history into periods of time. Yes, at one time God did come to people and reveal Himself directly through angels, dreams, visions, prophecies, etc. However, He doesn't need to do this anymore, because Jesus had come and now we had the Bible. So I memorized large portions of Scripture as a child, and as an adult I studied the Bible using my theological bias until the following dream got my attention:

My New Bible

The inside of my Bible is gone. Alarmed, I stand holding only its cover. My friend, Ralph Nault says to me, "I will give you a new Bible."

The man in the dream was a key to understanding it. In dream work, we ask ourselves who or what does the person symbolize for me? What are the characteristics and functions of the person in the dream?

Several years earlier, God had sent Ralph Nault to my home in answer to my prayers. He functioned differently than other Christians I knew, so when he appeared in my dream, I knew it was from God. This man knew the voice of the Father, the leading of the Holy Spirit, and received dreams and visions from God.

The dream was sent by God to show me that I was going to learn the Bible all over again. Instead of reading the Bible under the "law of sin and death"—which always brought me condemnation (Ro 8:2)—I needed to read it under "the law of the Spirit of life in Christ Jesus." It was important for me to look to the Holy Spirit to quicken truths and make them alive in my heart.

PART TWO The Christian Basis Of Dreams

Guidance From The Dream

(Judith): At the time, dreams were still new to me, and I had many questions about dreams. I kept praying to God, asking Him to reveal to me His truth about dreams. Then I dreamed…

I am looking at a file cabinet with one drawer pulled open. I see two files, one titled, "Guidance from dreams," and the other, "Guidance from the shadow."

This dream brought me clarity as to how God was going to give me guidance through my dreams. It also gave me faith that I could trust the dream as a reliable way to hear from God.

Divine purpose of Judith's dreams

God used the first dream to get my attention and show me what He was about to do. I had learned to read the Bible using the natural eyes, not by revelation given by the Holy Spirit. Nault was a person who knew how to hear God's voice for himself and be led by the Holy Spirit. We had invited him to hold meetings in our home..

God used my second dream to answer my questions about dreams and to point me to learning about the shadow figure in dreams.

4. Interactive learning

☐ Describe the divine purposes of Judith's two dreams.
☐ Has Judith received guidance from God through her dreams?
☐ Any ideas about what "guidance from the shadow" means?

Dream Treasure

To Gerald's Sunday School class

When I was a kid, I believed all the Bible stories. The characters were real people, they heard from God; their world—and eventually, indirectly, mine—was changed, things happened in the spiritual dimension. But that was then; God functions quite differently in the 20th century, according to the King James Bible (Scofield's notes said so, and they were right up there on a par with the scriptural canon).

So I enjoyed the stories of Moses, Joshua, David, and Daniel. Their exploits fired my young imagination, they moved in the power of some mysterious dimension of which I had no clue. However, the story of their lives had nothing to do with the real world we lived in. Threat of annihilation by the evil Soviet empire; increases in teen pregnancies; divorce rate in the church approaching that of the secular society in which we tried to live our faith without a spiritual clue as to what it was all about.

Don't look so sanctimonious. You didn't know what spirituality meant, either. Nobody did. We grew up in an age of reason, where head thinking trumped heart belief. Christians generally (if you'll pardon the expression) faithfully attended church on Sunday and prayer meetings on Wednesday, but lacked any grounded belief in the reality of the spiritual world. We played church, we sang, we read the Bible, we listened to sermons, but we had no inner spiritual reality. It was all in our heads—it never reached our hearts.

> We played church, we sang, we read the Bible, we listened to sermons, but we had no inner spiritual reality.

The church has lost contact with people and doesn't have much to say to their lives in our society today. No wonder so many people would rather golf or fish on Sunday mornings. We've got a mess here, and I think there are two fundamental reasons for these problems.

Experiencing the love of the Father

The first major problem I see is that most Christians have not really experienced the love of God as a reality in their lives. I can attest to the importance of this in my own life. Over the years I struggled with numerous issues that held me back, and kept me from embracing everything my Heavenly Father has for my life. At last, at age 55, tired of fighting with God, I lifted my arms toward heaven and said, "Abba, Father, I belong to You," and I experienced in a deep, profound way the love of my Father God.

This definitely is the watershed experience of my life—as a result, I began to change dramatically. No longer leaving two resistant heel marks dragging behind me on my life's pathway, I began to move in God's direction for my life. I know in a deeply satisfying, inexplicably wonderful way that I am loved unconditionally by my Creator. I am no longer the same man I was before.

Dream Treasure

Because I believe this is so fundamental, so vital to our lives, I pray that you also would be rooted and established in love—an experiential love of Christ that surpasses knowledge of him (Eph. 3:17-19). Jesus Christ showed us the Father, and we can experience His love deep within our hearts and souls. It changes everything.

Touching the spiritual dimension

In my view, the other chief problem in the Church is this: we do not know how to touch the spiritual dimension in an effective, meaningful way. We're still behaving as if we lived in a mechanistic world, directed and controlled by our rational behavior. Science is probably ahead of much of the Church in this regard.

For several centuries Newtonian physics was accepted as the proper notion of the universe (that's what I learned while earning an MSEE at Purdue University). All physical systems, all events, were seen part of a vast mechanistic process. Not so anymore. Physicists have traded their science of determinism and prediction for a more flexible, dynamic view of the universe.

Newton, chaos and dancing

The marvelous cosmos is more chaotic than predictable—even influenced by being observed. Our world is not so much a thing as it is a continuous dance of energy.[7] Today physicists take an almost spiritual approach, holistically including aspects of the unknown and immeasurable. A modern physicist sounds more like a mystic than a mechanic of the universe.

> We're still behaving as if we lived in a mechanistic world, directed and controlled by our rational behavior.

The Church cannot continue to define its structure and run its processes using the machine imagery created in the 17th century by Sir Isaac Newton. I believe it is time to wake-up and be led by the Spirit. As with every spiritual issue, we need to pray as did St. Paul for the Spirit of wisdom and revelation, that our spiritual eyes and ears will be opened by the power of God so we can know Him better and begin to function as spiritual men and women (Eph. 1:17-18).

Dreams help us touch the spiritual kingdom

I believe we can be awakened to the spiritual dimension through the dream. Basically our lives are pretty hopeless until we are touched deeply by the Holy Spirit. Dreams give us a contact with spiritual reality. We can begin to experience the power of God in the dream! And it transforms us.

My dreams helped open my spiritual senses, making the reality God more alive for me. Dreams enabled me to be more aware that God was working in my life. Dreams helped shape my view of God and change it. I believe my dreams brought the spiritual world closer to me. This is enormously important for us today!

Some of my dreams helped me deal with my inner psychological neurotic problems. When my house foundation was crumbling in my dream, when flood waters edged close to my house, I knew some things had to change! When my soul was in trouble, falling apart, my dreams gave me the inner resources to throw open the doors of my heart and say, "OK, God, I've got to change!"

My dreams helped me touch the spiritual dimension in such a way that I became increasingly open to the love of God for me, culminating in the Abba, Father experience. Some years later in my dream, Pope John Paul II met me and—it felt as if it were Jesus Himself—gave me the deepest, most meaningful hug I've ever experienced.[i]

Divine Hug From Pope

(Gerald): Walking along a quiet garden pathway, I meet Pope John Paul II, and we embrace. When I begin to draw back, he continues to embrace me firmly. I decide to return the embrace. It feels as if I am receiving a divine hug. It is the deepest, most heart-touching, profound, meaningful, satisfying hug I have ever experienced.

When I awoke and described the dream to Judith, I told her it felt as if Jesus Himself had embraced me, and I began to weep with great joy.

> *Lord, I pray that I may encounter You directly in my heart.*

---

[i] Gerald Doctor, personal journal entry, June 5, 2008.

Dream Treasure

Applied Learning

✎ *Your Response*

- ☐ Retake the *Survey of Attitudes & Beliefs About Dreams* (see Appendix A).
- ☐ How have your attitudes and beliefs about dreams changed thus far?
- ☐ Does your worldview allow you to receive information from the spiritual dimension while asleep? Yes/No
- ☐ Using a scale of 0 to 10 (0 not at all; 10 absolutely), how willing are you for God to update your worldview? Your response_____
- ☐ Reword I Cor. 2:12 into a prayer of response to God.
- ☐ Affirm aloud: "During sleep I am especially open to spiritual reality. I like that!"

☼ *Dream work strategies, skills & techniques*

- ☐ If Gerald's *Divine Hug From Pope* dream were yours. What might it mean to you?
- ☐ What area of Gerald's life is his dream concerned with?
- ☐ What EMOTIONAL FEELING did Gerald experience in his dream? (#1)
- ☐ Did Gerald FULLY EXPERIENCE his feeling or withhold, deny, or stuff it? (#2)
- ☐ Do you think Gerald experienced an "Aha!" moment? (#3)
- ☐ What blessing did Gerald receive through his dream?
- ☐ What was the divine purpose of his dream?

Explaining new dream work strategies, skills & techniques

#1 Identify the EMOTIONAL FEELING the dreamer felt in the dream.

#2 Note if it was FULLY EXPERIENCED or withheld, denied, or stuffed.

#3 Learn to recognize the "Aha!" moment; i.e., the witness in your spirit.

> **"Aha!" Moment**
>
> The "Aha!" feels like an inner resonance, inner click, or intuitive knowing. Because symbols are linked to energy deep within us, we can feel the sparks fly when the connection is made. We experience a subtle—and sometimes not so subtle—shift in mood. The "Aha!" indicates we have tapped into the symbolic meaning of a dream element.

Practicing your skills

- ☐ Select a dream to work with.
- ☐ What area of your life do you think your dream is concerned with?
- ☐ Identify the EMOTIONAL FEELING you experienced in your dream. (#1)
- ☐ Did you FULLY EXPERIENCE your feeling or withhold, deny, or stuff it? (#2)
- ☐ Pay attention to the "Aha!" when working with your dream. (#3)
- ☐ What blessing might your dream contain for you?
- ☐ What might the divine purpose be in your dream?

> **Dream Work Terminology**
>
> Can you explain the following terms?
> - Supernatural phenomenon
> - The "Aha!"
> - Guidance from dreams
> - Guidance from the shadow (see Chapter 16)

Dream Treasure

Part Three
Christian Approach to Dreams

Why you will find Part Three helpful

At this point we have come to appreciate that an historic perspective acknowledges supernatural phenomena as part of our faith experience. However, because dreams have been ignored for a long time, many of God's people have no framework in which to safely approach and evaluate their dreams. In this part you will build a knowledge base of principles that form the core beliefs about dreams as a way to hear from God.

You will understand the biblical purposes of dreams. Illustrations from Scripture will enhance your understanding of each of these purposes, helping you to rightly interpret what God is saying in your dreams. You will learn that the message of a dream is conveyed using a special language of inner pictures and symbols.

In discussing common concerns about dreams, you will acquire scriptural guidelines for testing the soundness of a dream interpretation. Because spiritual discernment is critical in understanding dreams, you will be encouraged to trust the Holy Spirit as your guide.

PART THREE chapters
- A God-Centered Lens (Chapter 9)
- Biblical Purposes of Dreams (Chapter 10)
- Scriptural Guidelines (Chapter 11)
- Spiritual Discernment (Chapter 12)

PART THREE Christian Approach To Dreams

A God–Centered Lens

9

"Almost the greater part of mankind get their knowledge of God from dreams." (Tertullian[1])

Core Concepts
In this chapter we offer a set of twelve belief statements we consider to be key to developing a Christian approach to dreams.
1. God speaks to people through dreams.
2. The Holy Spirit brings the dreams.
3. Dreams offer relationship with our Creator.
4. Dreams give us divine revelation.
5. Dreams carry divine purpose.
6. Dreams originate from an unseen realm within us.
7. Dreams contain hidden treasure.
8. Dreams use a language of pictures and symbols.
9. Dream interpretation belongs to God.
10. Dreams contain divine energy.
11. Dreams require a response.
12. Dreams are a gift from God.

Learning Objectives
At the completion of this chapter, you will be able to:
- [ ] List and describe the twelve core beliefs central to our approach to dreams.
- [ ] Discuss the *cornerstone* of our approach to dreams.
- [ ] Evaluate the concept of "intelligent intent."
- [ ] Explain the phrase "dark sayings" in Numbers 12:8 (NASB).
- [ ] Explore your dreams, guided by a Christian framework.

Because the Church essentially has not dealt with dreams for hundreds of years, God's people don't know how to pay attention to their dreams. New Age gurus seem quite eager to tell us how to approach dreams, but Church thinkers, theologians, and philosophers are largely silent on this important topic. Having no systematic theological treatise on dreams, Christians lack an appropriate framework for listening to God's voice in their dreams.

PART THREE   Christian Approach To Dreams

Before the 1960s, the last serious religious discussion of dreams took place in the late 18th century.

Anchored in the Holy Scriptures and supported by the writings of the Church Fathers, historical evidence and the Christian worldview, the following twelve beliefs collectively provide a lens through which we can safely view our dreams. Historically *Christian*, they keep us God-centered as we approach our dreams.

1. God speaks to people through dreams

The *cornerstone* of our approach to dreams is the belief that God wants to communicate with His creation. From the first chats with Abraham, all the way through the Biblical record, dreams were considered one of the standard ways God spoke to people.

There is no place in Scripture that says God rescinds His idea to use dreams as a way to speak to people.

Indeed God speaks once, or twice, yet no one notices it. In a dream, in a vision of the night, when sound sleep falls on men, while they slumber in their beds, then he opens the ears of men, and seals their instruction (Job 33:14-16).

There is no place in Scripture that says God rescinds His idea to use dreams as a way to speak to people. On the contrary, He promises that the Holy Spirit would bring dreams even in the last days.

Dreams have a divine author

The dream is not simply a pointless process of experiencing stimuli from our senses while we slumber—it has a divine author![2] Instead of thinking of dreams as coming from some part of ourselves, we view God as the source of our dreams. Christian psychologist David G. Benner describes dreams as communications from God containing messages intended to enhance our well-being. There is an "intelligent intent" behind our dreams, urging us toward wholeness.[3]

> *1. Interactive learning*
> ☐ Why do you think God wants to communicate with you?
> ☐ How does the concept of "intelligent intent" apply to your dreams?

2. The Holy Spirit brings the dream

Because the Church has been immersed for over 200 years in a rationalistic, materialistic, and mechanistic worldview, God's people often find it difficult to value the dream as coming from anything other than overeating tacos. Yet the Scriptures clearly say it is the Holy Spirit who brings us the dream.

God promised to send the Holy Spirit so He could make His words known to us (Prov. 1:23). The Prophet Joel and St. Peter tell us how the Holy Spirit will do this: through visions, prophecies, and…*dreams* (Joel 2:28-32; Acts 2:17). Some Christian teachers call these supernatural phenomena "the language of the Holy Spirit.[4]"

Dream Treasure

3. Dreams offer relationship with our Creator

Through dreams we can go beyond merely rational Christianity to experience personal contact with God in our spirits. The Bible relates many stories of people who experienced God personally. Frequently we read that *the Word of the Lord* came to so-and-so. How did this living Word come? Kelsey says he knows "no better way to achieve this experience, this confrontation with God, than through the dream."[5]

> *Athanasius, bishop of Alexandria, said that during sleep, "the soul... imagines and beholds things above the earth, and often even holds converse with the saints and angels who are above earthly and bodily existence."*[6]

In Genesis 15:1-21, the Lord God appeared to Abraham in both vision and dream, conversing with him about his future. Abraham's experiences show us that God uses the dream and vision to establish a direct on-going relationship between Him and His creation.

Later, the Lord established a conversation with Solomon *in a dream*, asking him what he wished God would give to him. Solomon answered the Lord directly in the dream (I Kings 3:5-15). In another interesting incident, God converses with Abimelech *in a dream* about Abraham's wife Sarah (Gen. 20:1-8).

Dream work is a vital spiritual practice that allows us to relate to the living God.

These events certainly challenge our understanding of dreams! Far more than just handing us bits of information, the dream helps us develop an authentic relationship with Our Lord, the very Source of our lives. Dream work is a vital spiritual practice that allows us to relate to the living God.

2. Interactive learning

☐ Read Abram's visionary/dream encounters with God (Gen. 12-22).
☐ How many ways did God use to speak to Abraham?
☐ What does it mean that God and Abram conversed together in the vision?

4. Dreams give us divine revelation

In the realm of the dream we are offered a place to hear God's voice and receive revelation from Him. God gave Daniel the wisdom to understand all kinds of visions and dreams, and he assured King Nebuchadnezzar that God reveals mysteries to us in dreams. Because Daniel received God's wisdom and knowledge (in a night vision), he was able to save not only himself and his friends, but his entire tribe! (Dan. 2:19).

Fourth century Greek Church giant, John Chrysostom, believed that dreams are one potential—and frequently used—source of revelation from the Lord.

Dream Treasure

He even suggested dreams are sufficient if we are finely tuned to God—we don't need visions and other dramatic divine revelations.[7] Irenaeus, bishop of Lyons, believed that the dream gives revelation of the spiritual world and is an indication of how very close to God one can be.

St. Paul wrote about "Christ in you, the hope of glory "(Col 1:27). Following is an example from our experience of receiving divine revelation in a dream.

It's Jesus

(Judith): At the time of this dream I was seeking God for revelation of this spiritual truth.

I am being followed by a shadowy-type figure near my childhood home. As I run toward the house, the shadowy figure continues to follow me. I run into the house and slam the door shut. Turning around, I see this figure in my house. I turn toward it, asking who it is. As I reach out to touch it, I say, I know who it is: "You are the ark of the covenant…and I know who the ark of the covenant is—it's Jesus!"

Divine purpose of dream

In this dream, I received divine revelation from God: Jesus is the ark of the covenant, and He lives in me. In the dream the house was the one my dad actually built in my youth. Now, it symbolized my heavenly Father's house, whose house I am.

5. Dreams carry divine purpose

Our Creator always has our best interests at heart, with plans for our welfare, to give us a future and a hope (Jer. 29:11). Testimony provides evidence that dreams are endowed with a divine purpose—to make us more fully alive, to call us to holiness, to make us complete, whole persons, and to bring us into a close relationship with God, our Father.

> *He became what we are in order that we can become who he is... The glory of God is humanity fully alive. (Irenaeus)*

To make us alive

We can know about God and yet have *no consciousness of God within us*. Jesus said, "I came that they might have life, and might have it abundantly" (John 10:10b). To become fully alive we must have contact with the Spirit from God, and one way this happens is by dreams in the night.

Call us to holiness

Dreams seek to call us to holiness. God's great plan is to make us His very own sons/daughters and joint heirs with Jesus Christ and sharers of His spirit and glory (see Rom. 8:17, Eph. 4:13b). The dream promotes this process, actively participating in our spiritual development and calling us to spiritual maturity.

> *Capturing the meaning of our dreams helps put us in touch with the divine purpose for our lives.*

To make us whole

Built into us is the potential for wholeness—to bring together all of the parts of the person into a complete, conscious self. Like an egg or an acorn, we contain tremendous potential seeking to be realized during our lives. Through symbols, dreams give us insight into this inner world and work to promote our psychological wholeness.

> *Augustine (354–430) taught that dreams were important for understanding both human psychology and also our relationship to God.*

Behind the dream is the divine purpose of enlarging us, increasing the depth and scope of our lives. Capturing the meaning of our dreams helps put us in touch with the divine purpose for our lives, showing us how God is working to lead us toward wholeness.

3. Interactive learning

- ☐ Explain the phrase "divine purpose" as it relates to dreams.
- ☐ Using a scale of 0 (*not at all*) to 10 (*very much*), how willing are you to allow your dreams to open you to God and the spiritual world? _____ Explain?

6. Dreams originate from an unseen realm within us

According to the findings of research, dreams originate from an unconscious realm within us. Viewing the unconscious as our interface with God, psychiatrist M. Scott Peck suggests it needs to be explored, because it is wiser than we are![8] Our dreams originate from this unseen place, enabling us to experience the spiritual realm that is difficult to contact any other way.

> **About the "soul"**
>
> Traditionally, religion thought of the soul as "an inner part of ourselves that connects us to the spiritual realm and leads us to God."[10] Embedded in the soul is God's divine pattern—*teleos*—for our lives. Modern man commonly refers to the soul as the "psyche."
>
> *Teleos*, a Greek word translated as *perfection, wholeness, completion,* or *maturity*. At its root is the idea of fulfilled purpose, implying the existence of a purposeful design or pattern that needs to be fulfilled. See *New Testament Words in Today's Language* by Wayne Detzler.

Thousands of years ago the prophet Daniel recognized the existence of this hidden unseen realm and its relationship to our dreams when he said Nebuchadnezzar's dream came to *reveal the thoughts and intents of his heart—an inner unseen place* (see Dan. 2:30).

Then the mystery (meaning of Nebuchadnezzar's dream) was revealed to Daniel in a night vision...It is He who reveals the profound and hidden things: He knows what is in the darkness... (Dan. 2:19-23).

Our view of dreams acknowledges the existence of an inner spiritual reality within us which can be known to us directly, intuitively.[9] Dreams originate from an unseen realm within our human soul.

Church Fathers recognized hidden inner realm

Early Church Fathers also affirmed the existence of this inner reality, asserting we have both a visible, *seen* side of our personality as well as an *unseen* side. While we recognize the outer realm of reality directly through physical senses, we experience the unseen reality through dreams, visions and our spiritual senses.

Jesus refers to unseen realm within us

Jesus talked about an unseen *place* within us, from which the Holy Spirit will flow: "...out of his innermost being (literally, *belly*) shall flow rivers of living water (John 7:38). The word *belly* refers to a cavity or hollow place within us.

> *Clement believed dreams come from the depth of our soul, which is always active—even during sleep. Dreams reveal spiritual reality...we are especially receptive to spiritual reality during sleep.*

In valuing dreams as people of faith, we recognize the existence of another level of reality, a spiritual reality, which we cannot reach with our reason.

4. Interactive learning

☐ Do you agree with Daniel's understanding of an unseen inner world? Yes/No

☐ Agree/disagree? Dreams come from within us, not from without. Explain?

Dream Treasure

7. Dreams contain hidden treasure

Central to our approach to dreams is the belief that our vast unconscious life, the hidden inner world our rational minds cannot find, is a storehouse of hidden treasure. The dream enables us to make immediate contact with God's wisdom and knowledge hidden in Christ Jesus.

> *...that is, Christ Himself, in whom are hidden all the treasures of wisdom and knowledge (Col. 2:2b-3).*
>
> *We have this treasure in earthen vessels (II Cor. 4:7).*
>
> *I will give you the treasures of darkness, and hidden wealth of secret places, in order that you may know that it is I, the Lord, the God of Israel, who calls you by your name (Is. 45:3).*

Viewing dreams as a manifestation of God's grace, psychiatrist M. Scott Peck says they reveal the existence of an immeasurable, concealed domain within us containing riches beyond imagination.[11] Dream work is about the search for this *great treasure* buried in the field of our souls (II Cor. 4:7). (Recall our discussion in Chapter 3 about the hidden treasure in dreams).

> *Clement of Alexandria said that at night, "the soul, released from the perceptions of sense, turns in on itself and has a truer hold of intelligence."*[12]

8. Dreams use a language of pictures and symbols

Most dreams communicate their messages using images, pictures, and metaphors in a *figurative* and *imaginative* way. Unfamiliar with metaphorical and allegorical language, our Western intellects are challenged—we want to take the dream literally. Yet, the Bible clearly says it is God Himself who chooses to make the message of the dream obscure. Here is what God says to Moses:

> *... I speak to him in a dream; not so with My servant Moses... I speak with him face to face, even plainly, and not in **dark sayings** (Num. 12:6-8 NKJV).*

According to *Strong's Exhaustive Concordance*[13], the Hebrew word for "dark sayings" is *chiydah*, which means a puzzle; i.e., a trick, a conundrum, some type of message tied in a knot, like a proverb or a riddle. God deliberately obscures His messages in puzzles and riddles—a language of symbols and images—that take some effort on our part to solve.

> *Basil the Great said this about dreams: "The enigmas in dreams have a close affinity to those things which are signified in an allegoric or hidden sense in the Scriptures."*[14]

> The Hebrew word for "dark sayings" is chiydah, *which means a puzzle; i.e., a trick, a conundrum, some type of message tied in a knot, like a proverb or a riddle.*

Dream Treasure

PART THREE Christian Approach To Dreams

Dreams use symbolic imagery
Here is a dream using symbolic imagery of babies.

My Two Babies
(Judith): in the late 1980s, I dreamed...

I am giving birth to a new baby; however the sac/a cowl is over its face. My friend Bob takes the sac off my baby's face and whacks the baby on its back. My baby comes to life and breathes. Scene shifts: I am again pregnant; however I am not sure if the baby is genetically correct. I send away for a test. Scene shifts: I am in the driveway of Bob's house. I go to his mailbox and open my mail, and learn that my baby is genetically correct. I call out to Bob's wife, "I am going to have another baby." She asks, "What about your schooling?" I answer, "Oh, it will be a long time before I finish my schooling. I will be busy raising these two babies."

My first baby, with the sac, signifies a divine birth, a supernatural act. I understood that I will birth and raise two babies—a divine child and a natural child—and both are of God. I eventually completed my BS in the 1990s and my MSW in 2005.

---

5. Interactive learning
- ☐ Define the meaning of "dark sayings."
- ☐ What was the divine purpose of Judith's dream?
- ☐ Brainstorm reasons why God deliberately chooses to conceal his dream messages in an obscure language.

---

9. Dream interpretation belongs to God

It is God who knows the meaning of our dreams—the understanding of the dream belongs to Him, not us. We depend upon the Holy Spirit to unlock the grace contained within our dreams.

> *Joseph said to them, 'Do not interpretations belong to God?' (Gen. 40:8).*

Under pressure to help king Nebuchadnezzar with his dream, Daniel looked to God for understanding, and in response God gave Daniel a vision.

Daniel actually received understanding of the king's dream through a vision in the night!

> *When I, Daniel, had seen the vision, I sought to understand it;... I heard the voice of a man...and he called out and said, 'Gabriel, give this man an understanding of the vision' (Dan. 8:15, 16).*
>
> *Then the mystery was revealed to Daniel in a night vision (Dan. 2:19).*
>
> *This mystery has not been revealed to me for any wisdom residing in me more than in any other living man (Dan. 2:30).*

Don't let this tiny detail escape you—Daniel actually received understanding of the

Dream Treasure

king's dream through a vision in the night!

After receiving the interpretation of king Nebuchadnezzar's dream, Daniel acknowledges that his understanding of the dream came from God:

> *Let the name of God be blessed forever…He reveals the profound and hidden things… You have given me wisdom and might, and have now made known to me what we asked of You, for You have made known to us the king's demand (Dan. 2:20-23).*

Look to the witness of the Holy Spirit

Revelation of spiritual realities must come by the Holy Spirit speaking truth into our hearts. Because the interpretation belongs to God, the Holy Spirit is the final witness as to the correct understanding of a dream.

> *Joseph and Daniel, through the gift of prophecy, used to interpret dreams (Morton Kelsey).*[15]

---

6. Interactive learning
- ☐ What qualified Daniel to interpret the dreams of others? (Daniel 1:17)
- ☐ What qualifies you to interpret the dreams of others?
- ☐ Describe what is meant by the *witness of the Holy Spirit*.

---

10. Dreams contain divine energy

Made in the image of God, we contain immense energy deep within us. By transforming the dynamic energy in our unconscious into images and symbols while we sleep, our dreams can re-energize us for everyday living.

> *The dream often imparts divine energy to us, because it contains a living Word—in picture form—from God.*

Because *God is the source of all energy,* our dreams often contain great power, capable of restoring and renewing us in our entire being. They can provide us spiritual and psychological liveliness we never knew existed. Psalmists often cried out for God's reviving life to come to them:

> *Revive me according to Thy Word* [a deposit, delivered in a visitation from God] *(Ps. 119:25b).*
>
> *My soul languishes for Thy salvation; I wait for Thy Word (Ps. 119:81).*
>
> *Undertake my cause, and come to my help, give me life, as you have said (Ps 119:154 MKJV).*

In our experience the dream often imparts divine energy to us, because it contains a *living* Word—in picture form—from God. By releasing God's divine energy through our dreams, we can be transformed in the way we see ourselves and the world around us. Our dreams can bring together the fractured pieces of our conflicted, divided heart. Help us complete an unfinished project. Provide additional enthusiasm to tackle new activities. Release divine creativity within us—discoveries and inventions have sometimes come through dreams.

Our dreams can help us achieve emotional balance and stability. At times, after a night of dreaming, we find ourselves waking up with our vigor renewed, our batteries recharged to handle the day's events. Following is an example of such a dream.

Disparate Pieces Coming Together
(Gerald): One night I experienced this simple dream:

Some disparate pieces of my self were somehow coming together.

When I awoke, I felt, wow! God can bring together the scattered pieces of my complex life and make me more whole. Even though the dream was vague, I received faith, confidence, and positive energy for my life.

7. Interactive learning
☐ Have you experienced awakening from a dream feeling energized?
☐ Begin to pay attention to the intensity of your dreams.

11. Dreams require a response

Dreams deserve a response from us. When people in the Bible awakened from a dream, they acted upon it—they understood the importance of responding to God. When Samuel heard a voice calling him in the night (an auditory vision), Eli instructed him to respond to the Lord.

An uninterpreted dream is like an unopened letter from God. (The Talmud)

Eli instructed Samuel to say to God during the night, "Speak Lord, for Thy servant is listening" (I Samuel 3:9).

Divine energy came to us in the dream, but now this energy needs to be released into specific actions and decisions in our waking life. Jacob, after receiving his legendary ladder dream, acknowledged God who gave it to him, and then built an altar using his stone pillow and poured oil on its top.

Once we have had the symbolic dream experience, we need conceptual thought—words and sentences—to make it conscious, to give it perspective, to release the energy it contains, to bring it into daily life.[16]

12. Dreams are a gift from God

Early Jewish scholars believed that an uninterpreted dream is like an unopened letter from God. In our dreams we receive personalized messages from God. Who wouldn't want to read a letter from our Creator and receive it with great thanksgiving?

When we receive a gift, the first thing we do is to thank the person who gave it. Our dreams are a wonderful gift from our Creator, and we welcome them with gratitude and expectancy. Psychiatrist M. Scott Peck views dreams as a manifestation of God's grace.[17] We are thankful to God who gives us this wonderful opportunity to relate to Him and the means to know ourselves better.

Toward a Christian theory of dreams

The theory of dreams has evolved over many millennia: from ancient civilizations of Babylonia and Egypt to the classical world of the Greeks and Romans; from the Far East and the Pagan Celts to Christian, Jewish and Islamic religions; from Indigenous Peoples and Native American Indians to the pioneering dream researchers of the last century. We find it compelling that, in most of these cultures, they connected their dreams with their spiritual beliefs.

For many centuries people have claimed that dreams are a useful basis to understand personal issues, solve problems, and provide a source for creativity.[18] Western scientists in depth psychology made a detailed attempt to understand and interpret dreams. These psychoanalytical theorists laid the groundwork for our modern eclectic approaches: Experiential, Gestalt, Cognitive-experiential, Object relations, Adlerian, Self-psychology, Brief theory, and PTSD treatment.[19]

Modern researchers assert that, because of the intimate link between mind and body, dreams are a product of our entire being: psychological, physical, and spiritual.[20] Nevertheless, in modern times the Christian community at large has neglected even to write about dreams, let alone offer a theory for the Christian use of dreams.

> *In modern times the Christian community at large has neglected even to write about dreams, let alone offer a theory for the Christian use of dreams.*

> *Our twelve belief statements establish that God is the author of our dreams. Life flows from out of our innermost depths, revealing the treasures deposited in our souls by God Himself. Based solidly on Scripture and supported by the teachings of the Church Fathers, these fundamental truths contribute to the development of a Christian theory of dreams for God's people living in the twenty-first century.*

8. Interactive learning

☐ Learn the 12 statements of beliefs.
☐ If you were writing a theory on the Christian use of dreams, what would you add or how would you change them?

> *Lord, I thank You for the gift of dreams. I am open to the invitation to wholeness that the dream brings.*

PART THREE Christian Approach To Dreams

Applied Learning

✎ *Your Response*
- ☐ See the earlier quote by Tertullian. If he is right, how could a knowledge of dreams help the work of God's Spirit among unbelievers?
- ☐ Write out your reasons for listening to dreams. This will help you know what you truly believe about dreams.
- ☐ Affirm aloud: "My dreams have a Divine purpose. I like that!"

☼ *Dream work strategies, skills & techniques*
- ☐ In Judith's "*It's Jesus*" dream, she TURNED AND FACED the thing she was afraid of, and in the process she discovered who she was running from. (#1)
- ☐ If Judith's "*My Two Babies*" were your dream, what QUESTIONS might the dream evoke in you? Choose a question and write a response to it. (#2)

Explaining new dream work strategies, skills & techniques

#1 TURN AND FACE IT. If you are running from something or if something is following you, it is possible to make a decision right in the dream to *turn and face it* and find out what you are running from.

#2 Make a list of QUESTIONS a dream might evoke in you. Choose the most compelling QUESTION, and spontaneously write out your response to the question. Did you experience some type of shift in your awareness as you wrote? How will your response influence your daily life?

✍ *Practicing your skills*
- ☐ Select a dream to work with.
- ☐ Are you running from something? Is something following you? If so, you can TURN AND FACE it. Plan to do this next time this happens. (#1)
- ☐ What QUESTIONS does your dream raise for you? Select one question and spontaneously write out your response to it. (#2)
- ☐ Which core belief/s might your dream be an illustration of?

Dream Treasure

Dream Work Terminology

Can you explain the following terms?

- Conscious ego
- Conversing with God in dreams
- Holiness
- Wholeness
- Human psychology
- Intelligent intent
- Dream energy/intensity
- Dark sayings (*Chiydah*)
- Symbolic imagery
- Auditory vision
- Turn and face it
- Your questions evoked by dream

PART THREE Christian Approach To Dreams

Biblical Purposes of Dreams   10

There is a God in heaven who reveals mysteries, and he has made known to king Nebuchadnezzar what will take place in the latter days. This was your dream and the visions in your mind while on the bed...and that you may understand your inmost thoughts (Dan. 2:28-30).

Core Concepts
1. Dreams make God known.
2. Dreams make God's words known.
3. Dreams provide divine counsel.
4. Dreams give godly instruction.
5. Dreams open our ears, get our attention.
6. Dreams adjust attitudes, keep us from pride.
7. Dreams change conduct, behavior.
8. Dreams keep our soul from death.
9. Dreams enlighten us with the light of life.
10. Dreams reveal divine mysteries.
11. Dreams foretell the future.
12. Dreams reveal our inner thoughts.

Learning Objectives
At the completion of this chapter, you will be able to:
- ☐ Know the Scriptures from which the biblical purposes are drawn.
- ☐ List and describe the twelve biblical purposes of dreams.
- ☐ Identify God's divine purpose in your dreams.
- ☐ Respond to your dream in light of its biblical purpose.

Early in our journey we learned that the dream is not merely a meaningless response to sense stimuli during sleep. From a biblical standpoint, the dream presents a way for God to speak directly to His people while they slumber in their beds. What types of messages does God use the dream for?

Using the following Scriptures as our source, we identify twelve divine purposes of dreams. Numerous biblical and illustrative examples are provided to enhance your understanding of each purpose. During the discussion you will notice the purposes often overlap.

Dream Treasure

*Hear now My words: If there is a prophet among you, I the Lord, shall make myself known (**1**) to him in a vision. I shall speak (**2**) with him in a dream... (Num. 12:6-8).*

*I will pour out my spirit on you; I will make my words known to you (**2**) (Prov. 1:23)—using prophesy, visions, and dreams (Acts 2:1-18).*

*I will bless the Lord who has counseled me (**3**); Indeed, my mind [inner man] instructs me (**4**) in the night (Ps. 16:7).*

*"...In a dream, a vision of the night, when sound sleep falls on men...he seals their instruction (**4**) (Job 33:14-16).*

*God speaks once or twice, yet no one notices it. In a dream, a vision of the night, when sound sleep falls on men...he opens the ears of men (**5**) (Job 33:14-16).*

*That he may turn man aside from his conduct (**7**), keep him from pride (**6**) (Job 33:17).*

*He keeps back his soul from the pit, and his life from passing over into Sheol (**8**) (Job 33:18, 28, 30).*

*That he may be enlightened with the light of life (**9**) (Job 33:30).*

*There is a God in heaven who reveals mysteries (**10**), and he has made known to king Nebuchadnezzar what will take place in the latter days (**11**). This was your dream and the visions in your mind while on the bed. As for you, O king, while on your bed your thoughts turned to what would take place in the future, and He who reveals mysteries (**10**) has made known to you what will take place (**11**) (Dan. 2:28-29).*

But as for me, this mystery has not been revealed to me for any wisdom residing in me more than in any other living man, but for the purpose of making the interpretation known to the king, and that you may understand the thoughts of your mind [lit., heart, your inmost thoughts] *(**12**) (Dan. 2:30).*

> *Hear now My words: If there is a prophet among you, I the Lord, shall make myself known to him in a vision. I shall speak with him in a dream... (Num. 12:6-8).*

1. Interactive learning

☐ Memorize the twelve biblical purposes of dreams.

☐ Be able to explain each purpose and distinguish it from the others.

☐ Identify a dream example for each purpose, drawing on the dreams in the Bible, authors' dreams, other people's dreams, or your own dreams.

1. Dreams make God known

According to Numbers 12:6-8, God uses dreams to make himself known to prophets. As we noted in Chapter 2, the prophets Isaiah, Jeremiah, Micah, Ezekiel, Zechariah, and Amos all experienced God and received his living Word through *visual* experiences—either dreams or visions. God also used a dream to make himself known to Jacob in his renowned angels-on-a-ladder dream (Genesis. 28:11-16).

In the New Testament, the Lord revealed himself using the angel of a dream to provide guidance for the father of the Messiah (Mt 1:20). The many stories of Jesus revealing himself in dreams to Muslims (for example, see Shayda's *Come, My Daughter* dream in Chapter 2) provide evidence God still uses dreams to make

Himself known to people today.

2. Dreams make God's words known to us

In the Old Testament, God promised to pour out His Spirit on us and make His words known to us (Prov. 1:23). Later, in the New Testament, the Apostle Peter connects the coming of the Holy Spirit with dreams, visions, and prophecies, providing the means for God to speak to people and make His words known to them.

Reveal the things God has for us

According to St. Paul, the Holy Spirit will make known the things that God has for us (I Cor. 2:12). Thus we can expect dreams to reveal the good things God has in mind for us. Following is an example of how God spoke to Judith in a dream. This dream is also an example of a direct voice of God dream.

Until You Do What I Told You

(Judith): For some months I sensed the Holy Spirit prompting me to become a Catholic, but I had procrastinated until I received this powerful dream from God.

I see no one, but only hear a voice saying, "Until you do what I told you, you won't hear from me again."

As I awoke I knew it was God who is speaking very directly to me, telling me exactly what He wants me to do—to become Catholic! There was nothing symbolic about this dream—no symbols to interpret. I obeyed the Lord, and this act of obedience opened up many good things for me—the door to Germany and later Catholic radio, as well as wonderful friends and great experiences with the people of God in Germany.

3. Dreams provide divine counsel

According to Psalms 16:7, we can expect to receive divine counsel, even during the wee hours when our brain is not conscious. During sleep the mind may be turned off, but the spirit is still active, listening as the Creator offers us guidance and direction. With God's help we can receive from these dreams God's wisdom and knowledge for our life problems, issues, and decisions.

Herman Riffel discovered in his personal life that the dream is an invaluable counselor: "It is with us every night and charges no fee…there is no better way to get to the heart of a person's problems than through the dream."[1] Following are two examples of biblical men receiving God's divine counsel in their dreams.

Jacob received counsel in his relationship with Laban via a dream, telling him what to do with the flock (Gen. 31:10-29).

Joseph dreams of an angel telling him to not be afraid to take Mary as his wife, even though she is with child. The angel tells him that Mary's conception was by the Holy Spirit (Mt 1:20).

> The Holy Spirit makes Gods words known to us through dreams, visions and prophecies.

Dream Treasure

PART THREE Christian Approach To Dreams

Problem-solving dreams

An example of a dream offering counsel is one providing specific help in solving a problem. Solutions for scientific problems have sometimes been revealed through a dream. When a dream presents us with a problem, the solution is often rooted right in the dream itself.

Although the meaning may be shrouded in the symbols and metaphors, the dream's wise counsel is there to for us to receive if we pay attention to it. For example:

Give Me Something From Your Purse

(Judith): A prestigious Christian woman was offended with me and was speaking negatively about me to others. I asked the Lord how He wanted me to respond. Then I dreamed:

I am in a Christian meeting, and the offering is being taken. A voice says to me, "Give me something from your purse." I look in my purse and find a needle and thread and a magnifying glass. I put them in the offering basket.

The needle and thread symbolized for me that I was not to try to mend the relationship. The magnifying glass indicated I was not to focus on the broken relationship.

4. Dreams give godly instruction

In Job 33:16, Elihu told Job that when sound sleep falls on men, God seals their instruction. According to Psalms 16:7, God also instructs us in the night. Unless we plan to stay awake all night long, we'll have to receive this nightly instruction through dreams.

Dream Treasure

Although many dreams offer guidance, there seems to be a difference between counsel and instruction dreams. For example, instruction dreams give us very *clear* information or instruction concerning something we need for our lives. Such a dream may be telling us what to do or where to go, or emphasizing something important.

> When Joseph was instructed to take Mary as his wife, and was given the name to call his son, he received his marching orders in a dream in the night (Mt 1:20-21).

Instruction dreams are simple—not a dramatic story—with only one theme, perhaps even consisting of only a voice, with no visual images. One young man was instructed in his dream to study theology—and also told where he was to study.

Instruction dreams give us very clear information or instruction concerning something we need for our lives.

Typically we awake from such a dream with an *inner knowing* that God has spoken to us. Following is an example of an instruction dream.

Study Psychology

(Judith): *In the early 1980s, I told the Lord that, if there was something He wanted me to do, I was willing to do it. Then I dreamed this simple dream:*

> An unseen person is speaking to me, saying, "Study psychology; it will pay you rich dividends."

I shared the dream with a friend, and he immediately said, "It means metaphysical psychology!" I went to a dictionary and learned it has to do with essential reality—the nature of being, the supernatural, the origin of things. In response to this dream, I spent hours studying materials related to the message in my dream. Over time, I experienced divine revelation and transformation deep inside, and also was able to help others.

Direction dreams

Another type of instruction dream is one giving us direction for our lives. It offers us general guidance, perhaps not quite as specific as a typical instruction dream.

Consider how St. Paul's vision-in-the-night pointed him in the right direction:

Dream Treasure

> *...a vision appeared to Paul in the night: a certain man of Macedonia was standing and appealing to him, and saying, "Come over to Macedonia and help us" (Acts 16:9).*

Gerald's *Bluebird of Happiness* dream in Chapter 1 used symbols to point him in the direction he needed to go—outside the corporation. Here is another example:

Come, We Are So Hungry

(Judith): We were praying for clarity on where to live in Germany. Several opportunities were open to us. Then I dreamed:

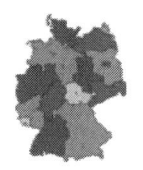

A woman is calling out to me, with her arms outstretched. She says, "Come, we are so hungry!"

As I awoke, I knew she was from Braunschweig, Germany. So this is exactly where we went.

5. Dreams open our ears—get our attention

Resistant to change, we often need help to open our ears to hear what God wants to say to us. According to Job 33, one way God gets our attention is through dreams. When we are not able to hear the still, small voice, God uses dreams.

Frightening dreams and nightmares

Another way God gets our attention is through highly-charged themes, such as frightening dreams and nightmares. Elihu, Job's advisor, asserts that God speaks to us in dreams, even multiple times on the same subject, trying to get our attention. Failing this, the Almighty may turn up the heat, bringing us frightening dreams or nightmares that jolt us into awareness (Job 33:14-18).

> **Dream Work Tip:**
> God uses the dream to help us release our unlived (denied or repressed) emotions.

A nightmare—being chased, attacked, drowning, falling, dying, or fighting in a war zone—is a type of dream that causes us to wake up feeling terrified. Palms sweating, heart pounding, we thank God it was only a dream! Usually the experience is not completed in the dream, suggesting we have unresolved issues in our lives. Elihu's counsel to Job suggests that the author of our scary dreams may be God, bringing us face to face with the things we are ignoring.

A nightmare can be viewed as an invitation to come to our Heavenly Father for healing and deliverance. According to Scripture, God has a purpose for us: "that the light of life may shine on him" (Job 33:30). (See Chapter 14, "*Classifying Dreams,*" for more discussion of nightmare dreams.)

When we are not able to hear the still, small voice, God uses dreams.

Trauma dreams

Some especially traumatic dreams cause the dreamer to repeatedly re-live a life-threatening experience such as war, natural catastrophe, abuse, or violence. Packed with emotional energy—helplessness, grief, and terror—they cause the dreamer to re-experience the traumatic event until it is integrated into conscious awareness and everyday life.[2] Recurring, severe nightmares are a signal that something is unhealed in our hearts.

A recurring nightmare

A woman who had been brutally assaulted while working at a shelter for runaways experienced this nightmare for months afterward:

A faceless girl chased me through a room and into a hallway. I am fleeing down the hallway, a pungent and bittersweet odor stings my nose, my arm becomes cold, and there is something about a red light. I feel sure it means my death. I awake sobbing in terror.

With the help of her pastor, the woman revisited the scene of her assault—smelled similar odors, felt the cool cinder block wall, and saw a red exit sign down the hall. Shortly afterward, her nightmares ceased.[3]

2. Interactive learning
- ☐ What is the purpose of a nightmare?
- ☐ List some things we can do if we have a nightmare.

6. Dreams adjust attitudes—keep us from pride

Beyond our conscious minds, our attitudes are deeply embedded in the memories of our past, branded into our soul by our life's experiences. Attitudes determine our view of ourselves and the world around us—we live the existence permitted by our attitudes and beliefs. If our attitudes are loaded with lies and illusions, they need replacement by healing, life-giving words from God.

As indicated in Job 33, sometimes we need a dream to change our attitudes—in Job's case, to prevent him from developing pride. Our dreams offer us a wonderful resource for exposing our negative belief systems about ourselves and our place in the world. Here is an example from Jacob's life.

Fearful of taking his family to Egypt to visit his son Joseph, Jacob received a dream that changed his attitude. God promised to go with him into Egypt and bring him back out again. Moreover, knowing he had a future, Jacob broke free from his fear (Gen 46:1-7).

This type of dream offers us the possibility to see in a new way our negative attitudes that need adjustment by the Divine Adjustor so we can alter our conduct and come into more life. They are trying to bring to consciousness our inner thoughts and motivations. By revealing the problems in our hearts we won't allow ourselves to see, these dreams try to help us change attitudes, behaviors, and negative beliefs. Following is an example of a dream that shows a need for attitude adjustment.

PART THREE Christian Approach To Dreams

Last of The Big Bruisers

My (Gerald) wife had tried many times to help me see that the way I spoke to her and to my children was too harsh, but I had difficulty accepting it. Then the following dream jolted me.

Bill Lambier (former center for the Detroit Pistons, a man known for his rough basketball tactics) was shooting baskets and I was tossing the balls back to him. I said, "You know, they call you the last of the Big Bruisers." Although he didn't like it, I insisted this is what they call him.

It is clear to me that this dream spoke to my condition. I was the big bruiser, wounding my family, hurting my relationship with my wife, alienating my children. Resolution of the issue awaited another later dream.

> **Dream Work Tip:**
> A same-sex figure often represents an unfamiliar part of us called the shadow, which can symbolize either positive or negative aspects (attitudes, capabilities, traits, etc.) of ourselves.

7. Dreams change conduct—behavior

Elihu told Job he was privileged to hear from God in his dreams because it enabled him to change unacceptable conduct. Dreams, the ever-present nighttime counselor, call our attention to attitudes, behaviors, values, and emotional reactions that are no longer life-giving. Because of the intensity of the dream images—the evoked emotion, God's divine energy—they are able to help us really see our inner motivations and thus enable us to change our behavior.

Following are two incidents from the Bible in which people's behavior was changed by a dream.

God warned the heathen king Abimelech not to touch Sarah, because she was Abraham's wife (Gen 20:1-18). Abimelech changed his plans and released her to Abraham.

A dream warned Laban to be careful how he spoke to Jacob (Gen 31:24).

I Cry Out My Sorrow To God

(Gerald): Some months after I dreamed I was the "Big Bruiser," I had another dream in which I realized deep inside that I was indeed a bruiser.

Feeling overwhelming remorse, I looked for a place where I could cry it out to God. I found a bed, knelt there and poured out my heart to God, weeping uncontrollably with extremely deep remorse—a true repentance.

I awoke with a sense that the dream showed me the approach to healing in this area of my life. I also realized the possibility of being the last *of the Big Bruisers in my family. By God's grace, I have chosen to bring restoration to my relationships.*

8. Dreams keep our soul from death

One of Elihu's arguments to Job was that heeding the warnings in his dreams might keep his soul from tumbling into the pit—to keep him in the land of the living (Job 33:18). Dreams may serve to warn us in some way to keep our lives from death and destruction.

> *In order to save Israel and Egypt, king Pharaoh dreamed of standing by the Nile River. Seven fat cows came up, followed by seven lean cows, which ate up the fat cows (Gen 41:1-49).*

Warning dreams

Although people's dreams sometimes indicate potential injury to themselves, this does not necessarily mean it will happen. Warning dreams are given so the event foreseen does not come to pass—there's no predictive power that makes evil things happen. However, if dreams are ignored or misunderstood, real accidents could happen.

> *Warning dreams are given so the event foreseen does not come to pass—there's no predictive power that makes evil things happen.*

> *Receiving a dream warning him of danger, Joseph diverts his family to Nazareth (Mt 2:22).*

> *The Lord God protects the Christ Child by warning the Magi in a dream, telling them not to return to Herod (Mt. 2:12).*

A would-be passenger of the infamous Titanic steamship promptly canceled his voyage after dreaming of disaster at sea—likely saving his life.[4] Shortly before his assassination, Abraham Lincoln dreamed about the death of a president.[5] Perhaps if Lincoln had heeded the dream, his life would have been spared.

Contemporary example

> *While employed as a truck driver, Ralph Nault dozed in a chair and experienced three vivid, terrifying dream/visions. Shortly he was involved in a bad accident that happened exactly as forewarned by the first dream/vision—he miraculously survived. Later, although he was not wrecked himself, he observed another accident exactly as depicted in his second dream/vision. In a third incident his truck hit a drunk driver (uninjured) just as he saw in another premonition dream/vision.*

> *Nault also relates a recurring dream he experienced during this time: after he was part way across a high bridge, something would go wrong with the front of the truck, and he would plunge over the edge of the bridge into the river below. Nault felt that God was using all these dreams to warn him to stop driving truck. When he quit truck driving, the horrifying accident dreams— including the recurring one—all stopped.*

> ▶ *Dream Work Tip:*
> Death of the self in a dream usually is a metaphor for a necessary psychological change—something within us needs to die.

Health dreams

We may experience dreams offering warnings or suggestions on caring for our physical bodies. Although understanding these dreams is often challenging, they may provide insight into the condition of our bodies. Dreams about our bodies may be trying to alert us to impending illness or imminent physical problems—long before symptoms are evident to us. If so, we need to seek medical help.

Fix the waterworks

A friend's doctor said she needed to have her female organs removed. However, she wanted to wait for God to heal them—until she dreamed that her house was in danger of sliding off its foundation and something was wrong with its water system. This dream symbolically condensed her current problem. She scheduled the surgery!

Regrettably, a scientific approach to diagnosing illness through dreams has not yet been developed. Fortunately, death of the self in a dream usually is a metaphor for a necessary psychological change—something within us needs to die.

9. Dreams enlighten us with the light of life

Continuing the dream theme Elihu introduced earlier, Job 33:30 indicates that God may shine His living light on us right in the dream. We are made more fully alive and able to do far more than we ever imagined!

Dreams carry divine energy that can create hope and faith in our hearts to empower us for living.

As discussed in Chapter 9, by transforming the energy contained in our unconscious into images and symbols while asleep, our dreams can re-energize us for everyday living. We find ourselves addressing challenges with renewed enthusiasm, finishing incomplete projects, and sensing new creativity for our lives.

Gifts of grace dreams

Because life can be tough, we need encouragement along the way. In the dream, God may grace us with gifts of encouragement or comfort. We may also be graced with spiritual gifts, such as faith, wisdom, or anointing for ministry. Dreams carry divine energy, creating hope and faith in our hearts to empower us for living.

A Baby Is Born

After several miscarriages, a woman found herself pregnant with another child. Paranoid she would lose this baby too, she asked the Lord to give her reassurance that whatever happened, He would be with her. That night she saw herself giving birth to a baby girl with pale skin, round little face, and full head of black hair. She heard the words, "All will be well." She awoke, with peace flooding her spirit—and months later, her baby girl was born on Christmas day.[6]

Transformed Basement

(Gerald): Here is a dream that graced my life with encouragement because I realized it spoke of the transformation God had accomplished deep in my soul:

The dark, dingy basement of my childhood home had been transformed into something bright, attractive and livable.

Comfort (gift) dreams

Although most death dreams are subjective (about ourselves), occasionally people may dream of a recently deceased loved one. Also called "gift dreams," they bring comfort and peace into the heart of a bereaved person.[7]

Christian psychiatrist Len Sperry relates the story of a client who had an extraordinary dream within the first few days of her son's death. In heaven her completely healed son bounded across an open, sunny field to greet her. He told her he was with two elderly loved neighbors; he "was doing fine, that God was okay." [8]

Holding Our Deceased Son

(Judith): After our sixteen year old son died, my mother's arms continued to ache for him. I prayed about this to the Lord, then I dreamed…

I am holding him one more time, telling him that he is going to leave us and how it will be for him to leave the earth. I compared it to his birth, what it was like for him to come here, how he had to pass through a narrow dark passage before emerging into the light.

When I awoke, my mother's arms no longer ached to hold him!

Growth and healing dreams

Many of our problems are caused by the destructive lies we believe. Growth and healing dreams throw light into those darkened areas, giving encouragement to weak parts of our personality, deflating the ego, and building up the true self.[9] The dream can deftly skirt around our defense mechanisms and drill down rapidly to the heart of our problems, perhaps even indicate a solution.

Growth and healing dreams come to bring changes in our lives that cause us to move toward our destiny, becoming what God meant us to be. When, in a dream, we are "enlightened with the light of life," healing comes into our souls and we become more alive. We can trust the Holy Spirit to guide us in this sometimes perilous adventure.

Following is an example of how a dream can lead to healing—even answering a prayer!

Three Embedded Lies

In 1985, for six months prior to this dream, I (Judith) had been praying, "Lord, there is a lie somewhere in the depths of my being; would you heal it?" On a Friday night, I dreamed…

I was looking at a small pimple on my thigh. Then the pimple opened up, and I saw my whole thigh was filled with infection down to the bone.

I knew God was about to do something, and my faith was quickened. Two days later, He did! We were discussing the idea that our earliest memory often reveals how we look at the world and our place in it. As I recalled my earliest memory (age 2 ½), the Lord exposed three lies embedded in this traumatic memory: 1) I am not loved; 2) I am not important or valuable; 3) self rejection and self hatred. As the Lord put His hand on each lie and pulled them out of the fabric of my personality, I saw that they were not true; I had simply believed the lies. My life has been forever changed because of this healing experience!

10. Dreams reveal divine mysteries

Mystery refers to something we cannot understand with our rational minds—it can be known to us only through insight and experience. The Kingdom of God contains mysteries (Mt 13:11).

In the Greek, "mysterion" was something to be known, but it was an initiated knowledge that one could acquire only through individual insight and experience—it could not be communicated through an ordinary educational process.[10]

According to St. Paul, God's wisdom is hidden (Eph. 3:3, 4). We need revelation to comprehend the mysteries of spiritual truth—we are unable to see it through our intellect and reason. Daniel assured King Nebuchadnezzar that God reveals mysteries to us in dreams (Dan. 2:28-30).

The mystery of God establishing a covenant with a group of people who would become the Israeli nation was revealed to Jacob in his ladder dream (Gen. 28:12).

Spiritual growth and revelation dreams

Spiritual growth and revelation dreams come from beyond the structure of our soul—from the Spirit of God. We recognize this type of dream because the symbolism is charged with energy and often has divine connotations—crucifix, Bible, church, cathedral, monastery, religious service. Because they bring revelation about spiritual matters, these dreams result in some type of transformation within us.

Gabriel Teaches Me To Fly

(Judith): I received this dream after approximately seven years of intense healing and spiritual growth. I was learning how to flow with the Holy Spirit as I worked in my ministry.

The angel Gabriel is with me, teaching me to fly. I had wings strapped on my arms and I was being taught to fly using the currents and the winds. I was very afraid, but I was flying. When I took my eyes off the angel's instruction, I fell.

Dream Treasure

Angel Gabriel Teaches Me To Fly

This dream gave spiritual revelation of what it means to be led by the Spirit and my level of expertise in doing so.

11. Dreams foretell the future

Another exciting type of dream prepares, announces, or warns about future situations before they actually happen. Also called anticipatory dreams, they may give answers or offer solutions, while others may suggest a pessimistic, even disastrous, turn of events. (See Chapter 14, "*Classifying Dreams*," for more explanation of extrasensory perception dreams.)

A young field hand named Joseph received two dreams from God about his future destiny sure to endear him to his brothers:

> *There we were, binding sheaves in the field. Then behold, my sheaf arose and also stood upright; and indeed your sheaves stood all around and bowed down to my sheaf. (Gen. 37:7)*

> *Look, I have dreamed another dream. And this time, the sun, the moon, and the eleven stars bowed down to me. (Gen. 37:9)*

These dreams may come to tell us about specific future events, possibly our life's purpose, or to give us information outside of our own experiences. Perhaps, instead of predicting the future, the purpose of this type of dream is more to help us be aware of what God is doing when something happens.

Benefit an individual

Dreams revealing information about future happenings come to prepare us for necessary action and call us to intercession. Or they could be simply telling us what

---

Warning!
Do not use prophetic dreams to control or manipulate others, or to bring them under your authority. Neither let others use their dreams about you to direct your life or to place burdens on you.

will happen *if we don't change* in some way. Understanding this type of dream is sometimes quite difficult. Is it symbolic, precognitive, or forecasting the future? Is it about someone else?

Perhaps it's well to remember that most dreams are about us and the development of our souls. A simple test of dreams purporting to forecast the future is whether or not they come true. Here is an example:

I Am In Rome!

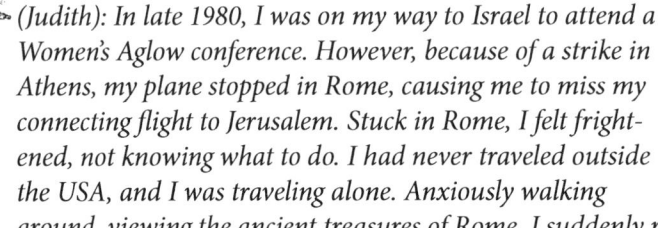

(Judith): In late 1980, I was on my way to Israel to attend a Women's Aglow conference. However, because of a strike in Athens, my plane stopped in Rome, causing me to miss my connecting flight to Jerusalem. Stuck in Rome, I felt frightened, not knowing what to do. I had never traveled outside the USA, and I was traveling alone. Anxiously walking around, viewing the ancient treasures of Rome, I suddenly remembered a little dream from some months earlier. It was a very simple dream:

I am walking the streets in Rome.

My faith quickened. Everything was in God's hands! In His faithfulness, He had given me this dream six months before—so I would recognize His hand in gifting me with this life-altering experience!

Benefit tribe (prophetic dream for community, church, nation)

While most of our dreams are ordinary, coming from our everyday lives, some may have far-reaching significance for whole groups of people. Known as "big" dreams or prophetic dreams, they foretell in accurate detail specific future events of importance to more people than just the dreamer. Based on extrasensory perception, they demonstrate an existing foreknowledge of events.

> *Prophetic dreams may appear when some dimension of God's plan is at stake, so people will know what to do when unexpected difficulties arise.*

An East African once told Dr. Jung that they were not receiving many big dreams anymore, because "now they had the colonial governor who gave directions for the tribe."[11]

Pharaoh's dream made him aware of approaching famine and gave him time to prepare for it—so whole groups of people could be preserved.

Pharaoh stood by the river. Suddenly out of the river came seven fine looking fat cows. Then seven ugly and gaunt cows came out of the river and ate up the seven fine looking fat cows. (taken from Gen 41:1-4)

Prophetic dreams may appear when some dimension of God's plan is at stake, so people will know what to do when unexpected difficulties arise. Just prior to WWII, Carl Jung dreamed of a map of Europe being dipped in blood. The only parts of the map not covered in blood were the areas in Europe that did not become Nazi occupied. Prophetic dreams are extremely rare. If you think your dream is intended for the larger community, first pause and take a deep breath—it's probably about yourself. Ask the Lord to show you how your dream relates to your own personal struggles. Also seek advice from wise people who are sensitive to God's Spirit.[12]

3. Interactive learning
☐ How will you know if a dream is foretelling the future or prophetic?
☐ What will you do if someone you know is in your dream and in danger?

12. Dreams reveal our inner thoughts

One purpose of King Nebuchadnezzar's dream was to cause him to know his thoughts and the intentions of his heart—what was going on in his inner life—and perhaps repent and change.

> *This was your dream and the visions in your mind while on the bed…that you may understand the thoughts of your mind* [lit., heart, your inmost thoughts] *(Dan. 2:28–30).*

This is the biblical purpose of *most* of our dreams—to reveal what is going on deep in our heart, in our inner spiritual life. By knowing what is happening in our heart, the dream enables us to make a connection between our inner spiritual life and the choices we make in our outer life.

God seems to weave together the messages about the state of our inner world with our various life experiences into dreams designed for our well-being. Because it makes us aware of our innermost thoughts, the dream helps us discover what is really in our hearts.

> *This is the biblical purpose of most of our dreams—to reveal what is going on deep in our heart, in our inner spiritual life.*

> *Basil the Great, way ahead of modern psychology, understood that the inner workings of the personality—which our conscious self is not in touch with—is often revealed in dreams.*

Following is an example of how a dream revealed what was going on in my (Gerald) inner world.

Waif Unplugs Me
While I worked on a graphic illustration on my computer, a waif woman tried unsuccessfully to get my attention. When I snapped at her, she reached over and unplugged my computer!

> *My dream symbolically illustrated my current problem—my new computer wasn't working, my relationship with my wife was deteriorating, things generally were going sour. Through discerning dream work, I saw that I was not relating properly to my inner world, disconnected from my emotions, not living in the flow of life.*

Search me and know my heart

Symbolically, the heart refers to the core and center of everything, the source of the hidden springs of our personal life. Everything we do works out from the heart—the place of contact with the Divine. Genuine faith is in the heart, not the intellect. God promises to give us a new heart, a heart of flesh, not stone.

The psalmist prayed, "Create in me a clean heart, O' God" (Ps 51:10). The Bible makes it clear that God will search our hearts for the purpose of cleansing and healing them.

> *I the Lord search the heart… (Jer. 17:9-10; I Ch 29:17; Jer. 11:20; I Thes. 2:4).*
>
> *Lord, search me and know my heart; Try me and know my anxious thoughts…see if there be any hurtful way [way of pain] in me, and lead me in the everlasting way (Ps. 139:23).*

> ➤ *Dream Work Tip:*
>
> In personification, some trait, emotion, attitude, characteristic, or aspect of our self is placed on an inanimate object, animal, or person.

Through personification, a dream reveals thoughts, emotions, desires, and motivations we are unable to see. It also may alert us when we are ignoring our own souls or our spiritual lives.

Conflict resolution

Dreams are a resource from God, bringing to light our inmost thoughts and motivations of our heart, enabling us to bring them to God for healing. Using symbols, images and metaphors, our dreams reflect the outward circumstances of our lives, our self-concept and its relationship to our behavior.

Our dreams are often loaded with conflicts and unresolved situations—something is chasing us, we find a malnourished baby, a monster is staring at us, we can't seem to finish something, we are lost, we miss an airplane flight. By bringing the dreamer into touch with the unconscious to restore balance with in the person, dreams can help heal the soul.

> *4. Interactive learning*
> ☐ Are you more interested in dreams foretelling the future or in dreams revealing the contents of your heart? Explain?

Summary statements

The Holy Scriptures tell us God uses dreams for many purposes in our lives. Some dreams teach us what we need to know at a particular phase of our lives, perhaps giving us direction for a decision we need to make. If God wants to communicate something to us, a dream can penetrate our awareness while our conscious mind cannot interfere. As we illustrated, a pillow vision can initiate attitude adjustments or behavior changes.

We come to know about ourselves in a deeper way through dreams that reach beyond what our rational mind can grasp. God uses the dream to reveal insight about spiritual matters that brings about needed transformation within us. By shining the light of life right into our dreams, God brings the grace that heals our souls, causing us to become more fully alive.

5. Interactive learning

Can you identify the biblical purpose/s of the following dreams?
- ☐ *Bluebird Of Happiness* (Chapter 1)—
- ☐ *Without a Degree* (Chapter 1)—
- ☐ *Come, My Daughter* (Chapter 2)—
- ☐ *Dancing Skeleton* (Chapter 3)—
- ☐ *Flood Waters Rising At My Doorstep* (Chapter 4)—
- ☐ *Jacob's Legendary Ladder Dream* (Chapter 5)—
- ☐ *Director Of Marketing* (Chapter 6)—
- ☐ *House Foundation Is Sick* (Chapter 7)—
- ☐ *My New Bible* (Chapter 8)—
- ☐ *Divine Hug From Pope* (Chapter 8)—
- ☐ *It's Jesus* (Chapter 9)—
- ☐ *My Two Babies* (Chapter 9)—
- ☐ *Sleeping Giant* (Chapter 18)—
- ☐ *Phone Call* (Chapter 14)—

> *Lord, I want to be made spiritually alive and whole.*
> *I need You to reveal the thoughts and intentions of my*
> *heart. Please enlighten me with the light of life.*

Applied Learning

✎ *Your Response*
- ☐ Meditate on Daniel 2:28-30, asking God to give you revelation of its meaning for you.
- ☐ Which of the biblical purposes would you like your dream to have? Why?
- ☐ Affirm aloud: "Dream work calls me to turn my life more and more towards God."

✲ *Dream work strategies, skills & techniques*
- ☐ Did Gerald fully release his emotions in "*I Cry Out My Sorrow?*"
- ☐ Describe the BIBLICAL PURPOSE of Gerald's "*Last of The Big Bruisers*" dream. (#1)
- ☐ Choose a dream in this chapter, imagining it is your dream, and use the LISTENING-PRAYER TECHNIQUE. Or use Jacob's ladder dream, imagining it is yours, and listen for what God might say to you. (#2)

Explaining new dream work strategies, skills & techniques
#1 Discerning the BIBLICAL PURPOSE of a dream can help clarify its message.

#2 Use the LISTENING-PRAYER TECHNIQUE. Enter into the Lord's presence through prayer, and invite Him to accompany you as you re-enter the dream. Using your imagination, allow Jesus Christ to be with you in the dream and resolve it.

✎ *Practicing your skills*
- ☐ Select a dream to work with.
- ☐ Did you fully release any emotion in it, or did you withhold, deny, or stuff it down?
- ☐ What might be the BIBLICAL PURPOSE of your dream? (#1)
- ☐ Use the LISTENING-PRAYER TECHNIQUE to re-enter your dream and listen to what the Lord Jesus might say to you in it. You can use this with any trauma or nightmarish dreams. (#2)

Dream Work Terminology

Can you explain the following terms?
- Biblical purpose
- Problem-solving dreams
- Direction dreams
- Nightmares—trauma dreams
- Warning dreams
- Health dreams
- Gifts of grace dreams
- Comfort dreams
- Growth and healing dreams
- Divine mystery dreams
- Extra-sensory dreams
- Prophetic dreams
- Big dreams
- Personification
- Listening-prayer technique

PART THREE Christian Approach To Dreams

Scriptural Guidelines 11

Joseph said to them, 'Do not interpretations belong to God?' (Gen. 40:8).

Core Concepts
- Take dreams seriously.
- Most dreams cannot be taken literally.
- Interpreting dreams requires effort.
- Dream work requires applying the heart.
- Dreams convey messages important to the heart.
- Pay attention to dreams when seeking God on an issue.
- Repetitive themes indicate importance.
- Share your dreams with friends.
- You are the decision-maker.
- Recognize the witness of the Holy Spirit
- Dreams require action.

Learning Objectives
At the completion of this chapter, you will be able to:
- ☐ List and describe the twelve scriptural guidelines.
- ☐ Explain why dream work is a "spiritual practice."
- ☐ Discuss the *importance of the heart* in dream work.
- ☐ Describe what it means to take a dream literally.
- ☐ Define "dream interpretation."
- ☐ Understand how to respond to your dream messages.
- ☐ Work with your dreams using scriptural guidelines.

As we said in the introduction, we found we have secret, hidden riches deposited by God within us. However, because they are buried beyond the reach of our conscious minds, we needed to learn how to draw them out. This is what dream work is all about: the art of drawing out the wisdom, knowledge and guidance in the dream. The Scriptures have much to say about how to break open the dream and discern its message for our lives.

In this part we highlight scriptural guidelines to help you draw out the meaning of your dream. Also, you will gain an appreciation for why we treat dream work more as an *art*, instead of a *science*. This approach is far more important than pounding the force of reason and logic against the dream, trying to understand it intellectually. We can't open up most dreams rationally.

1. Take your dreams seriously

If we believe God lives in the realm of the unseen part of our being and wants to speak to us, we will begin to give sincere attention to our dreams. Clearly decide you want God's help and direction for your life, and are willing to seek it by listening to your dreams.

> *Our attitude toward dreams, which are as delicate, complex, and alive as human beings, is of paramount importance. When we do take our dreams seriously, we discover that they have some powerful and transforming messages for us. (Morton Kelsey)[1]*

Nothing of great value comes easily. The more attention and respect we give our dreams, the more we will receive back from them. Gold and diamonds having the greatest value lie deepest in the earth. If you want to mine the field of your dreams for the glorious hidden wisdom of God, you must want it with all your heart.

> *If you **seek** her as silver, and **search** for her as for hidden treasures; then you will... discover the knowledge of God (Prov. 2:4,5).*

A spiritual practice

Consider your dream journal as a spiritual practice, enabling you to keep a record of the things God speaks to you personally in the night. Make an act of faith by placing your notebook, dream journal, or recorder near your bed.

> We can find few better ways of coming into contact with the Holy Spirit, "than by writing down our dreams and meditating upon them and bringing them before the One who gave them to us. If we should complain that He should speak more clearly, it is helpful to remember that Jesus spoke His deepest truths of salvation in the language of images, in parable." (Morton Kelsey)[2]

2. Write down your dream

We cannot take our dreams seriously unless we record them in some way—our memories are not so dependable, especially for details. As soon as possible, write a detailed description of your dream, or tell it to your partner or a friend. Dream research shows that 95% of the dreams not written down or told within five minutes are forgotten.

> ➤ *Dream Work Tip:* Honoring the dream improves the quality of our dreams.

Writing down what God gives us in our dreams is not new. Daniel gives us the biblical precedent for recording a dream:

> *Daniel saw a dream and visions in his mind as he lay on his bed; then wrote the dream down and related the words of it (Daniel 7:1).*

Habakkuk, Jeremiah, Ezekiel and Isaiah were also told to write down what they had heard and experienced when God spoke to them:

I will keep watch to see what he will speak to me...Then the Lord answered me and said, 'Record the vision and inscribe it on tablets' (Hab. 2:1-2).

Thus saith the Lord...'Write all the words which I have spoken to you in a book' (Jer. 30:2). 'Take a scroll and write on it all the words which I have spoken to you concerning...from the day I first spoke to you...even to this day' (Jer. 36:2).

'Take for yourself one stick and write on it' (Ez. 37:16)

The Lord said to me, 'Take for your self a large tablet and write on it in ordinary letters' (Is. 8:1)

Of itself, the act of recording your dream is significant—even if you never work with it. Writing it down honors both the dream and the One who gave it to you.

> Writing it down honors both the dream and the One who gave it to you.

3. Most dreams cannot be taken literally

Since the dream message is obscured, we cannot take most dreams at face value. A fundamental premise is that the meaning of the dream is conveyed in an imaginative, figurative or symbolic way. We do not take the dream literally. A *bear* in your dream is not referring to a real bear. Thus, we must learn how to unravel it, like a proverb or a riddle or a puzzle.

The following word study will help us understand what it means to "interpret" a dream. In Judges 7:15, the Hebrew word, *shêber,* means "to fracture," to find a solution to a dream by cracking it open. In Genesis 40:8, the Hebrew word, *pithrôn,* refers to "opening up," to open up our understanding.

> *...when Gideon heard the account of the dream and its interpretation (shêber), (Judges 7:15).*

> *Joseph said..."Do not interpretations (pithrôn) belong to God?" (Gen. 40:8).*

According to these Scriptures, a dream needs to be *fractured*—crack open its encoded message—before its meaning is revealed to us. Ponder for a moment... how do we open up something, how do we fracture or crack it open? The following dream symbolically portrayed the possibility of a transformation of how I (Gerald) could view my capabilities.

> **Hebrew meanings for "interpretation"**
>
> *Shêber* means to fracture a dream, to find a solution to it by cracking it open. *Pithrôn* refers to opening up a dream so it can be understood.

Back Door Counselor

(Gerald): Judith had just recently received her MSW degree, and was contemplating how to find work as a counselor. I wondered how I could be effective working with her in this area of our ministry, because I lack formal education in counseling. Then I dreamed...

An older downtown building was used as an office by a counseling agency. Judith was applying for a job through the front door. Noticing a sign by the back door offering a free tour of the agency, I decided to enter. A woman briefly described the operation, and then led me to a therapist's office for a more detailed explanation. The therapist was an old school buddy (who, after retiring from teaching school, drove an OTR truck for several years). He told me he recently had received an MSW degree, and said he enjoyed his work as a therapist.

My truck-driver-turned-counselor friend is a part of me, capable of participating in counseling activity in some way, in spite of not being educated in this arena (in through the back door). Since the Lord is my helper, I have the Spirit of God within me, I am able to offer life-giving thoughts to people in need. I have experienced this in our ministry in both the USA and Europe.

4. Interpreting dreams requires real effort

> *If you seek her as silver, and search for her as for hidden treasures; then you will...discover the knowledge of God (Prov. 2:4,5).*

Yes, the interpretation of a dream belongs to God. Keep in mind that God has hidden it from us for a very good reason. Thus the meaning of a dream does not come easily—without applying real effort. God deliberately keeps His wisdom hidden from us, and something is required of us in order to find it. We must seek it out.

It is the glory of God to conceal a matter, but the glory of Kings is to search out a matter (Prov. 25:2).

If you seek her as silver, and search for her as for hidden treasures; then you will... discover the knowledge of God (Prov. 2:4,5).

Most of us are lazy. Unwilling to do the work of hearing God personally, we want someone else to give us words of knowledge and wisdom from God. We stand in line for words of prophecy, but have not yet learned how to hear God ourselves. The biblical principle of reaping what we sow is true also for dreams—the benefit we receive is proportional to the amount of effort we put into understanding them.

Of course an easy way is to pick up a dream symbols book, flip to the right page for a ready-made symbol formula, and, presto, the meaning of a dream is revealed. While these books are helpful for *ideas to consider*, assigning a fixed meaning to a symbol only confuses anyone who is genuinely trying to understand their dreams.

Takes two to tango

Reasoning abilities are a gift from God, just as are our imaginative capacities. While they are quite different, both are important in dream work. Christian dream work must work at both levels; the analytical brain needs to function well, and also an understanding of the dream must flow from the heart.

Writing down a dream, sorting out the details, keeping track of dream figures, explaining our dream to someone else—these involve rational brain functioning. Analyzing, sorting, bringing order out of the chaos of bits and pieces, all require the efforts of our conscious mind.

Analytical brain activities complement the all-important function of engaging the dream with our heart, paying attention to the flow of images and feelings engendered by the dream figures. The message God has for us is for the heart—His words are designed to touch the heart. The synchronized dance between head and heart results in the total process of deciphering the mystery of our dreams.

Consider Daniel's education

Impressed by the Lord, Herman Riffel—a Baptist pastor—studied dream interpretation at the Jung Institute in Zurich. Some Christians find this troublesome, but don't forget Daniel. His ability to interpret dreams did not just descend upon him from nowhere—the Lord had prepared him by enabling him to become educated and skilled in all literature and wisdom. Because of Daniel's keen intellect, vast knowledge and skill, Nebuchadnezzar selected him to study extensively the language and literature of the Chaldean culture in which he lived (Dan. 1:4-5, 17, 20).

Our natural mind is simply unable to comprehend things belonging to the spiritual dimension. Although we are practiced in the language of logic and reason, we are quite ignorant of how to unravel the language of pictures, images, and symbols. Joseph and Daniel were skilled in it. However, most Christians have never even heard a sermon on dreams, let alone had any training on how to understand them.

Educated in a rationalistic worldview, we use analytical reasoning, the language of the mind. We need all the help we can get to appreciate the language the Lord uses in our dreams—the language of the Holy Spirit.

> **Warning:**
> *Dream experts say we should not interpret other people's dreams until we have spent at least five years learning to understand our own. We can suggest ideas about the meaning of someone's dream, but not as an expert!*

5. Dream work requires applying the heart

King Solomon, the wise dreamer, enlightens us on how to draw up the treasure in our dreams. Apply our hearts!

> *Make your ear attentive to wisdom, apply your heart* [stretch your heart out] *to understanding (Prov. 2:2b KJV).*

As God's people, we need to do dream work His way. If we don't learn how to apply our hearts, we can make a lot of mistakes and do damage to those around us. Solomon very deliberately tells us not to look to our analytical reasoning, but to use our hearts (Prov. 3:5).

Jesus' words were designed to reach our hearts. There must be a connection to our hearts resulting in an *intuitive knowing* or witness to the truth of something. It might be a bubbling up from within that says, *yes, this is it*. Or it might feel like we've touched a live wire, and we just know, *yes*, I see it with the eye of the spirit. So we don't have to depend upon another person, whether pastor, priest, or prophet—it's right there in our own hearts.

Meditate, muse, ponder

We are told in the Bible to remember everything God says to us and to meditate on it.

> *My mouth will speak wisdom; and the meditation of my heart will be understanding (Ps 49:3).*

In this Scripture, the English word "meditation" comes from a Hebrew word meaning to muse, ponder, imagine. The heart communicates differently than the mind—in meditation, we do not use our left brain to intellectually reason or analyze.

Quieting ourselves

Tuning into our heart requires us to learn the art of quieting ourselves. For ideas on how to become still on the inside, see Morton Kelsey's *Adventure Inward* and *The Other Side of Silence*, and also *Communion With God* by Mark and Patti Virkler.

Use intuition and imagination

The heart's language is pictures, images, and symbols. To unlock their meaning, we must use more of our *imaginative, pondering, intuitive* capabilities. Logic will fail us. We must tap into *intuition* if we ever hope to understand the symbols gracing our dreams.

> *We must tap into intuition if we ever hope to understand the symbols gracing our dreams.*

When we have a "hunch" or a premonition, it comes seemingly out of nowhere, from somewhere deep inside. This is the intuition at work. The key to understanding dreams is not in mastering dream interpretation methods. Instead we discover how to approach dreams by experiencing many of them and learning to use our intuition and imagination.

The art of dream interpretation is the art of intuition[3]. We must learn to quiet our minds and push aside the argumentative brain box. To access imagination and intuition try music, art, or perhaps singing softly in the Spirit. Or try using some imaginative techniques. (For fuller discussion, see Appendix F, "*Intuitive & Imaginative Faculties*.")

> Learning dream interpretation techniques is not the whole key to understanding dreams. You gain a general sense of how to approach dreams by experiencing many dreams, by learning how to cultivate your imagination and gaining confidence in your intuition.[4]

1. Interactive learning

☐ Read Appendix F, "*Intuitive & Imaginative Faculties*."

☐ Explain the difference between studying a Scripture passage and meditating on it.

6. Dreams convey messages important to your heart

Most dreams speak to us about the things important to our hearts: Our questions about who we are and our place in the world. Current situations and happenings at home and work. Concerns for family members and our relationships. Our emotional, mental, physical and spiritual well-being. Our failures, limitations, guilt and sins. Our choice of career, our calling.

When recalling a dream, always consider concerns or questions your heart was struggling with at the time of the dream. What was on your mind? What was troubling your heart? What issues needed to be resolved? Also think about the prayers you have been praying and how they may be related to the dream.

7. Pay attention to dreams if seeking God on an issue

Saul's enemies were gathered around the Israelites. Terrified, Saul inquired of the Lord, then checked if God was answering him through the usual ways—Urim, prophets, or dreams (I Sam, 28: 6,15). When the Lord did not answer him with these methods, Saul lamented that God had departed from him.

Likewise, when we seek the Lord about an issue, we can expect Him to answer—sometimes in our dreams. For example, an Arkansas sharecropper sought the Lord for the right wife. Determined his future children would escape a hand-to-mouth existence, he asked God to bring him the right life-partner. One night down on his knees he asked God to help him find her. That night he dreamed:[5]

> **Dream Work Tip:**
> Ask, how does my dream relate to my prayers, situations and circumstances troubling my heart?

I'm Your Wife

In his dream, the Arkansas sharecropper saw a young woman wearing pointed green-suede shoes and a plaid coat. The young woman kept saying to him, "I'm your wife." A few weeks later, he was introduced to a pretty girl wearing pointed green-suede shoes and a plaid coat.

8. Dream work requires a prayerful approach

Recognizing that the interpretation belongs to God, we must approach our dreams in a prayerful way, trusting Our Lord to guide and direct us as we seek for their meaning. Consider dream work as time spent in the presence of God.

> *He reveals the deep* [profound] *and secret* [concealed]) *things; he knows what is in the darkness (Dan. 2:22).*

Our dreams bring us very close to the living God, helping us build a deeper relationship with Him. We can imagine that Daniel stayed in a very close relationship to God when asked to interpret the dreams of the king. We, too, must maintain our reliance upon the Lord as we handle our dreams.

Ask the Lord for His Spirit of wisdom and knowledge

Consider St. Paul's prayer for wisdom and revelation (Eph. 1:17-19), noticing how he prays for the eyes of the heart to be opened. St. James adds that if we need wisdom, we are to ask for it, expecting God to answer.

> *If any of you lacks wisdom let him ask of God, who gives to all men generously and without reproach, and it will be given to him (James 1:4).*

Apply faith

As with all aspects of our Christian experience, working with our dreams requires us to use genuine heart faith.

> *Let him ask in faith without any doubting…let not that man expect that he will receive anything from the Lord (James 1:6, 7).*

We cultivate faith, knowing that, since it is God who gave us the dream, he will illumine the significance of the dream message in the right time—if we do our part. Jesus taught us to ask–seek–knock, and the door shall be opened (Luke 11:8-14)!

Morton Kelsey tells of a woman who brought her dream into the church before receiving the reserved sacraments. Before the altar she prayed for understanding, and it was given to her. When understood in prayer, the dream helped her know how to pray and gave her faith.[6]

9. Share your dreams with friends

It is good practice to share our dreams with another supportive person—spouse, partner, or friend. Telling someone the dream fixes it in our memory, making recall easier. This action also signals our heart (and the Lord) we are taking the dream seriously. There is biblical precedent for sharing our dreams:

Daniel saw a dream and visions in his mind [of the head] *as he lay on his bed; then wrote the dream down and related the words of it (Dan. 7:1).*

Often we can gain a better understanding of our dreams by sharing them with friends. Recall how the Midianite soldier (enemy of the Israelites) received the interpretation of his dream when he told it to his buddy.

A loaf of barley bread was tumbling into the camp of Midian, and it came to the tent and struck it so that it fell, and turned it upside down so that the tent lay flat. ... "this is nothing less than the sword of Gideon...God has given Midian and all the camp into his hand." (Judges 7:13-15).

> *People around us often can recognize the meaning of our dream symbols better than we ourselves.*

Moreover, we benefit from the insights and ideas of others. Since the dream expresses what is buried deep inside us, it's largely inaccessible to our rational mind. We are blind to the "log" in our own eye, but people around us often can recognize the meaning of our dream symbols better than we ourselves—especially if they are honest, intuitive, and open to the Holy Spirit.

I (Judith) received more understanding of my dream "*Study Psychology*" when I shared it with a friend and spiritual mentor (see Chapter 10).

The wise suggestion of a friend is sweet to the soul (Prov. 27:9)

Work with dreams in context of community

Stressing the value of working with our dreams in light of the larger community, Louis Savary, Patricia Berne and Strephon Williams suggest, "We journey, not as individuals, but as part of an interrelated network of other individual journeyers."[7]

The paradox of dream work is that the dream, the product of our most private and intimate being, can best be brought to fullest realization through being shared with another or others.[8]

Catherine Marshall cites an amazing example from a prayer group in Chappaqua, New York. A woman suffering from exhaustion and insomnia reported a strange dream about a baby who needed milk. Upon hearing her dream, two other prayer group members gasped—each of them had independently received the word that the woman herself needed milk. Also, one group member reported receiving Numbers 12:1-10 that very morning—a passage saying the Lord speaks in dreams.

When the exhausted woman consulted a nutritionist, she learned she suffered from a serious calcium deficiency, easily remedied by—you guessed it—milk. Here we see how the charisma of the Holy Spirit (prophecy, wisdom, knowledge) can be vital in our dream work.[9]

> **Dream Work Tip:**
> If you are not able to log your dream immediately, tell it to someone as soon as you can.

2. Interactive learning
- ☐ Do you have someone you can share your dreams with? If not, pray and ask Our Lord to give you such a person.
- ☐ How might dream sharing be integrated into your Church or fellowship group?

10. You are the decision-maker, not your dream

Embracing our dreams as invitations from our Creator to live a more integrated, whole life, we can make choices that help actualize the potential shown us in our dreams. Usually dreams don't provide direct answers: they raise issues, present alternatives, and suggest possibilities, encouraging further inquiry.

Our awareness and capacity for self-reflection is a function of our conscious mind, our ego—it's our choice-maker. No matter what we do or choose in a dream, we still need to make our own *conscious choices* in waking life. God has given us free-will, and He wants us to use it; He will not choose for us.

God's people find it difficult to make decisions. Especially for major, life-changing decisions such as vocation, ministry, or moving our home, we want God—or someone else—to decide for us. Even in the famous dream announcing Mary's pregnancy to Joseph, the angel did not direct Joseph to marry her; he only told Joseph he *did not need to be afraid* to take her as his wife (Mt. 1:20).

We must never give up our decision-making power to our dreams or to anyone else. Even if the dream reveals a direction or potential possibility, we must *decide* how we will carry it out. If we're going to become co-creators with God, we need to learn how to decide for ourselves.

Let your heart respond

Sometimes phrases such as "the prophetic interpretation of dreams," or "anointed interpretation" intimidate some people. They give power to prophets and teachers instead of trusting their own hearts. The Holy Spirit is in *you*—your own heart must witness to the interpretation of your dream. It's up to you to accept the responsibility to make your own decision on what your dream means. If you give this authority to someone else, you give away your power—and you remain a victim until you have the courage to allow your heart to respond.

Affirms decision making

Usually we must *first* decide about an issue, and then the Holy Spirit will confirm or deny it in our hearts. Many people get it backwards. *Lord, please tell me what to do. I'll just sit here and wait for you to answer.* After a while, they conclude God is hard of hearing.

However, our Lord seems to want us to decide an issue before He confirms it in some way. Normally, we first need to make a conscious decision about a situation before a dream will comment on it. Once we make up our minds, God may send a dream or other means to corroborate our decision. Following is an example of this concept.

> ▶ *Dream Work Tip:*
> Do not make major decisions solely based on a dream. Expect the Lord to confirm it in other ways.

No Fish Dinners For Me

(Judith): In 2006 I made the Lord aware I had decided to schedule a trip to Germany in the near future. However, I asked Him, if it was the wrong decision, to please let me know. That very night I dreamed:

I am flying in a plane, and a stewardess serving dinner informs me they have just run out of fish dinners. Then the plane suddenly lands in Idaho—without any warning or reason. Nobody knew why we had landed or how long it would take us to get out of there.

Awakening, I knew it was not the right time to go. If I did, I would not have any fish to feed the people with. Here, the fish is a symbol of Christ. Moreover, I would get bogged down in Idaho—a pun for "I dug a hole."

Interestingly, over the years the Lord had always used the symbol of an airplane in my dreams to signify it was time to make another trip to German.

> One of the earliest creeds of Christianity, "Jesus Christ, son of God, Savior," came from an acrostic consisting of the initial letters of five Greek words forming the word for fish (ICHTHYS).[10]

3. Interactive learning

☐ Ask, "Lord, why do you not want to make decisions for me?" Write out the thoughts that spontaneously flow through your mind.
☐ Why must we not make decisions based solely upon a dream?

11. Recognize the witness of the Holy Spirit

Since the interpretation belongs to God, the *Holy Spirit must be the final witness as to the interpretation of the dream.* Working with our dreams requires us to exercise our spiritual senses, just as we do with prophecies, visions, and audible voices. If we fail to use spiritual discernment, Satan can mislead us with wrong interpretation.

The work of the Holy Spirit is to lead us into all truth and bring to our remembrance everything Our Lord has said—even when it hurts or brings correction. The Holy Spirit is also responsible to bear witness in our spirit that we are children of God. Because the Holy Spirit bears witness to the *truth* of something, when we hear the right interpretation in dream work, our heart will leap (*Aha!*) in agreement. This is the witness (*intuitive knowing*) of the Holy Spirit in our hearts (John 16:13, Rom. 8:15-16, II Cor. 1:21).

12. Dreams require action

> ▸ *Dream Work Tip:* Never accept an interpretation that your heart doesn't respond to.

Many dream communications from God are conditioned upon our response to them. God is trying to get our attention in the dream, encouraging us to grow up in Christ, become mature, find our destiny. By responding positively to the dream, we honor God and the message He brings us.

Failure to act in response to the guidance from God can have interesting consequences (see Job 33). Repeated dreams may occur because we didn't act on the message of the first dream. If this goes on too long, it can open the closet door where the monsters hide. Yes, if we refuse to listen to a series of dreams trying to get our attention, God may be the source of our nightmares.

Because symbols are complex and multi-dimensional, they are not as easily manipulated by our rational mind as are words or concepts. However, having experienced a dream symbolically, some *conceptual thinking*—words and sentences—is needed to make it conscious and release its energy into our daily lives.[11]

Dreams demand a response

Dreams often challenge us to take some *action* that is important to our personal growth. Remember Jacob, after he dreamed about the ladder stretching from heaven to earth, first thanked God, then constructed an altar and poured oil over it (Gen 28:11-16). What will you do with the information you received from your dream? What *action* will you take to apply the insight from your dream to your life?

Taking some kind of symbolic action does something that affects your soul.

Kelsey says we need to actualize the dream by taking the necessary action it calls for.[12] Robert Johnson suggests we affirm the dream message by doing something to move it from the abstract level of the spirit into the here-and-now reality of daily life. Some physical action, such as lighting a candle or even walking around the block—if done intentionally—can help ground the meaning of the dream in our practical everyday experience.[13]

This is the value of performing religious rituals, where repetition of words and phrases adds the intensity of feeling so important to symbolism. The dramatic enactment of words accompanying ritual actions impresses us deeply enough to reach our inner world. Taking some kind of symbolic action—more than just thinking or dreaming—does something that affects and changes your soul.

Dream Treasure

> **4. Interactive learning**
> ☐ Explain to a friend why it is important to respond to a dream.
> ☐ Make a list of ways you might use to respond to your dreams.
> ☐ Think about how you can actualize your dream by actively meditating on, and bringing God directly into, this part of yourself.

Give God the thanks

Christianity makes possible a living relationship with the Creator, our Heavenly Father. When He speaks, we respond, acknowledging that we heard Him and we are grateful for this. As the meaning of a dream begins to open up to us, we need to recognize it was God who gave us the understanding. Like Daniel, we then rejoice in the Lord, giving Him the glory.

> *After interpreting the King's dreams, Daniel rejoiced, saying that the Lord "reveals the profound and hidden things; he knows what is in the darkness" (Dan. 2:22).*

Lord, I want to listen to my dreams and understand what You are trying to say to me through them. Please give me Your Spirit of wisdom and knowledge as I learn to work with my dreams.

Applied learning

✎ *Your Response*
- ☐ Write a short letter to God, telling him of your gratitude for the gift of dreams.
- ☐ Affirm aloud: "God has given me every spiritual blessing in heavenly places. I like that!" (See Eph. 1:3.)

✺ *Dream work strategies, skills & techniques*
- ☐ What questions might Judith's "*No Fish Dinners For Me*" dream evoke if it were your dream?
- ☐ DRAW A PICTURE of Judith's "*No Fish Dinners For Me*" dream or Gerald's "*Back Door Counselor*" dream. (#1)
- ☐ Look at your drawing, and say "IT IS AS THOUGH…" (#2)
- ☐ If "*Back Door Counselor*" were your dream, think about how you could actualize it by actively meditating on it and bringing God directly into a part of yourself.

Explaining new dream work strategies, skills & techniques

#1 DRAW-A-DREAM technique asks you to put on paper the things you saw in your dream. Using a nonverbal approach releases you to express the dream imaginatively. The act of drawing may help you recall more details. Don't be afraid to use crayons and stick figures.

#2 Say, "IT IS AS THOUGH…," and then see what spontaneously comes to you. Comparing the dream with something else may help you receive insight into its meaning. Use this technique by itself or with a drawing.

✎ *Practicing your skills*
- ☐ Select a dream to work with.
- ☐ Read your dream aloud.
- ☐ Think about the dream, just feel it. Then DRAW A PICTURE of your dream. (#1)
- ☐ Reflect on your drawing by saying, "IT IS AS THOUGH…"(#2)
- ☐ Think about how you could actualize your dream by actively meditating on it, and bring God directly into this part of yourself.

Dream Treasure

Part Three Christian Approach To Dreams

> **Dream Work Terminology**
> Can you explain the following terms?
> - Spiritual practice
> - Intuitive knowing
> - Repetitive dream themes
> - Spirit of wisdom and knowledge
> - Religious ritual
> - Actualizing a dream
> - Symbolic action

Spiritual Discernment

12

It is He who reveals the profound and hidden things; He knows what is in the darkness, and the light dwells with Him…For Thou has given me wisdom and power; even now Thou hast made known to me what we requested of Thee… (Dan. 2:22-23).

Core Concepts
- Ignorance of dreams breeds fear.
- Dreams help us wage spiritual warfare.
- Testing accuracy of interpretations using biblical principles.
- Dream work requires trained spiritual senses.

Learning Objectives
At the completion of this chapter, you will be able to:
- ☐ Evaluate your common fears and concerns about dreams,
- ☐ Explain how your dreams can help you in spiritual warfare.
- ☐ List and describe the spiritual principles you will use to test the validity of your dream's interpretation.
- ☐ Explore the concepts of "spiritual discernment" and "spiritual maturity."
- ☐ Discuss the value of dream sharing within a Christian community.
- ☐ Determine if your dreams are a reliable source of divine wisdom.

Throughout history, especially during the Middle Ages, some people have been afraid of their dreams. What if I sin during my dreams and I have no control over it? What if the devil gives me dreams? Someone said St. Augustine, concerned because certain aspects of his mind were beyond his control, worried about God holding him responsible for his dreams. Good news: I'm not responsible for my dreams—God is.

In this chapter, hoping to allay fears some people express about embracing this love gift from our Heavenly Father, we will address common dream concerns and issues, and discuss principles of spiritual discernment. Perhaps it's time to set aside medieval notions and open ourselves to hear from God in our dreams.

Addressing the fear of dreams

Many people in the Western world have been afraid of dreams for a long time. Along the way we learned that dreams are…natural phenomena, superstitious, forbidden, useless, occult, satanic, or simply the result of eating too much pizza. What

Dream Treasure

did you hear? The dream is a mirror, reflecting the attitudes, thoughts, and intentions of the heart. What's your attitude?

Can dreams be dangerous?

While, in a few places, the Bible at first appears to caution God's people against listening to dreams, the context indicates that the concern is over false prophets. People are being told to be wary of listening to *others'* dreams, not their own. As we developed in Chapter 5, the biblical warnings about dreams are about correctly distinguishing the Word of God.

> *Warnings in the Bible about dreams are not about real dreams, but delusions of the mind, false visions, or other people's dreams.*[1]

From a biblical standpoint, the preponderance of evidence is on the safe side—most references to dreams in Scripture are positive. Moreover, God attempts to make clear through His prophets that He views dreams as so important that we must learn to understand them properly, and not allow false religious leaders to mislead us by distorting their meaning. Here, as often is the case in battle, the best defense is a good offense—learn to rightly discern dreams.

Sleep is ... a friendly curtain behind which dreams continue to speak and to send out messages (Henri Nouwen)

Recognizing that our dreams come from a Source wiser and more loving than ourselves helps us accept dreams and visions as a trustworthy source of God communicating into our lives. Encouraging us not to fear the realm of the night, Henri J. M. Nouwen, in his treasured prayer guide, *With Open Hands,* says "sleep is…a friendly curtain behind which dreams continue to speak and to send out messages which can be gratefully received. The paths of our dreams become as trustworthy as the paths of our waking hours."[2]

Are all dreams from God?

This is a common question we hear. We believe the capacity to dream is a gift from God, just as all of our other capacities are. Dreaming is as much a part of our human makeup as is the immune system—God built systems into our bodies to keep us healthy.

> ► *Dream Work Tip:*
> Dreams always have something to say to us. They are accurate, honest, and frank.

If your thumb gets a sliver, soon white cells gather around to reject it. Similarly when the flu bug bites, you develop a fever and shortly the bug is defeated. God who created us with these capacities is also the originator of the ability to dream.

It is important to emphasize again that, although dreams have a divine origin, they are not all equally significant. Some dreams carry much more consequence than others for our lives. Dreams revealing mysteries have a numinous power that clearly gives them more importance than routine maintenance dreams.

Can Satan access our dreams?

Frequently the question is raised, "Can Satan give us a dream or influence our dreams?" Opinions are mixed. Not enough is known about the mechanism of dreaming to be absolutely certain. This seems to be a thorny question with no easy answers. Following are some thoughts and opinions on the topic, concluding with our personal observations.

Tertullian, the ancient Church Father, believed dreams have three sources: our fears and anxieties, revelation from God, and temptation from Satan. Paul Meier & Robert Wise say that, although early Christians wrote much about "encountering God in dreams, they wrote virtually nothing about meeting the devil. Centuries of dream work infer such confrontations are very rare." Still, evil is a reality and can occur in dreams.[3]

Herman Riffel felt dreams are God's safe instrument to show mankind the hidden secrets. If the devil could access dreams, surely he would have tried to do so when God gave Abraham the great covenant (Gen. 15:1-21). Also, if the dream was safe when God spoke truth to Nebuchadnezzar in idolatrous Babylon, it ought to be safe for us.[i]

> *If the devil could access dreams, surely he would have tried to do so when God gave Abraham the great covenant. (Riffel)*

Of course, if we deliberately ignore scriptural warnings by seeking knowledge through occult means, we're in trouble, dreams or no dreams.

1. Interactive learning
- [ ] Write a list of your fears about dreams.
- [ ] List questions about dreams you need answers to.
- [ ] Why will God not hold you responsible for the content of your dreams?
- [ ] Think of reasons why Satan didn't access the dreams of Abraham, the boy Joseph, Gideon's enemy, or the idolatrous Nebuchadnezzar.

Dreams can help us wage spiritual warfare

We certainly know that our dreams can reflect a spiritual battle and intrusion of the enemy in our waking lives. From his experience in foreign lands Riffel found even these dreams carry a divine purpose, alerting us to our problem. An African pastor once brought him this dream:[4]

Little Men
I was in my village trying to reach out for God, but I could not get through to him because some little men were hindering me. All my efforts to break through to God were of no avail. Then a ladder was set up for me, and I used it to reach God.

Sensing this dream was not about pygmies, Riffel learned that the men exercised witchcraft by placing "little men" sticks as an offering to the gods. Similar to Jacob, the pastor was offered a ladder as a symbol of the power of God overcoming the evil, and he was soon able to reach God in a new way.

Meier and Wise note, while such experiences happen, they should not hinder our

---
[i] Personal communication with Herman Riffel, March 13, 2008.

dream work. Despite the possibility of evil intruding, dreams continue to be a gift from God. As believers, we can trust the work of Jesus Christ at the cross and claim victory over the darkness.[5]

> *There is no evidence Satan can access a person's dreams. But the question remains, if people have been involved in the deep things of Satan, could their dreams be accessed by Satan?*

Dragons and devils

Even when dragons or devils appear in our dreams, they may be symbolic. Our experience is more along the lines of the advice given by Meier & Wise, who suggest satanic representations should be dealt with like all other dream imagery. The devil figure in our dream generally isn't the real creature, but rather is an embodiment of some aspect of ourselves. Here is an example:

> *Warning!*
> *Be careful not to project your fears of Satan onto dream images like dragons, monsters, etc.*

A young man dreamed he was fighting a giant dragon, trying to hit its weak spot in the throat. Some people felt his dream warned him not to play dungeons & dragons video games. Others suggested the dream was prophetic of the church's fight against Satan. However, when we inquired about his relationship with his mother, he immediately recognized that the giant dragon represented his mother. Although she had all the power, he knew where to hit her to hurt most. Using images from his own life experience, his dream mirrored a defiant, attacking behavior toward his mother.

It's mostly about me

In our experience, we have never heard a story where the demonic influenced a dream. The key is discernment—if we interpret a dream wrongly, it could present problems. Today there is a lot of interest in the prophetic, including prophetic dreams, ones alleging to foretell future events. Especially in this area we need to be careful, because—let's say it again—*most of my dreams are about me.*

However much I might want my dreams to be prophetic and to profoundly impact the whole world, most of my dreams are about me. Familiar figures in my dream that lead me to think I'm experiencing a clear dream about the events depicted are most likely a personification of parts of me! God is interested in urging me to grow up and mature. Perhaps this in itself is profound.

Dreams about our friends and loved ones are sometimes tricky. See Judith's dream of her ill brother arriving at our doorstep (Chapter 16, p. 217).

> ▶ *Dream Work Tip:*
> Dreams about specific events, especially predictive dreams, have a different quality to them. You just seem to know they mean something out of the ordinary!

2. Interactive learning
☐ How can your dreams be helpful in waging spiritual warfare?
☐ Do you think dreams can warn you about demonic attacks?
☐ Identify a common mistake in dream interpretation.

Fear of the unconscious

Many people fear anything to do with the unconscious. Can't see it, can't touch it, don't trust it. However, the spiritual realm is the realm of the unconscious, another dimension beyond rational functioning. The way to enter this territory is to ask the One who has been there to accompany us: Our Lord, Jesus Christ came from the Father, conquered the forces of darkness, and reigns in the heavenly kingdom at the right hand of the Father.

Fear of me

A primary reason for not remembering our dreams is because we fear they will tell us something unpleasant we do not want to know. Dreams bring us into contact with our self, with how we're relating to other people in our lives, and how we're handling life's challenges and tasks. Many of us don't *really* want to know this—we are running away from ourselves.

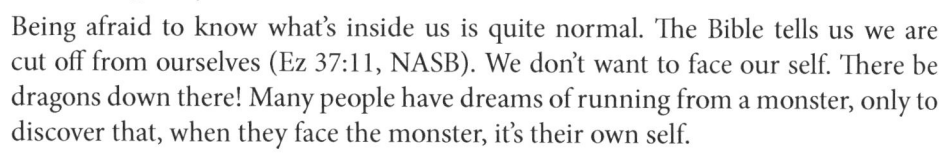

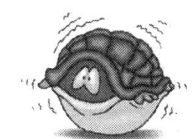

Being afraid to know what's inside us is quite normal. The Bible tells us we are cut off from ourselves (Ez 37:11, NASB). We don't want to face our self. There be dragons down there! Many people have dreams of running from a monster, only to discover that, when they face the monster, it's their own self.

Freudian slips

One reason for a fear of dreams has been the influence of Dr. Sigmund Freud. His emphasis on dreams revealing sexual repression makes us wary of looking at our dreams—they might reveal something about us we don't want to know. Ignorance of what is down inside keeps us as guilt-ridden neurotics, easy to manipulate and control.

Jesus said *whatever is hidden must come to the light* (Mark 4:22). St. Paul prayed for believers that God would sanctify them and they would be preserved blameless in body, soul, and spirit (I Thes. 5:23). Jesus came to heal the brokenhearted. The dream deals with the issues of the heart.

> *The dream is the counsel of the Lord or the instruction of our hearts during sleep.*[7]

Fear of imagination

We thank God for our reasoning capabilities; the development of rational thinking has been a great gift to civilization. This thing I (Gerald) have facetiously referred to as an "educated brain box" is a marvelous gift God has given us. Our ability to reason has taken us out of the morass of instinctive functioning prevalent in times past that kept many people in slavish obedience to dominant spiritual authorities, whether they were led by the Spirit or led by their own egos.

Quite different from our intellectual and reasoning capacity, there is another part of us that enables us to dream, to imagine. Christians may be afraid of involvement in the imaginative faculty if they value their dreams. However, is vitally important to be aware that our ability to think and see pictures in the imagination is given to us by God—not Satan. Even though the evil one attempts to mess with our visual capabilities, more importantly, so does our loving God.

The solution is not to turn from any image involvement, but instead to continually look to the Almighty Creator who gave us this capacity in the first place. Dream work is a vital spiritual practice that allows us to receive spiritual guidance and wisdom from God. Remember, we can trust the Holy Spirit to lead us to truth.

Fear of God

Dreams bring us into contact with God, our Heavenly Father. Many of us are afraid of God, afraid of what He might ask of us. Indeed, God does ask us to die to the natural man, the fallen man born of Adam. So it is a bit scary. If I die, what's out there? How will I be able to cope with life if my old way of functioning is dead?

Spirit guides

According to spiritualist churches, "spirit guides" that have lived former lives, gaining wisdom and insight, are assigned to help people with their lives. They claim the spirit guide meets them in dreams or the astral plane as a counselor. We need not fear this counterfeit spirituality.

We have the Holy Spirit as our guide in all areas of our lives. Before his ascension, Jesus Christ promised that the Holy Spirit would come to lead us into all truth. We can trust the Holy Spirit, who is the Spirit of truth.

Test interpretation for accuracy

When we are faced with any supernatural phenomenon, we must examine it carefully according to the principles revealed in the Bible. Compare your ideas with the Holy Scriptures as you seek understanding of the meaning of your dream—no interpretation is valid if it contradicts basic spiritual principles revealed in the Bible. Whatever truth is shown to us personally in our dreams, it never replaces or supersedes the written word of God.

> *No interpretation is valid if it contradicts basic spiritual principles revealed in the Bible.*

When a believer is faced with any supernatural phenomenon, he ought to examine it carefully according to the principles revealed in the Bible before he decides to accept or to reject it. (Watchman Nee)[8]

Here are some key Scriptures you can use as the basis for testing your interpretations (you may think of others):

1. *Jesus said it is not coming with observation [something you can see with your natural senses]; nor will they say, 'Look here it is;' or 'There it is'.... behold the Kingdom of God is in your midst [within] (Luke 17:21).*
2. *The Kingdom of God is...righteousness and peace and joy in the Holy Spirit (Rom 14:17).*
3. *I came that they might have life and have it more abundantly (John 10:10b).*
4. *My yoke is easy, my burden is light (Mt 11:30).*
5. *The law of the Spirit of life in Christ Jesus has made me free from the law of sin and*

death (Ro 8:2).

6. *Who also has made us able ministers of the new covenant; not of the letter, but of the spirit; for the letter kills, but the Spirit gives life (2Co 3:6).*

7. *For God has not given us a spirit of timidity, but of power and love and discipline* [sound judgment] *(II Tim.1:7).*

8. *The fruit of the Spirit is love, joy, peace, patience, kindness, goodness, faithfulness, gentleness, self-control (Gal. 5:22).*

Dreams do not condemn

One way to know if our interpretation is correct is whether or not it condemns us. Because of the work of Jesus Christ on the cross, we are no longer under condemnation—we are free from the law of sin and death. As you begin to work with your dreams, here is an extremely important principle: a dream's interpretation should bring us encouragement, instruction, guidance, enlightenment—even if it does bring us correction.

Herman Riffel taught us that the dream reveals the truth—what the mind cannot or will not accept—but it *never* condemns us. Many mistakes with interpretive dream work can be made at this point—if an interpretation is accusatory and brings condemnation, it is likely not correct.

> ▶ *Dream Work Tip:*
> The dream reveals the truth—what the mind cannot or will not accept—but it *never* condemns us.

Interpretations should not appeal to our ego

Although dreams certainly encourage us on our journey, they are not aimed at stroking our ego, telling us what magnificent creatures we are. If the understanding of a dream appeals to the ego or resists being tested, it is suspect immediately. A correct interpretation produces good fruit and humility. Dreams are intended to help us develop and mature into the whole person God desires us to be.

In testing dreams, avoid these two pitfalls:

1. Projection; i.e., don't project your wishes onto the dream.
2. Divination; i.e., don't set about trying to make your dream come to pass, or to make your desires happen.

Ask questions like the following:

- How am I functioning inside, my inner world?
- How am I functioning in relationship to my outer world, to external events?
- What does God want to reveal to (the world, tribe, whatever) through my dream?

> **Warning!**
> *Never say with absolute authority, "This is what your dream means." Always suggest in a tentative way, "Do you think it might mean this?"*

Seek confirmation from intuitive friends

In learning how to listen for the voice of God in our dreams, we do not ignore the many other ways God may speak to us, including His Word, the sacraments, and prayer. We also seek confirmation from intuitive, frank friends who are sensitive to the Holy Spirit, especially if the dream seems to indicate a major change of direction. Benner recommends we approach dreams within a context of the Christian disciplines and community.[9]

PART THREE Christian Approach To Dreams

> **Try this test for interpretation**
>
> To check if an interpretation is from God—not the dream itself, but your interpretation of it—assess it using the following biblical principles.
>
> Does the interpretation…
>
> 1. Give you comfort, or torment you? Bring hope, or despair?
> 2. Produce pride, or humility in you?
> 3. Bring peace, or pressure and anxiety?
> 4. Bring inner freedom, or lay a heavy burden on you?
> 5. Increase your faith?
> 6. Answer prayer? Relate to your current concerns?
> 7. Encourage, instruct, or enlighten you, without lifting up your ego?
> 8. Minister life or death?
> 9. Show you how to solve a problem?
> 10. Violate the nature of Christ or "the law of the spirit of life in Christ Jesus?"
> 11. Evoke a witness in your heart?

3. Interactive learning
- ☐ List the scriptural principles you plan to use.
- ☐ Which principle seems the most important to you?
- ☐ Why is the inner witness of the Holy Spirit, the "Aha!," vital in dream interpretation?
- ☐ Can you think of more Scriptures to use in evaluating the validity of an interpretation?

Illustrative dream example
The following dream is an example of the importance of testing our dream interpretations. It is also an example of why it is dangerous to take dreams literally!

My Brother Calls Me
(Judith): Background: In 1983, a little bearded Jewish man prophesied that the Lord had a ministry for me in Germany and other European countries. Having no clue about how to do this—never having been to Bible School—I surrendered the call back to God. But God had His way! In 1987, I received this very simple dream:

My brother who was living in Frankfurt, Germany, called me and said he wanted to have sex with me.

From the dream, I knew that my brother needed something from me. To check this out, I telephoned him and learned he was in depression. His wife said they needed spiritual encouragement. I talked it over with my husband and with a good friend. Both agreed that I should travel to Frankfort. On the basis of this dream—and confirmation from others—I flew to Frankfurt.

Before I left home, a friend telephoned me, strongly urging me to call his psychiatrist friend in the Black Forest and offer to take him out to eat. After we got acquainted over lunch, I was invited to be a short-term intern in his clinic. Later that year, I spent several weeks in his clinic, and again in 1988. This one trip opened the doorway to Europe, and enabled fulfilling the prophetic call of God. Imagine, just a little dream, seemingly not very important!

At the time, I understood the dream was just about my brother. Much later I recognized another layer of meaning. As a young man out of university, my brother had left America to make his home Europe. My dream symbolized not only a cry for help from my brother, but also a call from Europe.

> ▶ *Dream Work Tip:*
>
> Sex in a dream is most often not literally about sex, but about something else; i.e., a type of union or connection with whatever the other person symbolizes to you.

To unlock the messages in our dreams, we *really* need to learn another language—the language of pictures, images, and symbols, commonly used by Jesus. In Chapter 15 we explain in-depth how this language works.

4. Interactive learning

- ☐ What principles would you use to test the validity of Judith's interpretation?
- ☐ How do we decide if the brother symbolizes himself, a part of Judith, or something totally different—like a country?
- ☐ Recognize that a dream may have several levels of meaning.
- ☐ What might Judith have missed if she hadn't recognized God's voice in her dream?

Become spiritually mature

As mentioned earlier, clearly the Early Church Fathers valued the dream as an important way in which God communicated with people. However, eventually Church thinking regressed to where dream interpretation was discouraged. For many of us today, dreams don't make it through our theological grid.

Coming as they do from the spiritual realm, dreams thus become another issue causing confusion in the Church. As dreams become increasingly valued by God's people, this will be a big area of uncertainty and consternation for the Church.

Dream Treasure

PART THREE Christian Approach To Dreams

Reclaiming the importance of dreams requires us to challenge our theology, what we have been taught about what God would or would not do. We do not have much experience of, or experience with, the spiritual realm. To make matters worse, we're afraid of it.

Proper understanding of dreams, visions, and prophecy requires spiritual maturity, an ability to discern what the Holy Spirit is saying.

Ignorance of dreams breeds fear. There's lots to be afraid of, from the evil out there to the sin in me. What if the devil gives me a dream? What if I sin during my dreams and I have no control over it? All those things leave me feeling very uncomfortable with trusting my dreams.

Moreover, what if God does something unexpected with my dreams? I might be challenged beyond my theological comfort zone. If God escapes from the box I've put Him in, I'll run the other way in fear.

Sharpen our senses

Our problem is similar to that of early believers in the church at Corinth—we are not yet spiritual, i.e., our spiritual senses are not fully trained to recognize good and evil. The solution is for us to become spiritual people. Proper understanding of dreams, visions, and prophecy requires spiritual maturity, an ability to discern what the Holy Spirit is saying.

God has given us spiritual eyes and ears to develop and use. For us to know what is of God and what is not, we must learn to recognize the witness of the Spirit and to see with the eyes of the heart.

Wake up

Perhaps part of our problem is that we are asleep. We go through life without really living, without embracing our life fully, with both its pain and its pleasure.

Awake, sleeper, and arise from the dead, and Christ will shine on you (Eph. 5:14).

We need to pray for courage to enter the realm of the spirit—the natural mind is not adequate for the voyage.

Awakening is a challenge because it means we must accept responsibility for our own life and destiny. We need to pray for courage to enter the realm of the spirit—the natural mind is not adequate for the voyage. Listening to our dreams requires a tremendous amount of courage. Pray for God to give you courage—it is essential for any pilgrim who wants to journey into the land of the Spirit, the kingdom of God.

You can trust the Holy Spirit

Our personal testimony is this: we have found nothing but good things from our dreams. We have experienced God speaking to us in our dreams; we have learned His language; we have begun to understand what He is saying to us. So, we say it to you with confidence: you can trust the Holy Spirit.

Dream Treasure

> **A word about spiritual maturity**
>
> In this book we often refer to the importance of spiritual maturity, meaning the capacity to discern what the Spirit of God is saying to us. Using our spiritual senses, we are able to discern good and evil, to know what is from God and what is not. Through the eyes of the heart we can see and know what God is showing us. We can see pictures, visions, spontaneous images sent by God, in the day or night (see Eph. 1:17-19).
>
> We are living souls, containing a spirit. When we receive Jesus Christ, our spirit becomes activated through the indwelling Spirit of Christ. It is not just our spirit anymore, but God's Spirit becomes fused with our spirit, causing a new creation. This new creation has spiritual senses. It is not blind or deaf. It can hear; it has ears. It can see; it has eyes. It can speak; it has a voice. We call these senses *intuition, inward voice, inner guidance, inward witness*. We can recognize the witness of the Spirit in our spirit.[i]
>
> At Corinth, St. Paul lamented that he could not speak to Christians as spiritual people; they did not know how to understand the things belonging to the Spirit of God (I Cor. 3:1; 2:14-15). Dull of hearing, their spiritual senses were not fully trained (Heb. 5:11-14) to know what comes from the soul or what comes from the spirit.
>
> Because the soul and spirit are similar in nature, having similar capacities, we need to be able to distinguish between them. This is crucial in spiritual growth and valuable in dream work. We need to pray for the Spirit of the living God to differentiate them for us (Heb. 4:12).
>
> ---
>
> [i] We recommend *The Spiritual Man* by Watchman Nee. This book has helped many people learn what it means to become a spiritual Christian, able to discern the living word from God that transforms us.

Lord, please open the eyes of my heart so I can know what You are saying to me. Divide my spirit from my soul so I can function as a spiritual person.

Dream Treasure

Applied Learning

✎ *Your Response*

- ☐ Write out your understanding of Daniel 2:22-23.
- ☐ What is the Holy Spirit's role in discerning the meaning of your dreams?
- ☐ Re-take the "*Survey of Attitudes & Beliefs About Dreams*" (Appendix A). Have your attitudes and beliefs about dream continued to change?
- ☐ How did this chapter help allay your fears about dreams?
- ☐ Are dreams reliable instruments of God to guide and instruct you? Yes/No
- ☐ Affirm aloud: "God created me with a capacity to dream and to imagine. I like that!"

✧ *Dream work strategies, skills & techniques*

- ☐ What was the BACKGROUND to Judith's "*My Brother Calls Me*" dream? (#1)
- ☐ How would knowing more about Judith's BACKGROUND help you understand her dream? (#1)
- ☐ SUMMARIZE what God is trying to say to Judith in "*My Brother Calls Me*" dream. (#2)
- ☐ What did Judith do in response to her dream?
- ☐ What was the biblical purpose of Judith's dream?

Explaining new dream work strategies, skills & techniques

#1 Dream BACKGROUND asks you to sweep back over your life and reflect on your long-standing hopes, conflicts, divine promises, and old experiences as well as your current concerns (CC). Consider why this dream comes at this time of your life.

#2 When you finish exploring your dream, SUMMARIZE in a single sentence your considerations of what God might be trying to say to you through it. This helps you clarify the meaning of your dream.

Practicing your skills

- ☐ Select a dream to work with.
- ☐ Reflect on your BACKGROUND and current concerns and how they could relate to your dream. Ask, why am I receiving this dream at this time in my life? (#1)
- ☐ How would you consider the meaning of a dragon in your dream?
- ☐ What do you think might be the biblical purpose of your dream?
- ☐ SUMMARIZE what you think God might be trying to say to you in your dream. (#2)
- ☐ List ideas about how you can respond to your dream.

Dream Work Terminology

Can you explain the following terms?

- Spiritual discernment
- Spiritual maturity
- Dreamer's background

PART FOUR
The World of Dreaming

Why you will find Part Four helpful

We launch this part with a brief look at the science of dreaming. We examine what dream research has learned about the nature of dreams, the source of our dream images, and how these findings verify the importance of dreams.

We discuss ways to categorize your dreams, along with some personal examples. This will enable you to sort out the more important dreams from the common dreams we all have as part of our participation in the human experience.

A critical element in understanding dreams is learning to value the symbolic language used in most dreams. Jesus Christ used symbolic language in his parables and teaching to help us discover the hidden truths he wanted us to see. When you finish our "Symbolism 101" discussion, you will be well on your way to unlocking the counsel and wisdom contained in the symbols and imagery in your dreams.

You will learn common dynamics operating in symbolic communication. Also you will be able to identify the primary dream characters everybody encounters in their dreams. Finally, we discuss ways to determine whether a dream is objective (dream images refer to objects and situations in the external world) or subjective (images represent a picture of what is going on within ourselves).

PART FOUR Chapters
- Science of Dreaming (Chapter 13)
- Classifying Dreams (Chapter 14)
- The Language of Dreams (Chapter 15)
- Dream Dynamics (Chapter 16)

PART FOUR The World Of Dreaming

Science of Dreaming

13

Dreams are one of nature's miracles, not the result of a wandering mind in sleep. A dream is an interface between the process of life and our conscious personality. (Tony Crisp)[1]

Core Concepts
- The nature of dreams.
- Dreaming essential to mental health.
- Dreams are concerned with fundamental life issues.
- Sources of dream images.
- Structure of the personality.
- Four-part dream structure.

Learning Objectives
At the completion of this chapter, you will be able to:
- ☐ Explain the phenomena of dreaming.
- ☐ Describe the relationship of dreams to your well-being.
- ☐ List and discuss the five life issues your dreams are most likely to be about.
- ☐ Identify the source of the images appearing in your dreams.
- ☐ Explore your dream, using the four-part dream structure.

Brief history of dreaming

As evidenced by paintings on cave walls from the Neanderthal period and clay tablet journals dating back to around 3000 BC, the human race has been dreaming for a long time. Dreaming was an important element in the lives of the ancient civilizations of Sumer, Assyria, Babylonia and Egypt. Cuneiform script on tablets discovered in Mesopotamia reveal fragments of the Gilgamesh Epic, describing the dreams of the legendary Sumerian warrior.

> *Gilgamesh was assisted in interpreting his dreams by his mother (perhaps the first dream therapist on record).*

Cradle of civilization
Dream books of the Assyrians and Babylonians were discovered at Nineveh in the royal library of the Assyrian king Ashurbanipal (c. 650 BC). Some of these works have even been translated in the Transactions of the American Philosophical Soci-

ety.[2] These people took their dreams seriously. Dream interpretation was elevated to the status of a religion—huge temples in Babylon were dedicated to Mamu, the goddess of dreams.

Among the Egyptian papyri we find an early prophetic dream dating from around 1400 BC—recorded on a sheet of granite, held between the paws of the great sphinx of Giza. Because they believed dreams contained numinous power, Egyptians practiced dream incubation—a ritualistic procedure to encourage an especially informative dream from the gods. A papyrus dated around 1350 BC includes records of more than 200 dreams, plus details of interpretation methods that anticipate similar principles used much later by Freud.

Classical dream records

Greek and Roman civilizations viewed dreams as a way to gain insight into the dreamer's mind and also as a form of prediction. Influenced by Homer, the ancient Greeks distinguished two types of dreams: significant dreams that they felt came from the gods; insignificant dreams more personal to the dreamer. Hippocrates, the father of modern medicine, tried to use the symbolism of dreams as an aid to diagnosing his patients. Oracle dreams were incubated at the famous site in Delphi (believed by the ancients to be the center of the world).

The ancient Greeks distinguished two types of dreams: significant dreams that they felt came from the gods; insignificant dreams more personal to the dreamer.

Ancient Rome seemed to be especially fascinated with prophetic dreams. According to Roman historian Plutarch, Julius Caesar's wife, Calpurnia, dreamed of his death the night before Brutus actually did the deed. Likewise, the night before he was assassinated, Caligula had a dream with symbolic indications of impending death. The 2nd century Roman, Artemidorus, wrote the first dream dictionary, a five-volume work including more than 3000 dream reports.[3]

The nature of dreams

What is a dream?

A dictionary defines the dream as "a sequence of images passing through a sleeping person's mind" (*Webster's New World Dictionary*). Or we might say, the dream is a dynamic flow of images, anecdotes, activities, emotions, and thoughts we experience while asleep. Dreams are an inner psychological experience, occurring inside the psyche, not outside of it.

A dream in the night is described in one book as "a spontaneous symbolic experience lived out in the inner world during sleep ... over which we seem to have little or no conscious control."[4] A dream is a vibrant montage of images, usually symbolic in nature, moving and flowing on the screen within our mind. The key concept here is *symbolic experience.*

Here are more descriptions of dreams:

- The dream is the voice of God speaking to us in the night while our conscious mind is stilled (Herman Riffel).[6]
- A dream is considered to be an expression of the objective psyche describing in symbolic language the nature of the current psychic situation. The understanding of dreams thus becomes a powerful aid in the growth of consciousness (Edward Edinger).[7]
- A dream is the attempt of our inner man to communicate with us (Mark & Patti Virkler).[8]
- A dream is one of nature's miracles, not the result of a wandering mind in sleep. A dream is an interface between the process of life and our conscious personality (Tony Crisp).[9]
- Dreams are "a combination of messages about the state of the inner world and fragments of life experiences that are shaped by God as a communication designed for our well-being (David Benner)."[10]

> *A dream has been poetically described as "a little hidden door in the innermost and most secret recesses of the soul, opening into that cosmic night." (Mary Ann Mattoon)*[5]

1. Interactive learning
☐ Which description do you most relate to? Explain?
☐ How would you explain what a dream is to someone who had never heard of dreaming?

Five years of dreaming

Don't think you dream, or don't remember those images flowing across your mind every night? No Matter. It has been proven beyond doubt that everyone dreams—often many times per night.

Generally speaking, sleep accounts for approximately one-third of our lives (give or take a few all-nighters during college exams). Experts in the field tell us that approximately *one-fifth of our slumber time involves dreaming*! So if you are thirty years old, you've slept for ten years—and two of those years were spent in that mysterious dream space.[11]

Research shows we typically dream about five to seven times during an ordinary night's sleep! Periods of dreaming get progressively longer, starting at less than a minute, culminating in sessions as long as an hour. This amounts to about one to two hours of dreams every night, adding up to approximately *five years of dreaming* in a typical lifetime.

This amounts to approximately five years of dreaming in a typical lifetime.

The brain neither slumbers nor sleeps

In the 1950s, researchers made a startling new discovery: the brain remains active even during sleep. Using EEGs (electroencephalogram), they found that during sleep our brain wave patterns cycle through periods of heightened and slow-wave activity, but never stop.

Dream Treasure

165

PART FOUR The World Of Dreaming

While we participate in the nighttime drama of our dreams, our mind is very much alive, showing intense activity in electronic brain scans. Throughout a particular stage of sleep known as REM (rapid eye movement) sleep, our eyes move back and forth rapidly beneath our eyelids, like we are watching an action movie!

> REM (rapid eye movement): a stage of sleep in which our eyes move back and forth rapidly beneath our eyelids, like we are watching an action movie.

REM sleep

REM sleep results in two different types of dreams. The first type, *occurring later* in the sleep cycle, is strongly visual and active, with limb spasms, facial twitching, jerky eye movements, and changes in breathing. These dreams deal with more important or even threatening issues we struggle with (such as nightmares). During the second type of REM sleep, *occurring earlier* in the sleeping period, the dreamer is calmer and more relaxed, experiencing more peaceful and feeling-oriented dreams.

Right side keeps right on working

Whether we are awake or asleep, the brain keeps right on working. Much activity is happening during sleep of which we are unaware. The gray matter stays active! While sleeping, our dream content is perceived through the deeper layers of the unconscious mind. The exact brain mechanism is not yet clear. However, scientists have discovered that dreams flow along visual and verbal pathways or nerve channels to the right side of the brain, the side associated with intuition and imagination.

Key to understanding dreams is the idea that the deep hidden part of our being does not communicate in words or through reason, but uses visual images to stimulate intuition and feeling. According to Dimnet, "Every time we really succeed in watching our mental process we discover the presence of images."[12] We experience the presence of images first, then our ideas! Interestingly, in the Greek, *idea* and *image* are the same word.

Dreams

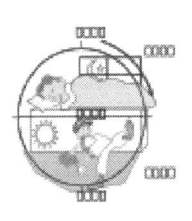

As we dream, a succession of images—from a single snapshot to a lengthy, involved saga—flows through our mind. Then some kind of conceptual activity transpires, where the brain translates perceptions into thoughts and ideas when it's not busy with dreams. These two processes work together to form thoughts and activities affecting our waking hours.

Visions

On the awake side of things, there is the vision—a sort of waking dream, if you will—occurring when we see pictures, spontaneous images, with the inward eye of the spirit while we're awake. These images are apparently quite like the ones we see in sleep, except they reach our awareness while we are awake.

Never-never land

In between, just on the cusp of falling asleep (*hypnagogic* state) or awakening (*hypnopompic* state), we may experience spontaneous images appearing out of nowhere.[i]

---

i   The *hypnagogic* state is a rather strange subjective experience at the onset of sleep that involves brief visual or auditory illusions. Complex patterns flow across the field of vision—seemingly random speckles, lines or geometrical patterns, typically changing rapidly. A similar condition, *hypnopompic* state, occurs as sleep recedes into the waking state.

Dream Treasure

Similar to dreams, these sensations appear without our ego making them happen. Sometimes they are so vivid we can't distinguish whether we are awake or asleep.

Studies suggest that dreams affect waking consciousness far more than previously believed.[13] Robert Johnson even asserts the world of dreaming—where the unconscious is working out its powerful dynamics—"has more practical and concrete effect on our lives than outer events do."[14]

Fantasy, daydreams, hallucinations

Dream activity differs from fantasy, daydreams, and hallucinations. *Fantasy* refers to anything our mind makes up while awake. *Daydreams* are not spontaneous, rather they consist of a flow of *images directed by the ego, the conscious center of personality*. Daydreams are not of the same fabric as the dream, which "happens" beyond our conscious control.

> *Warning: Be sure you know the difference between dreaming and hallucination.*

Unlike a true vision (which gives knowledge of the "dream" world, the inner world), in a *hallucination* the "dream" world is mistaken for the physical world of sense experience. People who hallucinate have lost the ability to distinguish between these two kinds of experience, so they *project inner images directly upon the outer world*. When the boundaries between normal waking life and another dimension dissolve and merge in this way, it is considered pathological.

2. Interactive learning
- ☐ How will the findings of dream and sleep research influence your attitudes toward dreams?
- ☐ Dreams are a gift from God. Agree/Disagree?

Dreaming essential for mental health

Researchers hold widely different opinions about the purpose of dreams. Some say dreams may simply serve a mundane function of dealing with daily accumulated data. Others contend dreams may possess divine import we'd be lost without.

Findings from dream research and sleep labs add emphasis to the psychological importance of dreaming. Sleep research has established the fact that dreaming is essential to mental and physical health. People awakened the moment REM sleep starts become irritable and anxious. If a person is awakened every time they enter a dreaming phase, after about three nights they begin to show signs of having a nervous breakdown.[16]

Dreams are essential to our mental stability, helping to balance us emotionally and keep us sane. Sometimes we think our dreams are driving us crazy. It's the other way around—if we can't dream, we go bonkers!

Vital to our well-being

Other REM research discovered that dreaming prepares the brain and mind for its lifelong task of complex interconnecting.[17] The dream can also function as a vehicle for restoring a cohesive sense of self and regulation of affect.[18] From these and other studies, such as the research of Dr. Charles Fisher, we conclude that the process of dreaming is vital to our sense of well-being.[19]

Dreams have divine significance on every level.

Catherine Marshall found her dreams became inhibited or even absent during her struggle with insomnia and use of barbiturates for sleep. Conflicts and tensions began to build up in her inner world.[20] Thus dreams have divine significance on every level.

Problem-solving function

Austrian psychiatrist Alfred Adler (1870-1937) recognized dreams have a problem-solving function, offering us a new way to look at a situation. While we sleep, our brain busily sorts through our experiences, attempting to make sense of them. A problem may be identified and resolved, or the dream may offer us a new way to look at a situation. As discussed in an earlier chapter, important discoveries and new inventions have sometimes resulted from dream activity. Following is an example of a problem-solving dream

Umbrellas Aren't Legal

(Gerald): After returning from Germany, we rented a house in Massachusetts while I looked for work, but we left most of our belongings at our house in Michigan. For income tax purposes, I needed to decide whether our legal residence was Massachusetts or Michigan. My plan was to stay in Massachusetts and move our belongings out there. Then I dreamed:

As I was taking an umbrella out of my car, someone said, "Those are illegal now in Massachusetts. You can't use those in Massachusetts anymore." I replied, "Well, I guess this is another reason why I should maintain my residency in Michigan."

I felt the umbrella symbol meant, if I called Massachusetts our residence, it would not afford the correct legal protection we needed for our lifestyle.

Dream Treasure

3. Interactive learning
☐ What functions do dreams seem to serve?
☐ What will you do to nurture your ability to recall your dreams?

Typical dream themes

Because we all wrestle with many similar issues, some common dream motifs appear frequently in dreams: flying, falling, being naked, being chased, loose teeth, houses, examinations, cars, babies and children, and water. Many factors determine what we dream—our interpersonal relationships; the spiritual or personal growth stage we are facing; how daily events influence us; personal business from our past (such as childhood traumas) not yet integrated into our lives.[21]

> *Most dreams are about everyday concerns—not repressed or hidden conflicts.*[25]

After studying ten thousand dreams of ordinary people to learn what the average person dreams about, dream researcher Calvin Hall reported that most dreams are about everyday concerns—not repressed or hidden conflicts.[22] For example, we are concerned with our ideas about ourselves, other people, and the world around us.

Hall identified five types of issues typically occurring in the everyday dreams of normal people:

1. *Concerns with life & death*
2. *Personal freedom vs. security*
3. *Socialization vs. instinctual nature*
4. *Struggles with mother & father*
5. *Conflict between masculine & feminine*

Dreams are fundamental to relationships

Dream theorists French and Fromm suggest the primary function of dreams may be to work on our relationship issues. Linking dreaming with cultural & social issues, Montague Ullman asserted that our dreams are in some way concerned with our "interconnectedness" as a species.[23]

Therapist Clara Hill views dreams as replays—sometimes literal, sometimes symbolic—of events in our waking life, rather than coded messages for unconscious wishes. "They are reenactments of how people respond when awake."[24] Thus the dream can be a resource to help us see how we are relating to the people in our lives.

> ➤ *Dream Work Tip:*
> Ponder the drama going on in your dream. What comment is it making on everyday events to which the feelings are connected? In what ways might it relate to your everyday life?

Dream Treasure

> *4. Interactive learning*
> ☐ What five issues are your dreams likely to be concerned with?
> ☐ Which life issue do you feel the need for help with?

Dream language

A dream uses an imaginative language consisting of figures of speech, metaphors, similes, symbols, hyperboles, and puns to express its message. Seldom is a dream message conveyed unambiguously in clear, straight-forward speech. Most of the time, the message of the dream is obscure, consisting chiefly of picturesque symbolic images varying in complexity and vividness.

Dreams apparently arise in the right hemisphere of the brain. It's this part of our brain which is the source of images—the substance of our dreams. Dreams do not communicate rationally; they seem to lack logical coherence or continuity of development. They mix up the past, present, and future—seemingly justifying popular opinion that dreams are nonsensical and meaningless.

> *The mind speaks in thoughts and concepts. The dream speaks in pictures and symbols.*

Using dreams, God communicates in an *imaginative* or *symbolic* way, figuratively, rather than in a literal sense. Understanding symbolic language is key to interpreting dreams: we devote an entire chapter to helping you learn this language.

Warning:
Many mistakes are made when dreams are taken literally.

Color dreamers

Black and white is okay, but color certainly enriches a movie, a video, or a dream. Does it make any difference whether we dream in color or black/white? Hoss suggests that color is as much a symbol as is the imagery in a dream, and color provides a more complete representation of the content portrayed by the image. He also believes color contains emotional content relating to the emotional situation in the dreamer's life.[26]

Sleep lab research reports that, if people awakened at the end of a REM sleep period are questioned soon enough after experiencing the dream, most of them say they dream in color.[27] If recall is delayed, dreamers are less aware of colors. This sounds like the general principle for remembering a dream: *the sooner we write down the dream or recite it, the more details we recall.*

According to Mary Ann Mattoon, research in the 1950s reported that people who dream in color tend to be "more responsive to their environment and more likely to have richer affectional relationships than people whose dreams were reported as not being in color."[28] Other research has found little difference between the characteristics of people who report dreaming in color and those who do not.

Virkler & Virkler theorize that left-brain dominated people may observe visions in black/white, whereas right-brain folks are more likely to see things in Technicolor.

Maybe, but either way, we can trust God with our dreams and visions. He can communicate His loving guidance using whatever color palette we are able to receive.

Note: We do not agree with the troublesome idea that black-and-white dreams are demonic. We have experienced valuable dreams from the Lord that were either in black/white or, if color was present, it seemed unimportant.

5. Interactive learning
☐ How would you explain the language of dreams to someone?
☐ What might the following images symbolize for you? Red car? Red shirt? Red pencil? Red pair of shoes?

Sources of dream imagery

Perhaps surprisingly to many people, researchers have determined that external stimuli—even eating too much pizza—have very little effect on the formation of dream images.[29] So where do dream images come from?

Most often the images in our dreams are created from the crucible of our daily lives. Our dream images come out of our everyday experiences, from conscious sights, impressions, and thoughts passed on into the 90% of the psyche (soul) below the level of consciousness, then screened, condensed, and translated into dream imagery.[30]

However, some dreams seem to arise from much deeper layers in our psyche (soul), well below our every day consciousness. The result is the appearance of extraordinary figures such as talking tortoises, larger-than-life human figures, angelic beings, sleeping giants, and mythological motifs. Hardly the stuff of everyday events, but valuable for deeper insight.

Here's a list of sources of dream images we believe makes sense to the Christian worldview:

1. Conscious life—individual life experiences

Since most dream images originate from our daily environment and individual life experiences, these symbols are very *personal* to us. For instance, our occupation frequently occurs in our dreams. Educated as a nurse, I (Judith) often dreamed of hospitals, nurses, and medications. With a high-tech background, I (Gerald) often experienced images of offices and computers in my dreams. An example of dream images originating out of life experience is my (Gerald) "Umbrellas Aren't Legal" dream.

Dream Treasure

2. Personal unconscious—life experiences we no longer remember

We often see images involving memories of long past events, such as childhood experiences—very personal images coming from our personal unconscious, perhaps long forgotten. Memories of particularly traumatic episodes may be imaged repetitively—combat veterans may relive war experiences repetitively in dreams.

3. Cultural experiences—shared cultural experiences

Characteristics of the groups of people we identify with—family, religion, culture, nation, ethnicity—may form the images of our daily life dreams.[31] Yellow ribbons around oak trees evoke feelings for soldiers; the stars and stripes evoke national pride. These images tend to lose their symbolic power over time. Eventually, other commonly-shared cultural experiences evolve to take their place.

4. Universal knowledge—common experiences

Some dream images can arise from the shared experience of all people everywhere—fire, water, sun, moon, stars, cross, and other images common to all mankind. Fromm named these types of images universal symbols.[32] Most of these images originate from the earth and our experiences in it.

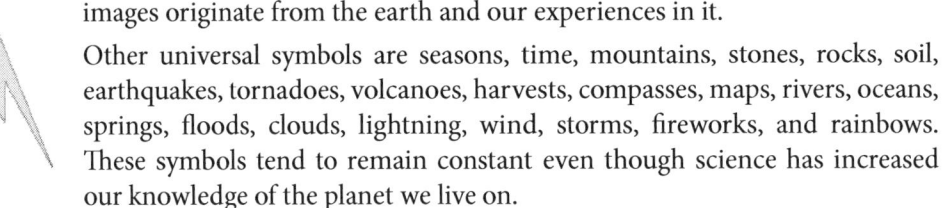

Other universal symbols are seasons, time, mountains, stones, rocks, soil, earthquakes, tornadoes, volcanoes, harvests, compasses, maps, rivers, oceans, springs, floods, clouds, lightning, wind, storms, fireworks, and rainbows. These symbols tend to remain constant even though science has increased our knowledge of the planet we live on.

5. Collective unconscious

Another type of dream image comes from a much deeper layer of reality than our everyday experiences, memories, and cultural experiences, conceptualized as the collective unconscious. Images arising from this deeper and larger area of the soul come to nurture our growth, to help us attain wholeness, reminding us we are more than the little selves of our everyday lives.

Some images may have never been in our awareness before, and we have no knowledge of them. Called *transformational* or *archetypal symbols,* they often possess great psychic energy, capable of transforming our view of ourselves and our place in the world. Frequently these images arise from the spiritual world of which we are a part, just as our bodies are a part of outer physical reality.[33]

In our dreams we may encounter giants working, exotic talking birds, oriental brides, ancient monks, and precocious babies.

6. The Spirit of God

As believers in Christ, we are not self-contained units, but we contain the eternally *living* life of God. Deep within us, we have a river of life, the Spirit of God (John 7:38-39), flowing through us. As the very root and ground of our being, the Holy Spirit is the underlying source of the images appearing in our dreams.

River Held Back
I (Judith) dreamed I was in a deep underground cavern being enlarged. I noted that the flow of a river of water was being held back, until the enlargement of the cavern was completed.

For more examples, see Judith's dreams, "*It's Jesus*" (Chapter 9) and "*Gabriel Teaches Me To Fly*" (Chapter 10).

Structure of the whole personality

In order to understand the discussion of where dream images come from, we need a little familiarity with the structure of the whole person. The following summary briefly lays out the current understanding of the mental, psychological and spiritual structures of a *living* Soul.

- *Personal consciousness (the ego)*: We refer to the conscious part of the soul as the *ego* (from Latin, meaning "I"), part of me which I am aware of, *my I*. The ego is the part of me that makes choices and carries my ordinary awareness of myself and life around me.

- *Personal unconscious or subconscious (our experiences)*: The *personal* or subconscious is the repository of our personal experiences—those remembered and those long forgotten or suppressed. Its basic contents include *complexes*—"groupings of related images held together by a common emotional tone"—such as the *inferiority complex* or *mother complex*.[34]

- *Collective unconscious (potentialities never made conscious)*: The *collective unconscious* refers to an unknown part of our soul possessing great energy. Containing a universal structure, apparently common to all mankind, it includes instinctual wisdom and common patterns of behavior, for instance the drive to find a mate. It also contains potentialities of the soul that *haven't yet* become conscious—seeds for development of future possibilities. Within the unconscious part, there appears to be an eternally *living,* creative layer in everyone.

- *A spiritual layer (Spirit of God)*: As Christians, we recognize the presence of the indwelling Christ and the Spirit of the *living* God (the river of life) who lives and flows within us. Our spirit in union with the Spirit of the *living* God has been quickened, made alive. Because God through His Holy Spirit chooses to dwell within the human soul, we contain a great treasure—God Himself, and His wisdom and knowledge for our lives.

Structures dreams take

Dreams can vary widely, from single images to complex, seemingly endless sagas. Whether they take the form of a simple still shot or an elaborate movie production, they may appear like a cartoon, an adventure story, or even a monster movie. Similar to stories, most dreams generally follow a familiar pattern of four parts:[35]

Typical dream structure

Dream experts refer to four stages through which most dreams progress—the setting, plot development, culmination of the plot, and conclusion.

1. **Setting:** First the dream sets the stage upon which a particular concern will unfold, introduces the location and the persons who will participate in the drama, and sets up the initial situation for the message.
2. **Plot development:** Next, the dream sets up the problem or issue to be faced. As the plot unfolds, we meet the struggle to resolve the issue. Thus, it is helpful to examine the plot to see what is suggests.
3. **Culmination of plot:** As the story unfolds, there is a pivotal point upon which the plot turns; something decisive happens or doesn't happen for some crucial reason.
4. **Conclusion:** Finally, the dream offers an approach to resolve the conflict, a way to address a tricky issue, solve a problem, or handle a challenge. All too often our dreams fail to reach a conclusion. However, even unresolved dream dramas offer us a key to understanding the message of the dream.

Of the many techniques for analyzing dreams, this simple four-part breakdown provides a systematic approach. Understanding these four parts gives us a basis for further exploration of the dream.

The *because* factor

In some dreams, events don't happen due to some crucial reason—I can't go somewhere *because* my Mother is upset; I can't get up a hill *because* it's too rocky; I miss an opportunity *because* I am afraid of what's ahead. Exploring the "because factor" may help you identify the source of an issue, perhaps even indicate a solution.

> ▶ *Dream Work Tip:* Exploring the "because factor" may help you identify the source of an issue, perhaps even indicate a solution.

6. Interactive learning
☐ List and describe the four common stages the dream progresses through.
☐ How will you recognize a "because factor" in your dreams?

> *Lord, I thank You that I am fearfully and wonderfully made. I thank You that You created me in Your image with a capacity to dream and to imagine.*

Applied Learning

✎ *Your Response*
- ☐ Review the quote by Tony Crisp and decide if dreams are something miraculous or just the result of a wandering mind.
- ☐ What does the long history of dreaming suggest to you?
- ☐ What was the most important idea for you in this chapter?
- ☐ Ask, "God, why did you create me with a capacity to dream?" Write out the thoughts that spontaneously flow through your mind.

✺ *Dream work strategies, skills & techniques*
- ☐ What life issue is Gerald's "*Umbrellas Aren't Legal*" dream concerned with?
- ☐ Can you identify a BECAUSE FACTOR in Gerald's umbrella dream? (#1)
- ☐ What was the *biblical purpose* of Gerald's "Umbrellas Aren't Legal?"
- ☐ Does Gerald's umbrella dream have a satisfactory CONCLUSION? (#2)
- ☐ Did his dream offer him a solution to a problem? (#2)

Explaining new dream work strategies, skills & techniques

#1 A BECAUSE FACTOR refers to something that happens or fails to happen, *because* of something else. Identifying the *because* factor helps us to recognize a problem and possible solutions.

#2 Explore the dream to see if it has a CONCLUSION and whether it is satisfactory or unsatisfactory to you.

✎ *Practicing your skills*
- ☐ Select a dream to work with.
- ☐ Can you recognize the source/s of your dream images?
- ☐ What life issue do you think your dream might be commenting on?
- ☐ Is your dream concerned about a relationship with someone?
- ☐ Does your dream progress through four stages?

Dream Treasure

- ☐ Does your dream have a BECAUSE FACTOR? (#1)
- ☐ Does the BECAUSE FACTOR shed light on a problem for you?
- ☐ Does your dream offer a solution to a problem?
- ☐ Does your dream have a CONCLUSION? (#2)
- ☐ Are you satisfied with the CONCLUSION? Why or why not? (#2)

Dream Work Terminology

Can you explain the following terms?

- Dream language
- Personal symbols
- Cultural symbols
- Universal symbols
- Archetypal symbols
- Transformational symbols
- Setting of dream
- Plot development
- Culmination of plot
- Dream conclusion
- The because factor

Classifying Dreams

14

Church father, Synesius of Cyrene, described the dream as an opening of the self to God and the spiritual world. He laid out sound reasoning for discussing dreams, and detailed the blessings we gain from studying our dreams.[1]

Core Concepts
- Common dream categories.
- Special types of dreams.
- Nightmares.
- Death and dying dreams.
- Balancing dreams.

Learning Objectives
At the completion of this chapter, you will be able to:

☐ List and describe seven dream categories.

☐ Discern dreams requiring differing techniques.

☐ Recognize dreams offering you transformation.

☐ Test whether your dream is prophetic.

☐ Describe the difference between clear and symbolic dreams.

☐ Realize the importance of nightmares.

Dreams have been classified in many different ways. Here are some we culled from other authors: housekeeping dreams, nightmares, message dreams, healing dreams, problem-solving dreams, mystical or visionary dreams, completion dreams, archetypal dreams, comfort dreams, numinous dreams, instruction dreams, transformational dreams, trauma dreams, warning dreams, and prophetic dreams.

As you will notice, a great deal of overlap exists between categories. Because dreams seem to defy definition, frequently it's difficult to determine to which category a dream belongs. Nevertheless, it is vital to recognize key types of dreams, because some of them need to be worked with differently.

Common dream categories

Adapted from many authors, here's our take on it: 1) *Routine maintenance* dreams; 2) *Current event* dreams; 3) *Historic event* dreams; 4) *Archetypal* dreams; 5) *Divine encounter* dreams; 6) *Extrasensory perception* dreams; 7) *Clear* dreams.

It's my house

To help you relate to these seven types of dreams, we suggest an analogy to a house. Much of our house activities center on daily cleaning and routine maintenance, just to keep the place functional. We may clean the windows so we get a clear view looking out.

Historically, our house is a repository of many memories from *prior years'* activities. Perhaps God has visited us on some special occasion. We have our *current* situation, actions happening right now in our house. We also prepare for *future* events.

Sometimes we need to change our house, either making major renovations or preparing it for sale. These decisions entail much effort as we clean, paint, and repair the building and surrounding grounds. Tremendous transformation may occur as we move to a new home.

1. Routine maintenance dreams

Keeping our house from deteriorating takes a lot of daily cleaning and maintenance. So, too, with dreams. Much of our nighttime imagery seems to be related simply to keeping our internal house functioning properly, perhaps sorting through all the new information we have collected and the emotions we've experienced during the day. We need dreams just to stay stable and steady, and to release unexpressed emotions and thoughts.

Dream research emphasizes the vital importance of dreaming to mental health and well-being. Deprived of dreaming in our sleep, tension builds inside, and we tend to become unstable and irritable. So, be thankful for all those dreams you barely remember, or can't make sense of, or aren't even aware of at all—they keep you sane.

> *Most of us are not even aware of our maintenance dreams; they don't seem to grab our attention when we awaken. However, if you become aware of one, take time to prayerfully reflect on it. We have found that even small, seemingly insignificant dreams can be very important!*

Gerald's "*Disparate Pieces Coming Together*" dream may be an example of a routine maintenance dream (see Chapter 9).

2. Current events dreams

Current events dreams comment on what's happening in the daily life of the dreamer. These dreams keep us centered in the middle of life's normal struggles, helping us work through the problems and issues in our daily lives. Sanford suggests they enable us "to see yesterday's events in a completely different light."[2] To understand this type of dream we must be familiar with our recent experiences and be able to reflect on our current concerns, prayers, dilemmas, and aspirations.

> ▸ *Dream Work Tip:*
> We must be familiar with our recent experiences and be able to reflect on our current concerns, prayers, dilemmas, and aspirations.

Here is an example of a current events dream.

Wet Concrete

I (Gerald) had been offered two job opportunities, one in England, one in USA. I chose the USA job, but was not allowed to accept it until I completed a critical product launch. I lost an argument with the CEO over this incident.

Although the unlocked doors of a warehouse seemed off limits, I plunged in recklessly. Walking seemed difficult. As I opened a door to a second room, I noticed in the semi-darkness that the floor was fresh, uncured concrete. Turning to retreat, I noticed the floor of the first room was also uncured concrete. Although I was embarrassed at my impetuosity, a woman from the office was outside to advise me on cleaning my shoes.

The first room represented the USA job; the second room, the England job. Whoops! England job not ready yet (uncured concrete); nor was the USA job (same problem). Despite my impetuous run-in with the CEO, a few months later he offered me a terrific job based in England (which I turned down because of another dream!).

3. Historic events dreams

Some dreams deal with unresolved, forgotten, or repressed experiences in our lives. Understanding this type of dream requires us to honestly reflect on our past history—remember childhood events, relationships with parents, traumas, attitudes and beliefs learned in childhood or perhaps a previous marriage or a destructive relationship. Historic event dreams help us find the truth about long-ago events, make peace with unresolved conflicts, or find relief from traumatic experiences, enabling us to bring them into the light of God's love and truth.

> *Understanding historic events dreams requires us to honestly reflect on our past history.*

Exploring historic events dreams is like looking through old photos, allowing your personal memories and feelings to float to consciousness. Here is an example of a historic events dream.

I Am An Inch Worm

(Judith): After the Lord showed me my broken condition, He used this dream to focus my attention on the historic events in my childhood.

I am in the backyard of my childhood home; a large tree (with no branches; only the trunk) is walking toward me. It has eyes and is looking at me. I run into the house, trying to get away from it. The tree follows me inside. I am terrified. I run out the door and down the sidewalk. As I run, I become an inch worm.

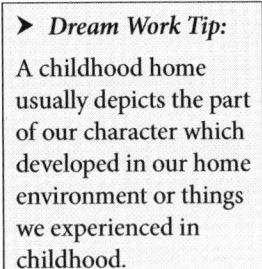

> ➤ *Dream Work Tip:*
>
> A childhood home usually depicts the part of our character which developed in our home environment or things we experienced in childhood.

I had lived in this house, until I was 12. This house symbolized what I learned or experienced there during those years. The tree symbolized my family tree. The dream was showing me that I need to turn and explore my family history and experiences I made during that time—if I want to become fully alive and set free.

4. Archetypal dreams

Long ago St. Augustine labeled as "archetypes" the psychological patterns of energy within each individual recently identified by depth psychology. These patterns of energy symbolize universal ways of feeling and behaving we all experience, regardless of our culture—such as the urge to find a mate, become a mother or father, or find higher meaning in life.

God's great plan is to make us fully alive, whole, fulfilling our divine destiny; *archetypal dreams* emerge to aid us at different points along the journey. Archetypal dreams obviously come from a deeper place, and seem to be associated with the inward movement of energy within us. Presence of archetypal images in our dreams indicates the possibility of new development or transformation within our selves.

Archetypal dreams are more concerned with our fate and destiny than with our current circumstances.

These dreams are more concerned with our fate and destiny than with our current circumstances. They enlarge our personality and help us realize our potential. Understanding archetypal dreams may require knowledge of archetypal and transformation symbols, which often have parallels in fairy tales, mythology, and religious symbolism.

Even though an archetypal image indicates the need for some major change, we cannot force the transformation with our will or mind. Instead we must both *experience the emotion* (only emotion has the energy to cause the necessary changes in us) and *understand the significance of the symbolic dream images* (the way the emotional content brings our choices to consciousness). (See Chapter 17 for more discussion of archetypes.)

> ➤ *Dream Work Tip:*
> Understanding archetypal dreams may require knowledge of archetypal and transformational symbols.

5. Divine encounter dreams

Unlike dreams from ordinary life, these dreams transcend our personal lives. They come from deep in our own spirit or from the Spirit of God and affect us deeply because they bring insight and revelation about spiritual matters.

Sometimes referred to as *spectacular dreams*, or *numinous dreams*, they "go beyond dealing with every day events and concerns to access the dreamer's spirituality."[3] We seem to have a direct encounter with something from the outer spiritual world—God, angelic beings, or Jesus in human form.

When we awaken, we intuitively know the dream was unusual because it affects us so deeply. Recall Shayda's *Come, My Daughter* dream (see Chapter 2), where Jesus spoke to her and brought her safely across a chasm. Also see Gerald's *Divine Hug From Pope* dream (Chapter 8).

> ➤ *Dream Work Tip:*
> Understanding divine encounter dreams requires a deep spiritual sense and knowledge of our inner world.

Dream Treasure

Understanding dreams of this type requires a deep spiritual sense and knowledge of our inner world. Often they are associated with major life changes and, sometimes, with religious conversion.

6. Extrasensory perception dreams (ESP)

Extrasensory perception dreams enable us to access information outside our own experience, across time or space. This type of dream fascinates us humans locked in a time-space box. Many dream authors cite riveting accounts of dreams announcing, warning or preparing something in advance. Catherine Marshall relates the compelling story of a woman with a brain tumor, who did not know it until it was revealed to her in a dream that saved her life.[4]

> *Many dream authors cite riveting accounts of dreams announcing, warning or preparing something in advance.*

Jung, in his scientific research, observed "the unconscious is capable…of manifesting an intelligence and purposiveness superior to the actual conscious insight."[5] He understood this type of phenomena as basically religious. Examples of extrasensory perception dreams include a) anticipatory, b) precognitive, c) telepathic, d) clairvoyant, e) mutual, and f) prophetic dreams.

Anticipatory dreams—"prepare, announce, warn about certain future situations often long before they actually happen."[6] Some anticipatory dreams may give answers or offer solutions, while others may suggest a pessimistic, even disastrous, turn of events.

Precognitive dreams—reveal in accurate detail what will happen in the future.

Telepathic dreams—contain direct communication between the dreamer and another person.

Clairvoyant dreams—reveal events or objects existing in waking life of which the dreamer has no foreknowledge, which turn out to be precisely the same as it appeared in the dream (similar to a "*déjà vu*" experience).

> ▶ *Dream Work Tip:*
> A simple test of prophetic dreams is whether or not they come true!

Mutual dreams—refer to two or more people having similar dreams on the same night.

Prophetic dreams—foretell in accurate detail specific future events of importance to *more* people than just the dreamer. Based on extrasensory perception, they demonstrate an existing foreknowledge of events. A simple test of this type of dream is whether or not they come true!

Following is an example of both an anticipatory dream and a precognitive dream.

Phone Call

(Judith): In 1992, I dreamed of a phone call from my oldest brother, telling me my mother was dying and her skin was yellow.

Six months later I received a phone call from my brother exactly like the dream. My mother had six weeks to live! Her skin was yellow. I took comfort, because the Lord had prepared me for this shock!

7. Clear dreams

Clear dreams need no interpretation. We refer to this type of dream as receiving a *direct* message from God, connecting us with His divine purpose. Very rare, clear dreams often use just a single image or scene. St. Paul recognized his nighttime vision as a clear, divine message—Macedonia simply meant Macedonia—and he hopped the next ship from Troas (Acts 16:9,10).

Judith's *Without a Degree* dream (Chapter 1) is an example of a clear dream. Another is Judith's *Until You Do What I Told You* dream (Chapter 10). Clear dreams are completely understandable because they simply are what they are. Understanding this type of dream requires *spiritual discernment.*

Remember, dreams can be characterized as either direct or indirect communication from God. If a dream is a direct communication from the living God, we know we are being addressed directly by the Lord!

On the other hand, an indirect communication personalizes God's communication with us in a way that helps us become more whole in body, soul, and spirit. Experts tell us (and from our experiences we agree) most of our dreams entail indirect communication from God, urging us toward completeness and fulfillment. Both types of dreams can transform our lives, demonstrating how committed our Creator is to our wholeness!

> *1. Interactive learning*
> ☐ List and describe the seven dream categories.
> ☐ Review your dreams and decide which type of dream they may be.
> ☐ Contrast and compare these types of dreams with the biblical purposes of dreams in Chapter 10.

Special types of dreams

In introducing this chapter we noted that there is much redundancy in the various classifications of dreams. In this section we discuss another way to describe special types of dreams.

Lucid dreams

In this type of dream, we realize *in the dream* that we are actually dreaming. Not very well known in our culture, lucid dreaming offers us the possibility of taking a certain action or making a decision in the dream. Wouldn't it be nice if this happened during a nightmare? Oh, thank God, it's only a dream! Recently I (Gerald) had the following lucid dream.

> *This Dream Is Going Nowhere*
> After a complex, convoluted series of events, I drive my old Mercedes sedan down a long, sweeping hill, realizing that I know neither where I am nor where I am going. I decide to turn the car around and go back up

Dream Treasure

the hill to see if I can at least determine where I am. When the car simply refuses to go, I say, "This dream is going nowhere; I'm getting out of it!" I immediately wake up.

Nightmares

In a nightmare, the dreamer is some kind of danger or observes a horrible event. Often paralyzed by fear or shock, in a nightmare we feel lost, helpless, manipulated by something beyond our control. Nightmares can have a positive intention, alerting us of the need to become more aware of something going on in our waking life.

Nightmares may be revealing our torments or replaying traumatic experiences we have not processed—veterans often relive their war experiences this way. Other factors such as drugs, illness, and stress may also provoke nightmares. Recurring, severe nightmares are a signal that something is unhealed in our hearts.

What causes nightmares?

Since understanding a problem is the first step toward a solution, Tony Crisp suggests the following possible causes of nightmares:[7]

- Childhood fears— being lost or abandoned; loss of a parent; attack by a parent or a stranger.
- Unconscious memories of intense emotions, e.g., a child being left in a hospital without mother.
- Adult fears connected with internal drives—sexuality, aggression, processes of growth and change.
- Precognition of fateful events.
- Serious physical illness.
- Intense anxiety-producing life situations, such as unresolved war scenes or sexual assault.

Since most nightmares don't just conveniently go away, we can take them to Our Lord to receive his healing and deliverance. Jesus was very comfortable dealing with this kind of thing—and He told us to do what He did.

See *Divine Purposes of Dreams* (Chapter 10) and *Strategies & Interpretation Techniques* (Chapter 20) for ways to deal with nightmares.

Since most nightmares don't just conveniently go away, we can take them to Our Lord to receive his healing and deliverance.

Dreams of death or dying

A spiritual principle of Christianity says the old must die so the new can emerge. This is the message of Easter: *life comes out of death*. The same power that brought Jesus out of the grave works to bring resurrection in us. Our dreams often mirror this process.

Since only death can bring about profound transformation of the personality, people dying or dead in our dreams often symbolize this process. I (Judith) dreamed many times about my mother dying, long after she was dead; or I dreamed she was alive, giving birth to a baby in her old age.

Dream Treasure

Our dreams about death usually are not about impending physical death—typically a dream would inform us of this symbolically. For example, just before a friend's wife became terminally ill, he dreamed of her looking down at him from a balcony.

Balancing (compensatory) dreams

God gives us dreams to move us toward wholeness and the realization of our potential. Dream writers use the term *compensatory* for dreams that show us the sides of ourselves we are usually unaware of, as a *balance* to our conscious attitudes.

Researchers found that most dreams are trying to change us in some way— adjust lopsided attitudes, express what we are not aware of, tell us what we do not want to know. They are called compensatory because they offer another point of view, allowing us to shift from a one-sided perspective. Our dreams are trying to equalize, balance, or adjust our consciousness in a purposeful manner—helping restore inner equilibrium and release our psyche/soul energy.

Balancing act

A basic function of dreams is to express the guidance, counsel, and advice coming from the unseen part of ourselves— the deepest layers of the unconscious, the hidden man of the heart—to cause us to see some truth about ourselves we don't easily see any other way.

A dream can show us what we have not yet been able to verbalize or bring into conscious thought, bringing to our attention aspects of our personality we deny or disown. *It is because of its compensatory function that the dream heals.*

Positive or negative

If a dream augments what is healthy within us, it is called a *positive* compensation dream—life is somehow improved, enriched, made more creative by the dream. A positive compensation dream protects what's healthy and strengthens us, enlarging our view of life and its possibilities. It adds some value to our conscious attitudes and may help stimulate us to greater creativity, refining and enriching our lives.

However, a *negative* compensation dream comes to correct illusions, distortions and lies inside us. It helps restore to consciousness some of the stuff we repressed 'cuz it ain't so nice, often dating way back—even to childhood emotions still hiding inside us. We might consider if the dream is trying to compensate for some wrong or inadequate conscious judgment we've made about something recently. A wrong attitude we hold about someone else or ourselves? Perhaps a wrong decision?

> *A basic function of dreams is to express the guidance, counsel, and advice coming from the unseen part of ourselves.*

For an example of a negative compensation dream, see my (Gerald) *Last Of The Big Bruisers* dream in Chapter 10. For a full discussion on compensatory dreams, we refer you to Mattoon or Hall.[8]

Dream Treasure

PART FOUR The World Of Dreaming

> **Dream Work Tip:**
>
> In dream work, it is helpful to ask, "What area of my life is the dream dealing with?" Sometimes, just in asking the question, we intuitively know the answer.

Non-compensatory dreams
Although most dreams are classified as balancing or compensatory, the following types of dreams are non-compensatory: anticipatory dreams, traumatic dreams and extrasensory dreams.

2. Interactive learning
☐ Explain the importance of the dreamer's background in dream interpretation; i.e., dreamer's life situation and current concerns.
☐ What factors will you consider when working with each type of dream?

How's that again?

Confused? No wonder! Sometimes it's difficult to know exactly which type of dream we experience. Interestingly, a dream message can be communicated in a number of ways. Following is an example of a dream we could classify as a current events dream, clear dream, anticipatory (ESP) dream, divine counsel dream, and objective dream (see Chapter 16).

I Am Not Going To Hire You

After working six months in a German clinic (1991), there was talk of making me a permanent staff member—and of course I wanted it, until I dreamed:

The owner and I are talking together. He says, "I am not going to hire you, because I need to hire a therapist, and you speak no German. You will have to leave."

I awoke with a jolt and, waking Gerald, I told him my time was done at the clinic and we would be returning to the USA. A few days later, the exact conversation with the owner occurred—no interpretation needed!

> *Lord, I thank You for the blessings I can gain from discussing and studying my dreams.*

186   Dream Treasure

Applied Learning

✎ *Your Response*
- ☐ Review the quote by Church father, Synesius of Cyrene. Do you agree or disagree with his ideas? Explain?
- ☐ Using the dream types explained in this chapter, list the possible blessings your dreams could bring you.
- ☐ What new understanding did you receive from this chapter?
- ☐ Affirm, "God created me with a capacity to dream and to imagine. I like that!"

✲ *Dream work strategies, skills & techniques*
- ☐ List the ELEMENTS in Gerald's "Wet Concrete" dream? (#1)
- ☐ Identify any DETAIL in Gerald's dream. (#2)
- ☐ What AREA OF LIFE was Gerald's "Wet Concrete" concerned with? (#3)

Explaining new dream work strategies, skills & techniques

#1 Identify dream's distinct ELEMENTS; i.e., all distinguishable persons, figures, wild/plant life, landscapes, weather conditions, nature, situations, places, buildings, objects, vehicles, colors, sounds, feelings, actions, words or thoughts in a dream.

#2 Identify all DETAILS in a dream. The tiniest detail may offer clues as to the meaning of the dream or the area of life the dream is about.

#3 Asking yourself, "what AREA OF MY LIFE is this dream about?" often brings an intuitive knowing. Note the thoughts that come in response to the question.

✎ *Practicing your skills*
- ☐ Select a dream to work with.
- ☐ List the ELEMENTS in your dream. (#1)
- ☐ Identify the tiniest DETAILS in your dream. (#2)
- ☐ Ask, what AREA OF LIFE is my dream concerned with? (#3)
- ☐ Pay attention to an inner click or "Aha!" (See Chapter 8 to review the "Aha!")

Dream Treasure

PART FOUR The World Of Dreaming

> **Dream Work Terminology**
>
> Can you explain the following terms?
> - Routine maintenance dreams
> - Current events dreams
> - Historic dreams
> - Archetypal dreams
> - Divine encounter dreams
> - Extrasensory perception dreams
> - Prophetic dreams
> - Anticipatory dreams
> - Clear dreams
> - Lucid dreams
> - Nightmares
> - Death and dying dreams
> - Balancing (compensatory) dreams
> - Dream elements

The Language of Dreams

15

Hear now My words…I shall speak with him in a dream, not so with My servant Moses…with him I speak mouth to mouth…and not in dark sayings (Num. 12:6-8).

Core Concepts
- Symbolism 101.
- Ruling categories of symbolism.
- Symbolic communication in the Bible.
- Why God uses symbolic language.
- Symbols touch the heart of man.

Learning Objectives
At the completion of this chapter, you will be able to:
- ☐ Explain the nature of symbolic language.
- ☐ Describe the two ruling factors in symbolism.
- ☐ Give examples of the use of symbolism in the Bible.
- ☐ Differentiate between the two ways we process information.
- ☐ Discuss reasons why God chooses to *conceal* His dream messages.
- ☐ Understand the significance of "religious symbolic experience."
- ☐ Unlock the meaning of your dream's symbolic elements.

Earlier we learned that the Scriptures described dream language as "dark sayings," riddles, seeming enigmas, puzzles. In other words, the dream speaks in pictures and symbols, whereas the mind speaks in thoughts, ideas, and concepts.

As we look to our dreams to help us discover the hidden treasure within us, we must become conversant in the pictorial, imaginative way in which dreams bring their message to us. In this strange new dimension of communication, we process information conveyed through word pictures, metaphors, puns, stories, and figures of speech.

It's quite normal to be uneasy about learning new things, especially learning a new language. So when we embrace this symbolic language of parables, riddles and poetry, we are entering unfamiliar territory. For this journey, we need to be able to trust the Holy Spirit.

Symbolic language is the language of the Holy Spirit; it belongs to God. Since it's God's language, we can expect His Spirit to guide us, help us, and tutor us as we learn it. You can trust God.

Dream Treasure

Blame God for the confusing language

The Bible provides compelling evidence that it is *God* who makes dreams difficult to understand. In Numbers 12:6-8 (NASB), God says *He* will speak in dreams using a language of "dark sayings." Modern Bible translations use the word "puzzle" because the meaning refers to mysterious speech presenting an enigma, a knotted message to be unraveled, like a proverb or a riddle.

God has chosen to conceal his messages in riddles requiring effort to unlock their meaning—for *our* benefit. When the God-man walked the earth, he said pretty much the same thing:

> *I speak to them in parables, because, while seeing they do not see, and while hearing they do not hear, nor do they understand (Matt. 13:13).*

Called to search out a matter

Listen to this Scripture: "It is the glory of God to conceal a matter, but the glory of Kings is to search out a matter" (Prov. 25:2). There is tremendous deeper meaning to Jesus' teaching—for the person who takes the time to seek it out.

Our friend Ralph Nault suggests God deliberately conceals His dream messages because He wants to reach our heart: "Dreams use a symbolic type of language that speaks directly to my heart, bypassing my mind and intellect, in a way that God can get through to me without my logic and reason getting in the way."[i]

> *It is the glory of God to conceal a matter, but the glory of Kings is to search out a matter (Prov. 25:2).*

Western ignorance

Many people of faith in the Western world have lost touch with religious symbolic experience. De-symbolized, we do not know how to allow the symbolic material in our dreams to come alive with meaning.

This was me (Gerald). Raised as a Protestant, I was clueless about the valuable, life-giving symbols of our faith. The cross, bread, wine, water, stained glass rose windows, altars, bell towers—these objects didn't carry much meaning for me. I had no idea what a symbol meant. Because of this and other reasons, for many years I lived a life of ignorance and spiritual poverty.

To sort through the array of images presented to us in our dreams, we must go to language school—learn to read the language of dreams.

About Symbolic Language

The essence of symbolic language is this: something concrete is used to make present something not easily perceived. To help us understand invisible spiritual realities, in his teaching Jesus used ordinary tangible things: fire, trees, fish, candles, seeds, bread, wine, houses, rocks, wind. Some things cannot be understood until they are clothed in picture language. Stories, myths, fairy tales, poetry, science fiction, fantasy, art, and architecture also use symbolic language.

In our dreams, people, characters, animals, objects, etc. from our outer world are

---

i   Personal conversation with Ralph Nault, 2004.

used in an imaginative or symbolic way. Thus, the objects in our dreams are not to be taken literally, because they are symbols of the operative forces within our soul, the dynamics in our outer lives, and the unseen realities in the spiritual dimension.

Consider poor Pharaoh trying to make sense of his dream using purely rational thinking:

> Joseph, listen to this dream. I'm standing by the Nile when seven fat cows crawl up out of the river, followed by seven scrawny cows who proceed to eat the seven fat cows. What do you make of that? (see Gen. 41:2-4; 17:21)

Symbolism 101

Our lives are filled with symbols—wedding rings, baby shoes, family heirlooms, photo albums, personal mementoes and keepsakes, trophies, souvenirs, relics, Easter lilies, apple pies, patriotic emblems. These special objects are important to us because they evoke emotional response deep within us. By embodying invisible truths and experiences in symbolic form, these material objects make present to us another unseen reality.

What is a symbol?

A symbol is a visible (material) representation of something invisible. However, it is something far more than this. Although a symbol points to another reality, it also participates in the reality to which it is pointing. This larger, unseen reality is thus made alive to us.

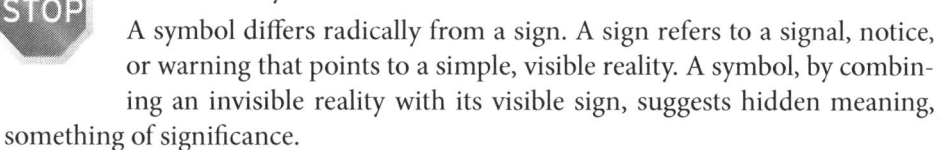

A symbol differs radically from a sign. A sign refers to a signal, notice, or warning that points to a simple, visible reality. A symbol, by combining an invisible reality with its visible sign, suggests hidden meaning, something of significance.

Symbols evoke emotional response

Savary, Berne, & Williams say, "a symbol refers to any dream image which evokes an emotional response, either during the dream or after it. … It is the energy inherent in a symbol that causes it to catch our attention."[1] Charged with emotional energy, a symbol becomes a message capable of delivering a profound religious idea or concept through our senses—imparting a religious symbolic experience. A dream symbol may be a visual image, a sound, or a smell. Activities and experiences such as flying or falling can also be treated as symbols.

Basis of symbolism is analogy

The basis of symbolism is analogy—something difficult to communicate is understood by association with something concrete. A symbolic object represents and makes present to us, a greater, invisible reality of which we are not aware of. While retaining its own form and content, a symbol links our conscious and unconscious selves, serving as a window through which to view truth.

Analogy is the basis of symbolism—something difficult to perceive is understood by association with something concrete.

Dream Treasure

191

A symbol as two aspects: A concrete, material reality, a "this world" element, the part of which we are conscious; and an unconscious, or unseen, reality to which it points, but also makes present.

A symbol links two realities

In dream work, the symbol acts as a bridge between the conscious and the unconscious parts of ourselves—making a spontaneous, *live* connection to our deep heart.

Dreams embody unseen truth in symbols. Symbolic imagery can quickly portray an abstraction that would take hours to describe. Symbols help us communicate our feelings, moods, emotions and values. For example, how would you explain love?

While love is a primary value and experience for people, you can't describe it as yellow and weighing ten pounds. It takes a story—using symbolic imagery—to communicate what love is. Here is how poet Robert Burns carries us into his experience of love:

> O, my luve's like a red, red rose; That's newly sprung in June. O, my luve is like the melodie; That's sweetly played in tune.

Symbols do not have a fixed meaning

Every symbol has many possible meanings and associations. For example, a fish can represent: something coming from the depths of the unconscious; the feeding of five thousand; or the healing Christ living in the deep ocean of our heart. For me (Judith), growing up in a third generation commercial fishing family, the fish might symbolize my family's livelihood, my father who smelled of fish every evening, or my love of water.

Admittedly, since symbols can have different meanings, they can be difficult to comprehend (four horsemen of the apocalypse in Revelation). Noteworthy is the fact that symbols can have either a positive or a negative meaning. For example, the color green can mean either growth or it can represent envy.

> *A symbol does not have a fixed meaning—a symbol can represent many things.*

1. Interactive learning
☐ How would you explain a symbol to a friend?
☐ Slowly read Burn's poem. Does it arouse any spontaneous feelings in you?

Right-brain dreaming

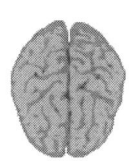

The right brain/left brain theory popularized in the 1980s says we have two brain hemispheres that function *very* differently. More recent research shows that the brain is not nearly as dichotomous as once thought—what matters is how the two sides of the brain *complement and combine*. Never-the-less, the right brain/left brain concept is useful for discussing how symbolic language works.

Dream Treasure

The *left brain* enables us to think logically, conduct research, reason, analyze, sort facts, give order to chaos. Left side leads, it's active, speaks linear thoughts. On the left side we speak and write using language, read, do math, and apply reasoning. To build a skyscraper, I'd depend on the left brain.

Out of the *right brain* comes symbolic thought, imagination, intuition, poetry, music & art appreciation, religion. Connecting us to the unconscious part of ourself, the hidden man of the heart, the language of the right side of the brain is images and symbols evoking association, emotions and feelings. From the right brain, we dream, tell stories, myths and fairy tales, and make up science fiction.

Left Brain	Right Brain
Rational, analytical thinking	Symbolic thinking
Science & logic	Art, poetry, religion, myth, fantasy, parables, dreams, visions
Linear thoughts & concepts	Pictures & symbols
We are active—lead the process	We are passive—led along
Processes "parts"	Adept at "wholes"
Speaks to our logic, reason	Speaks to our inner self, deep heart
Language of the conscious	Language of the unseen part, the deep heart

The brain can think in two ways

With a split brain we think and process information in radically different ways. For example, what might a picture of a tiger and an eagle fighting mean? If the picture comes from *Nature* magazine, it's likely a natural bird/animal battle. However, if the picture is an international political cartoon, we might guess it implies a China/USA conflict.

Here's the difference:
- Nature magazine: we use *rational interpretation & thinking process* to understand the information—this is left brain.
- Political cartoon: we use *imaginative sense or symbolic thinking*—definitely right brain.

Imagination creates our dream symbols

Imagination is the underlying phenomenon of dreaming—it creates the images we see in our dreams. We don't make up symbols intellectually—instead they emerge spontaneously using our imaginative capacity. Symbols arise from our *feeling and intuitive* functions, so we cannot approach them with rational thinking or fix their meaning intellectually.

Dream Treasure

PART FOUR The World Of Dreaming

> *Material appearing in dreams has to originate in the unconscious... imagination is a channel through which this material flows to the conscious mind... Imagination is a transformer that converts the invisible material into images the conscious mind can perceive (Robert Johnson).*[2]

How does symbolic language work?

> ▶ *Dream Work Tip:*
> *To understand a symbol we need to pay attention to both the intensity of the symbol and our association to it.*

Characteristics of symbolic thinking

In symbolic thinking we are passive, led along by images and our feeling response. Our mind is spontaneously flooded by images and symbols which evoke association, feeling and emotion deep within us. When we spontaneously connect with the symbolic imagery in our dreams, we experience an "Aha!" moment, where the dream comes alive with meaning for us.

Cardinal principles of symbolism

To understand this new language of symbolism, we cannot work with the usual categories of time and space, which apply in a rational dimension. To unlock the meaning of a symbol, we must consider two quite different categories: the *intensity* of the symbol and our *association* to it.

Intensity refers to emotional energy the symbols carry, having the capacity to evoke our feeling response. If we awaken from a dream charged with energy for some task, or we feel bogged down because of a dream, this is the important feeling response at work. It is the intrinsic power embedded in the symbol that enables transformation of our energy.

Association means the personal significance of the objects, animals, and people in our dreams. As we *amplify* a symbol, what feelings, sensations, experiences, intuitions or memories come to us?

During wartime people have tied yellow ribbons around trees. The *association* of the ribbons to returning military personnel gives it symbolic significance; the strong emotional power of love and worry gives it high *intensity*.

Dream example of symbolic language

Helping Michael Jordan With Basketball Camp

(Gerald): Usually content to bumble along in my ignorance and self-doubt, I resisted God's efforts to transform my worldview so I could function at a much higher level. Because God had work for me to do in his kingdom, He needed to challenge my self concept and make me bigger inside. Knowing that I valued my dreams, and recognizing I could not resist with my conscious mind while I slept, God sent me this dream:

Michael Jordan asked me to help him with some basketball camps in England. At first I balked, feeling I had nothing to offer. Jordan was a basketball superstar, while I only played scrub basketball in my youth. I hadn't even shot a basket in many years, and I know very little about the game. However, before the dream ended, I decided to apply whatever I know to the

194   Dream Treasure

task, and I agreed to go with Jordan to help him.

I feel this dream speaks to transformation of my way of seeing my self and my place in the world. It challenges my view of myself, and pushes me to acknowledge I have far more potential than I usually realize. I am capable of functioning at a much higher level—if I can come out of agreement with the negativity in my life.

Symbolic Communication in the Bible

Symbolic communication is not new to God's people. It is used throughout the Old and New Testaments. Prophets spoke in symbolic images, as well as in concepts. Jesus Himself did much of His teaching in "story-pictures."

As we said before, the "*Word of the Lord*" doesn't mean just ideas and words. In many Scripture passages God equates image-based visions with His *Word*. Much biblical truth is presented as image—vision, dreams, and figures of speech.

Jesus Christ frequently clothed His most powerful messages in the language of symbolism.

> *The enigmas in dreams have a close affinity to those things which are signified in an allegoric or hidden sense in the Scriptures (Basil the Great).*

Jesus, paradoxes & parables

Jesus Christ frequently clothed His most powerful messages in the language of symbolism, not the language of linear thinking and rationalistic thought. Employing parables and paradoxes in His teachings, Jesus conveyed His iconoclastic truths using allegories, figures of speech (metaphor, simile, hyperbole), personification, and even humor, such as puns and irony.

> *I will open My mouth in parables, I will utter things hidden since the foundation of the world (Matt. 13:35).*

> *Jesus used this figure of speech, but they did not understand what he was telling them (John 10:6 NIV).*

By using symbolic language broadly and frequently in His teaching, Jesus showed us that He understood effective communications often requires skirting around the conscious mind to engage the unconscious directly.

Kingdom of God is *like* a...

He seemed to make special effort to avoid using the language of concepts and reasoning. Relying upon His imaginative faculty, He conveyed His most important teachings concerning the Kingdom of God in the language of symbolism. He described the kingdom of God as being *like*:

- Treasure hidden in a field (Mt 13:44)
- Merchant looking for fine pearls (Mt 13:45)
- Mustard seed growing into a huge tree (Mt 13:31)

Dream Treasure

Symbolic imagery expressing invisible realities

Here are some of the myriad ways objects, wildlife, and natural elements were used symbolically to convey unseen realities. Notice how many use the word *like*.

Objects
- Nations *like* a drop in a bucket (Is. 40:15)
- Our righteous deeds are *like* a filthy garment (Is. 64:6)
- Select arrow, hidden in his quiver (Is. 49:2)
- Seven golden lamp stands for seven churches (Rev. 1:20)

Wildlife
- Thou hast chastened me *like* an untrained calf (Jer. 31:18)
- Its inhabitants are like grasshoppers (Is. 40:22)
- They will mount up with wings *like* eagles (Is. 40:31)
- Like sheep gone astray (Is. 53:6)
- Growl *like* bears, moan sadly *like* doves (Is. 59:11)

Natural elements
- The wicked are *like* the tossing sea (Is. 57:20)
- Your light shall break out *like* the dawn (Is. 58:8)
- He grew up before him...*like* a root out of parched ground (Is. 53:2)
- Morning star arises in your hearts (II Pet. 1:19)
- Seven stars for the angels of seven churches (Rev. 1:20)

The sons of Jacob

Interestingly, in the Old Testament, Jacob gave his twelve sons names with symbolic meaning for their lives (see Gen. 49:9-23). Judah is characterized as a lion's whelp; Zebulon, a haven for ships; Benjamin, a ravenous wolf; Joseph, a fruitful bough; etc. (Reuben, Simeon and Levi received negative characterizations because of previous bad behavior).

Characterization of God's people

Here are some positive symbolic images used for believers in the Bible: branch, light of the world, clay pot, temple of God, tree, living stone, house on a rock, sheep. You can probably find more.

Our basic language is picture language.

Our basic language is picture language. We need pictures to nurture our growth. Our self-image is built up of symbolic imagery. These pictures in our deep heart determine what we are going to be. Over the years, Our Lord has given us several pictures of how he sees us: Judith is *like* a sunflower full of seed, a treasure chest filled with treasure; Gerald is *like* a star shining brightly.

The nature of Jesus Christ

A similar language was used to convey the nature and essence of Jesus Christ: Lamb of God, Good shepherd, Living water, Vine, Incorruptible seed, Bread of life, Rock of salvation, Physician, Serpent lifted up in the wilderness, Cup of salvation, Bright morning star, Sun, Great light.

Dream Treasure

3. Interactive learning
- How do you *see* yourself? What picture do you hold of yourself?
- Ask God to give you His picture of how He sees you.
- Read Luke 11:11-13 and Matthew 7:9-11. Why did Jesus choose the loaf of bread & stone, fish & snake, and egg & scorpion in his teaching?

Biblical dreams using symbolic language

Besides Jacob's ladder dream, we have referenced many of the famous dreams in the Bible. Here are a few of those dreams from the perspective of symbolic language.

Joseph is the leader

Joseph had two significant dreams with similar themes. First he dreamed that while he was binding sheaves in a field, his sheaf stood erect while his brothers' sheaves bowed to his (Gen. 37:7). In a second dream, the sun, moon, and stars bowed to Joseph (Gen. 37:9). Not terribly popular with his brothers, these dreams were key to the unfolding of Joseph's life, symbolizing how God would arrange for Joseph to become a high-ranking leader in Egypt.

Pharaoh and the cows

The Pharaoh of Egypt dreamed he stood by the Nile River. Up came seven fat, handsome cows, followed by seven bedraggled, starving cows who ate the fat cows (Gen. 41:4-21). Joseph, a man intimately familiar with God's dream language, recognized the cows were a symbolic representation of the Egyptian economy. His wise counsel likely saved many lives in the Egyptian kingdom.

Gideon's enemy predicts defeat

While spying on an enemy camp, Gideon overheard an enemy soldier telling his dream of a loaf of barley bread rolling into camp, crushing their tent. The soldier interpreted the bread as symbolic of a rout of his army by Gideon's tiny army. When Gideon heard this, his faith rose up and he proceeded to defeat Israel's enemy in battle (Judges 7:13-25).

King Nebuchadnezzar's statue

King Nebuchadnezzar dreamed of a huge, bright statue comprised of various metals, with feet of part clay, part iron. When a rock hewn from out of a mountain crushed the statue's feet, it crumbled into dust (Dan. 2:31-35). The statue was a symbol of King Neb himself, a great leader who would experience a great fall.

Daniel and the beasts

Daniel dreamed of four great, terrible beasts arising from the churning sea—lion with eagle's wings; bear with three ribs in its mouth; leopard with four wings and heads; ten-horned monster (Dan. 7:1-27). Such a complex dream (references to "the son of man", "Ancient of Days", saints of the Most High, everlasting kingdoms) is too complicated for this discussion, but obviously it's loaded with symbolic meaning.

> **Butler's and baker's dreams**
>
> While living in a gated community—courtesy of the Pharaoh—Joseph's butler and baker each dreamed, and shared their dreams with Joseph (Gen. 40: 1-22). The wine taster dreamed he saw a grape vine with three branches that shot forth blossoms and buds and clusters of fruit. Pressing the grapes, he presented the cup of wine to Pharaoh.
>
> The dream used familiar symbols from the butler's own life, showing that life would again flow for him. Joseph interpreted this to mean that in three days the butler would leave prison and be restored to his former job—which came to pass.
>
> Since that went so well, the baker decided to share his dream in group. He dreamed of three white baskets stacked on his head, filled with baked goods for Pharaoh. However, the birds got there first and ate the goodies. Here also, the symbols come from the baker's chosen profession, representing, likely, the results of his work. Bird symbols can be good messengers, or bearers of ominous news. It's best not to eat the Pharaoh's favorite cinnamon rolls—this is not a good sign. Joseph interpreted this dream to mean the baker would die, and this also came to pass.

4. Interactive learning
- ☐ List the elements in the butler's dream. In the baker's dream.
- ☐ What might grapes symbolize for you? Birds?
- ☐ What did the birds in Jesus' parable on the seeds symbolize (Mt. 13:4, 19)?
- ☐ How did the baker's dream reveal his coming death?

Why the Language of Symbols?

Why does God use such a difficult language we can't easily understand? Perhaps it is because God desires fellowship with us, more than just giving us information—He wants to reach the human heart. Truths communicated through figurative speech and imaginative language are far more likely to engage our heart than rational propositions can.

Paul Tillich said, "Man's ultimate concern must be expressed symbolically, because symbolic language alone is able to express the ultimate."[3] Anything in life that cannot be grasped by intellect strives for realization through symbolism (Unknown).

Dream Treasure

Symbols touch the heart of man

Jesus Christ revealed that *the reality of the kingdom of God can be experienced within us*. He knew the message of Christianity was for the heart of man, not his intellect, calling us to a spirituality of the heart, not a religion of the head.

We can't grasp spiritual reality with just our reasoning and intellect—it must be perceived through "the eyes of the heart." By using the symbolic language the heart understands, Jesus hopes to help us experience spiritual reality and discover the truths hidden within.

Man's ultimate concern must be expressed symbolically, because symbolic language alone is able to express the ultimate.

> *The force of reason by itself is not powerful enough for getting at truth (Basil the Great).*[4]

New covenant is written in our hearts

Originally God wrote down His Word with His finger on the stone tablets Moses lugged down from Mt. Sinai. Later God said He'd make a new covenant with His people in which He would write His Word in their hearts (Jer. 31:31-33). The Word we now have inked on paper tells us clearly God has established this promised new covenant with His followers *in their hearts* (Heb. 8:10).

It's done, completed—and Jesus is the mediator of the new covenant (Heb: 9:15). So where should I look to discover the living Word God wants me to hear?

> *Trust in the Lord with all thine heart, lean not to thine own understanding; in all thy ways acknowledge him and he shall direct thy paths (Prov. 3: 5,6 KJV)*

Christianity is meant to touch our hearts—the core and center of our entire being. Emphasis in the Bible is on the contents of the heart. The living word of God penetrates to the heart, dividing soul and spirit, discerning the "thoughts and intents of the heart" (Heb. 4:12).

Dreams, language of the heart

Communications experts tell us we think first in images and pictures, then ideas and words.[5] The Holy Spirit uses images and symbols because this is the language of the heart. Picture language is the most basic way we grasp something.

> *The language of symbolism is the one universal language that the human race has developed (Erich Fromm).*

Symbolic images allow us to interiorize concepts rather than reason them out, because these images reach into the depth of our being where faith resides. With the "eye" of faith—imaginations, visions, dreams—we receive the things hoped for.

Picture this—flowing images, thoughts, emotions

The Virklers suggest the language of the heart consists of flowing thoughts (John 7:38), pictures (Acts 2:17), emotions (Gal. 5:22-23), supported by pondering and meditation (Ps. 77:6). Picture language engages our heart at a much deeper level than our intellectual reasoning can possibly penetrate.[6]

Most of us have had little experience with flowing pictures and thoughts arising

Dream Treasure

from our deep heart. Not being poets or song writers, we are more comfortable with linear, rational reasoning, but totally lost with heart language. We are starved for the language of the Spirit. If we don't want our souls and spirits to wither and die, it's vital for us to draw up water from *the river of life* within us.

Religious symbolic experience

There are many ways we can *know* something, and knowledge can be communicated in a variety of forms—words, symbols, actions, art, sounds, movement. However, much of what we know cannot be fully expressed—religious symbolic expression conveys truths impossible to articulate verbally.

God is able to speak directly to us through symbolic experiences. As already noted, the Scriptures are full of symbolic material. Jesus relies upon it to convey eternal truths. Why? Because religious symbolic experience is capable of empowering us with vision and purpose, mediating the presence of God and imparting spiritual gifts, revelation, and healing to us.

Symbolic imagery is linked to energy deep within us. We explore a dream for the purpose of drawing out its meaning and connecting with God's divine purpose in it. By interacting with its symbolic imagery, we enter into a kind of dialogue with God, allowing the images to spontaneously spring alive with meaning for our lives.

> *Nothing speaks to us more profoundly than our symbols (Paul Tillich).*

When a symbol connects to your heart, you experience an inner "Aha!"—divine revelation, intuitive knowing. The "word" has been made alive in you! When you sense this intuitive witness, you have discovered the symbolic meaning of the image.

> Many Churches limit themselves unnecessarily by addressing their message almost exclusively to those who are open to religious impression through the intellect and reasoning, whereas … there are at least four other gateways—the feeling response, the imagination, the aesthetic feeling, and the will—through which they can be reached.[7]

Dream symbols promote wholeness

When there are deep, destructive conflicts in the soul, rational analysis simply cannot bring healing. For changes to occur there must be a connection between theoretical solutions and the emotions quickened by symbolic experience. We all contain a well of images within us, created out of our own struggles and suffering, that engender meaning for our lives.

Many of us don't know who we are or why we exist. Our inability to separate and form our own personal identity leaves us with dark, empty spaces inside. This void created by lack of bonding can only be filled by life-giving creative images symbolically expressing who we are inside our hearts. We must nourish inner imagery, our inner pictures, in order to become transformed.

Our power to make images enables us to "see" what's in the unconscious. Our imagination *transforms* material from the unconscious into images, symbols and pictures that our conscious mind can perceive. Because dreams and the imagination have power to change us at deep levels and realign our attitudes, they may have more practical effect on us than do our outer experiences.[8]

> *Dreams and the imagination... may have more practical effect on us than do the outer events of our lives.*

5. Interactive learning

☐ Identify three objects you cherish. What thoughts or memories do they bring to mind? What spontaneous feelings do they arouse in you?

☐ In your own words, explain the meaning of "religious symbolic experience."

☐ Ponder the role of religious symbols in your own life.

Get a good book on symbols

Especially in the early stages of our dream journey, our understanding of symbolism can be inadequate to bring us very deeply into the meaning of many dreams. A dictionary that discusses archetypal and universal symbols, covering many shades of meaning, can be useful. However, we encourage readers to be wary of any approach to dream symbols that offers only a single, fixed meaning for a symbolic dream element. Fixed meanings fall short of what the Bible says about dreams and dream interpretation—God conceals His wisdom from us, requiring us to work at unraveling the meaning of a dream.

Here is a list of books on symbols we have found helpful at various times in our odyssey—especially the Clifts' book on symbols of transformation. We urge you not to lean too heavily upon symbol books; instead only use them to help you learn how to think symbolically. Symbols can have many meanings, and determining what a dream means is up to the dreamer.

- J.E. Cirlot, *A Dictionary Of Symbols 2nd ed.* (New York: Philosophical Library, 1972).
- Tom Chetwynd, *A Dictionary Of Symbols* (London: Paladin Books, 1982).
- Jean Clift & Wallace Clift, *Symbols of Transformation in Dreams* (New York: Crossroad, 1986).
- Anthony Crisp, *Dream Dictionary: A Guide To Dreams And Sleep Experiences* (New York, NY: Dell Publishing, 1990).
- Boris Matthews, Ed., *The Herder Symbol Dictionary of Symbols: Symbols from Art, Archeology, Mythology, Literature, and Religion* (New York: Continuum International Publishing Group, 1993).

Dream Treasure

PART FOUR The World Of Dreaming

6. Interactive learning
- [ ] List reasons why we must not apply fixed meanings to our dream symbols.
- [ ] Do you think we can manufacture our own symbols? Why or why not?

> *Lord, give me the courage to understand the inner meaning of the symbols in my dreams. I thank You that I can trust the Holy Spirit to be my teacher.*

Applied Learning

✎ *Your Response*
- ☐ Review this chapter, underlining the most important idea in it for you.
- ☐ List reasons why God chooses to conceal His messages in most dreams.
- ☐ Describe the benefits of symbolic language.
- ☐ Affirm: "God has given me symbol-making capacity. I like that."

✻ *Dream work strategies, skills & techniques*
- ☐ Identify the distinct elements and details in Gerald's dream, "Helping Michael Jordan."
- ☐ AMPLIFY the elements in Gerald's dream, describing their chief characteristics and functions. (#1)
- ☐ Continue to AMPLIFY the elements by making PERSONAL ASSOCIATIONS to them. (#2)
- ☐ What might Mr. Jordan suggest to you?
- ☐ What might basketball camp in England suggest to you?
- ☐ What is the biblical purpose of Gerald's "Helping Michael Jordan" dream?

Explaining new dream work strategies, skills & techniques

#1 AMPLIFYING an element consists of first *describing its chief* characteristics and functions *and then making* PERSONAL ASSOCIATIONS *to it*. This technique will yield a large storehouse of information from which the meaning of a dream can emerge.

#2 Making PERSONAL ASSOCIATIONS involves clarifying what a symbolic element means to you in your unique inner world. What feelings, ideas, mental pictures, memories, or thoughts spontaneously spring to mind when you think of it? What does its function or characteristics suggest to you?

✎ *Practicing your skills*
- ☐ Select a dream to work with.
- ☐ Identify the distinct elements and details in your dream.

Dream Treasure

PART FOUR The World Of Dreaming

- ☐ AMPLIFY each element, describing its characteristics and functions. (#1)
- ☐ Then make PERSONAL ASSOCIATIONS to this element. (#2)
- ☐ Look for the "Aha!" an intuitive knowing in your spirit, as you make associations.
- ☐ What is the biblical purpose of your dream?

Dream Work Terminology
Can you explain the following terms?
- Symbol
- Analogy
- Symbolic thinking
- Intensity
- Association
- Amplification
- Religious symbolic experience

Dream Dynamics

16

This figure of speech Jesus spoke to them, but they did not understand what those things were which he had been saying to them" (John 10:6).

Core Concepts
- Figurative expressions.
- Personification in dreams.
- Role of projection in dreams.
- Common dream characters.
- Objective or subjective dreams.

Learning Objectives
At the completion of this chapter, you will be able to:
☐ Name types of figurative expressions likely to appear in dreams.
☐ Examine your dream for puns.
☐ Explain the difference between personification and projection.
☐ Draw out the meaning of different people in your dreams.
☐ Recognize the difference between your dream ego figure and *you* in real life.
☐ Consider whether your dream is to be taken objectively or subjectively.

Before working with our dreams, we need to learn more about how dreams communicate their messages. We first explain three basic mechanisms used in symbolic communication: *figurative expressions, personification*, and *projection*. Then we describe five characters likely to appear in dreams—figures used to personify patterns of dynamic energies within our soul. Lastly, we address one of the most difficult tasks in dream work: deciding if a dream is about external situations or the dynamics operating in our inner lives—or both.

Three Basic Mechanisms

Symbolic language is not difficult to understand if we take time to understand basic mechanisms at work in symbolism. In this section we will identify kinds of figurative expressions, and describe *personification* and *projection*.

Dream Treasure

1. Figurative expressions

As we have just seen, from beginning to end the Bible is loaded with symbolic expressions. God continues using this way of communicating today—in dreams, visions and prophecies. However, because of our limited ability to use the right side of our brain to think imaginatively and figuratively, many of us need a crash course in figurative expressions. We have forgotten the poetic language we learned in high school literature class. Here is a sampling:

Figures of speech

A figure of speech is any expressive use of language in which words are used in other than their literal sense, in order to suggest a picture or image or for other special effect. Figures of speech are used to provide freshness of expression, special emphasis, or unseen realities.

Metaphor—a term is applied to something to which it is not literally applicable, in order to suggest a resemblance: *I am the good shepherd* (John 10:11); *You are the salt of the earth* (Mt. 5:13).

Irony—using words to convey a meaning quite opposite of their literal meaning: *Have I the strength of stones, or is my flesh bronze?* (Job 6:12).

Synecdoche—a part is used for the whole, or the whole for a part; the special is used for the general, the general for the special: The *law* was our schoolmaster to bring us unto Christ (Gal. 3:24); May the *nations* be glad and shout for joy (Ps. 67:4).

Simile—two unlike things are explicitly compared: *Judah is* like *a lion's whelp* (Gen. 49:9); *Goliath's spear shaft was* like *a weaver's beam* (II Sam. 21:19).

Biblical example of simile—"like a fruitful tree"
The Bible uses the imagery of a tree as a means to communicate a spiritual truth. The Psalmist compares a person who delights in the law of the Lord to a tree:

> *How blessed is the man who...his delight is in the law of the Lord...he will be like a tree firmly planted by streams of water, which yields its fruit in its season, and its leaf does not wither; and in whatever he does, he prospers (Ps. 1:3).*

Amplifying the symbolic images helps us more fully understand what the Psalmist wants us to *see* and *feel*.

Hyperbole and litotes

Dreams may try to draw our attention to some aspect of our lives by either exaggerating or minimizing it. *Hyperbole* and *litotes* are figures of speech used to make an overstatement or an understatement.

Hyperbole is an extravagant statement made to evoke strong feelings or create a strong emphasis—but not intended to be taken literally. This literary device is often used in poetry, political cartoons, casual speech, and in the Bible.

> *How sweet to my tongue is your promise, sweeter than honey to my mouth (Ps. 119:103).*

> *These books weigh a ton.*

Hyperbole can also be used as a visual technique by deliberately exaggerating a particular part of an image, such as embellishing facial features in a political cartoon.

Litotes is a form of understatement in which an affirmative is expressed by the negative of the contrary (e.g., She is "not a bad singer," or I am "not unhappy"). Instead of making a statement directly, we express it more effectively (or to achieve emphasis) by negating or denying its opposite. We sometimes express our appreciation of something by describing it as "not bad."

Parables, allegories, puns

These are some more types of figurative expressions you may come across in your dreams:

Parable—a short story designed to teach some truth, conveying meaning indirectly by use of comparison or analogy.

Allegory—a symbolic narrative with an underlying meaning, representing abstract or spiritual meaning through concrete or material forms. Jesus often used allegory to teach about the kingdom of God, using stories about concrete things to illustrate what the kingdom was like.

Pun—a figurative expression, a humorous use of a word or phrase in such a way as to suggest a completely different meaning; a play on words; humorous use of words that sound nearly alike but have a different meaning. Following is an example of a dream using a pun:

Moving to Tucson

A while before this, we had an intuitive knowing that a move was coming—Gerald felt it was to Michigan. When we learned that a son and his family might be moving to Tucson, we thought we might go to Tucson instead of Michigan. Then I (Judith) had the following dream:

Gerald comes into the room and says to me, "We are moving to Tucson."

I made the mistake of taking "Tucson" literally. I figured my dream was showing us we'd be going there too. However, when our son's family did not move to Tuscan, I was confused. I prayed about the confusion, and suddenly I experienced an "Aha!"—the witness of the Holy Spirit. "Tucson" was a pun, meaning we would be moving near our "two sons"—in Michigan!

> *Now you can understand why we emphasize the importance of not taking our dreams literally, unless there is a quickening, a witness, in our spirit—not merely excitement in our soul!*

1. Interactive learning

☐ List each element used in Ps. 1:3.
☐ What are the main characteristics and functions of a tree? Streams of water?
☐ What is the purpose of each part of a tree? Of streams of water?
☐ Sum up the meaning of this verse for you.

Dream Treasure

2. Personification

Poetry, music, the Bible, and dreams use personification as a way to communicate unseen elements. In personification, some trait, emotion, attitude, characteristic, or aspect of our self is placed on an *inanimate* object. Prophet/poet Isaiah says mountains and hills will break forth into shouts of joy while trees applaud (Is. 55:12). Although mountains are not considered good vocalists, and trees don't have hands, they express poetically the joy we experience as we venture into the world in the Lord's presence.

> *In personification, some trait, emotion, attitude, characteristic, or aspect of our self is placed on an inanimate object.*

Dreams are not trying to hide information, but express it in much the same way we use imagery in everyday speech.[1]

In dreams, unconscious aspects of ourselves are personified as dream figures portraying our inner feelings, attitudes and behaviors. By personifying our inner feelings and attitudes as dream figures, we can stand back and examine them as qualities or aspects of ourselves. Hopefully this makes it a little easier to begin making changes in our lives suggested by our dreams.

2. Interactive learning
- Ask questions to help unlock the meaning of a personified object:
- What are the positive and negative characteristics of this object?
- When am I behaving this way?
- What attitude, value, belief system, or feeling might they be personifying?
- What might a speeding red car crashing through a road barrier personify for me?

3. Projection

Projection is the placement of our own unknown attitudes, feelings, qualities, and abilities on another person. We see in someone else what we cannot see in ourselves. Jesus Christ recognized this when he said:

> ▶ *Dream Work Tip:*
>
> Another person appearing in a dream may be representing an aspect of your own psyche, rather than themselves.

Why do you look at the speck that is in your brother's eye, but do not notice the log that is in your own eye? ...or say to your brother, Let me take the speck out of your eye and behold, the log is in your own eye? (Mt. 7:1-5).

Any issue we are not aware of within us possesses energy that must be released. One way we release it is to project it onto another person. However, this prevents us from identifying our own stuff—unrecognized or rejected characteristics remain hidden in our unconscious. Projection also ruins any possibility of a relationship with that person!

What we cannot see in ourselves, we project on others.

Energy locked up in the projection can be released by becoming more aware of our own negative or positive qualities. Running away from an unpleasant person in our dream likely shows us we are running from this characteristic in ourselves. Face it, and we can discover what we're hiding from and become more whole.

Dream example of the use of projection

In my (Gerald) *Last Of the Big Bruisers* dream (Chapter 10), my unknown attitudes and feelings were embodied in the basketball player who I didn't like in my outer life. By engaging my dream figure, I could begin to see the truth about myself.

3. Interactive learning

- ☐ How does projection differ from personification?
- ☐ Use questions to help you understand why a person is in your dream.
- ☐ What are the positive and negative characteristics of this person?
- ☐ How would you describe his or her personality? Disposition? Temperament? Idiosyncrasies?
- ☐ What part of me could this be?
- ☐ When do I behave this way?
- ☐ Where can I find this in me?
- ☐ Where else do I feel this way?

Common Dream Characters

As we work with our dreams, we soon recognize the different types of characters who portray the deeper parts of our inner self. Most dream characters, while not archetypal, spring from our *personal energy systems,* giving visual form to our *personal* values, attitudes, feelings, and psychological complexes.

Other, more infrequent archetypal figures symbolize the psychological patterns of energy common to people everywhere—waiting for us to live out in life-producing ways. Similar to the basic blueprint that genetics play in our physical development, these in-born energy patterns establish the model for the process of unfolding the human personality. Archetypal figures offer us the possibility of a new development or transformation of some part of our self.

To benefit from these symbolic characters in our dreams, we work to unlock their meaning. Our goal is to make conscious their connection to the dynamic energies living within us—thus enabling us to become more fully developed and alive human beings.

Following are common figures you will recognize in dreams: *dream ego figure, persona figure, shadow figure, opposite-gender figure,* and the *Self figure.* All these figures personify some dynamic energy operating within us.

Dream Treasure

PART FOUR The World Of Dreaming

1. Dream ego figure

The dream ego is a figure in our dream representing our conscious self when we are awake. Most often, it looks *exactly* like us. Remember, the ego refers to our center of consciousness—our "I," our conscious awareness. In dream work we observe the actions and emotions of the dream ego figure, and compare them with our actions and emotions in daily life. Are we pleased with their choices, actions and behaviors.

Seize The Opportunity

(Gerald): I worked with computer terminals at Honeywell years ago. For many years, my way of functioning was to hesitate until I felt sure I knew what I was doing. As our ministry developed, I was increasingly required to step up into unfamiliar, unclear situations and do whatever is necessary.

> **Dream Work Tip:**
> Are you pleased with the choices, actions and behaviors of your dream ego figure?

I was traveling to Zurich to assess the status of a terminal program for Honeywell. I entered a city, thought I knew where to find the office, but didn't. A woman volunteered to drive me and several colleagues to the office. We traveled some distance, but the first city was not Zurich. Next, at a dinner table the woman asked me to tell the group what I'm doing. In spite of not being at all clear about my mission, I decided to seize the opportunity and run with it. Winging it, I did a good job of spinning my story.

From this dream I see that I have the capacity within me to seize the moment and make something positive happen—even in unfamiliar situations. When lacking clear direction, I must function from my heart and make the best of the situation. When I do, life flows and people are blessed.

One day as we were conducting a retreat at a German convent, some nuns came to us for prayer. In spite of feeling clueless, I accessed the energy God deposited in me from my Honeywell dream, and I ministered comfort and healing to their souls.

2. Persona figure

Early in our journey toward wholeness, we will most likely come upon *persona* figures in our dreams. Originating from the Greek word for mask, persona refers to the roles we play in daily life, the face we show that is presentable and acceptable to others.

True Christianity demands authenticity, calling us to be genuine people whose aliveness can touch others. In the Gospels, Jesus called us to let our lights shine in the world and not hide them. However, many of God's people keep their lights hidden behind defense mechanisms, religious faces, and false humility. We smile, say the right words, act spiritual, but we feel radically different than what we do and say—we wear a mask.

Dream Treasure

Our persona should accurately reflect who we really are on the inside. When it doesn't, God may use our dreams to help us see this. Persona dreams help us see how we meet and adapt to the people and situations in the world around us. The persona is often symbolized as clothing or some other outward aspect of the dreamer, like nakedness. Here are examples of such dreams.

Fig Leaves

(Judith): I am admiring new floral slipcovers a friend had made to cover her old, worn sofa.

I shared this dream with a friend and immediately he said, "fig leaves." The floral design was fig leaves! God was showing me my problem—I had covered myself with fig leaves just like Adam did in the Garden, hiding my true condition. It was time to let Him bring into the light things hidden inside me.

Naked On Route 9

At the time of this dream, I (Gerald) was working hard to get in touch with things inside. Although fearful of facing my inner dragons, I was beginning to open up and become honest.

(Gerald): I am walking along a major thoroughfare wearing only my bath robe. I feel naked and exposed, despite having on my robe.

Another type of persona problem is wrapping our identity in our societal position—unable to separate ourselves from the opinions of other people. Professions often present this problem: a nurse is always on duty; an actress is always on stage; a professor always lectures instead of engaging in real conversation. Our goal is a flexible persona that protects our basic identity while allowing us to respond appropriately to any given circumstance.

> ➤ *Dream Work Tip:*
>
> In persona dreams, consider the purpose of each clothing item—hat, jacket, skirt, slacks, shoes, etc. What function does it serve?

Dream Treasure

PART FOUR The World Of Dreaming

What Do I Wear?

(Judith) After I graduated with my master's degree and could work as a therapist, I dreamed:

I was in a hotel room with my friend (a professional therapist in waking life), but I didn't know what to wear. We were preparing to leave and fly home, but my clothing was strewn all over the room. I couldn't seem to put it all together into my suitcase or decide what I was going to wear.

Clearly, I was having difficulty in developing an adequate persona to handle my new professional status.

4. Interactive learning

- ☐ Recall Gerald's "*Flood Waters Rising At My Doorstep*" dream? (See Chapter 4). What type of dream is this?
- ☐ What type of figures are in this dream?
- ☐ What did his *leather jacket* symbolize?

3. Shadow figure—same gender figure

Another dynamic in the unconscious is the *shadow*, which appears in the dream as a person of the same gender as the dreamer. Its purpose is to show us neglected parts of ourselves of which we are unaware—parts we need to recognize and allow Christ to transform and integrate into ourselves.

The shadow figure frequently represents the unconscious part of ourselves we have failed to live out, because it requires too much responsibility of the ego—or because it would alter our Little Orphan Annie self-image. Often these unknown aspects of ourselves are seen as tendencies in other people in the psychological process of *projection* (seeing in someone else the characteristics of ourselves of which we are unconscious).

Usually the shadow presents itself as a negative or inferior personality characteristic. In my (Gerald) dream, *Last of The Big Bruisers* (Chapter 10), Bill Lambier symbolized a part of me my ego denied. However, the shadow can also be positive, revealing unrealized potential and capabilities, such as my (Gerald) dream, *Helping Michael Jordan With Basketball Camp* (Chapter 15).

> **Dream Work Tip:**
> Amplifying shadow figures helps you recognize your own unknown attitudes, feelings, qualities, and abilities. Ask, do I unconsciously exhibit the same attitude or behavior? Do I have the same gifts, talents or possibilities in me?

5. Interactive learning

- ☐ How would you explain the shadow figure in dreams?
- ☐ What questions will you ask to discern the meaning of the same-gender figures appearing in your dreams?

Dream Treasure

4. Opposite-gender figure

More difficult for us to understand are the other-gender figures appearing in dreams—they also are personifying the dynamic energy systems at work within us. Various terms are used for these perplexing figures. Many dream experts refer to them as the *anima/animus* (Latin for soul or spirit). Christian dream authors Meier and Wise call them *alter-gender figures*. We use the expression *opposite-gender figures* as we discuss the meaning of these figures in our dreams.

Traditionally, religion thought of the soul as "an inner part of ourselves that connects us to the spiritual realm and leads us to God."[2] St. Paul notes that in Christ, we are considered neither male nor female. Psychology says that, instead of manifesting itself by gender, the human soul contains both masculine and feminine aspects.

Principal gender characteristics

In some dreams, opposite-gender figures could be simply personifying masculine or feminine traits we all carry. Typical masculine characteristics are logic, abstract thought, authority, determination, and goal-oriented action. Classic feminine characteristics are creativity, receptivity, relationship, symbolic thought, gentleness, nurturing, and unconditional love.

Every man carries within his dominant masculine soul some largely unconscious feminine aspects that he needs to relate to; every woman's soul possesses some unconscious masculine aspects she needs to make conscious. Jesus expressed His feminine aspect when He compared Himself to a mother hen, wanting to hold her chicks under her wings.

Potential for wholeness

Opposite-gender figures are extremely valuable in our journey to wholeness. A feminine figure in a man's dream may be calling him to relate to his more unconscious emotional life, or the willingness to love and be loved. A masculine figure in a woman's dream may be calling for the development of her more outer, goal-oriented self.

The dream is a wondrous gift from God, because it reveals to us the things God has prepared for us to become, as His very own sons and daughters. To become fully alive and the completely whole person that God planned for me, I need to discover the potentialities He embedded in me before I was ever born. Drawing up these things from my inner world, the dream offers them to my conscious self—usually in symbolic form.

In Bed With My Male Friends

(Judith): I am in bed with two male friends, one a psychologist and the other a psychiatrist. Someone hands us a baby to raise together.

I am not dreaming about these male friends as they are in my outer world. I am dreaming about some masculine aspect, role or characteristic that I need to discover, relate to and bring into my conscious self. If I can do this, I will be handed a baby to raise (representing some new potentiality in my life).

Dream Treasure

Personifying our soul

In some dreams the opposite-gender may be personifying our soul. In a woman's dreams, the soul appears as a masculine figure. A woman encounters the unconscious masculine aspect of her soul either *positively* (constructive initiative) or *negatively* (opinionatedness). A woman who underemphasizes her inner masculine will likely become extremely self-condemning and cowering, or she will become an aggressive crusader, stubborn and opinionated.

In a man, the soul appears in dreams as a feminine figure. A man experiences his unconscious feminine aspect either *negatively* (moodiness) or *positively* (creativity). If a man ignores his feminine side, he gets depressive, has fits of uncontrolled emotional outbursts, gets sentimentally sloppy, maudlin, glum.

Consequences of ignoring opposite-gender figures

If we ignore these powerful opposite-gender energies within us, we may project them into areas of our lives where they don't belong. For instance, a man may place his largely unconscious soul-image onto another woman or onto his work, obsessing over them. Or a married woman falls in love with another man who *really* gets her, unaware of her failure to relate properly to the unconscious masculine part of her soul she has denied knowing.

For an example of an opposite-gender dream personifying the soul, see Gerald's dream, *Waif Unplugs Me* in Chapter 10. In this dream my (Gerald) neglected inner feminine soul quickly got my attention, graphically illustrating my problem! To actualize the dream I sought counseling, wrote letters to myself, and eventually God got me back on track.

> ▶ *Dream Work Tip:*
> You do not need to be afraid of opposite-gender figures in your dreams. They are only personifying unknown dynamic energies within you.

6. Interactive learning

☐ Who was the opposite-gender figure in Gerald's "*Flood waters*" dream? (Chapter 4)

☐ What did the opposite-gender figures in Judith's "*In Bed With Male Friends*" represent?

> *Learning to ask ourselves questions helps us see how an image might relate to an actual dynamic taking place within us.*

Dream Treasure

> *Drawing out the meaning of shadow figures & opposite-gender figures*
>
> - Do you know the figure/s in outer life?
> - Who or what do they bring to mind?
> - Where and when did you know them?
> - What were you involved in at that time?
> - What are their characteristics, traits?
> - What roles do they play?
> - What do they do for work?
> - What are their relationships with their families?
> - Are they a positive or negative figure for you?
> - What set of beliefs do they function from?
> - What behaviors or attitudes are they mirroring?
> - What part of you might be like this?
> - Why are they appearing in your dream at this time?

5. The Self figure

One type of figure appearing in dreams is called the *Self* (perhaps an unfortunate term, because ordinarily the word *self* is used for the conscious personality, the ego). Built right into us by God is the potential for wholeness, where every part of us is integrated into a whole, conscious self, a complete person. The *Self* figure symbolizes this full, complete person, the larger totality.

But we're not born this way. Will Larson offers a fascinating look at the Hebrew word for "image," *tseh'lem*, (Gen. 1:27), suggesting "God created us as an unrealized potential, a shadow that has the potential of becoming something more, a real, complete person."[3] Once we are born of the Spirit of Jesus Christ, we become new creations, and the journey commences to become this completed, whole person.

However, since it takes many years for the new creation to become fully operative within us, the Self figure may appear in dreams to show us our progress toward wholeness. Self figures may materialize in dreams as unknown people who seem larger than life or carry a sense of God-like power or wisdom. Other examples: a giant, a wise old man/woman, a divine child. Following are two dreams that symbolize the process of inner transformation.

Rotten Inside

Judith: In the mid seventies, I was praying for the Lord to show me my true condition. Then I had the following dream.

Part Four The World Of Dreaming

I was lying on a table, split open down the middle. My insides were filled with rottenness, and hands were packing me with salt.

At this point I realized my condition and surrendered it to God. I remember saying, "God, I am sick from head to toe; I do not know how to heal myself. You are the great physician, would you heal me?" Even though I had many emotional and psychological symptoms indicating my need for healing, I did not focus on my condition. I just kept looking to God for what He wanted to do in my life as He brought me through one healing experience after another.

Most Alive Woman

About seven years later, I experienced the following, most wonderful dream.

I was lying on a pedestal table, again split open down the middle. Out of the center of my being stepped a most beautiful woman, vibrant, dancing with life.

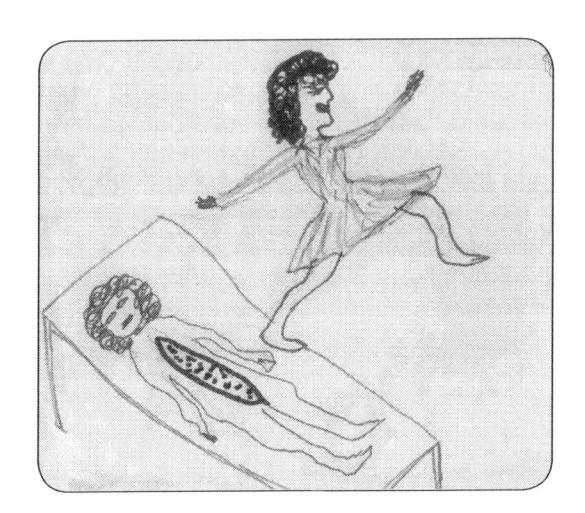

216 Dream Treasure

7. Interactive learning
- ☐ Who are the two women in Judith's "*Most Alive Woman*" dream?
- ☐ Be alert to other types of figures appearing in your dreams.

Objective or Subjective Dream Characters?

Dream work can be confusing at first, because we are unsure who or what the dream is about—other people, the external situations and direction of our lives, or about our inner life, our own soul. Are the figures about real people, or facets of our personality? Here is an example of a dream offering Judith a challenge:

My Ill Brother Arrives

(Judith): Just a few weeks prior to my brother's death in France, I dreamed that he arrived on our doorstep. He said, "I went through detox so I could come to you." He wanted my sons to be taken to the office of a church so he could meet with our friend Ralph Nault.

I didn't know what to do with this dream. We were praying hard for my brother's recovery. So is my dream telling me that he will live? After he died, I spent some time looking at the symbolic meaning of the dream. What does my brother symbolize to me? I think back to how he was used in an earlier dream. What aspect or quality of myself does my brother depict? What does detox mean to me? As I asked these questions, I found the meaning of my brother in this dream!

Dream experts outline two ways to view the figures in our dreams: *objectively* and *subjectively*. Although it is sometimes difficult to achieve, it is extremely important to distinguish between subjective dreams and objective dreams if we want to benefit from the treasure they contain for us. This is why we must rely upon the witness of the Holy Spirit.

Brief summary
- Objective: dream contents refer to objects in the external world or to our relationship with them.
- Subjective: dream contents refer to processes within our own soul—they represent qualities or parts of our personality.

Taking an objective approach

When we look at a dream from an *objective* approach, the dream images/figures refer to objects and events in the *external* world of the dreamer. The dream images/figures refer to people, circumstances, situations, and relationships in the waking world of the dreamer.

In our dreams about familiar people, they display characteristics of those people

Dream Treasure

in our lives and our attitudes and feelings about them. The people represent themselves, and the dream tells us something about them that *is* actually true. This can be slightly tricky, because in this case, the unconscious conveys to the dreamer a *perception* of a specific person or external situation that's probably different than the dreamer's conscious viewpoint.

Although in some cases the dream figure may be a person close to us who represents something about ourselves (*subjective* dream), generally we say a dream figure is characterized as *objective* when it appears in the dream as an actual person in an actual relationship with the dreamer.

While there are several different types of objective dreams, most of them deal with our own life issues. Sometimes the people and situations in the dream may involve actual events beyond our own individual lives, perhaps an entire community. However, by far the most common type of objective dream comments on our exterior life and our relationship to it.

What's happening around us?

An objective dream may be like watching a movie of a real situation—the setting and structure are related to what is happening in our immediate environment. When familiar people show up in our dreams, too often we try to make the dream be about them. Most of the time it's not about those people—it's about ourselves!

We can ask, what does the dream suggest about our relationship to the person in our dream? If we dream about our neighbor, our dream probably is calling attention to something in our relationship with them, perhaps an attitude we hold toward them.

Suggested ideas for identifying an objective dream:

1. All details of the dream are virtually the same as in waking life.

2. Person in the dream is an immediate family member.

3. Dreamer is emotionally related to the person in the dream.

4. Dream figure is depicted as it is in waking life.

5. Dreamer is an observer, not participating in the action.

6. Dream simply doesn't fit subjectively.

Taking a subjective approach

When we look at a dream from a *subjective* approach, the dream images/figures refer to objects and events in the *internal* world of the dreamer. The dream refers to *dynamic processes* taking place within the dreamer's own soul—dream images/figures represent some qualities or parts of the dreamer's inner structures held by the image.

Ascertaining subjective vs. objective can be very challenging, especially when we are emotionally related to the person in our dream. Riffel noted that in his 65 years of experience, whenever his wife, Lillie, appeared in his dreams, she represented a feminine part of himself.[i]

Hey, that's part of me!

A dream figure is characterized as subjective when it portrays part of the dreamer's personality, inner dynamics of the soul. Thus a dream image of a particular person taken subjectively means the dreamer possesses (potentially, at least) some characteristic of this person.

Images in a subjective dream are personified aspects of our own personality—the external people, objects or situations characterize our own internal feelings and thinking structure. These images express dramatically how we feel and react to everyday life circumstances, allowing us to experience them, even though we don't recognize them consciously.

I'm like that?!

A subjective dream addresses our inner life and shows us in some exterior form how we are functioning within ourselves. Each part of our dream may represent previously unknown parts of our personality—a part of our life we have not yet discovered. This kind of dream is tough to understand because we are unaware of our blind spots the dream is trying to expose.

Urging us toward wholeness

Recall that a key biblical purpose of a dream is to reveal our innermost thoughts (Dan. 2:30). Recognizing our inner feelings and attitudes personified as figures in our dreams enables us to view them as aspects of ourselves. Understanding dream figures as parts of ourselves increases our personal responsibility.

Recognizing our inner feelings and attitudes personified as figures in our dreams enables us to view them as aspects of ourselves.

Subjective dreams urge us to dig down below the surface to see what's inside, making us function the way we do. This type of dream helps focus issues in our lives on the goal of becoming more whole, integrated people, properly related to God, others and ourselves.

---

[i] Personal communication with Herman Riffel, 2008.

PART FOUR The World Of Dreaming

> **Some ideas for identifying a subjective dream:**
>
> 1. Person in the dream is not emotionally important to the dreamer.
>
> 2. Person in the dream belongs to dreamer's distant past or is a distant relative.
>
> 3. Person in the dream is a famous person.
>
> 4. Person in the dream is depicted differently than in waking life—some distortion occurs.
>
> 5. Person in the dream is a stranger to the dreamer.

Sorting it out

To be thorough, explore your dream both ways, objectively and subjectively. Even though *most* dreams are *subjective*, some dream experts recommend trying on the *objective* approach first.[ii] If you are not sure if a dream is objective, it is best to err on the side of subjectivity.

> *Here is the basic question to ask: Is my dream to be taken inwardly? Or is my dream about real people, real events and real experiences? If it is, I should try an objective interpretation. On the other hand, if my dream is about the real parts of my soul, the inner dynamics of my personality, I should try for a subjective understanding of my dream.*

When we dream about other people, often it's difficult to determine whether they represent themselves (objective) or some part of ourselves (subjective). Since the overwhelming majority of our dream imagery is subjective, it's probably best to take this approach (sometimes difficult because it reveals parts of ourselves of which we may not be aware). Infrequently, a dream can be taken as *both* a comment on our relationship to someone else and as a picture of what is going on within us.

If we think our dream is an objective dream about another person, we should take it to God in prayer for guidance. Generally these dreams shouldn't be told to the other person. Virkler & Virkler suggest this wise bit of guidance: "we do not hear from God about people over whom we have no influence, authority or accountability."[4]

> *Whether a dream should be taken on the subjective or objective level is seldom unambiguously indicated by the dream itself. The decision is much more a question of feeling on the part of the dreamer or of his consultant.*
> *(von Franz)* [5]

God used this next dream to give me (Judith) guidance about how to handle a difficult situation.

---

ii   Robert Johnson suggests the opposite: "Always begin by applying your dream inwardly. Start by assuming that your dream represents an inner dynamic..." (*Inner Work*, p. 68).

Dream Treasure

Cut The Cord

(Judith): I was forming another Woman's Aglow Chapter, when suddenly the Lord spoke into my heart that I was not to be president. I informed the group; however, I stayed very much involved in the picture, even though another president had been chosen. Then I dreamed:

A woman is giving birth to a baby girl at home. I and some women from the Aglow chapter are standing around the bed and assisting in the birth. After the baby is born, I am holding the baby up, but the umbilical cord is still attached to the mother. I realize that the cord needs to be cut, so I ask for scissors and cut the cord, handing the baby back to the mother.

> **Dream Work Tip:**
> The dream enables us to make a connection between our inner spiritual life and the choices we make in the outer life

As I awoke, I knew the message of the dream. Yes, I had given birth to a baby, the Aglow chapter. It was "my baby," but now I had to set it free, let it go. Get out of the way, so the new president could be free to lead. At the same time, I was aware of the "Aha!," the witness in my spirit that this was the right interpretation of the dream's message.

Notice that this dream used people and events from my outer world: The woman in the dream was actually a friend, and she had just given birth to a baby girl at home. But how did I know the dream was not about her, but about me?

One way is to determine if all the details in the dream are exactly like the real life experience. No, they were not. Then we look to see if any of the dream elements provide us with clues. In this dream, it was the Aglow women. From them, I could easily answer the question, "What area of my life is this dream commenting on?"

Dream Treasure

PART FOUR The World Of Dreaming

8. Interactive learning
- [ ] What are the differences between objective and subjective dreams?
- [ ] List the types of objective dreams.
- [ ] What might the death of someone you know in your dream mean to you?
- [ ] Write out the questions you will use to discern the objectivity or subjectivity of dream characters.

> *Lord God, I thank You for the wonderful ways You can reveal truths to me. Give me courage to allow You to show me the thoughts and motives in my heart, and set me free from this fear of knowing myself better.*

Applied Learning

✎ *Your Response*
- ☐ Reflect on the meaning of "soul" and your relationship to your soul.
- ☐ How might the soul appear in dreams?
- ☐ Do opposite-gender figures always represent the soul? Why or why not?
- ☐ Explain why you need to know the witness of the Holy Spirit in your spirit— the "Aha!"—in dream interpretation.
- ☐ Affirm aloud: "God wants to reveal to me new things. I like that!"

✧ *Dream work strategies, skills & techniques*
- ☐ Identify the elements in Gerald's "*Seize The Opportunity*" dream.
- ☐ Identify the types of DREAM FIGURES in this dream. (#1)
- ☐ What is Gerald's DREAM EGO FIGURE doing? (#2)
- ☐ Was Gerald pleased with the choices his DREAM EGO FIGURE made in the dream? (#2)
- ☐ What QUESTIONS would you ask to help Gerald amplify and make personal associations to the elements in his dream: Honeywell, Zurich, terminals, computers? (#3)
- ☐ Could "Honeywell" be a PUN in Gerald's dream? If so, what might it mean? (#4)
- ☐ What QUESTIONS would you ask Gerald to help him discern if his dream is OBJECTIVE or SUBJECTIVE? (#5)

> ▶ *Dream Work Tip:*
> If a dream is long and complicated, try selecting significant factors, just a single scene, or minimize the dream to its essential elements and work with that.

Explaining new dream work strategies, skills & techniques

#1 Identify the types of DREAM FIGURES in your dreams: dream ego, persona, shadow, opposite-gender, the self.

#2 *Follow the* DREAM EGO FIGURE (the I) technique, observing the actions of the figure representing your conscious self, noting what it is doing. How similar are its actions, attitudes, and feelings to you in waking life? Are you pleased with its choices? This technique helps you look at how your ego is functioning in the dream versus how it functions during the day. It also helps you to connect your choices in the day time with what is going on within your soul.

Dream Treasure

#3 Learn the QUESTIONS to ask in amplifying and making personal associations to your dream elements. (See above questions.)

#4 Examine the dream for PUNS; i.e., figurative expressions using words or phrases in such a way as to suggest a completely different meaning; or humorous use of words that sound nearly alike but have a different meaning.

#5 Learn what QUESTIONS to ask to help you discern if dream is OBJECTIVE or SUBJECTIVE.

Practicing your skills

- [ ] Select a dream to work with.
- [ ] List the elements in your dream.
- [ ] Determine the type of FIGURES appearing in your dream. (#1)
- [ ] Follow your DREAM EGO FIGURE (the "I"), noting how its choices compares to your choices in the day. (#2)
- [ ] Use QUESTIONS to help you amplify and make personal associations to the elements you choose to work with. (#3)
- [ ] Examine your dream for PUNS? (#4)
- [ ] Determine if your dream is about your external circumstances (OBJECTIVE) or inner life (SUBJECTIVE). (#5)

Dream Work Terminology

Can you explain the following terms?

- Figurative expressions
- Puns
- Personification
- Projection
- Ego figure
- Persona figure
- Shadow figure
- Opposite-gender figure
- The Self figure
- Objective and subjective dreams
- Inner dynamics

PART FIVE
Unlocking The Meaning of Dreams

Why you will find Part Five helpful

Part Five establishes cardinal rules of dream work that will offers some useful guidelines to enable you to approach your dream work with more confidence. Here you will find some helpful, very practical ways to explore your dreams. We emphasize the importance of engaging your heart in dream work, and encourage you not to forget to use the scriptural principles you learned in Chapter 11.

You will learn the steps of dream exploration and the questions to use in working with your dreams. We offer suggestions on how to choose the technique you feel most comfortable using. You will understand ways to personalize your dream work to fit your style and knowledge.

As you begin to take responsibility for your dream images, you will appreciate that the meaning must come from dreamer. In addition to learning how to identify, amplify, and make personal associations with your dream images, you will gain an appreciation for the benefits of using imaginative techniques for more insight.

PART FIVE Chapters
- Cardinal Rules (Chapter 17)
- First Steps (Chapter 18)
- Exploring The Dream (Chapter 19)
- Strategies & Interpretation Techniques (Chapter 20)

Part Five Unlocking The Meaning Of Dreams

Cardinal Rules

| | 17 |

Give instruction to a wise man, and he will be yet wiser: teach a just man, and he will increase in learning (Prov. 9:9).

Core Concepts
- Most dreams are about you.
- Dreams reveal something you do not know.
- All dreams are not equally valid.
- Repetitive themes indicate importance.
- Take responsibility for your dream images.
- Most dream images come out of your own life.
- Pay attention to details.
- Begin by assuming dream is symbolic.
- Pay attention to intensity of a dream image.
- Make personal associations.
- Be alert to word plays and puns.
- Recognize archetypal figures.
- Dreams may carry meaning for different levels of life.
- Meaning must come from dreamer.

Learning Objectives
At the completion of this chapter, you will be able to:
- ☐ List and describe the cardinal rules of dream work.
- ☐ Recognize your more important dreams.
- ☐ Know what to pay attention to in your dreams.
- ☐ Use the right questions in your dream work.
- ☐ Recognize that dreams may have multiple layers of meaning over time.
- ☐ Explore the meaning of your dreams on five levels.
- ☐ Work with the archetypal figures in your dreams.

Dreams are not intended to be simply passive mechanisms that hand us facts and information—they invite us to become involved with them. In dream work we focus our attention on a particular dream, giving it a conscious, intentional response. Using a variety of strategies and techniques, we interact with the dream material, trying to discover its hidden treasure.

> *If we oversimplify dream interpretation or try to reduce our dreams to pat meanings, their value and vitality will elude us. (Morton Kelsey)*[1]

Dream Treasure

Don't become discouraged with the seemingly tedious process as you begin. Eventually, it becomes quite natural—you know *intuitively* which dreams need your attention and what strategies or techniques to use with them. Remember your experience of learning to ride a bike? Wobbly at first, you were soon calling out confidently, "Look, Mom, no hands!"

> **Dream work or dream interpretation?**
>
> Dream interpretation is usually understood as a process aimed toward interpreting a dream. As the end result of all your work, an interpretation is a summary statement of what the dream means to you as a whole.
>
> Instead of *dream interpretation*, we often use the term *dream work*, because it offers more ways to interact with dreams—including non-interpretive techniques. Putting us in touch with resources other than our ego, *dream work* goes beyond merely intellectual exploration—it facilitates our relationship with God. When we work with a dream, it is important to be aware we may be encountering the living God.

General rule: the dream should not be told to the person of whom we dream.

1. Most dreams are about you

Once we understand how dreams work, we will notice that they speak most often about the events and circumstances of our own life—*our ideas* about ourselves, other people, and the world around us. Whatever we think or feel, even in the depths of our inner being, is materialized in our dreams. Dream researchers tell us that the vast majority of our dreams are about our own concerns and problems.

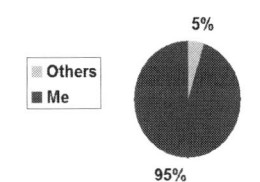

Your dreams are working to helping *you* resolve your conflicts and grow. Even though the dream may be about an external circumstance, its purpose is to help you see how your attitudes and behaviors are impacting your life.

This is the most challenging difficulty in working with our dreams. The dream seems *so* real, it must be about that person. But more than 95% of the time it is not!

Dreams are highly personal, uniquely reflecting the individual dreamer. Begin with the assumption the dream is probably about something you are, or should be, dealing with in your own life right now. Most likely, it is dealing with specific events in your recent experience and your inner response to them.

Who Are My Dreams Concerned With
- Others: 5%
- Me: 95%

> ▶ *Dream Work Tip:*
> To what area of my life is this dream pointing?

Work with dream in context of your life situation

Our dreams must be understood within the context of our own whole life situation. Always consider the timing of the dream and its relationship to what is happening in your life. See Appendix B, *"What Is Your Life Situation?"* to help you reflect upon your life situation.

> **Warning!**
>
> Be careful in thinking that dreams about cities on fire, or dragons coming out of the earth, are prophetic or about end times. Most of the time they are about our inner selves, giving us a mirror as to how we are functioning. War dreams are about an inner enemy, a destructive power at work holding us prisoner.

2. Dreams reveal something you aren't aware of

Dreams don't waste our time; they tell us something we need to know—about ourselves, about our relationships with others, with God, and the world around us. Since most dreams are about ourselves, typically a dream will act as a mirror to reveal how we're functioning deep inside. *This is a fundamental principle of dream work.* The purpose of the dream is to show us something existing within us at the deeper unconscious (heart) level, urging us to open ourselves to the unknown.

A dream can show us what we have not yet been able to verbalize or bring into conscious thought—calling to our attention aspects of our personality we deny or disown. Reassuring thought: dreams usually don't disclose more than we can comfortably handle.

> *Cardinal principle: The dream is trying to show us something existing within us that we are unaware of.*

Cardinal principle: The dream is trying to show us something existing within us that we are unaware of.

This principle applies whether the dream deals with *external events* in our lives or addresses *internal issues*. My (Judith) dream about being in Rome, and my dream portending my Mother's death both revealed important issues of which I was unaware.

Dreams usually don't disclose more than we can comfortably handle.

3. All dreams are not equally valuable

Although all dreams are valuable, certain dreams are *far* more significant. Some dreams are simply "routine maintenance," helping us stay mentally balanced in our personality, centered in living our daily lives (see Chapter 14 *"Classifying Dreams"*). The *most* important dreams are sacred, because they contain divine messages for us from God.

PART FIVE Unlocking The Meaning Of Dreams

> *The more attention we give our dreams, the more they yield valuable information to us.*

Although we believe dreams have a divine origin, they are not all equally noteworthy. Some dreams carry much more consequence than others for our lives. In our experience, the more attention we give our dreams, the more they yield valuable information to us.

More significant dreams can be identified simply because they *feel* important and are so unforgettable. Or perhaps some elements just pop out at you, something about them seems out of place or inappropriate. Okay, bizarre, maybe. Dreams causing you to wake with anxiety, or occurring during periods of stress, anxiety and ambivalence may be more significant.

Sleeping Giant

(Gerald): In a workshop some years back, Judith asked everyone to draw an image of how we see ourselves. I drew a hand saw, sharp, jagged, cutting. When she encouraged us to ask God how he sees us, the image he placed in my imagination was a star, shining brightly (see Phil 2:15). I accept this image in faith, but sometimes it takes a long time for these things to settle deeply into our hearts. God keeps working on me, urging me to greater and greater things. A few years ago God gave me this dream:

A sleeping giant was slumped over the bell in a cathedral bell tower. He slid out of the north side of the tower onto a flatbed truck/trailer. The giant was paraded around the block and returned to the south side of the bell tower. As he returned, I discovered his cloak lying in the bottom of the bell tower. I was going to simply hand the giant his cloak, but a priest off to my left suggested I demand access to the giant in exchange for return of his cloak.

Dream Treasure

Although this is a relatively recent dream, I think it has something to do with my true Self. Incorporated right into our inner being by God is the potential to become a whole, conscious personality, complete according to God's design for our lives—the true Self. I believe this giant represents my potential—asleep, unaware, right in the bell tower pointing toward God. I have discovered his cloak, his mantle of authority.

Dream experts suggest we be particularly alert to dreams that happen at times of significant events, such as marriage, divorce, graduation, job change, major illness, birthdays, anniversaries, holidays, and religious celebrations. Another time to be especially attentive is when we're involved in therapy, or just being extraordinarily attentive to our inner work.

> ▶ *Dream Work Tip:*
> Don't feel compelled to work with every dream—we don't need to understand the meaning of every dream. Allow the Holy Spirit to lead you.

To avoid becoming overwhelmed with too many dreams, choose just one dream or dream element per week to work on. If a dream is long and complicated, try selecting significant factors, just a single scene, or minimize the dream to its essential elements and work with this.

1. Interactive learning

☐ Why do you think Gerald's dream "*Sleeping Giant*" is a significant dream?

4. Repetitive themes indicate importance

Pay special attention when a dream or dream motif keeps showing up. A repetitive dream is usually flagging its importance to us. Some dreams may be repeated because they are prophetic or visionary, vital to God's greater purposes. Other dreams may repeat variations of a theme, because God is patient and waits until we get it.

Repetition may occur because we failed to receive and act on the dream's message the first time it came. Here come the nightmares!

Repeated *themes* between dreams in the same night may indicate these dreams are using different images to get our attention on the *same issue*. Even when multiple dreams in the same night seem unrelated, they may be addressing the same issue—each dream may help explain the others.

> *In Gen. 41, repeating the dream twice to Pharaoh meant that the matter was determined by God, and God would quickly accomplish it.*

Repetition may occur also because we failed to receive and act on the dream's message the first time it came. According to Elihu's advice to Job, God uses a three-step approach to get our attention: first by a "still small voice;" if this fails, we are treated to troubling dreams or nightmares; failing this, the Scripture suggests God may employ more unpleasant methods (Job 33:14-22).

Since one dream can throw light on another dream, it may be helpful to consider your dreams in a series. After you've been logging your dreams for a month or so, review them for any repeating patterns or themes, such as being chased or held

Dream Treasure

captive. Perhaps these recurring themes indicate you have something happening in you that wants to be expressed or needs attention.

5. Take responsibility for your dream images

A dream is highly personal—only you are involved in the process. It's your dream, you created it, and therefore you need to take responsibility for everything in it, even if it makes you uncomfortable. Don't worry if your dream ego does something embarrassing. Your dream ego is simply expressing your inner dynamics in symbolic form so you can see what's going on more clearly.

You do not need to feel guilty over the images in your dreams. When disturbing images appear, it does not mean you are sinning. Do not take them literally, but consider their symbolic meaning using the amplification and association techniques (see Chapter 19).

> *Never accept an interpretation of a dream blaming others or indicating where they need to change.*

Caution

Keep your attention on the dream itself. Don't use your dreams to complain about other family members or to try to change them. It's not about them—it's *about you* and *for you*. The following example is from a cartoon I (Gerald) saw somewhere.

> *A little girl dreams she is walking with her father. As he moves out ahead of her, she can't keep up with him. She awakens crying, and tells her father the dream. Then she chides him, "Next time you're in my dream, you be nicer"!*

6. Most dream images come out of your own life

The symbols in our dreams come out of our own lives, not someone else's. In (OT) Joseph's dream the symbols came from his years as a shepherd.

In my (Judith) dreams, hospitals and nurses have appeared repeatedly because of my years as a nurse. Since I had given birth to babies, neglecting my baby became a signal that I was not nurturing my spiritual self.

In my (Gerald) dreams, the corporate office, computers or a briefcase have been reappearing symbols. Repeated dream themes about not knowing what to do in the office reflected my feelings of inadequacy.

Office For Writer

(Gerald): For a couple years after I left my high tech career, I worked for a Christian camp and conference center, to wind down and get mentally reset. Then I began searching for new direction for my life. Although people had commented favorably on my writing over the years, I had never remotely considered the idea of writing professionally. In this dream...

I was returning to work, and a woman had arranged my office. Two easy chairs, a small table, lamp, desk, windows, a comfy arrangement, but no file cabinets, no places for the usual things I'd worked with when I was in industry. The environment seemed ideal for a writer. As I looked through my work assignments, all "technical" things, I had a sinking feeling. I searched for tasks involving only writing.

Office For Writer

This dream encouraged me toward my next career path—writing. Spurred on by the images in this dream, and greatly energized by Bill Cosby whispering in my ear in another dream, I launched a new career as a technology writer. When my high tech vision for my life was no longer viable, God had graciously given me a new purpose and direction for my life and confirmed it through a dream!

Most dream images and symbols are highly personal, coming out of the context of our own life experience and particular personality. Therefore we need to explore what they mean to us in our inner world. Since we know our own experiences better than anyone else, who can better identify how our dream imagery connects to our present and past life experiences?

Become familiar with your own dream images

Symbols have a capacity to communicate the deepest meaning, depicting what would take hours of abstract talk to describe. Our task is to discover the personal meanings and messages *our own symbols* have for us. We need to become familiar with the language of our dreams and the images they most frequently use. For example, what do airplanes typically mean in your dreams?

Over the years, in my (Judith) dreams, airplane dreams usually signal it's time to schedule another ministry trip to Germany. Clothes often indicate my conflicts in how I present myself to the public.

> ▶ *Dream Work Tip:*
>
> You may want to build your own dream dictionary based upon the symbols and their meaning in your dreams.

What were the images in the cupbearer's dream? A vine, three branches, buds, blossoms, clusters of ripe grapes, and Pharaoh's cup. Did not these images come out of his work with tasting Pharaoh's wine?

7. Pay attention to details

All of the details in a dream are important, serving as clues to the meaning of the dream. Nothing is insignificant, including weather, time of day, lighting, condition of buildings, colors, hair styles, eyes—it's all helpful. As in mystery novels, little hints are embedded in the dream that can lead us to its meaning. Perhaps these clues also suggest when or where the issue that surfaces in the dream first occurred in the dreamer's waking life.[2]

I Can't Go Through With The Wedding

(Gerald): A few months prior to this dream, I had been denied an opportunity to take a job in Europe because I first needed to finish a critical product introduction. As the product launch neared completion, I was offered a terrific job in England. Then I had this dream:

It is ten minutes to seven, I am about to get married, but decide I cannot go through with the wedding. The pastor/priest is vice president of marketing where I work. Scene shifts, the bride and I are sitting on the edge of a bed, and I try to explain why I am canceling on such short notice. She is distraught, openly sexually frustrated. Scene shifts, we are in the bridal chamber, she wants me strongly. She is naked—except for a sanitary napkin.

I sense that the woman represents the very desirable job in England offered to me. Vice president of marketing represents corporate establishment trying to join me to this job. Since my heart was leading me in another direction, I refused the England job, knowing it wasn't right for me—it was the wrong time for this union to be fruitful.

The clock indicating ten minutes to seven—a seemingly small detail in an intense drama—signified it was time to follow God's direction for my life.

2. Interactive learning
- ☐ Why is Gerald's dream related to his job offer?
- ☐ Did his dream offer him divine counsel?

8. Begin by assuming dream is symbolic

Start with the assumption the dream images are symbolic representations of parts of yourself, your inner structures and the independent energy systems moving below your conscious ego. People, animals, and objects in your dreams all represent parts of you, depicting your internal feelings and inner structure. Whatever we think or feel, even in the depths of our inner being, is materialized in our dreams.

Benner observes that, when your father appears in your dream, the dream figure is likely not your external father, but the *internal* father who lives in you. If the figure really *does* represent your external father, the dream is telling you something about your relationship with Him, trying to help you see something about yourself.[3]

To understand a symbolic dream, we must think figuratively, not literally, incorporating the imaginative and intuitive functions of the brain. In symbolic thinking, we are passive; the mind is flooded by images and symbols which evoke association, feeling and emotion.

However, take courage. Our unconscious already knows the meaning of the symbol it has given us in our dream; all we need do is learn to make our personal associations to it.

9. Make personal associations

Pay attention to the associations that come to your mind as you describe the dream or ponder a particular image in it. Key to unraveling the meaning of a dream are your associations, i.e., any word, idea, mental picture, feeling or memory that pops into mind.

Personal associations involve clarifying what an element means to you in your *unique* inner world and connecting it to the dynamics operating within your soul. Be sure you learn how to amplify and make personal associations to your dream images! See Chapter 19 for more clarity on how to do this.

Learn how to amplify and make personal associations to your dream images!

10. Pay attention to intensity of a dream image

Instead of trying to obtain an arbitrary interpretation of a dream symbol, pay attention to its vitality and vividness. Intellectualizing symbolic material reduces its intensity. In dream work, the intensity of our images is more important to us than their precision and clarity!

Dream Treasure

Dreams contain God's divine energy, which can empower, heal, and transform us by creating faith and hope—and energy. Moreover, the images and symbols in our dreams can transform the energy in our unconscious into our conscious life, re-energizing us for everyday living. The more intense the symbols, the more important and urgent the dream message is.

The more intense the symbols, the more important and urgent the dream.

Charged with intense energy, the symbols arouse strong feelings of awe, terror, delight and deep peace, which linger long after we awake. They capture our emotional attention with an intensity that forces our energy into certain paths. Here's an interesting thought: a dream can bring us energy *whether or not we understand the dream at all!*

Dream symbols offer us transformation, precisely because of the divine energy embedded in them. Trying to force an interpretation of a dream analytically causes the symbols to lose intensity, subverting their power to impact your life.

11. Be alert to word plays and puns

Although we take the message seriously, sometimes it takes a sense of humor to decipher dreams, which often use word plays and puns. Looking at your dream imagery, does a word or an object have another completely different meaning? It helps to loosen up a bit and take a light approach when we look at our dreams.

▶ *Dream Work Tip:* When you work with a dream, go to the symbolic imagery that contains the most energy for you.

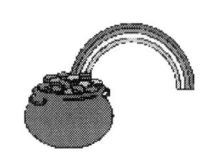

Become familiar with the way you use metaphors and phrases in everyday speech. Even though I've never been in the military, I (Gerald) often used military terms with my family ("come on, troops").

(Gerald) In one of my dreams, when Bill Cosby whispered in my ear what sounded like "Rhodes Scholar," perhaps it was a pun on road scholar. Over the 20-some years since this dream, I have traveled and learned much about living life God's way.

12. Recognize archetypal images

Fundamental to dream work is an understanding of the different archetypal images likely to appear in our dreams. Universal in nature, these dynamic "psychological building blocks of energy" actually join together to create your unique individual soul/psyche.[4]

Archetypal images in our dreams are more concerned with our fate and destiny than with our current circumstances. Presence of archetypal images indicates the possibility of new development, a major change, or transformation of our inner self. Because archetypal dreams enlarge our personality and help us realize our potential, it is important to learn how to recognize their powerful symbolic images. An archetype may appear as a character, animal, bird, object, or activity.

- Archetypal *characters* include giants, wise figures, precocious children, kings and queens, angels, monks, priests, pregnant women, and talking skeletons.
- Archetypal *animals or birds* could be unicorns, mythical animals, brilliantly plumaged birds, talking animals and snakes.
- *Objects* in dreams that could be archetypes: chalice, rainbow, caves, churches, lightning, or church bells.
- *Activities* likely to be archetypal in dreams: marriage ceremony, ocean journey, mountain climbing, treasure hunting, city under siege.

Sometimes common dream symbols can serve an archetypal purpose. Driving a strange vehicle, or discovering a room we didn't know existed in an unknown house, likely means we've entered the realm of the archetype.

An archetypal image in a dream may indicate the necessity for inner transformation, but we cannot make the required changes by our willpower. Rather, we must first *experience the emotion* triggered by the dream images, which provides the energy to cause the changes needed. Then we must *understand the symbolic significance* of the dream images, which is the only way the energy from the emotion can help bring our choices to consciousness.

Instead of being simply one-dimensional beings, we are rich combinations of all the archetypes. Yes, there's a hero inside, but there's also a villain; we are part saint, but also part sinner. It is important for us to acknowledge all these archetypal characters inside us as real parts of ourselves. Johnson notes that as we begin to live out the energy of these archetypes positively, "we make inner work a great pilgrimage of the spirit."[5]

> ➤ *Dream Work Tip:*
> Dream experts suggest we toss out our dream dictionaries, and instead learn all we can about archetypal symbols and motifs. We recommend *Symbols of Transformation in Dreams* by Jean & Wallace Clift (available through online book sellers).

3. Interactive learning
☐ What is the origin of the sleeping giant image in Gerald's dream?
☐ Do you think Gerald's *"Sleeping Giant"* dream is archetypal? Why?

13. Dreams may carry meaning for different levels

Dreams provide access to various levels of the soul, and also to the nature and causes of our individual problems. Thus dreams often are multidimensional, revealing many levels of truth all at the same time. Savary, Berne, and Williams suggest we learn to view dreams and work with them on five levels:[6]

- Personal and attitudinal
- Relational
- Spiritual
- Communal or political
- Universal

Live with the dream over time

The symbolic power of its images may enable a dream's energy to continue for a long time. Moreover, the meaning of a dream may continue to unfold or deepen for many years. In our experience, we have understood some symbolic elements of a dream immediately, but didn't realize other aspects until many years later. If you can't interpret a dream, you may need to live with it for a while.

Several years after I (Judith) dreamed "Cut The Cord" (Chapter 16), I recognized another level of meaning: I was psychologically tied to my internalized mother. My dreams helped me see this: I'm dragging my mother up a hill, pulling her out of a fire, carrying her on my back. My identity was fused with hers. Note that these dreams are about me, not my mother.

14. Meaning must come from the dreamer

Because the dream belongs to the dreamer, each person is the interpreter of their own dreams. By depending upon the Holy Spirit and asking skillful questions, other people can help draw out the meaning of our dream from our own heart. However, *we should never accept ideas for understanding our dream that our heart does not respond to.*

We will intuitively know we have tapped into the energy behind the dream. Symbols are linked to energy deep within us, and when the connection is made, sparks fly. There needs to be an *"Aha!"* moment, an inner click or intuitive knowing, letting us know we are close to the meaning of the dream.

> **Warning!**
> *Never allow anyone else to decide for you what your dream means.*

Our interpretation of the dream should answer the question: What is the central, most important message this dream is trying to communicate to me? What is it advising me to do? What is the overall meaning of the dream for my life?

Most importantly, the interpretation should arouse energy and strong feelings in you. This might be a good way to test the validity of your interpretation—if there is no energy, perhaps it is not the correct interpretation.

Keep in mind that the dream wants to show you something you don't know or are unaware of. The dream comes to nurture your growth, psychologically and spiritually, to expand your possibilities and wake you up to your potential.

You have the final word on what your dream means to you. The only dictionary of correct meanings for your dream symbols is the one you devise over time as you look again and again for patterns of symbols and meanings in your dreams. Don't let anybody else decide for you what your dream means.

Avoid straining for the meaning

Avoid putting yourself under strain to find the meaning of a dream. This is a key principle in God: never put your personality under pressure! Only when we lower our ego energy (humble ourselves) are we able to hear or sense what the Spirit of God is saying.

Sometimes the meaning of our dreams is very obvious the moment we awaken. The dreams are clear-cut, we intuitively know their meaning. However, in most cases we need to work with our dreams, or to allow them to simply rest in our minds, until understanding comes. Admittedly, there are many dreams we do not understand or even care to work with. When we do not understand a dream, we have learned to simply leave it in the hand of God. Nevertheless, the dreams God has given us the grace to understand have enriched our lives at every level.

> ▶ *Dream Work Tip:* Try writing a succinct statement of the central idea that you think the dream is trying to convey to you, and noting whether it arouses any feelings in you.

Lord God, I honor You as the very source of my dreams. I choose to believe that You want to speak to me through them.

Dream Treasure

Applied Learning

✎ *Your Response*
- ☐ Can you list the 14 cardinal rules of dream work?
- ☐ Which rule seems most important to you?
- ☐ How will you recognize your more important dreams?
- ☐ Why will you not accept another person's interpretation without your "*Aha!*"?

✧ *Dream work strategies, skills & techniques*
- ☐ Identify the elements in Gerald's "*Sleeping Giant*" dream.
- ☐ Which element seems to hold more ENERGY for Gerald? (#1)
- ☐ Rate the INTENSITY of the cloak—as if it were your dream. (#2)
- ☐ Draw a sketch of the cloak and meditate on it.
- ☐ Amplify and make personal associations to the sleeping giant and cloak—as if they were in your dream.
- ☐ What does the giant's cloak suggest to you? The sleeping giant?
- ☐ RE-ENTER *Gerald's dream* in order to put on the cloak and awaken the sleeping giant. (#3)
- ☐ Begin a DIALOGUE with the giant, asking him what he wants to say to you. (#4)
- ☐ Sum up what you think the divine purpose of Gerald's dream is.

Explaining new dream work strategies, skills & techniques

#1 When working with a dream, go where the ENERGY takes you, to the symbolic imagery containing the greatest amount of energy for you. Which element contains the most energy for you?

#2 Rate the INTENSITY of a dream element, using a scale of 0 (none) to 10 (maximum).

#3 The RE-ENTER technique asks you to re-enter a dream in order to explore some aspect or element of it.

#4 DIALOGUING with dream characters asks you to use your imagination to begin a conversation with them, allowing them to spontaneously speak to you. (See Chapter 20 to learn how to dialogue with a dream character).

✒ Practicing your skills

- ☐ Select a dream to work with.
- ☐ Identify the main action or activity in your dream.
- ☐ What element holds more ENERGY for you? Feels most compelling? (#1)
- ☐ *Rate the* INTENSITY of the element (#2)
- ☐ Sketch a picture of this element, allowing yourself to feel its ENERGY.
- ☐ What personal recollections does this element bring to mind as you look at the sketch?
- ☐ RE-ENTER *your dream* and explore some aspect of it (#3)
- ☐ Choose a figure to begin a DIALOGUE with. *(#4)*
- ☐ Summarize what you think might be the divine purpose of your dream.

Dream Work Terminology

Can you explain the following terms?
- Repetitive themes
- Archetypal objects
- Archetypal locations
- Archetypal animals
- Dream action/activity
- Dream intensity
- Dream energy
- Re-entering dream
- Dream dialogue

Dream Treasure

Part Five Unlocking The Meaning Of Dreams

First Steps

18

If you seek her as silver, and search for her as for hidden treasures; then you will… discover the knowledge of God (Prov. 2:4,5).

Core Concepts
- Basic steps of dream work.
- Recalling dreams.
- Writing down dreams.
- TTAQ technique.
- Dream journal format.

Learning Objectives
At the completion of this chapter, you will be able to:
- ☐ List and describe six basic steps of dream work.
- ☐ Learn ways to cultivate and recall your dreams.
- ☐ Know what to include when writing down your dream.
- ☐ Be alert to your immediate reaction (R) to your dreams.
- ☐ Apply the TTAQ with confidence.
- ☐ Develop a consistent format for recording your dreams.

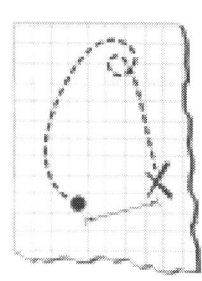

In this chapter, we lead you step-by-step to help you get started with your new adventure of finding God's counsel and wisdom in your dreams. Approach dream work with confidence in God's goodness toward you. He promises to do good for us: "For I know the plans that I have for you, declares the Lord, plans for welfare and not for calamity, to give you a future and a hope" (Jer. 29:11).

> *Dream work is not about playing with a new toy in your Christian living kit, but about a diligent search to find the counsel and wisdom from our living Lord.*

Keep in mind that dream work is not about playing with a new toy in your Christian living kit, nor divining the future, but about a diligent search to find the counsel and wisdom from our living Lord. Enter the treasure hunt with joyous expectation!

Dream Treasure

PART FIVE Unlocking The Meaning Of Dreams

Six Basic Steps

In this first section you will learn the six basic steps of dream work, enabling you to keep a written record of the dreams God gives you.

Step 1—Make a commitment

> *Lord, today I make a decision to seek Your voice and to listen to what You have to say to me through my dreams. I choose to pay attention to my dreams, honoring them as gifts from You.*

The first important step is to *make a decision to take dream work seriously*. We have examined the solid scriptural evidence for dreams as a way God speaks to us, the testimony of the Church Fathers, and the preponderance of historical belief in the value of dreams. Now it's time to make a decision to commit yourself wholeheartedly to listening to your dreams.

Decide that you want and need God's help and direction for your life. One way you will seek it is through a determined effort to find His voice in dreams.

> *Step 1—Making a commitment*
> ☐ Write down reasons for making a commitment to listen to your dreams.
> ☐ Affirm aloud, "I choose to attend to my dreams, honoring them as gifts from God."

Step 2—Cultivate dreams

There are some very practical ways we can prepare ourselves to hear God's voice in our dreams. For starters, get a good night's sleep. Set a go-to-bed time and a wake-up time—this seems to encourage more dream recall.

Also, don't set an alarm—at least on weekends. Alarms shatter dream recall. Train yourself to recall a dream when the alarm goes off by making positive affirmations, such as: "When the alarm goes off, I will remember my dreams and record them."

Share your hopes with someone—your spouse or roommate—that you may have a dream tonight. If you live alone, reflect back over any dreams you remember from the past, or meditate on the importance of dreams to you.

> *Ho everyone who thirsts, come to the waters…incline your ear and come to me, listen that you may live (Is 55: 1-3).*

Do something to take your thoughts away from life in the fast lane. Shift to a more reflective posture, perhaps by listening to soft, contemplative music—anything that promotes a peaceful reflective atmosphere. Read a meaningful novel or poem, allowing you to get in touch with its symbolic expression.

As you fall asleep, tell the Lord that you believe He wants to speak to you through your dreams, and you are listening. This act signals your heart that you are earnest and serious about your dream work.

Dream Treasure

Chapter 18 First Steps

Speak Lord, for Thy servant is listening (I Samuel 3:9).

We have cultivated our readiness many times to receive dreams from God. We simply tell God at bedtime we are ready and willing to hear from Him in our dreams. Sometimes God speaks, sometimes He doesn't. Sometimes we hear when He speaks, sometimes we don't. The important thing is to be ready.

> *In the Scriptures, God's people believed God might answer them through their dreams. In one instance, King Saul first inquired of the Lord via dreams, Urim, and the prophets. When he could not sense God's guidance in dreams or by the prophets, he concluded (rightly) that God had departed from him and did not answer him anymore (I Sam 28:6,15).*

Step 2—Cultivating dreams
- ☐ Before going to bed, listen to meditative music or read a psalm, novel, or poem for a half hour.
- ☐ Meditate on a dream like Solomon's (I Kings 3:5-28) or Jacob's (Gen. 28:11-15).
- ☐ Carry out a meaningful custom that you choose to associate with dreaming—such as turn on a special night light or meditate on a religious painting.
- ☐ Speak aloud: "I believe God wants to speak to me through dreams."
- ☐ Place your dedicated dream journal or audio recorder near your bed.

> *Lord, I need to hear Your voice—I cannot live on bread alone. I am open to You speaking to me in my dreams tonight, and I look to You to bring them to my mind in the morning. Thank You.*

Step 3—Remember your dreams

You've seen those whimsical "dream catchers" in novelty stores? Wispy little nets, wouldn't hold a butterfly. Dreams are elusive, otherworldly, difficult to grab from the ether.

When you first awaken in the morning, *wait to see if the Lord communicated with you while you slept.* Cultivate the habit of asking the Lord if He spoke to you during the night, and to bring it to your remembrance.

Here's a suggested approach: As you come out of your sleep, don't allow yourself to become fully alert—don't open your eyes, don't even move. Cast your thoughts back over the night, lingering to see if the memory of a dream begins to float into your consciousness. If a dream memory surfaces, thank the Lord, then get up immediately and log it. "You snooze, you lose" certainly applies here. Even if only a small fragment floats into your consciousness, latch onto it! More pieces will probably come as you write.

Not dreaming?

If you can't remember your dreams, use your journal to explore why. Write out the following questions: "Lord why don't I recall my dreams? Is there something wrong

> ▶ *Dream Work Tip:*
> If you can't get up during the night to record a dream, repeat it to yourself a few times before going back to sleep, to anchor the dream in your memory.

Dream Treasure

245

with my life that I am refusing to face? Am I holding back something I am afraid to look at? Do I want to stay passive, letting others hear You for my life?" Then listen inside, and begin to write down the thoughts coming to you.

Step 3—Remembering dreams

- ☐ Try writing a question in your journal you'd like God to answer that night.
- ☐ When you awake, before allowing your mind to move forward into the coming day, linger in the twilight zone between night and day. Wait on the Lord to see if a dream comes to mind.
- ☐ Practice recalling your dreams upon awakening—or as you're drinking coffee.
- ☐ If you can't recall a dream, ask, "Lord, why am I unable to remember my dreams?" Listen for His answer, and write out the thoughts that flow into your mind in response.
- ☐ If you don't remember dreams at all, try recording the mood or feeling you have when you awaken— often these are the result of our dreams.
- ☐ Don't place too much pressure on yourself to remember your dreams. Trust God!

> *Lord, remove any barrier keeping me from recalling my dreams. I confess I have been afraid of listening to my dreams. I ask You to forgive me for this.*

Step 4—Write down your dreams

As soon as possible, write a detailed description of your dream (see Ch. 11, *Biblical Guidelines,* for explanation of why we write down dreams.) Early in our dream odyssey we learned that we need to write down our dreams. Dream experts recommend this, so we did it. We both have piles of books stuffed with dreams we've journaled. Based on our experience, we suggest buying a good journal or a spiral notebook in which to record your nighttime visions.

Nuts & bolts of recording dreams

Assuming you're convinced of the value of logging your dreams, here are some ideas for how to go about it. You can capture your dream in a number of ways. One method is to record the dream simply, just capture the essence, and go back later to write the details. If you're late to catch the commuter train or the kids are yelling for breakfast, this can work.

> *A U.S. Navy dream research lab in San Diego found that 95% of dreams not written down or told within five minutes are forgotten.*

Write without evaluating

If at all possible, write a detailed description of your dream as soon as you've got on your robe and slippers. Experts suggest using a narrative, non judgmental, reporting style, writing it quickly without correcting grammar and punctuation. Write down every detail you can remember—this record becomes your data for subsequent dream work. However, be careful not to evaluate the dream, try to understand its meaning, or interpret it as you write.

Simply recording the dream will make it grow more vivid, and help you to remember more details. Think of it like fishing—just pull on the line and see what you reel in.

Present tense is helpful

Try reporting the dream in the present tense as if it is happening *now*—in the moment. It makes the dream come more alive, and helps you access the feelings and energy in the story. For example, past tense is like this: *I was swimming. I saw a shark. People were yelling, "help." I felt guilty.* Present tense is like this: *I am swimming. I see a shark. People are yelling, "help." I feel guilty.* See the difference?

Every detail is important

Describe the dream in detail, not only visual, but the other sense impressions as well. Every detail offers us clues as to the message of the dream. Here are some elements for you to take note of when writing down your dreams:

- **Setting**—the elements that set the stage for the drama; location, scenery, season, time, weather, environment, etc.
- **Buildings**— rooms, floors, elevators, stairs.
- **Characters**—people who appear in dream; how many; appearance, gender, age, posture, hair, clothing, etc.
- **Dream ego**—if you are in the dream, what are you doing, feeling, wearing, or saying. Are you active, passive, observer?
- **Wildlife**—animals, birds, fish, reptiles; number, what they look like.
- **Objects and other elements**—how many, what they looked like, anything unusual about them.
- **Vehicles**—types, movement, color; who is driving; where you are in vehicle.
- **Emotions and mood**—emotional feelings; what people or animals are feeling, sensing.
- **Physical sensations**—smells, sounds, tastes, textures, colors, movements.
- **Action**—choices, movement; what people or animals are doing or choosing.
- **Spoken or unspoken words**—any dialogue, thoughts, statements, conversations of any character, animal or object.

> ▶ *Dream Work Tip:*
> Use loose paper or speak into a recorder for your first draft of the dream, and then transfer later to your dream journal—perhaps when you're fully awake.

PART FIVE Unlocking The Meaning Of Dreams

Step 4—Writing dreams down
☐ Choose a dedicated place in which to sit and record your dreams.
☐ Write out a detailed description of your dream in your dream journal.
☐ Did you include all the elements listed above?
☐ Did you avoid editing or trying to understand your dream?
☐ What tense (past/present) did you use?
☐ If you don't have time to write down the entire dream, write down the highlights or draw a rough sketch of the dream.
☐ Take a few minutes simply to think about your dream, just *feel* it. This brief attention honors the giver of the dream, and allows time for additional meaning to pass through your mind.

Step 5—Note your immediate reaction (R) to dream

Next, log your immediate *reaction* to the dream as you awoke. Your reactions might offer you clues as to the meaning of the dream. What impression did it make on you as you awoke? What feelings were still present in you? What mood were you in? Invigorated? Exhausted? Tense? Relaxed? What thoughts came to you?

Note if the dream immediately brought to mind memories, recollections, or associations. Have you been in this place before? Have you seen any of the dream images recently in your waking life?

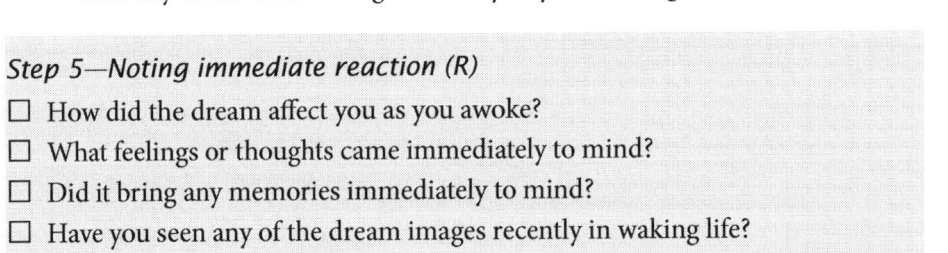

Step 5—Noting immediate reaction (R)
☐ How did the dream affect you as you awoke?
☐ What feelings or thoughts came immediately to mind?
☐ Did it bring any memories immediately to mind?
☐ Have you seen any of the dream images recently in waking life?

Step 6—Log your current concerns (CC)

How does the dream relate to your *recent* life experiences? This step is an absolutely vital link to understanding the message of your dream. We can't stress this enough. People come to us for help with a dream they had weeks, months, even years ago, but they have no idea what their hearts were struggling with at that time. Remember this key fundamental in dream interpretation: *most dreams speak to us about the things important to our hearts.*

Write down what was going on in your life in the days before the dream—life events, circumstances, decisions, conflicts, crises, and problems you encountered.

Dream Treasure

What are the concerns or questions your heart is struggling with? What prayers are you praying? What issue or question is your heart concerned with? Do any aspects of your current concerns connect to your dream imagery?

Step 6—Logging my current concerns (CC)
- [ ] Write out what is happening in your life at the moment.
- [ ] What current concerns (CC)—problems, prayers, or issues press on your heart?
- [ ] What decisions need to be made? What questions are you asking?
- [ ] Anything upset you or worry you? Any recent traumas or illnesses?
- [ ] How do you think the dream might relate to your current life situation?

Use The TTAQ Technique

Congratulations! You have completed the basic steps of dream work. Now we urge you to use the *one* dream work technique we find most helpful: the TTAQ, which is short for Title, Theme, Affect, Question. Our personal experience shows that merely recording our dreams and using this technique provides significant insight into our dreams. We suggest using the invaluable TTAQ right after recording your dream. Described in the book, *Dreams And Spiritual Growth*,[1] this technique consists of the following four tasks:

1: Title (T)—give dream a title

Most dream experts suggest you give the dream a title as soon as you record it. Titling not only helps you identify the dream in your journal, but it also can give you keys to unraveling the mysteries of the dream. As with all dream work, we encourage you to ask the Lord for His thoughts.

Here are suggestions to help you establish a title. Try asking the dream: "Dream, by what name or title do you wish to be addressed?" This approach takes the pressure off your overworked left brain. Pretend you're an artist and you want to title your freshly hung painting. Or imagine you just wrote a short story that needs a title.

Another idea is to choose a title capturing the single most unusual element of the dream. If there is a specific message or key statement in the dream, you can turn this into your title. Since titling the dream seems difficult for some people, you may prefer to title it *after* you have determined its theme.

1: Giving my dream a title (T)
- ☐ Ask the dream what title it wants.
- ☐ Sketch the dream in your journal. Ask the drawing what title it wants to have.
- ☐ Ask the Lord for His thoughts on titling the dream.

2: Theme (T)—determine theme of dream

Usually the main issue, conflict, or problem is quite clear. If not, try answering the question, "What is this dream mainly about?" "What is the key issue the dream is addressing?" Examples of themes might include: reading a book, taking a test, making a meal, feeling lost, climbing a hill, losing teeth, missing a bus/plane, preaching a sermon, forgetting something, or losing something.

If several themes seem to be involved, note all of them, prioritizing and emphasizing the most important ones. Now try to determine if one theme or motif dominates the dream. If so, you have a clue as to what meaning the dream is trying to convey to you. For a particularly complex dream, separate the pieces and identify the main issue in each one.

2: Determining dream theme (T)
- ☐ What theme runs through the dream?
- ☐ What is the main issue the dream addresses?
- ☐ State briefly the basic theme, noting the key issue it triggers in you.

3: Affect (A)—identify affect in dream

Often the feeling factor is the most important clue in our discovery process.

Next, determine the primary emotion or basic feeling in the dream. We find this very valuable—often the feeling factor is the most important clue in our discovery process.

What are the dominant feelings, emotional responses, and moods experienced in the dream? What did you feel about what was happening in the dream? Does the behavior of the other characters suggest what feelings they may be experiencing? Is anyone glad, sad, mad, afraid, or loving?

3: Identifying dream affect (A)
- ☐ Identify the different emotions expressed in the dream.
- ☐ Determine the one that feels the strongest or most dominant.

4: Question (Q)—discern question dream asks

This step asks you to consider the dream as if it brings you a question from God, not an answer. Approaching the dream as if it contains a question shifts the focus off ourselves and directs our attention toward God. We begin to relate to the Source of our dream. God never violates our choice, He is not a dictator. He more often asks questions of us than He gives us answers.

Dreams can be viewed as inviting our engagement, rather than a form of passive communication simply presenting information. Try approaching the dream as if it were a friend bringing you a question. "Hey, Joe, what do you think I should be reflecting on or considering?"

4: Discerning dream question (Q)
- ☐ Lord, what question are you asking me in this dream?
- ☐ Discern possible questions; choose the most compelling one.

Develop A Dream Journal Format

Finally, you will want to develop your personal format for chronicling your dreams. Using a consistent format makes it easier to go back and find things in the future. We suggest you include the items listed in the following exercise.

Develop a consistent format
- Date: write the date in the same place.
- Dream entry number: number consecutively.
- Dream description: write down everything you can remember about the dream.
- R (Your Reaction): your reactions and thoughts upon awakening.
- CC (Current Concerns): what's going on in your life, issues, concerns, prayers?
- T (Title): select a title and write it at the top of entry.
- T (Theme): state the basic theme in one sentence.
- A (Affect): identify the dominant feeling/emotion expressed in dream.
- Q (Question): Log question the dream may be asking you.

Example of how to chronicle dreams

Here is an example of how I (Judith) logged a dream and used the TTAQ technique *directly* in my journal.

You've Got A Good Thing Going Here March 23, 2006

I am in my house. A small group of women are staying with me for a couple of days. They mill around in my dining room, waiting to eat. The meat is already prepared, on a platter on the table. I am in the kitchen hurriedly trying to prepare the rest of the meal, because they can't seem to wait any longer. They begin to pick at the meat hungrily. I tell them to wait, because "I am not ready yet." I am trying to hold them off. I say to my guests, "Perhaps you would like to stay another night." I seem to enjoy having them here, however, I feel a bit pressured to complete my meal preparation.

Early evening, I step out of the front door and stand on the steps. My house feels like it is at the end of a cul-de-sac or in some type of courtyard. An unknown man looks up at me and says, "You have got a good thing going here." I nod in agreement. But I have a question in my mind, "Do I need to have official approval (permit/license) to have these guests in my home?"

R: When I awoke, I felt excited. I felt the man at the bottom of the steps was bringing me a message from God. The house reminds me of a lovely Victorian we once redid and sold to a retired couple who turned it into a Bed & Breakfast.

CC: I am at a pivotal point in my life. I feel unsure of what I want to do, now that I have my MSW degree. Old ways are gone, but I do not know the next step into the new. I have been asking the Lord to show me the direction to take and to clarify ideas I hold, even though I don't feel ready for the next step. I have many questions. The last few years in grad school have been rough. I wonder if I have energy for the future. My age and my stamina concern me. Reviewing my journal from 3/06/06, I had written, "Lord, I need a new vision for my life."

T: "You've Got A Good Thing Going Here"

T: Trying to finish my meal preparation

A: Pressure, anxiety, concern

Q: "Are you willing to feed my sheep?"

> *Lord, I ask You to give me Your Spirit of wisdom and knowledge as I learn to work with my dreams. Thank You.*

Dream Treasure

Applied Learning

✎ *Your Response*
- ☐ Are you recording your dreams? Yes/No
- ☐ What do you find difficult about writing your dreams down?
- ☐ Affirm: "I like logging my dreams. I do it for me."

☼ *Dream work strategies, skills & techniques*
- ☐ Identify the dream elements in Judith's *"You've Got A Good Thing Going. Here"*
- ☐ Identify the MAIN ACTION or activity in her dream. What is she doing in it? (#1)
- ☐ Where in her life is she doing, or about to do, this ACTION or activity? (#2)
- ☐ What type of figure is the unknown man?
- ☐ How does meat differ from the other food she wants to prepare?
- ☐ Is there a key statement in her dream? A BECAUSE FACTOR?
- ☐ Is there a relationship between her dream, current concerns & prayers?
- ☐ What is the treasure contained for Judith in her dream?

Explaining new dream work strategies, skills & techniques
#1 Identify the MAIN ACTION or activity taking place in the dream.
#2 When or where are you DOING this activity in your outer life?

Dream Treasure

PART FIVE   Unlocking The Meaning Of Dreams

☙ Practicing your skills

- ☐ Practice using the above steps to record your dreams.
- ☐ Are you using a consistent format style in recording your dreams?
- ☐ What tense do you prefer to use? Why?
- ☐ When logging dreams, *always* note your current concerns.
- ☐ Use the TTAQ after recording your dream.
- ☐ Identify the MAIN ACTION or activity in your dream. (#1)
- ☐ Where are you DOING this ACTION/ACTIVITY, or about to do it, in your life? (#2)
- ☐ Summarize what God may be trying to say to you in your dream.
- ☐ What treasure might your dream contain for you?

Dream Work Terminology

Can you explain the following terms?

- Recalling dreams
- Recording dreams
- Your reaction (R)
- Dream journal format
- Dream action or activity

Dream Treasure

Exploring The Dream

19

It is the glory of God to conceal a matter, but the glory of Kings is to search out a matter (Prov. 25:2).

Core Concepts
- Five steps for exploring a dream.
- Identifying dream elements/images.
- Amplifying elements/images.
- Making personal associations.
- Connecting the elements to your inner life.
- Summarizing meaning of dream.

Learning Objectives
At the completion of this chapter, you will be able to:
- ☐ List and describe the five steps of dream exploration.
- ☐ Explain the goal of amplification.
- ☐ Amplify and make personal associations to your dream elements/images.
- ☐ Know how to connect the dream element/image to your inner life.
- ☐ Learn the questions to use in exploring your dreams.
- ☐ Sum up the meaning of your dreams.

We explore the dream for the purpose of drawing out its meaning and connecting with God's divine purpose in it. By interacting with its symbolic imagery, we enter into a kind of dialogue with God that allows the images to spring spontaneously alive with meaning for our lives. As our heart is touched, an *"Aha!"* may bring a sudden quickening, a *knowing*, that releases an overflowing emotion, welling up in our eyes as tears.

In this chapter, we will show you how to explore your dream using a series of questions and dream work techniques. The goal is to find out what the element means to you symbolically and then connect it to your inner life. To explore your dream you will work through the following five steps:

Step 1—Identify dream elements.
Step 2—Amplify a dream element, describing its characteristics and functions.
Step 3—Make personal associations to an element.
Step 4—Connect the dream element to your inner life.
Step 5— Summarize the meaning of the dream.

> Use the *Dream Exploration Guide* in Appendix G as a tool to help you explore your dreams.

PART FIVE Unlocking The Meaning Of Dreams

Step 1—Identify dream elements

Before working with the dream symbolically, identify the specific elements/images already apparent in the dream—all *distinguishable* features. This will give you a clear understanding of the exact details of the dream; even the tiniest detail offers clues about the area of your life the dream is commenting on. Use the following twelve categories to help you identify the different elements in your dream.

> ▶ *Dream Work Tip:*
> The setting may symbolize particular moods, certain time periods, or inner states of mind.

1. The dream setting

Typically the first part of a dream sets the stage on which the dream characters appear and events unfold, providing the *setting* for the theme or issue on which the dream wants to focus your attention. This initial part includes scenery, location, time, and weather forming the environment in which the story plays out. According to Mark O'Connell et al., the setting not only forms the backdrop for the dream action, but also it's an integral part of the content of the dream and its message.[1]

2. Buildings, houses

Identify any buildings, houses, rooms, floors, elevators, stairs, colors, and describe their appearances and conditions. Are they known or unknown to you?

O'Connell et al. note that the most common dream setting is in a building, typically a domestic place, such as a living room, kitchen, or bedroom. Houses, especially unknown ones, usually represent our inner self. If the house is known, then it probably has a different meaning, perhaps our relationship with people in it at that time or what we learned or experienced in the house.

Typically large public buildings—churches or hospitals—represent the functions for which they are used. Churches may refer to our relationship to organized religion, to God, to our religious beliefs, or to our inner sanctum.

3. People, characters, figures

Identify who the people or characters are in the dream. Describe their appearance. Unfamiliar or familiar? Any helper figures, celebrity guest stars, casual acquaintances, uniformed or composite figures? Can you identify any archetypal characters? Who do you think is the central or most important figure in the dream? Dream research indicates that strangers appear more often than family and friends, and typically three characters appear in a dream.[2] If you are in the dream, what are you doing, feeling, wearing, or saying?

4. Wildlife—animals, birds, marine life, reptiles

Identify and describe any wildlife. Any composite animals, or animals which changed to another animal during the dream? For example, a wild lion roaring viciously suddenly becomes a ferocious bear.

5. Objects

Identify any objects or decorations—size, color, age, location, condition.

6. Vehicles and transportation

Identify and describe any vehicles in the dream—cars, buses, trains, airplanes, boats, bicycles, ships, etc. Note its condition, color, age. Who is driving, where you are in vehicle?

7. Action, activity, role, movement

Identify the main action or overall activity in the dream. Describe what people or figures are doing—searching, running, escaping, flying, traveling, sleeping, eating, following, fixing, or driving? If there is a series of actions, identify all of them.

What exactly are you doing—your primary activity? The most prominent actions in dreams are running or walking, followed by talking, sitting, socializing and playing.[3] Identify other types of movement, such as blowing wind, rushing waters, swirling clouds, exploding fire, or growing plants.

What role did you or the principal character play?
Are you a nurse, mother, father, engineer, programmer, salesperson, teacher, advisor, victim, etc.? What roles do the other characters play? Is anyone wearing a uniform?

Are you active or passive in the dream?
Do you take a leading role or are you passively observing what is happening?

8. Feelings, emotions, physical sensations

Similar to the TTAQ, identify the feelings and emotions experienced or expressed in dream. This helps to make clear the major feeling area the dream is dealing with—sad, mad, glad, fear, and love. The feelings and actions of the dream may help you clarify the area of your life it is about. O'Connell, et al. say that apprehension and anger are the most common dream emotions, followed by happiness and excitement.[4]

What you are feeling in the dream? Some people have trouble recognizing their own emotions. If this is you, try asking someone else to help you identify an emotion. Common feelings include the following: helpless, rejected, abandoned, powerless, rage, angry, embarrassed, shamed, guilty, remorseful, grieved, terrorized, sad, envious, fearful, anxious, resentful, surprised, joyful, pleasured, relaxed, tense, excited, or curious.

Don't ignore the physical feelings. Identify and describe any physical sensations experienced in the dream: physical pain, tired, exhausted, cold, at ease, or hungry.

9. Spoken or unspoken words, thoughts

Sift through the dream, identifying spoken and unspoken words, thoughts, impressions, phrases, or statements. Who says or thinks the words or expresses the thoughts? Do *you* say or think anything?

Key statement
Is there any one particular statement that stands out more than the others?

10. Dream theme—issue, plot, problem

Similar to TTAQ, describe the basic theme in a brief sentence, noting the key issue it triggers in you. What motifs are introduced? How does the dream present an issue for you to consider? Identify what the dream is trying to make you aware of, get your attention to consider.

11. Identify any *because* factors

The third part of a dream typically contains a "because" factor. In many dreams, something happens, or fails to happen, *because* of something. Something appears, or fails to appear, *because* of something. Identifying the "because" factor will give you important clues about the nature of the problem in the dream and its possible solution.

> ▶ *Dream Work Tip:*
>
> Identifying the "because" factor will give you important clues about the nature of the problem in the dream and its possible solution.

12. Identify if problem or issue was resolved

Typically the last part of the dream conveys the solution. Was the problem or issue in your dream left unresolved? Is there unfinished business in the dream, or something you would like to know more about? Does the dream identify conflicts or inconsistencies not dealt with in the dream?

Step 2—Amplify dream elements

After identifying your dream elements/images, you are ready to choose one you want to "*amplify,*" i.e., to clarify what you *already know* about it. Amplification asks you to describe an element and clarify its objective connotation to you. The goal is to shed light on the dream and create a larger warehouse of information from which the insight or "Aha!" may emerge.

Amplification asks you to describe an element and clarify its objective connotation to you.

Describe its chief characteristics and functions

This is a more logical, left brain function, where you will identify the typical characteristics and functions of each element you choose to work with. Before you bias your thinking by doing subjective associations, explore the main characteristics and functions of each element using the following questions.

- Review your list of elements, and choose the one you want to *amplify*.
- Describe its chief characteristics: What/who does it look like? What are its characteristics? How does it differ from others? Explain it to someone who has never seen it.
- Describe its chief function: What is its purpose? How is it used? Why does it exist?

> *Interactive learning*
>
> ☐ Practice putting meaning on the things around you. What does this *mean* to me?

Step 3—Make personal associations

Now you are ready to work with the element/image symbolically by *making personal associations* to it. This answers the question: "What does this remind *you* of?" or "What comes to mind when *you* think of it?" This helps to clarify what the element *means* to you in your *unique* inner world.

Remember what it is like to look through a stack of old pictures or your old school yearbook? As your mind drifts through past experiences, memories and feelings keep coming to your awareness. This is similar to what we do in making associations to a dream image. We allow the subjective part of our mind to freely take us to other associations as we think of them. Spontaneous thoughts, feelings, sensations, intuitions, and memories simply bubble up into our awareness as we reflect on, or relate to, the dream element.

All that's needed is a willingness to "let oneself go." Go through the dream, and write out every personal association you have with each element. Then note how intense your emotional response is to each symbol. This is key!

Note that making personal associations differs radically from the Freudian technique of free association (not commonly used today).

> *Dreams are created out of energy…go where the energy is—go to the association that brings up a surge of energy.*[5]

Alert for the "Aha!"

Continue to associate, until you experience a resonance or "Aha!" within you. You are looking for an inner click or intuitive knowing. Because symbols are linked to energy deep within us, we can feel the sparks fly when the connection is made. We experience a subtle—and sometimes not so subtle—shift in mood. Karen Signell says, "We can feel the change in our bodies: a release of tension, surprise, amusement, laughter, or crying. To find out something you didn't know before, even if it's negative, usually brings a flow of life and energy."[6]

Step 4—Connect dream element to inner life

If the dream is subjective, we need to consider how a dream element/image connects to what is going on inside us—to relate the element to some behavior, personality trait, emotion, value, attitude, potentiality, strength, gift, or capacity we have within us. We ask ourselves: When do I behave like this? In what situations am I like this? What part of me has this capacity, potential, quality?

For example, in my (Gerald) dream, "Last of The Big Bruisers," I might ask, "When am I like this NBA player?" In "Back Door Counselor," I could ask "Where can I find this therapist potential within me?"

> ▸ *Dream Work Tip:*
>
> Since most of your dreams are about you, first try to see if the person represents some part of you.

We also need to consider what to do with the information we gained. How will we apply the insights to our daily life? What actions do we need to take?

Step 5—Summarize the meaning of the dream

The final step in exploring a dream asks us to sum up its possible *meaning*, its interpretation or the message it has for us. Before summing it up, review the following

Dream Treasure

considerations: your life situation, your current concerns; objective or subjective; and dream purpose. Use the questions in the *Dream Exploration Guide* in Appendix G to guide you through this step.

1. Consider your life situation – current concerns

All dreams need to be considered within the *context* of our life—the circumstances of our current situation (some dream experts refer to this as the *background* to the dream, others the *environment* of the dream). What is going on in our lives around the time of the dream, what's *happening* in our life at that moment—significant events, concerns, decisions, conflicts, crises, circumstances, challenges?

Prayers?

We firmly convinced God uses our dreams to bring us answers to our prayers. The dream comes in response to the issues and concerns our hearts are struggling with. Consider the problems you need help with, the prayers you have been praying, the concerns your heart carries.

2. Consider if dream figure is objective or subjective

Here you are being asked to determine if the dream is objective—about real people, real events and outer experiences. Or is it subjective—about the real parts of your soul, the inner figures in your personality. (Sorry, it might be both!). This is discussed in detail in Chapter 16, *Dream Dynamics*.

Ascertaining this can be very challenging, especially when we are emotionally related to the person in our dream. For example, if your wife appears in your dream, is it about her and your relationship with her, or is it about a feminine part of yourself? Because there is often a lack of clarity, you must rely on the witness of the Holy Spirit.

Write out a clear statement of what you think God is trying to say to you in your dream.

3. Consider its biblical purpose

Another helpful strategy is to consider the dream in the context of its biblical purpose (see Chapter 10, *Biblical Purposes of Dreams*). What do you think the purpose of your dream is? Keep in mind that a dream may be rich with meaning on several levels.

4. Summarize what God is saying to you in your dream

Consider the information you have gathered, reflecting on how it relates to your life, and then summarize your considerations by writing them down—allowing the insights to flow. Write out a clear statement of what you think God is trying to say to you in your dream. Include any final insights you felt during this process.

The simplest, shortest interpretations are often the best ones. Probably we're closest to the right understanding when we can condense the meaning of the dream into a single statement.

5. Test the interpretation

Test your *interpretation* against biblical principles. Always ask the Lord for substantiation—He promises to confirm every word He speaks to us. If your interpretation involves major life decisions, we strongly suggest you discuss your dream with spiritually-sensitive friends. If you think the dream is about future events in our nation, submit it to recognized Christian leaders for their viewpoint.

> *Lord, bless me with spiritual discernment as I test the interpretation of my dreams.*

> ▶ *Dream Work Tip:*
> Don't try to force understanding—let the meaning come to you.

Use the following dream for the Applied Learning exercises on the next page.

People Are Hungry To Learn About Dreams

(Gerald): Leading up to this dream, I had been thinking a lot about the topic of dreams. While editing our dreams book, I had been reflecting on how a pastor recently told us he did not understand his dreams. Even though I have worked with Judith many times, helping people find what God is saying to them in their dreams, I felt inadequate to address dreams in a public venue.

In a public place, seeming like a city square, a woman asked me about her dream. A few people (mostly women) gathered round as I wrote things on a whiteboard about the dream. I started to tell the woman her dream meant encouragement, but I stopped in mid-sentence, and instead told her that the meaning of the dream had to come from her. Off to my right, another woman seemed upset because I did not explain what this dream meant; instead I asked questions of the dreamer to help her draw out the meaning of her dream herself. As I further discussed dreams, the crowd on my right swelled to perhaps 50 or more people, most of them men.

I awoke in the night sensing this was a powerful dream! It was an energizing, life-giving experience for me, teaching those people about dreams. It feels deep, full of spiritual and psychological energy to thrust me forward. It is an encouragement to me to continue learning and writing about dreams, perhaps do more in the public arena with dreams.

Dream Treasure

PART FIVE Unlocking The Meaning Of Dreams

Applied Learning

✎ *Your Response*
- ☐ Which step seems most difficult for you? Why?
- ☐ Clarify the difference between dream *setting* and the *context* or *current concerns* of your life situation.
- ☐ Affirm, "I am beginning to get the hang of this dream stuff!"

☼ *Dream work strategies, skills & techniques*
- ☐ Use the TTAQ technique with Gerald's "*People Are Hungry To Learn About Dreams*"—as if it were your dream.
- ☐ Explore Gerald's dream as if it were your dream, using Appendix G, *Dream Exploration Guide*.
- ☐ Write a clear statement of what you think God is trying to say to you if this were your dream.
- ☐ What you have gained from the dreams we shared in this book?

✍ *Practicing your skills*
- ☐ Use the *Dream Exploration Guide* (Appendix G) to help you explore a dream.
- ☐ Did you experience an "Aha!" or moment of insight or revelation?
- ☐ How will you apply this insight in your life?
- ☐ Did you test your interpretation of the dream?

Dream Work Terminology

Can you explain the following terms?
- Dream exploration
- Amplifying dream elements
- Making personal association to elements
- Connecting dream images
- Summarizing dream message

Dream Treasure

Strategies & Interpretation Techniques

20

An uninterpreted dream is like an unopened letter from God (The Talmud).

Core Concepts
- Eleven non-interpretive dream work strategies.
- Five imaginative dream interpretation techniques.
- Seven symbolic dream interpretation techniques.

Learning Objectives
At the completion of this chapter, you will be able to:
- ☐ Discuss three major types of dream work strategies & techniques.
- ☐ List and describe eleven non-interpretive strategies.
- ☐ Explain why it is important to engage your heart in dream work.
- ☐ Discuss the benefits of using imaginative techniques.
- ☐ Learn ways to work symbolically with your dream images.
- ☐ Choose the most appropriate technique/s for a specific dream.

A Christian faith approach to dreams views them as a manifestation of God's grace. We begin our journey to understand a dream by thanking God for the dream and asking the Holy Spirit to help us comprehend its meaning. As we work with our dream, we put into the hands of Our Lord all the dream content and all our interpretive methods.

In addition to direct revelation by the Holy Spirit, we also find God's grace in knowledge gained by social and psychological methods. *All truth is God's truth.* We may find useful methods from dream analysts and researchers who help advance truth about the way God blesses our dream activities and how the content of our dreams may benefit us.

Thus a broad approach allows for drawing upon the truth and utility contained in social/psychological methods to understand the grace inherent in dreams.[1] The Holy Spirit knows the meaning of every dream and the best way for us to approach understanding it, whether by a word of knowledge or by using other methods.

In this last chapter many of the techniques introduced throughout the book are reviewed and expanded. Although you've already worked briefly with them, now you will achieve a more in-depth understanding of how to use them. You also will learn some additional ideas to help you draw out the wisdom concealed in dreams.

We suggest some imaginative, non-interpretive strategies that present opportunities to be creative and playful with dreams to see what further insight they can provide. More adventuresome dreamers will discover new ways to interact with their dreams and discover the hidden treasure buried in them.

Mystery, not formula

Learning dream interpretation techniques is not the key to understanding dreams. We seek *insight and revelation*, not some formula to unlock the secrets of our dreams. That said, there are useful tools to help us work with our dreams, techniques which give us insight into the vast, complex interplay of images and themes coming to us in the nighttime.

There is no single correct method to figure out our dreams.

It is important to emphasize that *there is no single correct method to figure out our dreams*. Just become familiar with some of the techniques you can use, then select the ones you feel drawn toward—mix and match them any way you like. As you learn to pay attention to your dreams, you will develop a general sense of how to approach them.

Non-interpretive strategies

Non-interpretive methods can take us out of our analytical approach to dreams and discover alternate ways to work with them. Following are some suggested ideas.

1. Consider a dream as if it were parable

Jesus spoke many great truths in parables. Our experience with understanding parables in the Bible can aid us in our dream work. Obviously parables use a symbolic language our mind is not able to comprehend.

> *I speak to them in parables, because, while seeing they do not see, and while hearing they do not hear, nor do they understand (Matt. 13:13).*

If we simply understood a parable with our conscious mind, we would not discover its inner meaning—we'd just have more head knowledge. Parables are not direct statements we can grasp with our conscious ego—they're riddles.

A useful technique is to work with the dream as if it were a parable, trying to discern its overall theme, or question, rather than its one true meaning. This approach engages the heart in an experience that may yield important information. Dreams, like parables, "draw us into their story until suddenly their message is quite clear and usually remarkably simple."[2]

2. Consider the emotional feelings in the dream

A very simplified way of understanding your dreams is to disregard the imagery. Instead, look at what *feelings* you experienced in the dream and then see if you can recognize the glimmers of such feelings in your everyday life. If you can, then go back to the dream. Consider what the drama portrays, and see what comment it makes on the everyday events to which the feelings are connected.

> *1. Interactive learning*
> ☐ Does this emotion relate to something I am feeling in my daily life?
> ☐ In what area of my life am I feeling this same emotion?
> ☐ Where am I experiencing this emotion in my daily life?

3. Read dream aloud

Sometimes merely saying something out loud can help us understand it better. So also with dreams—simply hearing yourself read a dream aloud may lead to an insight and unlock its meaning.

Therapist Clara Hill says *retelling a dream in the present tense* can bring about cognitive and emotional insight. She suggests recapping the most important parts several times and allowing our feelings to surface.[3]

4. Share your dream

Try telling your dream to a friend, someone who appreciates the value of dreams as a way to hear from God. Then ask the other person what they see in your dream.

Say, "I am having some interesting dreams. I want to know what God is saying to me through them. I would appreciate your ideas of what it might be about. What do you see in my dream? What area of my life do you think the dream could be about?"

Don't forget to listen for the *Aha!* that confirms the relevance of what you hear.

5. "If it were my dream…" technique

To combat a professional arrogance—the notion that only experts can interpret dreams—psychoanalyst Montague Ullman developed an effective dream group technique enabling ordinary people to benefit from their dreams. Using this technique, group members or another individual is asked to comment on someone else's dream as if it were their own. To begin, they preface their remarks with the phrase, "If it were my dream…," so as to acknowledge that their ideas are merely suggestions.[4]

Listening to others say what your dream might mean to them allows you to feel more open to what others say, confident no one is trying to force their understanding on you. It also allows you to distance yourself from your dream, so you can listen for the inner *Aha!*, the response of your spirit as they share.

> *The act of imagining another person's dream as yours may help release you to use your imaginative capacity and to engage your heart. The pressure to get it right has been removed!*

6. "It is as though…" technique

To decipher symbolic imagery try saying, "It is as though…" and then see what

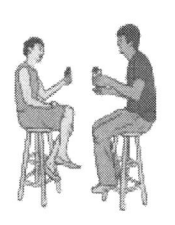

Dream Treasure

spontaneously comes to you. Comparing the dream with something else may help you receive insight into its meaning. Jesus did this in some of His parables when He said, in effect, "It is as though a man who hears and heeds my words is like a wise man who built his residence on rock." Use this technique by itself or with a draw-a-dream technique.

> *(Gerald) When I drove my little red car over a steep incline and plunged into the thickets below, I could say, "It is as though my life is just out of control!"*

7. Listen to the dream as if it were a play or movie

Because the dream comes from the unconscious, making it difficult to understand, it is helpful to relate to the dream as something totally outside of us. Any technique that achieves this can help provide a glimpse of its meaning.

Try approaching a dream as if it was a theater play or a movie. Observe its beginning, notice the unfolding of the situation, follow development of the action, and understand its conclusion. What feelings and human situations is it depicting? What message would this movie be giving? What type of movie it is—adventure, slapstick, comedy, romance, thriller? In what way does this movie correspond to your daily life, and how does it differ?

8. Draw-a-dream technique

Sometimes, it can be helpful to draw a dream—especially for a dream difficult to describe in words. Using a nonverbal approach, you can express it imaginatively on paper instead. Using colored markers, just put on paper the things you saw in your dream, or some element of it.

Don't be afraid to draw using stick figures. This will help you recall more details. Also, note the arousal of any feelings as you relate visually to the image and its energies in the dream.

Now step back and admire your artwork—even if it is only stick figures. It is *your* work! What do you see? Which element feels the most important? What does it bring to mind? What does it suggest to you? What feelings does it express? What feelings does it arouse in you?

When you finish processing your drawing, title it and place it where you can look at it for a while.[i] If you belong to a dream group, show it to them and ask for their feedback. Drawing out dreams can help both adults and children find a greater sense of mastery and control over frightful images in the dream.[5]

What would the artist be trying to convey if the dream were such a painting? One way to help you open up to this approach is to visit a gallery to view impressionist or symbolic paintings, especially those based on dreams: consider works by Chagall, or Dali.

---

i   Anyone intimidated by the idea of their drawings being scoffed at need only look at some of Gerald's dream drawings in this book to feel some comfort—obviously artistic ability is not a prerequisite to finding value in sketching one's dreams.

2. Interactive learning
- ☐ Look at your drawing as if it were hanging in an art gallery.
- ☐ What is this artist trying to convey?
- ☐ What message is this artist trying to communicate?
- ☐ In what way is this painting portraying my daily life?

9. Explore key questions evoked by the dream

Most people like to approach a dream as if it is giving them answers, advice or prophetic revelation. Perhaps we get more from our dream if we ask questions that *invite responses* instead of looking for answers. Focusing our attention on what questions the dream raises helps us establish a dialogue with its Divine Source.

> *A dream is an answer to a question we haven't yet learned how to ask. (Fox Mulder, The X-Files)*[6]

Try asking relational and functional questions, rather than informative ones. Then explore the question and its meaning to you. Try using the question to kick off an imaginative conversation with God to help draw out the meaning of your dream.

> *In my (Judith) dream "You've Got A Good Thing Going Here" I asked: 'Lord, what do you want from me? Why do I feel my meal is not ready? Will I ever feel fully prepared to feed others? What food do I need to prepare to be ready? Who is this man speaking to me?'*

3. Interactive learning
- ☐ List questions the dream raises in you—for example, why is this dream coming to me now? Why am I behaving like this?"
- ☐ Choose one or two of the most compelling questions to reflect on. Then spontaneously write out your response to the question.
- ☐ Reflect on how the questions and your responses will influence your daily life.
- ☐ Did you experience some type of shift in your awareness?

10. Follow-the-dream ego figure

This technique helps you compare how your ego is functioning in the dream versus how it functions during waking hours. Our night-time dramas are filled with actors (characters and objects) reflecting some part of us. One of the key actors portrays the ego, the part of us in the daytime we refer to as "I", our present point of view.[7]

The dream ego is the figure with whom you most identify. It may appear as the same or different sex, age, or race as yourself (could be an animal, even an object).

PART FIVE Unlocking The Meaning Of Dreams

By observing the attitudes your dream egos carries and how it makes choices, acts and reacts, you get an amazing perspective on how you are behaving in various situations in your daily life. The dream doesn't lie!

> *Benner suggests we pay particular attention to the ways in which the dream ego is different from us in waking life.*[8]

4. Interactive learning

- ☐ List in sequence the things your dream ego did—how it acted, what it said, what it chose, how it responded to the situation. You may have only a few actions to list, or many. Record the actions in a narrative style, or list them in a column.
- ☐ Next to each action, describe the attitudes and feelings the dream ego had toward this action or situation.
- ☐ Consider how the actions, attitudes, and feelings may be similar to, or different than, those of your waking ego.

Imaginative techniques

We can use our God-given imagination as a resource to help us understand our dreams. Imaginative techniques enable us to re-enter or re-enact dreams and observe the free flow of imagery across the screen of our imagination. If you try these techniques, keep a light touch, a playful spirit, and share your experiences with spiritually-attuned friends.

1. Imagine your dream belongs to someone else

It might be helpful to pretend your dream is not yours. Consider your dream as if it belongs to someone else, perhaps a close friend—or even a lesser known acquaintance. Ask, "If this dream were theirs, what might it be saying to them?" This approach may help relieve any pressure you may feel, enabling you to free your imaginative and intuitive capacities.

2. Meditational prayer or listening prayer

Use meditational prayer as a way to allow the presence of Jesus to be with you in a troubling or disturbing dream. God has gifted us with an imagination to put at His service. Using your imagination, reenter the dream, allowing Jesus Christ to be with you in the disturbing dream and resolve the pain in it or perhaps give you a creative solution to a troubling problem.

3. Re-entering a dream

Sometimes it is possible to bring an unfinished dream to a conclusion. In this technique, we use our imagination to re-enter a dream. Often in daily life we reflect on yesterday's experiences, thinking about how we handled them or what we wish we had done differently. Similarly we use our imagination to re-enter a dream.

This practice offers us a way to draw upon the positive energy in a dream. We may be able to complete an unfinished dream; rewrite an unsatisfactory ending; release negative energy such as anger; work through a traumatic experience.

4. Write a story

Writing a story based on a dream offers another playful way to relate to a dream and its imagery. Immerse yourself in the dream, and then allow its characters or images to spontaneously change or move forward in time. When finished, you will have created a new story, perhaps changing the end of the dream in a more positive, insightful way. (For more on this technique, see Savary, Berne and Williams, *Dreams And Spiritual Growth*.)[9]

5. Gestalt Approach: "What part of me is that, and what is it saying?"

Underlying this technique is the idea that everything in the dream is a representation of our personal experience, an aspect of ourselves. This approach involves "taking the part" of each person and thing in the dream, exploring what it feels like and what it means to be in this part. Because it allows experiencing parts of ourselves we may be rejecting or disowning, this technique may be helpful for people with recurring dreams.

Also used in therapy, this approach asks the person to role-play the different parts of their dream, enabling them to actually experience the feelings associated with their conflicts, instead of merely talking about them in a detached fashion.[10]

6. Creating scripts for each element

Dreams can help us accept ownership of our own issues instead of projecting them onto others or blaming others. Assuming the various parts of the dream are facets of ourselves—opposing and inconsistent sides—we spontaneously create a script for each one and allow it to speak. Using your scripts, play *each* element, acting and creating a dialogue with the other parts.

Creating dream scripts can help conflicted people see how they are responding to life and where they need to make changes. This technique allows us to see more clearly our way of being in the world and expose the way we avoid our lives.

Symbolic techniques

Although a dream can use both literal and symbolic language, most dreams use symbolic material. Remember, a symbol may be any image, sound, smell, or activity capable of eliciting an emotional response in you—either during the dream or following it. Symbols are multi-dimensional, functioning at a deeper, more primary level than words or even concepts. They belong to the language of our inner world and the spiritual dimension.

Symbols mean much more than they seem at first glance, and they cannot be precisely interpreted—there is no single meaning for a given symbol. They will always be a bit ambiguous, with multiple meanings. We must never attempt to force a specific meaning onto a symbol—it must be allowed free reign for its meaning to develop and evolve. Its meaning must remain alive and not be restricted to a fixed doctrine or formula.

Dream Treasure

Our rational minds are not able to easily process symbols. To unlock symbolic images, we use techniques that allow us to reach deeper into the meaning of the symbol, release its energy, and make it useful in our lives. Using these methods requires the ability to switch to the right side of our brain function and use our imagination and intuition—faculties also given us by the Creator. Because our imaginative faculty creates the images we see in our dreams, it is key to unlocking the symbolic meaning of a dream.

> *The force of reason by itself is not powerful enough for getting at truth (Basil the Great).*

1. Rate the intensity of the dream

To get started, it may be helpful to rate the intensity of the dream or symbol. In choosing a dream or symbol to work with, choose the more highly charged image, one which brought up a surge of energy in you. The more intense the symbols, the more important and urgent the dream message is.

Follow the energy that rises up from within; go to the symbolic image that has the most energy for you. Now rate the intensity of that energy using a scale of 0 (none) to 10 (maximum), and log the intensity number with the dream. Also circle the images that feel most intense to you.

2. Ponder and meditate on dream image

The *intensity* of our dream images is more important to us than their precision and clarity. Choose a dream image to work with and, instead of trying to define it, simply *relate* to it. Working with these images, contemplating their meaning, we make a connection between our outer conscious world and our inner disordered world.

When we put our everyday worries and concerns aside and meditate on our dream images, we gain new strength and peace. Simply musing on the dream is more important than attempting to grasp its meaning by using our rational mind. However, once we have experienced the dream symbolically, we need conceptual thoughts to give it perspective and to release the energy it contains, to bring it into daily life.[11]

If you want to learn more about the art of Christian meditation and how to use it in dream work, we suggest these excellent sources: *Dreams and Spiritual Growth* by Savary, Berne & Williams; *The Other Side of Silence* by M. Kelsey; and *Inner Work* by R. Johnson. Also review number five, "Dream work requires applying the heart," in Chapter 11, "*Biblical Guidelines.*"

---

5. Interactive learning
- ☐ Quiet yourself down.
- ☐ Meditate on dream as if it was a teaching given by Jesus, or as if it was a Scripture passage.
- ☐ Meditate on an image in the dream.

3. Draw-an-image

After choosing a dream image to work with, you may find it helpful to draw the image on paper. As you draw, pay attention to any thoughts coming to mind or any emotional feelings aroused by the image. Place the drawing where you will see it, and then use it as a tool to help you ponder and meditate on the image.

4. Make personal associations to a dream image

Making personal associations is about discovering what an image *means* to you in your inner world, as we discussed in Step 3 in Chapter 19, *"Exploring The Dream."* This is the heart of dream interpretation, unlocking the meaning of a symbol in our dream. Our reasoning and analytical thought processes alone will not give it to us.

Here we take a symbolic element holding much energy for us, lift it out of the dream, and ask ourselves, "what does this image mean to me in my inner world?" Although our unconscious already knows what it means, we must bring it to consciousness so we can benefit from the energy it contains.

This is the heart of dream interpretation, unlocking the meaning of a symbol in our dream.

Determining associations

Johnson suggests the following strategy for determining the associations for each dream element. First write down the symbolic element, noting your feelings about it. What ideas come to mind as you ponder the image?

Write down whatever associations pop up—feelings, memories, ideas, mental pictures—anything you spontaneously connect with this image. How intense is your emotional response to the element? When you finish with one element, go back and repeat the process for other elements.[12]

Feelings are important

Signell suggests, "It is important…to be aware of the feelings elicited by dreams… Finding the feeling that goes with an element (or the element associated with a feeling) adds depth and reality to the experience of your dream."[13]

We often experience a sudden tearing up in our eyes when the "Aha!" occurs. When you sense this intuitive witness, you have stumbled into the symbolic meaning of the symbol, and thus fractured the "dark saying" and released the dream's hidden treasure!

> ▶ **Dream Work Tip:**
>
> If an image seems not to come out of your personal experience, consider that might be an archetypal symbol.

Remember, making personal associations to a dream symbol is not about interpreting or analyzing it, but about finding out what the image *means* to you in your inner world. Most of the dream images come out of your own life experience. You chose them because they are capable of connecting you to the unseen parts of yourself.

Dream Treasure

5. Role play the symbol

To help you make associations to each symbol, you might like to try role playing. Essentially you act the part of each dream element, speaking on its behalf or holding an inner dialogue with it.

Perhaps you can get someone to ask you questions about the symbol to allow you to discover more information about the symbol as you explore it. You answer, of course, from the perspective of the *dream*, not your waking life. After you finish with the questioning, assess how your answers relate to your daily life.

6. Dream dialogue—converse with dream character or figure

Remember, Solomon conversed with God in his dream. Aquinas had a conversation with St. Peter and St. Paul in his dream. We also can enter into a conversation with a figure from our dreams. Don't be alarmed! Our personal experience verifies what other Christian dream experts say: having an imaginative conversational encounter with our dream figures can be a powerful resource for drawing out the meaning of the dream.

Benner says "dialogue with a symbol of our dreams may occur in our imagination and still be guided by God." He argues that our dream figures are a gift from God to bless us, and we should actively work to receive the gift —wrestle with them like Jacob did, if necessary.[14]

Keep to the right

Some more rational and analytical approaches demand the use of our left-brain functions. Other techniques require us to utilize the creative side of our minds. Dialogue with dream figures asks us to approach a conversation with a dream figure using our right-brain functions—the imaginative and intuitive capacities. This allows us to move out from rational control into the non-rational realm to open ourselves to new awareness.

Talk with ourselves

Dialoguing with our dream figures is much the same as daydreaming or having a conversation with ourselves. It is *not* talking to spirit guides or some demonic reality. Similar to the way we sometimes reflect out loud to ourselves, we can dialogue with our dream symbols. Since each dream character represents a facet of ourselves, we look to our imagination to strike up a conversation with these figures and ask them who they are or what they mean.

In the Christian use of dialogue we are having a two-way conversation between our dream figures and us. According to Savary, Berne & Williams, we can disagree with what the dream figure says, or even challenge it, as Peter did in his dream at Joppa (Acts 10:9-16). We have this freedom because we are in relationship to the figure, not controlled by it.[15]

Conversing with dream figure

We personify in our mind who or what it is we want to talk to. For instance, we can dialogue with other people, events in our life, our career, dream images, a famous person, our body, etc. First choose the dream figure you want to converse with, then think of several questions you will want to ask it.

> *Remember my (Gerald) "Bluebird of Happiness" dream? Using imaginative dialogue, I could ask the bluebird, "Where will you lead me?" "Why is my happiness outside the corporation?" "What do I need to do to follow you?"*

7. Personify a dream object or place

We can even personify dream objects (key, flashlight) or places (car, school, hospital) and engage them in dialogue to see where it leads. Choose some prominent dream object or place and personify it. Give the object/place a name as if it were alive, and using your imaginative faculty, set up a conversation with it. This technique helps to make conscious the energy inherent in this symbol, allowing you to creatively put it to use in your life.

> *For example, I (Gerald) dream of my alma mater where I received my engineering degree. To personify this place, I name it "Michigan Tech" and ask, "Why do you keep tantalizing me in my dreams?" "What is the energy you hold for me?"*

This technique helps to make conscious the energy inherent in this symbol—allowing you to creatively put it to use in your life.

Investigate further

For a discussion of the imaginative use of dialogue from a Christian perspective see the following authors:

- Savary, Berne, & Williams, *Dreams and Spiritual growth: A Judeo-Christian Way Of Dream work.*
- Benner, *Care of Souls: Revisioning Christian Nurture & Counsel.* He discusses the differences between pathological conversations, automatic writing practiced by some psychics and mediums, and Christian dialogue.
- Meier & Wise, *Windows Of The Soul: A Look at Dreams and Their Meanings.*

6. Interactive learning

- [ ] Find a quiet place, paper and pen.
- [ ] Sit back, close your eyes and let your self become quiet. Make sure you will not be interrupted.
- [ ] Welcome the presence of the Lord, asking for His guidance.
- [ ] After a moment or two, gradually open yourself to the dream and the dream figure, as if it is happening all over again. With your imagination, replay the dream scene where the dream figure was.
- [ ] Let your mind come into contact with the dream figure. Note that you do not have to develop a clear image of the figure, unless it comes easily. Just holding the idea of the dream is often sufficient.
- [ ] Don't try to direct your thoughts, just feel what is there. Greet who it is.
- [ ] Then in a playful way, you can ask a question to get the relationship started (in your imagination picture yourself asking it to your dream figure). Ask about what they are doing, why they appeared in your dream, what they represent of yourself, what they have brought you.
- [ ] Let them speak to you.
- [ ] Write down the response the figure seems to be giving you, but keep your attention focused inward. You can continue conversing with the dream figure until you want to stop.
- [ ] When you sense the conversation is coming to an end, you might what to ask if there is anything else the figure wants to say to you.
- [ ] Draw the conversation to a close, sit back and try to record how you felt as you dialogued.
- [ ] Reflect on your experience, noting any impressions, insights or feelings. What happened to you during the experience? What insights did you receive?
- [ ] Later, reread it. You may discover something new or find a shift in some attitude.
- [ ] Then focus on what you have learned.

Note: refer to the following dreams for your work in Applied Learning.

Don't Sell Out My Pattern

(Gerald): God has plans for my life, and His thoughts toward me are for peace and not evil, giving me a future and a hope (Jer 29:11). He also encourages me—sometimes gently, sometimes not so gently as I'd prefer—to embrace growth and change. Sometimes his plans exceed my natural capacity to accept readily.

As I go along a road, out on the road in front of me is a pattern for a giant suit. Behind me I sense that my youngest son, talking with a middle-aged business woman, is "selling out." I see how "they" are radically changing the suit pattern from its original design. I am concerned that he not sell out because the pattern would be ruined.

I believe this dream depicts the pattern God has for my life, which seems far bigger than I could possibly imagine. My youngest son symbolizes my possibilities. The pattern is for a suit much larger than I feel capable of wearing. The dream tells me to increase my understanding of God's plans for my life, which are far greater than my fears and my limited view of my capabilities. The dream warns me not to allow my more practical side to abandon life's magnificent possibilities and sell out the divine plan for my life.

Release The Anointing

(Judith): At this time, I'd been asking the Lord to touch me afresh with his Holy Spirit, to give me a fresh anointing for the ministry we have received from him. Then I dreamed…

I am on stage, leading a Christian meeting. My friend Ralph Nault comes up to me and teaches me how to release the anointing of the Holy Spirit in the meeting. When I did what he showed me, the Holy Spirit came down like a bolt of lightening and knocked us to the floor.

Obviously the Lord answered my prayer. Right in the dream, I experience an impartation of the Holy Spirit like never before.

Lord, may You give discerning hearts to Your people and the grace to understand their dreams.

Dream Treasure

Applied Learning

✎ *Your Response*
- ☐ List discoveries you made while working through this manual on dreams.
- ☐ Have you found hidden treasure in your dreams? God's counsel or wisdom in your dreams?
- ☐ Ask: "God, what do you want to accomplish in the world through dreams and dream work?"[16] Spontaneously write out thoughts that flow through your mind in response to the question.

☼ *Dream work strategies, skills & techniques*
- ☐ What technique could Gerald use with his "*Don't Sell Out My Pattern*" dream?
- ☐ What technique might you use with Judith's "*Release the Anointing*" dream?

✎ *Practicing your skills*
- ☐ Review your dreams, reading them in sequence.
- ☐ Do you see any similar themes in your dreams?
- ☐ Can you recognize any pattern emerging through them?
- ☐ Which emotional category—mad, sad, glad, fear, love—has appeared most often in them?
- ☐ How many of your dreams do not have a conclusion or resolution that pleases you?
- ☐ Select a technique and try it with your dream.

Dream Work Terminology
Can you explain the following terms?
- Dream dialogue
- Personify
- Role-play

Appendix A
Survey Of Attitudes & Beliefs About Dreams

Mark the following statements as true (T) or false (F):

1. Dreams belong to the world of too much pizza. _____
2. Dreaming is a not a God-given faculty. _____
3. Dreams carry clues for my future. _____
4. Dreams are not trustworthy and reliable. _____
5. Only superstitious people pay attention to their dreams. _____
6. Dreams mirror the condition of my soul. _____
7. Dreams are nonsensical and defy interpretation. _____
8. Dreams use a dark language belonging to the occult. _____
9. Dreams offer wise counsel. _____
10. Dreaming is a meaningless experience. _____
11. Dreams are a safe approach to correct deep-seated problems. _____
12. Dreaming is only a natural phenomenon. _____
13. Dreams help us understand human behavior. _____
14. Listening to dreams can open me to the demonic. _____
15. The fall of man corrupted our capacity to dream. _____
16. Dreams are fearful things. _____
17. Dreams can lead me to a deeper communion with God. _____
18. God may speak to me through my dreams. _____
19. Dreams carry clues for my future development. _____
20. Dreams have a divine origin. _____
21. Dreams are influenced by immediate stimulus. _____
22. Dreams promote growth and wholeness. _____
23. Valid knowledge can be received from dreams. _____
24. We don't need dreams to hear God; we have the Bible. _____
25. We may encounter God in our dreams. _____
26. Dreams can be from an evil source. _____
27. All nightmares are from an evil source. _____
28. Paying attention to dreams is useless. _____
29. Supernatural phenomena are dangerous. _____
30. The Bible warns me not to pay attention to dreams. _____
31. Dreams belong to New Agers, not Christians. _____
32. Dreams contain a biblical purpose. _____
33. Satan may mislead me through my dreams. _____
34. Dreams may foretell the future. _____
35. Dreams are reliable instruments of God to instruct and guide us. _____

Appendix B
What Is Your Life Situation?

In conducting dream work it is vital for us to have a clear understanding about our current situation in life. This is the context into which the dream enters our life.

Following are some questions to help you think about your life right now. Reflect on the questions, and then re-number them according to their importance to you. Take some time to journal about the most important ones, noting any emotions arising as you write.

- List the prayers you are praying.
- List current problems, troubling situations.
- What areas in your life do you feel most troubled about?
- What recent experience(s) is/are troubling you?
- List disappointments, losses, and failures you recently experienced.
- Are you in a life-threatening situation?
- Identify current health problems, issues, and concerns. Any chronic health problems?
- Identify life situations you are facing: Child moving out; moving; out of work; loss of money; divorce; death; etc.
- Identify troubling relationships.
- Identify persistent conflicts.
- What questions are you asking about your relationships?
- What people trigger a tightening or ping in your gut when you remember their faces?
- With whom do you feel in conflict?
- Are you currently being physically or emotionally abused, threatened, or violated by someone?
- Write a list of the fears, worries, or phobias you struggle with.
- What do you think your emotional needs and concerns are?
- Identify any unresolved conflicts, either in your past or present.
- Identify your hopes for the future.
- What short-term goals do you currently hold?
- What trips are you planning or wish you could plan in the future?
- What creative aspect of your life needs help?
- What is it you consciously seek in life?

Dream Treasure

APPENDIX C
The Holy Spirit

Who is the Holy Spirit?

Many people are confused about the Holy Spirit. We mistake Jesus for the Holy Spirit, or the Holy Spirit for the Father. Jesus is seated at the right hand of the Father, (yes He is with us through His Spirit, inside of us, this is how we are united with Him); yet, He is seated in heaven at the right hand of the Father. The Father is also seated in heaven. The Holy Spirit, the third Person of the trinity, is here on earth, and He is here for a purpose.

The Holy Spirit, the power of God

The Holy Spirit is the same person who brooded over the waters, who came down upon Jesus when he was baptized, who was upon the prophets of old, and who filled the people at Pentecost. It is the Holy Spirit of Power. The Holy Spirit is the power of God and He is here for many purposes, including teacher, guide, comforter, leader.

The Holy Spirit is a Person; it is not a force, power, or energy. As the third Person of the trinity, He has feelings (Eph. 4:30), a mind of infinite knowledge (Rom. 8:26, 27), and a will. He speaks (Acts 13:2; John 16:13). A force or power does not have these attributes and abilities!

The work of the Holy Spirit

In bringing us to salvation, holiness, and wholeness, each part of the Trinity has its work to do. The Father has his, the Son, Jesus Christ, has his, and the Holy Spirit of God has its. The general working of the Holy Spirit is to edify, transform, and lead us, and to fill us with God's power and authority, giving us spiritual gifts. The Holy Spirit is sent to us to help us develop fully into being that new spiritual person.

Spiritual maturity

In the journey to becoming who God intends us to be, we need the power of the Holy Spirit working within us. The Holy Spirit teaches us how to begin to see, hear, and speak spiritually, enabling us to respond spiritually to God. This is key. Without the working of the Holy Spirit we cannot come to a place of spiritual maturity.

Transform us

The Holy Spirit is the One who gives us the power, not only to do the works of Jesus and to be His witnesses, but to heal and transform us deep inside (see I Cor. 4:20

and I Tim. 1:7). Real Christianity goes beyond ceremonies, creeds and rituals and offers a source of power to transform and change lives.

Resurrection power is at work within each person who believes. This is one of the differences between other religions and Christianity. In man's religion, we try to be good, to have a morality, but end up with no morality. In Christianity, transformation occurs through the indwelling Christ and the power of the Holy Spirit working inside a person. He alone has to power to cause an inner transformation within us.[i]

Led by the Spirit

Both Jesus and St. Paul taught that we must learn how to be led by the Spirit. This is a key issue if we ever want to mature spiritually and grow up and break free—from dead religion—and experience something deeper. This can happen only by the Holy Spirit.

We must have the boldness and courage to be led by the Spirit, then we will mature spiritually and be transformed. God has made us adequate to be follow and serve the Spirit—but not the letter of the law (II Cor. 3:6). We are capable of being led by the Spirit. We can trust the Holy Spirit!

Longing for the Holy Spirit

At the end of 19th century, Pope Leo XIII wrote an encyclical letter on the Holy Spirit and dedicated the 20th century to the Holy Spirit. Shortly thereafter, the Holy Spirit was poured out in the Azusa Street revival in California, birthing the modern Pentecostal movement. Later, Pope John XXIII (1958–1963) prayed for the Holy Spirit to come and once more revive the Church as in a new Pentecost.

In 1960 Father Dennis Bennett experienced a new outpouring of God's Spirit, sparking a renewal in his Anglican church and producing life-changing effects on many people. In the fall of 1966, the Holy Spirit stirred the hearts of some Catholic believers and the Catholic Pentecostal movement began. This outpouring of the Holy Spirit swept across the Church, bringing a divine touch to millions of people across all Christian faith traditions .

The beloved Pope John Paul II (1978–2005) called for renewal in the Holy Spirit with accompanying charisma gifts. At *Jubilee 2000,* he called the church to prepare for a fresh work of the Holy Spirit, as the third day of Christianity arrived. He stood at the doors of the Vatican and said before a listening world, "We welcome you, Spirit of Jesus." His successor, Pope Benedict XVI, in his Pentecost homily on June 2006 invoked the Holy Spirit, "so that in our time too, we may have the experience of a renewed Pentecost."

---

i   Personal communication with Ralph Nault (2003).

Appendix D
New Testament Words For Dream & Vision

Following are descriptions of Greek words frequently used to describe the dream and vision. A deeper study of these words can be found in Jim Goll and Morton Kelsey.

- *Angelos*—denotes an angel, which can mean either a divine being or an actual physical messenger. Usually an angel refers to a visionary reality of great importance, which is seen and heard, but is not a physical reality. (Acts 10:3)
- *Blepo/eido*—to "see" or to "perceive." Similar in meaning to our word "see" in the outer sense. (Mark 9:9; Luke 9:36; Rev. 1:2, 11)
- *Enupniom*—a vision or dream seen in sleep; refers to events or happenings that occur during sleep. Carries a surprise quality. (Acts 2:17; Jude 8-9)
- *Horama*—often used for vision; however, it does not distinguish between dream and vision. The sense is something seen, a sight, a spectacle, the appearance of something. (Mt. 17:9; Acts 9:10-12; 10:3-4, 19-20; 11:5; 12:9; 16:9-10; 18:9-11)
- *Horasis*—can mean sight/vision in either physical or supernatural sense. It has to do with the way something appears, as if the Spirit helps us "see." (Acts 2:17; Rev. 4:3)
- *Optasia*—refers to a visionary state that implies a self-disclosure, or of allowing one's self to be seen. (Luke 1:22; 24:22-23; Acts 26:19; II Cor. 12:1-4)
- *Onar*—a common word for dream; any content that comes in sleep, as opposed to waking. (Mt. 1:20, 24-25; 2:12-14,19-22; 27:19)
- *Ecstatsis*—a displacement of the mind or "standing aside oneself." Connotes amazement, confusion, astonishment, or a state in which ordinary consciousness is suspended by God's action, such as being caught up in the Spirit to receive revelation. (Mark 5:42; 16:8; Luke 5:26; Acts 3:9-10; 22:17)
- *Apokalupsis*—has the sense of disclosure of something formerly hidden that has now been revealed. The most commonly used word to describe a visionary state, it signifies anything revealed by the Spirit. (I Cor. 14:6, 26; Rom 16:25-27; II Cor. 12:1, 7; I Pet 1:6-7)
- *Egenomehn ehn pneumati*—"to become in the Spirit." Signifies a state in which we can see visions and receive something directly by the Spirit of God. (Mt. 4:1; Mark 1:12; Luke 4:1-2; Rev. 1:9-10)

Appendix E
Biblical Blessings Of Dreams

Here are some ways God blessed people through dreams/visions in the Bible:

1. Establish covenants (Gen. 15:8-21; 28:12-22; 46:3-4; 48:3-4).
2. Make God known (Gen. 15:1, 7; 28:13; 46:2-3; Numbers 12:6-8).
3. Make known Jesus as the Christ (Acts 9:5, 7, 22).
4. Make God's words known, reveal things God has for someone (Gen. 15:4-5, 7, 18-21; 28:12-15; 46:3-4; 48:3-4; I Kings 3:12-14; I Sam. 3:1-15)
5. Converse with God (Gen. 15:1-21; 20:3-7; I Kings 3:5-14; Acts 9:3-6; 10:10-16): a) ask God questions, receive answers (I Kings 3:5-14; I Sam. 28:6).
6. Know what God is about to do (Gen. 41:25, 28; I Sam. 3:11-14).
7. Receive promise from God: a) for children & numerous descendants (Gen. 15:1-6; 28:13-14; 48:3-4); b) to make a great nation (Gen. 15:5-7; 28:13-14; 46:3); c) to give land to person's descendants (Gen. 15:7, 18; 28:13; 48:4); d) to expect a great reward (Gen. 15:1).
8. Receive promise from God: a) of riches & wealth (Gen. 15:14; I Kings 3:13); b) a long life (Gen. 15:15; 46:4; I Kings 3:14); c) to be with someone and keep them safe (Gen. 28:15; 46:4; Acts 18:10).
9. Receive a personal blessing from God and for one's descendants (Gen. 28:14; 48:3).
10. Receive divine counsel: a) solve problems (Gen. 31:10-29); b) what to do with a pregnant finance, who to marry (Mt. 1:20-24); c) whether to go to battle (Judges 7:13-15); d) how to protect family from harm (Mt. 2:19-23).
11. Receive wise counsel and instruction (Gen. 31:10-13; 41:25-36; Ps. 16:7; Job 33:16).
12. Receive godly instruction and direction: a) where to live (Gen. 31:13; Mt. 2:19-21); b) concerning what to do and where to go (Acts 9:5-9; 9:10-16; 10:1-6; 16:5-11).
13. Instructed not be afraid… a) but to speak and teach the word of God in a certain city (Acts 18:9-11); b) because no one would die (Acts 27:23-25).
14. Get a person's attention; open their ears (Gen. 41:8; Dan. 2:1-3; 4:4-5; Job 33:16; I Sam. 3:1-9).
15. Inform of impending death because of unrepented arrogance (Dan. 5:5, 17-30).
16. Inform of necessity to change attitude and keep from pride—to recognize God as ruler over man (Dan. 4:25; Job 33:17).
17. Warn to change conduct and behavior: a) to stop sinning & to show mercy to

the poor (Dan. 4:27); b) to keep from sinning against God (Gen. 20:3-7); c) to change behavior (Dan. 4:4-5; 5:18-21; Job 33:17); d) to stay away from someone (Mt. 2:12); d) to not hurt someone while speaking to them (Gen. 31:24-29); e) so someone doesn't get hurt (Gen. 31:24, 29).

18. Warn to: a) quickly get out of city and go to Gentiles (Acts 22:17-21); b) change direction and go to a different city (Mt. 2:19-23).

19. Warn of danger (Gen. 20: 3-7; Mt. 2:12, 13, 22; 22: 17-21; Acts 22:17-21).

20. Warn: a) the ungodly (Judges 7:12-14); b) of defeat in battle (Judges 7:13-14); c) not to kill someone (Mt. 17:19).

21. Preserve life: a) keep people alive during famine (Gen. 41:25-36, 54-57); b) keep from death (Mt. 2:12, 22); c) keep a soul from the pit (Job 33:18).

22. Enlighten with the light of God's life (Job 33:30): a) impart gifts of wisdom & a hearing heart (I Kings 3:12); b) keep from fear (Gen. 15:1); c) give courage (Gen. 46:1-7); d) impart strength and courage (Dan. 10:7-10, 12-19); e) encourage confidence in God (Judges 7:9-15); f) inform person his prayers have been heard (Acts 10:1-4, 31).

23. Prepare for impending death by revealing open heavens and Jesus at the right hand of God (Acts 8:55-60).

24. Know future things God has for a person: a) divine purpose & destiny (Gen. 37:5-10; Acts 9:7, 15-16); b) giftedness, calling, or anointing (Gen. 37:5-10; I Sam. 3:1-15).

25. Reveal divine mysteries (Dan. 2:29-30; Rev. 15:1-8; 21 & 22)

26. Reveal God's plan for Gentiles to receive the Holy Spirit (Acts 10:9-45; 11:4-18).

27. Reveal profound and hidden things, interpretation of someone's dream (Dan. 2:19, 22); insight and understanding of a vision (Dan. 9:21-23).

28. Foretell the future (Judges 7:9-18; Dan. 2:28, 39-49; 7:1-27; 8:15-27).

29. Foretell the future, inform about future events in time to prepare for them (Gen. 41:28-34).

30. Foretell the future: a) failure of enemy's battle plans (Judges 7:9-18); b) person's immediate future (Gen. 40:4-22); c) future of one's descendants (Gen. 15:13-14);

31. Foretell the future: a) God's victory at time of the end (Dan. 2:44; 7:1-27; Rev. 12:10; 17:14; 21 & 22); b) nature of end-times and battle (Dan. 8: 18-27; Rev. 1-21).

32. Reveal to a person their inner thoughts, conflicts and intentions in their heart (Dan. 2:28-30).

APPENDIX F
Intuitive & Imaginative Faculties

About intuition

Intuition is key in understanding the symbols in our dreams. The root for "intuition" is intuitus (Latin) and means "to look at." *The Webster's New Universal Unabridged Dictionary* (2003) says "intuition is the direct perception of truth, independent of any reasoning process."

In *The Spiritual Man, Volume Two*, Chinese Christian Watchman Nee (1968) describes the main functions of the spirit as intuition, communion, and conscience. Nee says intuition is similar to the law of God hidden in the ark, because it reveals God and His will to us.

Jewish scholar, Abraham Heschel, quoting Maimonides, says "the source of our knowledge of God is the inner eye, 'the eye of the heart,' a medieval name for intuition."[1] It is through the eyes of the heart that we perceive or see God.

The spirit man or inner man has its own senses, spiritual senses with which it can speak and see. Through the eye of the spirit, we see visions, spontaneous images and pictures. Through the inner voice of the spirit, we receive intuitive knowing, inner guidance, or inward witness. We receive the thoughts from God through our intuition. Thus God comes to us directly through our spirit and heart with dreams, visions, and prophecies.

Intuition is spiritual perception via the unconscious or deep heart. Similar to prophesy, intuition bubbles up from within, giving us the understanding of a dream symbol. It may feel like an unuttered, soundless voice or a wordless, noiseless monitor that urges, moves, confirms, or constrains us in some way.[2]

About imagination

Dreams and visions are the first of the two great channels of communication from the deep heart; the second is the imagination.[3] They consist of images that move and flow and which are symbolic in nature.

The imagination is a faculty created by God and called "good." Understanding this is important to our well-being. We must learn how to place our imagination in the service of God. It is a powerful source of healing and revelation. Einstein is famous for his statement, "the imagination is more important than knowledge."

Dream Treasure

Imagination is "the action or process of forming mental images, of what is not actually present, of what has never been actually experienced, or of creating new images or ideas by combining previous experiences; creative power. It is often regarded as the more seriously and deeply creative faculty..." (*Webster's New Twentieth Century Dictionary*).

The Holy Scripture tells us "to gird up the loins of our mind for action" (I Pet. 1:13). *Strong's Concordance* (1978/1894) informs us that the Greek word for "mind," dianŏia, also includes the imaginative aspect of the mind. Thinking symbolically, the loins refer to the reproductive organs where the seed is held, i.e., the creating part. When Scripture says "to gird up the loins of our mind for action," it is telling us to use the creative aspect of the mind in preparation for something!

The imagination as the generating and creating power of the mind, is either a tool for faith or for unbelief. A spiritual imagination works from our born-again spirit. A doubting, fearful imagination works from the outer, soulish realm and is open to attack and harassment from the enemy.

Our imagination is an inner eye, part of our intuitive capability that allows us to see the spiritual world. Imagination lets us see the invisible arena we cannot see with the natural, physical eye. In cooperation with our spirit, the imagination can create pictures of what the Holy Spirit is revealing to us.

We have a choice. We can put our imagination in the service of the Holy Spirit. We can utilize the tremendous power of our imagination in the context of God's presence and faith. Using our imagination allows us to break free from the controlling influence of our rational minds, and gives the Spirit of God a channel to bless us.

Appendix G
Dream Exploration Guide

The following is a step-by-step guide to help you: 1) *identify* the dream's elements; 2) *amplify* the elements; 3) *make personal associations* to elements, 4) *make connections* to your inner life, and 5) *summarize* the meaning of your dream.

Steps 1-4—Identify, Amplify, Associate, Connect

We have combined the first four steps in one section, hopefully making it easier for you to learn the process. Pay attention to any inter-connections between the amplifications and associations you make, as well as any insights you received.

1. Dream setting
- [ ] Where is the dream taking place? Inside or out?
- [ ] Are their any natural elements—water, sky, earth, or fire?
- [ ] Describe its chief characteristics & condition: scenery, landscape, environment, colors, weather, time, season, etc.
- [ ] Is this place familiar to you?
- [ ] Have you ever been there in a dream before? How often?
- [ ] Have you ever been there in real life? When?
- [ ] Does this place differ from the actual place you have been? If so, how?
- [ ] What is the setting usually used for? Leisure, work, daily life, worship?
- [ ] What is the purpose of this setting? What usually takes place there?
- [ ] How do its characteristics and function differ from others like it?
- [ ] What time period in your life might it relate to?
- [ ] Does it remind you of any place you have been before?
- [ ] What does this setting bring to mind? Memories, situations?
- [ ] What people, experiences, or places does it bring to mind?
- [ ] What words or ideas come to mind when you look at it?
- [ ] What does the setting make you *feel*?
- [ ] How *intense* is your emotional response to it?
- [ ] What does this place *mean* to you?
- [ ] What inner states of mind might it suggest?
- [ ] Did you experience an "Aha!" or click?
- [ ] Record any insights you felt during the process.

2. Buildings, houses
- [ ] Identify buildings, churches, hotels, houses, rooms, floors, elevators, doors, stairs.

Dream Treasure

- [ ] Describe its chief characteristics & condition.
- [ ] Is this building/house familiar to you?
- [ ] Have you ever been there in a dream before? How often?
- [ ] Have you ever been there in real life? When?
- [ ] Does this building/house differ from the actual place you have been? If so, how?
- [ ] Does it remind you of any building you have been in before?
- [ ] What is the purpose of this building? What usually takes place there?
- [ ] How do its characteristics and function differ from others like it?
- [ ] What time period in your life might it relate to?
- [ ] What does this building bring to mind? Memories, situations?
- [ ] What people, experiences, or places does it bring to mind?
- [ ] What words or ideas come to mind when you look at it?
- [ ] What does the building make you *feel*?
- [ ] How *intense* is your emotional response to it?
- [ ] What does this building *mean* to you?
- [ ] What inner states of mind might it suggest?
- [ ] Did you experience an "Aha!" or click?
- [ ] Record any insights you felt during the process.

3. People, characters, figures
- [ ] Identify the characters and figures in the dream.
- [ ] Describe the appearance of each one.
- [ ] Any uniformed characters, helper figures, celebrity guest stars?
- [ ] Are there any other worldly figures? Archetypal figures?
- [ ] Any composite figures?
- [ ] How do their characteristics and functions differ from other people?
- [ ] If unfamiliar figures are present, do they remind you of someone?
- [ ] Who do you think is the most important figure?
- [ ] Do you know any of the people in your dream? When? Why? Where?
- [ ] When have you seen this person before? Think of this person last?
- [ ] What time period in your life might they relate to?
- [ ] What memories, experiences, or situations do they bring to mind?
- [ ] What words or ideas come to mind when you look at them?
- [ ] What does this person/character make you feel?
- [ ] How intense is your emotional response to them?
- [ ] What does this person, character, figure *mean* to you?
- [ ] What inner states of mind, attitudes, or habits might the person suggest?
- [ ] How are you like this person?
- [ ] When do you behave like this? In what situations?
- [ ] What part of you has that capability, potential, quality?
- [ ] Where can you find this in you?
- [ ] Did you experience an "Aha!" or click?
- [ ] Record any insights you felt during the process.

4. Wildlife figures

- [ ] Identify the animals, birds, marine life, reptiles in dream.
- [ ] Any there any strange or exotic animals?
- [ ] Are they familiar or unfamiliar?
- [ ] Describe their condition and demeanor—age, color, gender, wild or free, caged, injured, docile or fierce.
- [ ] Describe their characteristics and functions.
- [ ] How do their characteristics/functions differ from others like it?
- [ ] Have you ever owned one? When? Where? How?
- [ ] What does this wildlife bring to mind?
- [ ] What memories does this wildlife recall for you?
- [ ] What people, experiences, or places does it bring to mind?
- [ ] What words or ideas come to mind when you look at it?
- [ ] What does this wildlife make you feel?
- [ ] How intense is your emotional response to it?
- [ ] What does this wildlife *mean* to you?
- [ ] What part of you might this wildlife represent?
- [ ] What attitudes, behaviors or habits might it suggest?
- [ ] What inner states of mind, attitudes, or habits might this figure suggest?
- [ ] How are you like this?
- [ ] When do you behave like that? In what situations?
- [ ] What part of you has this capability, potential, quality?
- [ ] Where can you find this in you?
- [ ] Did you experience an "Aha!" or click?
- [ ] Record any insights you felt during the process.

5. Objects

- [ ] Identify any objects, furniture, decorations, etc.
- [ ] Describe their appearance—colors, numbers, condition, location, age.
- [ ] Describe their characteristics and functions.
- [ ] How is it used in life?
- [ ] How do its characteristics/functions differ from others like it?
- [ ] Is it familiar or unfamiliar?
- [ ] When have you seen it before?
- [ ] Is it similar in number, color, shape or in value to something else?
- [ ] Are some aspects different from your real life experience?
- [ ] What memories does this object bring to mind?
- [ ] What people, experiences, or places does it bring to mind?
- [ ] What words or ideas come to mind when you look at it?
- [ ] What does this object make you feel?
- [ ] What does its color make you feel?
- [ ] How intense is your emotional response to it?
- [ ] What does this object *mean* to you?

6. Vehicles, transport systems
- [ ] Identify any vehicles—cars, trains, bus, planes, trucks, boats, bikes, etc.
- [ ] Describe its characteristics and functions.
- [ ] What is the vehicle doing?
- [ ] How does it differ from the other means of transportation?
- [ ] Where are you in the vehicle? Driving or back seat?
- [ ] What memories, experiences, people, or events does this vehicle bring to mind?
- [ ] How does this vehicle make you feel?
- [ ] What does its color make you feel?
- [ ] How intense is your emotional response to it?
- [ ] What does that vehicle *mean* to you?
- [ ] Where in your life are you doing/not doing what it is doing?
- [ ] What part of you is like this?
- [ ] What is happening inside you that is like that?

7. Action, activity, movement
- [ ] Identify actions and activities.
- [ ] Identify the main action or overall activity.
- [ ] Describe its purpose. How is it used in life?
- [ ] Which one is the primary or overall action?
- [ ] How does this action/activity make you feel?
- [ ] How intense is your emotional response to it?
- [ ] What memories does this activity recall for you?
- [ ] What does this action/activity bring to mind?
- [ ] What people, experiences, or places does this action/activity bring to mind?
- [ ] What words or ideas come to mind when you think of the action/activity?
- [ ] Are you active or passive in the dream?
- [ ] Are there any other types of movement in the dream?
- [ ] When or where do you act in that way?
- [ ] What does this activity *mean* to you?
- [ ] In what area of your life are you doing this now?
- [ ] Where does this show up in you?
- [ ] How do your actions (or those of anyone else) parallel your actions in daily life?
- [ ] How closely are they similar and how far are they different?
- [ ] If they are different, can you think of any reasons why this might be so?

Roles
- [ ] Identify any roles.
- [ ] What role are you playing? Are you pleased with your role?
- [ ] Have you ever done it before? When? Why? Where?
- [ ] How does this role make you feel?
- [ ] How intense is your emotional response to it?
- [ ] What does this role bring to mind?
- [ ] What people, experiences, or places does this role bring to mind?

- [ ] What does this role *mean* to you?
- [ ] When do you play this role?
- [ ] In what area of your life are you playing this role?

8. Feelings, emotions & physical sensations

- [ ] Identify feelings and emotions experienced, expressed, dramatized. Who felt them?
- [ ] Was the feeling given full expression or held back? If held back, why?
- [ ] Name physical sensations experienced—hungry, cold, tired, etc.
- [ ] Which feeling or sensation was primary?
- [ ] What is the purpose of that feeling or sensation in life?
- [ ] What does this emotion bring to mind?
- [ ] Have you ever felt it before? When? Why? Where? In what situation?
- [ ] What memories does this feeling/sensation recall for you?
- [ ] What people, experiences, or places does it bring to mind?
- [ ] What words or ideas come to mind when you feel the emotions/sensations?
- [ ] What does this emotion/sensation make you feel?
- [ ] How intense is your emotional response to it?
- [ ] What does this emotion/sensation *mean* to you?
- [ ] Are the emotions the same as you are experiencing in your daily life?
- [ ] Does this emotion relate to something you are feeling in waking life?
- [ ] In what area of your life are you feeling this emotion?
- [ ] Does it represent some condition in your life?
- [ ] Is there anything troubling you at the moment that is looking for emotional release?

9. Spoken or unspoken words, thoughts, key statements

- [ ] Identify words, phrases, or statements spoken or thought in dream.
- [ ] Who is it saying or thinking them?
- [ ] Do you say anything or think anything in the dream?
- [ ] Identify any key statements.
- [ ] Does any particular statement/word stand out more than the others?
- [ ] What does this word/statement make you feel?
- [ ] How intense is your emotional response to it?
- [ ] What do these words bring to mind?
- [ ] What words or ideas come to mind when you hear them?
- [ ] Where have you heard this word before?
- [ ] Do any words have a completely different meaning? (looking for puns)
- [ ] What memories do these words recall for you?
- [ ] What people, experiences, or places do they bring to mind?
- [ ] What comes to mind when you say those words?
- [ ] What does this word or sentence *mean* to you?
- [ ] Where in your life are you thinking or saying something similar?

Dream Treasure

- [ ] How does this word or words relate to your life?
- [ ] When or in what situation in waking life are you saying or thinking the same word?

10. Dream theme, issue, conflict

- [ ] What is going on in the dream?
- [ ] Have you ever seen this theme before? When? Where? In what situation?
- [ ] What does this theme bring to mind?
- [ ] What memories does it recall for you me?
- [ ] What people, experiences, or places does it bring to mind?
- [ ] What words or ideas come to mind when you look at it?
- [ ] What does this theme make you feel?
- [ ] How intense is your emotional response to it?
- [ ] What does this theme, issue, conflict mean to you?
- [ ] How does this theme, issue, problem relate to your life?
- [ ] In what area of your life are you feeling this issue or conflict?
- [ ] What is going on inside of you that this dream speaks of?
- [ ] Do some aspects of the theme connect to your daily life?

11. Because factor

- [ ] Is there a because factor in dream?
- [ ] How does the action begin?
- [ ] What is the result of each action?
- [ ] What becomes of it?
- [ ] What does it lead to?
- [ ] Is there a cause and effect?
- [ ] What created the because factor?
- [ ] Can you see any solution in the because factor?
- [ ] What does it bring to mind? Memories?
- [ ] What people, experiences, or places does it bring to mind?
- [ ] What does this because factor make you feel?
- [ ] How intense is your emotional response to it?
- [ ] What does this because factor *mean* to you?
- [ ] Where have you seen this because factor before?
- [ ] Can you identify a because factor in your present life?
- [ ] How does it relate to your life?
- [ ] What words or ideas come to mind when you think of it?

12. Resolution of problem or issue

- [ ] Identify the primary problem or issue in the dream.
- [ ] Was it resolved in a satisfactory or unsatisfactory way?
- [ ] Was it left unresolved or incomplete? If so, why was it left unresolved or incomplete?

- ☐ If completed, identify how it was solved or completed.
- ☐ What does it bring to mind?
- ☐ What memories does it recall for you?
- ☐ What people, experiences, or places does it bring to mind?
- ☐ What words or ideas come to mind when you think of it?
- ☐ What does the resolution or irresolution make you feel?
- ☐ How intense is your emotional response to it?
- ☐ What does this resolution/irresolution mean to you?
- ☐ How does it relate to your life?
- ☐ Where have you seen this resolution/irresolution before?
- ☐ Can you identify an unresolved issue in your life?
- ☐ How does the ending depict your waking life?
- ☐ What issues need resolving in your life?
- ☐ What problems do you need solved?
- ☐ Are you meeting the things you feared in your dream?

Step 5: Summarize the Message

The following is a step-by-step guide taking you through the summarizing process.

1. Consider dream context—your life situation
- ☐ What has been going in your life the last few days?
- ☐ What has your heart been struggling with? Concerned about?
- ☐ What prayers have you been praying?
- ☐ What problems do you need help with?
- ☐ What significant events are happening?
- ☐ Do any dream images have any connection to your life?
- ☐ Do any aspects of your life connect to the dream or its imagery?
- ☐ What aspect of your life may have impacted the dream?
- ☐ What area of your life might it be commenting on?
- ☐ Why is this particular dream coming to you now?
- ☐ How does the dream describe your waking life?

2a. Determine if an objective dream
- ☐ Are the dream details exactly the same as in your waking life?
- ☐ Is the person an immediate family member?
- ☐ Are you emotionally related to person in your dream?
- ☐ Is person depicted exactly as he or she is in your waking life?
- ☐ Are you an observer, not participating in the action?

2b. Determine if subjective dream
- ☐ Is person emotionally important to you?
- ☐ Does the person belong to your distant past or a distant relative?
- ☐ Is person famous?
- ☐ Is person depicting different than in waking life—some distortion occurs?
- ☐ Is person a stranger to you?

3. Consider biblical purpose
- ☐ What primary life issue is dream related to?
- ☐ What category of dream does it belong to?
- ☐ What biblical purpose does this dream have?

4. Summarize the meaning
- ☐ Do any of the words for the elements have a completely different meaning?
- ☐ Did you experience an "Aha!" or click?
- ☐ Record any insights you felt during the exploration process.
- ☐ What is the most important message, the central theme the dream wants to communicate to you?
- ☐ What is it telling you to do?
- ☐ What is the over meaning of the dream for your life?
- ☐ What gift or treasure is the dream bringing you from God?
- ☐ What is God trying to say to you in the dream?
- ☐ Write a simple summary statement about its message or meaning.
- ☐ Read aloud your summary of the meaning of the dream.

5. Test the interpretation
- ☐ Is the interpretation accusative?
- ☐ Violate biblical principles?
- ☐ Violate the nature of Jesus Christ or "the law of the spirit of life in Christ Jesus?"
- ☐ Does it produce pride, or humility in me?
- ☐ Does it bring me peace? Create pressure or anxiety?
- ☐ Is it giving me comfort or torment? Hope or despair?
- ☐ Share your interpretation with a spiritually-attuned person.

Endnotes

Preface
1. Eddie Hyatt, *2000 Years of Charismatic Christianity* (Lake Mary, FL: Strang Communications Company, 2002).

Chapter 1 Authors' Awakening
1. John A. Sanford, *Dreams, God's Forgotten Language* (New York: HarperCollins Publisher, 1968/1989). Sanford, son of the late Agnes Sanford, is an Episcopal priest and Jungian analyst.
2. Morton Kelsey, Dreams, *The Dark Speech Of The Spirit: A Christian Interpretation* (New York: Doubleday & Co, 1968). Kelsey is a former professor at the University of Notre Dame and an Episcopal clergyman.
3. Herman Riffel, *Your Dreams: God's Neglected Gift* (Lincoln, VA: Chosen Books Publishing Company, 1981), 16. For more on Riffel's insights on dreams, visit http://dreamsinfo.com.
4. Charles Zeiders, *Dreams and Christian Holism: Therapy and the Nocturnal Voice of God*, http://www.actheals.org/Publications/Full%20Reports/Clinical%20Inputs/06ClinicalDreams.pdf (accessed February 7, 2009).

Chapter 2 God Wants Us To Hear His Voice
1. Larry Kreider, *Hearing God 30 Different Ways* (Lititz, PA: House to House Publications, 2005), 13.
2. Brian Godawa, *Word Pictures: Knowing God Through Story & Image* (Downers Grove, IL: InterVarsity Press, 2009), 53.
3. Ibid., 56.
4. Derek Prince, *Blessing or Curse. You Can Choose.* (Grand Rapids, MI: Chosen Books, 1990), 32.
5. Henry & Richard Blackaby, & Claude King, *Experiencing God* (Nashville, TN: LifeWay Press, 1990/2007), 73.

Chapter 3 Dreams, A Way To Hear God's Voice
1. Herman Riffel (2007), http://www.dreamsinfo.com/ (accessed March 4, 2008).
2. Rufus Rockwell Wilson (ed.), "Intimate Memories of Lincoln" (Joshua F. Speed, 1880), as cited in *Abraham Lincoln and the Bible*, from the web site of the Lincoln Institute, http://www.abrahamlincolnsclassroom.org/Library/newsletter.asp?ID=111&CRLI=159 (accessed June 10, 2008).
3. Herman Riffel, *Your Dreams: God's Neglected Gift* (Lincoln, VA: Chosen Books Publishing Company, 1981), 23.
4. Morton Kelsey, *Dreams, The Dark Speech Of The Spirit: A Christian Interpretation* (New York: Doubleday & Co, 1968).
5. From *The Catholic Encyclopedia*, http://www.newadvent.org/fathers/0310.htm (accessed June 5, 2008).
6. Rufus Rockwell Wilson (ed.).
7. Len Sperry, *Spirituality In Clinical Practice, Incorporating the Spiritual Dimension in Psychotherapy and Counseling* (Philadelphia, PA: Brummer-Routledge, 2001).
8. Paul Youngi Cho. *The Fourth Dimension*, (Gainesville, FL: Bridge-Logos Publishers, 1979).
9. Ralph Nault, *How Are We Led By The Spirit* (Barton, VT: New Life Books, 1986). Read it free online: http://thenewlife.us/books/BK-05.html
10. Herman Riffel, *Dreams: Wisdom Within* (Shippensburg, PA: Destiny Image, 1990).
11. Sperry.
12. M. P. Hartmann, *Finding Meaning In Crisis: A Link Between Spirituality And Social Work Practice*, as cited in Judith Doctor, *Resource Manual Of Spiritual Interventions* (Grand Rapids, MI: unpublished, 2005).
13. Judith Doctor, *Resource Manual Of Spiritual Interventions* (Grand Rapids, MI: unpublished, 2005).
14. Helen M. Luke, *Woman Earth and Spirit* (New York: Crossroads, 1993), 1-3.
15. Athanasius, "Against the Heathen," *Christian Classics Ethereal Library*, http://www.ccel.org/ccel/schaff/npnf204.txt (accessed June 3, 2008).
16. John Sanford, *The Kingdom Within: The Inner Meaning of Jesus' Sayings* (New York: HarperCollins Publishers, 1987).
17. Herman Riffel, Presentation at a dream seminar, 1988.

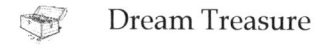

Chapter 4 Dream Robbers
1. Louis Savary, Patricia Berne and Strephon Williams, *Dreams And Spiritual Growth: A Judeo-Christian Way Of Dreamwork* (New York, NY: Paulist Press, 1984).
2. Chris Armstrong, "The Future Lies in the Past: Why evangelicals are connecting with the early church as they move into the 21st century," *Christianity Today*, February 2008, 29.
3. John Nuelsen, ed., *International Standard Bible Encyclopedia* (Grand Rapids, MI: Wm. B. Eerdmans Publishing Co., 1988), 874-5.
4. Tony Crisp, *Dream Dictionary: An A To Z Guide to Understanding Your Unconscious Mind* (New York: Dell Publishing, 2002), 245.
5. Morton Kelsey, *Dreams, The Dark Speech Of The Spirit: A Christian Interpretation* (New York: Doubleday & Co, 1968).
6. Catherine Marshall, *Something More: In Search of a Deeper Faith* (New York: McGraw-Hill Book Company,1974), 116.
7. Armstrong, 25.
8. Morton Kelsey, *God, Dreams, And Revelation: A Christian Interpretation Of Dreams* (Minneapolis, MN: Augsburg Fortress, 1991).
9. "Who is Isa al Masih?—the man in white," Isaalmasih.net web site, http://isaalmasih.net/isa/dreamsofisa.html (accessed April 15, 2010). This web site relates several stories about Muslims whose dreams led them to accept Isa al Masih (Jesus Christ) as their Savior. Also the web site describes a 2001 report on a survey of Muslims who placed their faith in Jesus: more than one-fourth emphasized dreams and visions as key to drawing them to the Savior and sustaining them during tough times.
10. Scott Breslin and Mike Jones, *Understanding Dreams From God* (Pasadena, CA: William Carey Library, 2004), 5.
11. Michelle Van Loon, "Willow Creek Pastor Admits 'Mistake'", *Charisma*, January 2008.

Chapter 5 Biblical Record
1. Herman Riffel, *Your Dreams: God's Neglected Gift* (Lincoln, VA: Chosen Books, 1981).
2. Louis Savary, Patricia Berne and Strephon Williams, *Dreams And Spiritual Growth: A Judeo-Christian Way Of Dreamwork* (New York, NY: Paulist Press, 1984), 16.
3. Morton Kelsey, *Dreams, The Dark Speech Of The Spirit: A Christian Interpretation* (New York: Doubleday & Co, 1968), 19-20.
4. Morton Kelsey, *God, Dreams, And Revelation: A Christian Interpretation Of Dreams* (Minneapolis, MN: Augsburg Fortress, 1991).
5. Stuart A. Kallen, *Dreams, The Mystery Library* (Farmington Hills, MI: Lucent Books, 2004), 49.
6. Riffel.
7. Mark Virkler & Patti Virkler, *Hear God Through Your Dreams* (Shippensburg, PA: Destiny Image Publishers, Inc., 2003/1985).

Chapter 6 Church Fathers
1. Morton Kelsey, *God, Dreams, And Revelation: A Christian Interpretation Of Dreams* (Minneapolis, MN: Augsburg Fortress, 1991).
2. From The Catholic Encyclopedia, http://www.newadvent.org/fathers/0310.htm (accessed June 5, 2008).
3. From the web site of Christian Classics Ethereal Library, http://www.ccel.org/ccel/schaff/npnf204.vi.ii.ii.iv.html (accessed June 3, 2008).
4. Kelsey, 128.
5. "S. Basilii Magni, Commentarium in Isaiam Prophetam," as cited in Mark Virkler & Patti Virkler, *Communion with God* (Shippensburg, PA: Destiny Image Publishers, Inc., 1991), 63.
6. Mark Virkler & Patti Virkler, *How To Hear God's Voice* (Shippensburg, PA: Destiny Image Publishers, Inc., 2005), 271.
7. Morton Kelsey, *Dreams, A Way To Listen To God* (New York: Paulist Press, 1978), 76.

Chapter 7 Historical Evidence
1. Herman Riffel, Notes from seminar on dreams. Grand Rapids, MI (1992).
2. Stuart A. Kallen, *Dreams, The Mystery Library* (Farmington Hills, MI: Lucent Books, 2004), 37.
3. R.A. Brown and R.G. Luckcock, "Dreams, Daydreams and Discovery," *Journal of Chemical Education 55* (1978): 696.
4. Lancelot Whyte, "The Unconscious before Freud," as cited in Morton Kelsey, *God, Dreams, And Revelation: A Christian Interpretation Of Dreams* (Minneapolis, MN: Augsburg Fortress, 1991), 158.
5. A.J. Gordon, http://www.lectionarysermons.com/ADV4-98.html (accessed March 1, 2010).
6. From the web site of Encyclopedia Britannica, 2008, http://www.britannica.com/eb/topic-383152/

Battle-of-Milvian-Bridge (accessed June 4, 2008).
7. Joe Nickell, as cited in Stuart Kallen, *Dreams, The Mystery Library* (Farmington Hills, MI: Lucent Books, 2004), 65.
8. Old Soldier, "George Washington's Vision," *The National Tribute* (1859), http://www.propheticroundtable.org/vision_of_george_washington.htm (accessed April 9, 2010).
9. Morton Kelsey, *God, Dreams, And Revelation: A Christian Interpretation Of Dreams* (Minneapolis, MN: Augsburg Fortress, 1991), 166.
10. Herman Riffel, *Your Dreams: God's Neglected Gift* (Lincoln, VA: Chosen Books Publishing Company, 1981), p.vii.
11. Catherine Marshall, *Something More: In Search of a Deeper Faith* (New York: McGraw-Hill Book Company,1974).
12. Ralph Nault, *Out of Confusion* (Barton, VT: New Life Books, 1986). (Read free online, *How Are We Led By The Spirit*, http://thenewlife.us/books/BK-05.html)
13. Anthony Crisp, *Dream Dictionary: A Guide To Dreams And Sleep Experiences* (New York, NY: Dell Publishing, 1990), 108.
14. J. Lee Grady, "When the next wave of the Spirit hits, let's pray that it will crash into all denominations," *Charisma*, June 2005.

Chapter 8 Christian Worldview
1. For more understanding of competing worldviews see *Christ Centered Therapy* by Neil Anderson, Terry Zuehlke, and Julianne Zuehlke. Grand Rapids, MI: Zondervan Publishing House, 2000.
2. David Benner, *Care Of Souls: Revisioning Christian Nurture & Counsel* (Grand Rapids, MI: Baker Books, 1998), 160.
3. John A. Sanford, *Dreams: God's Forgotten Language* (San Francisco: HarperCollins Publishers, 1968/1989).
4. Benner, 160.
5. Richard Woods, *Christian Spirituality: God's Presence Through The Ages* (Allen, TX: Christian Classics, 1989),19.
6. Morton Kelsey, *God, Dreams, And Revelation: A Christian Interpretation Of Dreams* (Minneapolis, MN: Augsburg Fortress, 1991), 104.
7. Fritjof Capra, *The Tao of Physics*, as cited in Margaret Wheatley, *Leadership and the New Science: Learning about Organization from an Orderly Universe* (San Francisco, CA: Berrett-Koehler Publishers, Inc., 1992), 32.

Chapter 9 A God-Centered Lens
1. From "The Catholic Encyclopedia," http://www.newadvent.org/fathers/0310.htm (accessed June 5, 2008).
2. John A. Sanford, *Dreams: God's Forgotten Language* (San Francisco: HarperCollins Publishers, 1968/1989), 102.
3. David Benner, *Care Of Souls: Revisioning Christian Nurture & Counsel* (Grand Rapids, MI: Baker Books, 1998), 165.
4. Personal conversation with Ralph Nault, 2004; Paul Youngi Cho, *The Fourth Dimension;* Rev. John A. Sanford, *Dreams: God's Forgotten Language*.
5. Morton Kelsey, *Dreams, A Way To Listen To God* (New York: Paulist Press, 1978), 100.
6. Athanasius, *Against the Heathen,* from the web site of Christian Classics Ethereal Library: http://www.ccel.org/ccel/schaff/npnf204.txt (accessed June 3, 2008).
7. Charles Zeiders, "Dreams and Christian Holism: Therapy and the Nocturnal Voice of God," http://www.actheals.org/Publications/FullReports/ClinicalInputs/06ClinicalDreams.pdf (accessed Feb 7, 2009).
8. Scott Peck, *The Road Less Traveled: A New Psychology Of Love*, Traditional Values And Spiritual Growth (New York: Simon & Schuster, 1978).
9. John Sanford, *The Kingdom Within: The Inner Meaning of Jesus' Sayings* (New York: HarperCollins Publishers, 1987).
10. Robert Johnson, *Inner Work: Using Dreams & Imagination For Personal Growth* (New York: HarperCollins Publishers, 1986), 46-48.
11. Scott Peck, *The Road Less Traveled: A New Psychology Of Love, Traditional Values And Spiritual Growth* (New York: Simon & Schuster, 1978), 243.
12. Morton Kelsey, *God, Dreams, And Revelation: A Christian Interpretation Of Dreams* (Minneapolis, MN: Augsburg Fortress, 1991), 106.
13. Strong, J. (1978/1894). *Strong's Exhaustive Concordance of the Bible.* Nashville, TN: Abingdon.
14. "S. Basilii Magni, Commentarium in Isaiam Prophetam," as cited in Mark Virkler & Patti Virkler, *Communion with God* (Shippensburg, PA: Destiny Image Publishers, Inc., 1991), 63.

15 Kelsey, 125.
16 Louis Savary, Patricia Berne and Strephon Williams, *Dreams And Spiritual Growth: A Judeo-Christian Way Of Dreamwork* (New York, NY: Paulist Press, 1984), 73.
17 Scott Peck, *The Road Less Traveled: A New Psychology Of Love, Traditional Values And Spiritual Growth* (New York: Simon & Schuster, 1978), 243.
18 Van de Castle, as cited in C.E. Hill, R.A. Diemer, & K.J. Heaton. "Dream interpretation sessions: Who volunteers, who benefits, and what volunteer clients view as most and least helpful." *Journal of Counseling Psychology, 44(1) (1997):* 53-62.
19 S. Ringel, "Dreaming and listening: a final journey." *Clinical Social Work Journal, 30(4)* (2002): 359-369.
20 Broadribb, as cited in A. D. Van Breda, "Parallels between Jungian and black African views on dreams." *Clinical Social Work Journal 27(2)* (1999): 141-155.

Chapter 10 Biblical Purposes of Dreams

1 Herman Riffel, *Your Dreams: God's Neglected Gift* (Lincoln, VA: Chosen Books Publishing Company, 1981), 127.
2 Hartman (1995), as quoted by Shoshana Ringel, "Dreaming and listening: a final journey," *Clinical Social Work Journal. 30(4)* (Winter 2002): 349-359.
3 Bryan Smith, "Who Am I", *Reader's Digest*, (September 1994): 131-134.
4 Paul Meier & Robert Wise, *Windows Of The Soul: A Look At Dreams And Their Meanings.* (Nashville, TN: Thomas Nelson Publishers, 1995), 171.
5 "The Death of President Lincoln, 1865," *Eyewitness to History*, 1999, www.eyewitnesstohistory.com (accessed June 4, 2008).
6 Joan Wester Anderson, *Woman's Day*, 17 December 1996, 156.
7 Jean Clift & Wallace Clift, *Symbols of Transformation in Dreams* (New York: Crossroad, 1986), 117.
8 Len Sperry, *Spirituality In Clinical Practice, Incorporating the Spiritual Dimension in Psychotherapy and Counseling* (Philadelphia, PA: Brummer-Routledge, 2001), 142.
9 Herman Riffel, *Dreams: Wisdom Within* (Shippensburg, PA: Destiny Image, 1990), 127.
10 John Sanford, *The Kingdom Within: The Inner Meaning of Jesus' Sayings* (New York: HarperCollins Publishers, 1987), 44.
11 Clift & Clift, 4.
12 To learn more about discernment of prophetic dreams and visions, we suggest reading *The Seer*, by Jim W. Goll and *Windows Of The Soul* by Paul Meier and Robert Wise.

Chapter 11 Biblical Guidelines

1 Morton Kelsey, *Transcend: A Guide to The Perennial Spiritual Quest* (Rockport, MA: Element, Inc., 1981/1991), 65.
2 Morton Kelsey, *Dreams, A Way To Listen To God* (New York: Paulist Press, 1978), 101.
3 Morton Kelsey, *God, Dreams, And Revelation: A Christian Interpretation Of Dreams* (Minneapolis, MN: Augsburg Fortress, 1991).
4 Karen Signell, *Wisdom Of The Heart, Working With Women's Dreams* (NY: Banton Books, 1990), 7.
5 Jack Kearney, "Father's Great Expectations," *Reader's Digest*, January 1994, 131.
6 Morton Kelsey, *Adventure Inward: Christian growth through personal journal writing* (Augsburg Publishing House: Minneapolis, MN, 1980), 111.
7 Louis Savary, Patricia Berne and Strephon Williams, *Dreams And Spiritual Growth: A Judeo-Christian Way Of Dreamwork* (New York, NY: Paulist Press, 1984), 175.
8 Montague Ullman, *Working with Dreams* (London: Hutchinson and Company, 1979).
9 Catherine Marshall, *Something More: In Search of a Deeper Faith* (New York: McGraw-Hill Book Company,1974).
10 Maurice Hassett, "Symbolism of the Fish," *The Catholic Encyclopedia*, Vol. 6. (New York: Robert Appleton Company, 1909), http://www.newadvent.org/cathen/06083a.htm (accessed June 5, 2008).
11 Savary, Berne & Williams, 73.
12 Kelsey, 119.
13 Robert Johnson, *Inner Work: Using Dreams & Imagination For Personal Growth* (New York: HarperCollins Publishers, 1986), 97-107.

Chapter 12 Spiritual Discernment

1 Herman Riffel, *Your Dreams: God's Neglected Gift* (Lincoln, VA: Chosen Books Publishing Company, 1981), 10.
2 Henri J. M. Nouwen, *With Open Hands* (Notre Dame, IN: Ave Maria Press, 1972/2006), 41.

3. Paul Meier & Robert Wise, *Windows Of The Soul: A Look At Dreams And Their Meanings* (Nashville, TN: Thomas Nelson Publishers, 1995), 207.
4. Riffel, 117.
5. Meier & Wise, 210.
6. Research by Witken & co-workers, as cited in Mary Ann Mattoon, *Understanding Dreams* (Dallas, TX: Spring Publications, 1984), 149.
7. Mark Virkler & Patti Virkler, *Hear God Through Your Dreams* (Shippensburg, PA: Destiny Image Publishers, Inc., 2003/1985), 50.
8. Watchman Nee, *The Spiritual Man* (New York: Christian Fellowship Publishers, 1977), 18.
9. David Benner, *Care Of Souls: Revisioning Christian Nurture & Counsel* (Grand Rapids, MI: Baker Books, 1998).

Chapter 13 Science of Dreaming

1. Tony Crisp, *Dream Dictionary* (New York: Dell Publishing, 1990), 1.
2. Morton Kelsey, *God, Dreams, And Revelation: A Christian Interpretation Of Dreams* (Minneapolis, MN: Augsburg Fortress, 1991), 54.
3. Mark O'Connell, Raje Airey, Richard Craze, *The Illustrated Encyclopedia Of Symbols, Signs & Dream Interpretation* (Fall River Press, NY, 2009), p 224-229.
4. Louis Savary, Patricia Berne and Strephon Williams, *Dreams And Spiritual Growth: A Judeo-Christian Way Of Dreamwork* (New York, NY: Paulist Press, 1984).
5. Mary Ann Mattoon, *Understanding Dreams* (Dallas, TX: Spring Publications, 1984), 32.
6. Herman Riffel (2007), http://www.dreamsinfo.com/ (accessed March 4, 2008).
7. Edward Edinger, M.D., "An outline of analytical psychology," *Center for Applications of Psychological Type*, http://www.capt.org/using-type/c-g-jung.htm (accessed April 9, 2010).
8. Virkler, Mark and Patti Virkler. *Hear God Through Your Dreams* (Shippensburg, PA: Destiny Image Publishers, Inc., 2003/1985), 52.
9. Crisp,1.
10. David Benner, *Care Of Souls: Revisioning Christian Nurture & Counsel* (Grand Rapids, MI: Baker Books, 1998), 165.
11. Stuart A. Kallen, *Dreams, The Mystery Library* (Farmington Hills, MI: Lucent Books, 2004),10.
12. Ernest Dimnet, *The Art Of Thinking* (New York: Fawcett World Library, 1928), 20.
13. Fred Alan Wolf, *The Dreaming Universe: A Mind-Expanding Journey Into The Realm Where Psyche And Physics Meet* (New York, NY: Simon & Schuster, 1994), 19.
14. Robert Johnson, *Inner Work: Using Dreams & Imagination For Personal Growth* (New York: HarperCollins Publishers, 1986), 19.
15. Kelsey.
16. Dement, 1972, as cited in Phyllis R. Koch-Sheras and Amy Lemley, *The Dream Sourcebook* (Los Angeles: Lowell House, 1995).
17. Paul Lippman, "Dreams and Psychoanalysis, A Love-Hate Story." *Psychoanalytic Psychology 17(4)* (Fall 2000): 627-650.
18. Shoshana Ringel, "Dreaming and listening: a final journey, *Clinical Social Work Journal. 30(4)* (Winter 2002): 349-359.
19. Dr. Charles Fisher, "Psychoanalytic Implications of Recent Research on Sleep," *Journal of the American Psychoanalytic Association 13* (April 1965): 20.
20. Catherine Marshall, *Something More: In Search of a Deeper Faith* (New York: McGraw-Hill Book Company,1974), 86-87.
21. Tony Crisp, *Dream Dictionary: An A To Z Guide to Understanding Your Unconscious Mind* (New York: Dell Publishing, 2002), 294.
22. Calvin Hall, *The Meaning of Dreams* (New York: McGraw-Hill Book Company, 1966).
23. Montague Ullman, M.D., "Interconnectedness: Species Unity and Dreaming," *Dream Appreciation Newsletter Vol 5 No 2, Spring 2000,* http://siivola.org/monte/Dream_Appreciation_Newsletter/2000-2.pdf, (accessed April 5, 2010).
24. Clara Hill, as cited in Garry Cooper, "Clinician's Digest," *Psychotherapy Networker 33*, no. 5 September/October 2009): 17.
25. Calvin Hall, *The Meaning of Dreams* (New York: McGraw-Hill Book Company, 1966).
26. Robert Hoss, author of *Dream Language: Self-understanding Through Imagery and Color* (2005), http://dreamgate.com/dream/hoss/index.htm#intro (accessed August 2, 2007).
27. Mattoon, 37.
28. Ibid.
29. Ibid., 34.
30. Source unknown.
31. Jean Clift & Wallace Clift, *Symbols of Transformation in Dreams* (New York: Crossroad, 1986), 17.

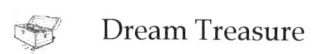

32   Ibid., 17.
33   Morton Kelsey, *Transcend: A Guide to The Perennial Spiritual Quest* (Rockport, MA: Element, Inc., 1981/1991), 63.
34   James Hall, *Jungian Dream Interpretation: A Handbook Of Theory And Practice* (Toronto, Canada: Inner City Books, 1983),10.
35   Paul Meier & Robert Wise, *Windows Of The Soul: A Look At Dreams And Their Meanings* (Nashville, TN: Thomas Nelson Publishers, 1995).

Chapter 14 Classifying Dreams

1. Mark Virkler & Patti Virkler, *How To Hear God's Voice* (Shippensburg, PA: Destiny Image Publishers, Inc., 2005), 271.
2. John Sanford, *Dreams And Healing: A Succinct and Lively Interpretation of Dreams* (New York: Paulist Press, 1978).
3. Phyllis Koch-Sheras, Amy Lemley, & Peter Sheras, *The Dream Sourcebook & Journal: A guide to the theory and interpretation of dreams* (New York: Barnes & Noble Books, 2000), 85.
4. Catherine Marshall, *Something More: In Search of a Deeper Faith* (New York: McGraw-Hill Book Company,1974), 103-105.
5. Jung, as cited in Mary Ann Mattoon, *Understanding Dreams* (Dallas, TX: Spring Publications, 1984), 140.
6. Ibid.
7. Tony Crisp, *Dream Dictionary: An A To Z Guide to Understanding Your Unconscious Mind* (New York: Dell Publishing, 2002), 265-266.
8. Mary Ann Mattoon, *Understanding Dreams* (Dallas, TX: Spring Publications, 1984); James Hall, *Jungian Dream Interpretation: A Handbook Of Theory And Practice* (Toronto, Canada: Inner City Books, 1983).

Chapter 15 The Language of Dreams

1. Louis Savary, Patricia Berne and Strephon Williams, *Dreams And Spiritual Growth: A Judeo-Christian Way Of Dreamwork* (New York, NY: Paulist Press, 1984), 72.
2. Johnson, Robert. *Inner Work: Using Dreams & Imagination For Personal Growth* (New York: HarperCollins Publishers, 1986), 22.
3. Paul Tillich, http://www.brainyquote.com/quotes/quotes/p/paultillic390301.html (accessed February 13, 2009).
4. "S. Basilii Magni, Commentarium in Isaiam Prophetam," as cited in Mark Virkler & Patti Virkler, *Communion with God* (Shippensburg, PA: Destiny Image Publishers, Inc., 1991), 63.
5. Ernest Dimnet, *The Art Of Thinking* (New York: Fawcett World Library, 1928), 20.
6. Mark Virkler & Patti Virkler, *Hear God Through Your Dreams* (Shippensburg, PA: Destiny Image Publishers, Inc., 1985).
7. A.J. Gossip, "Daily Quotation for February 5, 1996," http://cqod.gospelcom.net/index-02-05-96.html (accessed June 21, 2007).
8. Johnson, 19.

Chapter 16 Dream Dynamics

1. Tony Crisp, *Dream Dictionary: An A To Z Guide to Understanding Your Unconscious Mind* (New York: Dell Publishing, 2002), 245.
2. Robert Johnson, *Inner Work: Using Dreams & Imagination For Personal Growth* (New York: HarperCollins Publishers, 1986), 46-48.
3. Will Larson, "New England Conference, CD Series 050430," 2005.
4. Mark Virkler & Patti Virkler, *How To Hear God's Voice* (Shippensburg, PA: Destiny Image Publishers, Inc., 2005).
5. von Franz, as cited in Mary Ann Mattoon, *Understanding Dreams* (Dallas, TX: Spring Publications, 1984), 116.

Chapter 17 Cardinal Rules

1. Morton Kelsey, *Transcend: A Guide to The Perennial Spiritual Quest* (Rockport, MA: Element, Inc., 1981/1991), 63.
2. Karen Signell, as cited in Phyllis R. Koch-Sheras and Amy Lemley, *The Dream Sourcebook* (Los Angeles: Lowell House, 1995).
3. David Benner, *Care Of Souls: Revisioning Christian Nurture & Counsel* (Grand Rapids, MI: Baker Books, 1998), 172.
5. Robert Johnson, *Inner Work: Using Dreams & Imagination For Personal Growth* (New York: HarperCollins Publishers, 1986), 46.
5. Ibid., 35.

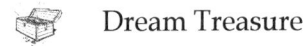

6   Louis Savary, Patricia Berne and Strephon Williams, *Dreams And Spiritual Growth: A Judeo-Christian Way Of Dreamwork* (New York, NY: Paulist Press, 1984), 152.

Chapter 18 First Steps

1   Louis Savary, Patricia Berne and Strephon Williams, *Dreams And Spiritual Growth: A Judeo-Christian Way Of Dreamwork* (New York, NY: Paulist Press, 1984).

Chapter 19 Exploring The Dream

1   Mark O'Connell, Raje Airey, Richard Craze, *The Illustrated Encyclopedia Of Symbols, Signs & Dream Interpretation* (Fall River Press, NY, 2009), 275.
2   Ibid.
3   Ibid.
4   Ibid.
6   Robert Johnson, *Inner Work: Using Dreams & Imagination For Personal Growth* (New York: HarperCollins Publishers, 1986), 56.
7   Karen Signell, *Wisdom Of The Heart, Working With Women's Dreams* (NY: Banton Books, 1990),17.

Chapter 20 Strategies & Interpretation Techniques

1   Charles Zeiders, *Dreams and Christian Holism: Therapy and the Nocturnal Voice of God*, http://www.actheals.org/Publications/Full%20Reports/Clinical%20Inputs/06ClinicalDreams.pdf (accessed February 7, 2009).
2   David Benner, *Care Of Souls: Revisioning Christian Nurture & Counsel* (Grand Rapids, MI: Baker Books, 1998), 170-171.
3   Clara Hill, as cited in Garry Cooper, "Clinician's Digest," *Psychotherapy Networker* 33, no. 5 (September/October 2009): 17.
4   Montague Ullmann, as cited in Phyllis Koch-Sheras, Amy Lemley, & Peter Sheras, *The Dream Sourcebook & Journal: A guide to the theory and interpretation of dreams* (New York: Barnes & Noble Books, 2000), 68.
5   Koch-Sheras, Lemley, & Sheras, 223.
6   Motivational quotes from the web site of *Happy Publishing*, http://www.happypublishing.com/blog/20-dreams-quotes, (accessed April 5, 2010).
7   Louis Savary, Patricia Berne and Strephon Williams, *Dreams And Spiritual Growth: A Judeo-Christian Way Of Dreamwork* (New York, NY: Paulist Press, 1984).
8   Benner.
9   Savary, Berne, & Williams.
10   Janie Rhyne, cited by Judith Rubin in *Approaches to art therapy: Theory and technique,* 2nd ed. (Brunner-Routledge: New York, NY, 2001).
11   Savary, Berne, & Williams, 73.
12   Robert Johnson, *Inner Work: Using Dreams & Imagination For Personal Growth* (New York: HarperCollins Publishers, 1986), 52.
13   Karen Signell, *Wisdom Of The Heart, Working With Women's Dreams* (NY: Banton Books, 1990),17.
14   Benner, 181.
15   Savary, Berne, & Williams, 60.
16   Ibid.

Appendix C The Holy Spirit

1   Kevin and Dorothy Rahagnan, *Catholic Pentecostals* (NY: Paulist Press, 1969).
2   Eddie Hyatt, *2000 Years of Charismatic Christianity* (Lake Mary, FL: Strang Communications Company, 2002).

Appendix D New Testament Words For Dream & Vision

1   Jim Goll, *The Seer: The Prophetic Power of Visions, Dreams, and Open Heavens* (Shippensburg, PA: Destiny Image Publishers, 2005), 57-68.
2   Morton Kelsey, Dreams, *The Dark Speech Of The Spirit: A Christian Interpretation* (New York: Doubleday & Co, 1968), 80-85.

Appendix F Intuitive & Imaginative Faculties

1   Abraham Heschel. *"God In Search Of Man: A Philosophy of Judaism"* (New York: Farrar, Straus & Giroux, 1955), 148.
2   Watchman Nee, *The Spiritual Man* (New York: Christian Fellowship Publishers, 1977).
3   Robert Johnson, *Inner Work: Using Dreams & Imagination For Personal Growth* (New York: HarperCollins Publishers, 1986).

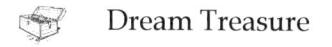

Bibliography

Anderson, Joan Wester. *Woman's Day*, December 17, 1996.

Anderson, Neil and Terry & Julianne Zuehlke. *Christ Centered Therapy*. Grand Rapids, MI: Zondervan Publishing House, 2000.

Armstrong, Chris. "The Future Lies in the Past: Why evangelicals are connecting with the early church as they move into the 21st century." *Christianity Today*, February 2008.

Pope Benedict XVI. "Faith, Reason and the University." speech at University of Regensburg, Germany, September 12, 2006, http://www.vatican.va/holy_father/benedict_xvi/speeches/2006/september/documents/hf_ben-xvi_spe_20060912_university-regensburg_en.html (accessed April 28, 2008).

Pope Benedict XVI. "Remarks to The Catholic University of America." April 17, 2008, http://publicaffairs.cua.edu/Releases/2008//PopeBenedictSpeech.cfm (accessed April 28, 2008).

Benner, David. *Care Of Souls: Revisioning Christian Nurture & Counsel*. Grand Rapids, MI: Baker Books, 1998.

Blackaby, Henry & Richard & Claude King. *Experiencing God*. Nashville, TN: LifeWay Press, 1990/2007.

Breslin, Scott and Jones, Mike. *Understanding Dreams From God*. Pasadena, CA: William Carey Library, 2004.

Brown, R.A. and R.G. Luckcock. "Dreams, Daydreams and Discovery." *Journal of Chemical Education 55* (1978): 696.

Capra, Fritjof. *The Tao of Physics*, as cited in Margaret Wheatley, *Leadership and the New Science: Learning about Organization from an Orderly Universe*. San Francisco, CA: Berrett-Koehler Publishers, Inc., 1992.

The Catholic Encyclopedia. http://www.newadvent.org/fathers/0310.htm (accessed June 5, 2008).

Chetwynd, Tom. *A Dictionary Of Symbols*. London: Paladin Books, 1982.

Chetwynd, Tom. *How To Interpret Your Own Dreams*. New York: Bell Publishing, 1980.

Christian Classics Ethereal Library: http://www.ccel.org/ccel/schaff/npnf204.txt (accessed June 3, 2008).

Cho, Paul Youngi. *The Fourth Dimension*. Gainesville, FL: Bridge-Logos Publishers, 1979.

Cirlot, J.E. *A Dictionary Of Symbols* 2nd ed. (New York: Philosophical Library, 1972).

Clift, Jean and Wallace Clift. *Symbols of Transformation in Dreams*. New York: Crossroad, 1986.

Cooper, Garry. "Clinician's Digest," *Psychotherapy Networker 33*, no. 5 (September/October 2009),17.

Crisp, Anthony. *Dream Dictionary: A Guide To Dreams And Sleep Experiences*. New York, NY: Dell Publishing, 1990.

Crisp, Tony. *Dream Dictionary: An A To Z Guide to Understanding Your Unconscious Mind*. New York: Dell Publishing, 2002.

Dimnet, Ernest. *The Art Of Thinking*. New York: Faucet World Library, 1928.

Doctor, Judith. *Resource Manual of Spiritual Interventions*. Grand Rapids, MI: unpublished, 2005.

Edinger, Edward. "An outline of analytical psychology." *Center for Applications of Psychological Type*, http://www.capt.org/using-type/c-g-jung.htm (accessed April 9, 2010).

Encyclopedia Britannica, 2008, http://www.britannica.com/eb/topic-383152/Battle-of-Milvian-Bridge (accessed June 4, 2008).

Eyewitness to History, 1999, www.eyewitnesstohistory.com (accessed June 4, 2008).

Fisher, Charles. "Psychoanalytic Implications of Recent Research on Sleep." *Journal of the American Psychoanalytic Association 13* (April 1965).

Godawa, Brian. *Word Pictures: Knowing God Through Story & Image*. Downers Grove, IL: InterVarsity Press, 2009.

Goll, Jim. *The Seer: The Prophetic Power of Visions, Dreams, and Open Heavens*. Shippensburg, PA: Destiny Image Publishers, 2005.

Gordon, A.J., http://www.lectionarysermons.com/ADV4-98.html (accessed March 1, 2010).

Gossip, A.J. Daily Quotation for February 5, 1996 from CQOD website, http://cqod.gospelcom.net/index-02-05-96.html (accessed June 21, 2007).

Grady, J. Lee. "When the next wave of the Spirit hits, let's pray that it will crash into all denominations." *Charisma*, June 2005.

Hall, Calvin. *The Meaning of Dreams*. New York: McGraw-Hill Book Company, 1966.

Hall, James. *Jungian Dream Interpretation: A Handbook Of Theory And Practice*. Toronto, Canada: Inner City Books, 1983.

Happy Publishing. http://www.happypublishing.com/blog/20-dreams-quotes, (accessed April 5, 2010).

Hassett, Maurice. "Symbolism of the Fish," *The Catholic Encyclopedia*, Vol. 6. (New York: Robert Appleton Company, 1909), http://www.newadvent.org/cathen/06083a.htm (accessed June 5, 2008).

Heschel, Abraham. *God In Search Of Man: A Philosophy of Judaism*. New York: Farrar, Straus & Giroux, 1955.

Hill, C.E., R.A. Diemer, & K.J. Heaton. "Dream interpretation sessions: Who volunteers, who benefits, and what volunteer clients view as most and least helpful." *Journal of Counseling Psychology, 44(1) (1997):* 53-62.

Hoss, Robert. author of *Dream Language: Self-understanding Through Imagery and Color* (2005), http://dreamgate.com/dream/hoss/index.htm#intro (accessed August 2, 2007).

Howard, Walden and Alice Howard. *Exploring the Road Less Traveled: A Study Guide for Small Groups*. New York: Simon & Schuster, 1985.

Hyatt, Eddie. *2000 Years of Charismatic Christianity*. Lake Mary, FL: Strang Communications Company, 2002.

Isaalmasih.net website, "Who Is Isa Al Masih—The Man In White?" http://isaalmasih.net/isa/dreamsofisa.html#1 (accessed April 15, 2010).

Johnson, Robert. *Inner Work: Using Dreams & Imagination For Personal Growth*. New York: HarperCollins Publishers, 1986.

Jung, C. G. *Psyche & Symbol*. Garden City, NY: Doubleday Anchor Books, 1958.

Kallen, Stuart. *Dreams, The Mystery Library*. Farmington Hills, MI: Lucent Books, 2004.

Kearney, Jack. "Father's Great Expectations." *Reader's Digest*, January 1994.

Kelsey, Morton. *Adventure Inward: Christian growth through personal journal writing*. Augsburg Publishing House: Minneapolis, MN, 1980.

Kelsey, Morton. *The Other Side of Silence: A Guide to Christian Meditation*. New York: Paulist Press, 1976.

Kelsey, Morton. *Dreams, A Way To Listen To God*. New York: Paulist Press, 1978.

Kelsey, Morton. *Dreams, The Dark Speech Of The Spirit: A Christian Interpretation*. New York: Doubleday & Co, 1968.

Kelsey, Morton. *God, Dreams, And Revelation: A Christian Interpretation Of Dreams*. Minneapolis, MN: Augsburg Fortress, 1991.

Kelsey, Morton. *Transcend: A Guide to The Perennial Spiritual Quest*. Rockport, MA: Element, Inc., 1981/1991.

Kirby, Peter. *Early Christian Writings* (2006), http://www.earlychristianwritings.com

Koch-Sheras, Phyllis and Amy Lemley. *The Dream Sourcebook*. Los Angeles: Lowell House, 1995.

Koch-Sheras, Phyllis and Amy Lemley and Peter Sheras. *The Dream Sourcebook & Journal: A guide to the theory and interpretation of dreams*. New York: Barnes & Noble Books, 2000.

Kreider, Larry. *Hearing God 30 Different Ways*. Lititz, PA: House to House Publications, 2005.

Lippman, Paul. "Dreams and Psychoanalysis, A Love-Hate Story." *Psychoanalytic Psychology 17*(4) (Fall 2000): 627-650.

Luke, Helen. *Woman Earth and Spirit*. New York: Crossroads, 1993.

Marshall, Catherine. *Something More: In Search of a Deeper Faith*. New York: McGraw-Hill Book Company,1974.

Matthews, Boris, Ed. *The Herder Symbol Dictionary of Symbols: Symbols from Art, Archeology, Mythology, Literature, and Religion*. New York: Continuum International Publishing Group, 1993. [Initially published as: Herder Lexikon, & Boris Matthews, *The Herder Symbol Dictionary*. Brooklyn, NY: Chiron Publications, 1986.]

Mattoon, Mary Ann. *Understanding Dreams*. Dallas, TX: Spring Publications, 1984.

Meier, Paul and Robert Wise. *Windows Of The Soul: A Look At Dreams And Their Meanings*. Nashville, TN: Thomas Nelson Publishers, 1995.

Nault, Ralph. *How Are We Led By The Spirit*. Barton, VT: New Life Books, 1986. [Read it free online: http://thenewlife.us/books/BK-05.html

Nault, Ralph. *Out of Confusion*. Barton, VT: New Life Books, 1986.

Nee, Watchman. *The Spiritual Man*. New York: Christian Fellowship Publishers, 1977.

Nouwen, Henri J. M. *With Open Hands*. Notre Dame, IN: Ave Maria Press, 1972/2006.

Nuelsen, John, ed. *International Standard Bible Encyclopedia*. Grand Rapids, MI: Eerdmans Publishing Co., 1949.

O'Connell, Mark and Raje Airey and Richard Craze, *The Illustrated Encyclopedia Of Symbols, Signs & Dream Interpretation*. Fall River, NY: Fall River Press, 2009.

Peck, Scott. *The Road Less Traveled: A New Psychology Of Love, Traditional Values And Spiritual Growth*. New York: Simon & Schuster, 1978.

Rahagnan, Kevin and Dorothy Rahagnan. *Catholic Pentecostals*. NY: Paulist Press, 1969.

Riffel, Herman. *Your Dreams: God's Neglected Gift.* Lincoln, VA: Chosen Books Publishing Company, 1981.

Riffel, Herman. *Dreams: Wisdom Within.* Shippensburg, PA: Destiny Image, 1990.

Riffel, Herman. (2007), http://www.dreamsinfo.com/ (accessed March 4, 2008).

Ringel, Shoshana. "Dreaming and listening: a final journey." *Clinical Social Work Journal.* 30(4) (Winter 2002): 349-359.

Rubin, Judith. *Approaches to art therapy: Theory and technique,* 2nd ed. Brunner-Routledge: New York, NY, 2001.

Sanford, John A. *Dreams: God's Forgotten Language.* San Francisco: HarperCollins Publishers, 1968/1989.

Sanford, John A. *Dreams And Healing: A Succinct and Lively Interpretation of Dreams.* New York: Paulist Press, 1978.

Sanford, John A. *The Kingdom Within: The Inner Meaning of Jesus' Sayings.* New York: HarperCollins Publishers, 1987.

Savary, Louis and Patricia Berne and Strephon Williams. *Dreams And Spiritual Growth: A Judeo-Christian Way Of Dream work.* New York, NY: Paulist Press, 1984.

Signell, Karen. *Wisdom Of The Heart, Working With Women's Dreams.* NY: Bantam Books, 1990.

Smith, Bryan. "Who Am I." Reader's Digest, September, 1994, 131-134.

Old Soldier, "George Washington's Vision." The National Tribute (1859), http://www.shalomjerusalem.com/prophecy/prophecy4.htm (accessed May 4, 2007).

Sperry, Len. *Spirituality In Clinical Practice, Incorporating the Spiritual Dimension in Psychotherapy and Counseling.* Philadelphia, PA: Brummer-Routledge, 2001.

Strong, J. *Strong's Exhaustive Concordance of the Bible.* Nashville: Abingdon. 1978/1894.

Stringfellow, William. *The Politics of Spirituality.* Philadelphia, PA: Westminster Press, 1984.

Taylor, Daniel. *The Healing Power Of Stories: Creating Yourself Through The Stories Of Your Life.* New York: Doubleday, 1996.

Tillich, Paul. *BrainyMedia.com,* http://www.brainyquote.com/quotes/quotes/p/paultillic390301.html (accessed February 13, 2009).

Ullman, Montague. "Interconnectedness: Species Unity and Dreaming." *Dream Appreciation Newsletter Vol 5 No 2, Spring 2000,* http://siivola.org/monte/Dream_Appreciation_Newsletter/2000-2.pdf.

Ullman, Montague. *Working with Dreams.* London: Hutchinson and Company, 1979.

Van Breda, A.D., "Parallels between Jungian and black African views on dreams." *Clinical Social Work Journal 27(2)* (1999): 141-155.

Van Loon, Michelle. "Willow Creek Pastor Admits 'Mistake.'" *Charisma,* January 2008.

Virkler, Mark and Patti Virkler. *Communion with God.* Shippensburg, PA: Destiny Image Publishers, Inc., 1991.

Virkler, Mark and Patti Virkler. *Hear God Through Your Dreams.* Shippensburg, PA: Destiny Image Publishers, Inc., 2003/1985.

Virkler, Mark and Patti Virkler. *How To Hear God's Voice.* Shippensburg, PA: Destiny Image Publishers, Inc., 2005.

Virkler, Mark and Patti Virkler. "Principles Of Christian Dream Interpretation." *Hear God Through Your Dreams* (2004), http://www.cwgministries.org/Principles-of-Christian-Dream-Interpretation.htm (accessed April 4, 2006).

Warren, Rick. *The Purpose Driven Life* Grand Rapids, MI: Zondervan, 2002.

Wilson, Rufus Rockwell, ed. "Intimate Memories of Lincoln" (Joshua F. Speed, 1880), as cited in *Abraham Lincoln and the Bible,* from the website of the Lincoln Institute, http://www.abrahamlincolnsclassroom.org/Library/newsletter.asp?ID=111&CRLI=159 (accessed June 10, 2008).

Wolf, Fred Alan. *The Dreaming Universe: A Mind-Expanding Journey Into The Realm Where Psyche And Physics Meet.* New York, NY: Simon & Schuster, 1994.

Woods, Richard. *Christian Spirituality: God's Presence Through The Ages.* Allen, TX: Christian Classics, 1989.

Zeiders, Charles. *Dreams and Christian Holism: Therapy and the Nocturnal Voice of God.* From the Web site of The Association of Christian Therapists, http://www.actheals.org/Publications/Full%20Reports/Clinical%20Inputs/06ClinicalDreams.pdf (accessed February 7, 2009).

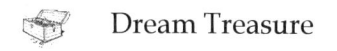

Index

Because the main topic of this book is dreams, and the word appears on nearly every page, it isn't always included in the index.

A

Abraham 14, 51, 55, 62, 100, 101, 120, 149
Abraham Lincoln 25, 26, 27, 77, 121
action, taking 42, 59, 63, 108, 125, 140, 143, 146,183, 259
activity/action, dream 241, 247, 253, 254, 257, 289, 292
actualize dream potential 141, 143, 144, 145, 146, 214
Adler, Alfred 109, 168
affect, dream (A) 34, 35, 250, 251, 293
(the) "Aha!" 94-95, 143, 154, 194, 200, 207, 221, 238, 255, 258, 259, 265, 271, 296
airplane 128, 142, 233, 250, 256, 292
allegory 67, 105, 195, 207
Ambrose 26, 67
amplification 194, 203, 204, 206, 212, 223, 225, 232, 235, 255, 258, 289-295, goal of 258
analogy 191, 204, 207
ancient civilizations 33, 38, 55, 62, 109, 163, 164
angels 9, 15, 16, 26, 27, 31, 40, 51-54, 56-59, 67, 85, 88; 101, 114, 141, 171, 181, 196, 237, 283; Gabriel 57, 124
anima/animus 213
animals 128, 190, 194, 196, 197, 235, 236, 237, 241, 247, 256, 267, 291; cow 191; donkey 14
anticipatory dreams 182
Aquinas, St. Thomas 38, 67, 68, 75, 272
archetype/archetypal 172, 176, 181, 201, 209, 227, 236-237, 256, 271; dreams 177, 181
ark of the covenant 102
arrows 196
association 191, 192, 193-194, 203, 224, 227, 232, 235, 248, 255, 258-259, 269, 271-272, 289
Athanasius 32, 67, 101
attitudes/beliefs about dreams 3, 6, 8, 37, 39, 43, 53, 77, 94, 134, 148, 167; biblical 51; Church fathers 65, 68; survey 8, 277
Augustine 26, 67, 68, 103, 147, 181

B

baby, birth 106, 122, 123, 128, 141, 169, 172, 184, 191, 213, 221, 232
background (dreamer's) 154, 158, 171, 186, 229, 260 (see current concerns, context, life situation)

balancing (compensatory) dreams 177, 185-186
basement 123
basic steps of dream work 244-249
Basil the Great 67, 105, 127, 195, 199, 270
basketball/camp 120, 194
bear 196, 197
because factor 174, 175, 258, 268, 294
bed 52, 61, 74, 100, 120, 134, 213, 221, 234
bell/bell tower 190, 230, 231, 237
benefits of dreams 21-39, 125, 126, 167-169, 185
Benner, David 85, 86, 100, 153, 165, 227, 235, 268, 272, 273
biblical basis 61- 62
biblical blessings of dreams 285-286
biblical dreams/visions 15-17, 53-55, 56-59, 101, 197-198
biblical guidelines of interpretation 7, 133-144
biblical purposes 113-129, 130, 260
big dream (prophetic) 126
bird/s 172, 196, 198, 236, 237, 247, 256, 291; bluebird 4, 41, 273
Bishop Bruno 75, 76
black & white dreams 170-171
Blackaby, Henry T. 20
blessing 18, 145, 186
blessings from dreams 26, 31, 34, 62, 67, 73, 177
body, head/hands/thigh 78, 122, 123, 215-216; umbilical cord 221
brain 136, 137, 138, 165, 170, 192-193, 206, 249, 258, 270, 272; brain activity 165-168
bread 57, 76, 140, 190, 196, 197
Breslin, Scott and Mike Jones 43
brother 55, 154-155, 182, 217
bucket 196; like a 32-33
buildings 4, 28, 135-136, 179, 210, 212, 230, 232, 247, 256, 273, 285-286, 289-290
Bunyan, John 27, 74-75
butler & baker dreams 57, 198

C

Calvin, John 38, 39
candles 143, 190
car/truck 121, 168, 169, 183-184, 208, 230, 237, 247,

Dream Treasure

309

Index

256, 266, 273, 289, 292
cardinal, principles/rules 194, 227- 241
casket/coffin 28, 77
cave 237; cavern 173
chalice 237
charisma (gifts of the Holy Spirit) 15, 16, 67, 84, 107, 122, 141, 200, 281-282
Christian beliefs about dreams 99-109
Christian symbols 190; 196
Christian theory of dreams 109
Chrysostom, John xiii, 67, 101
church, Vatican 45, 79, 196, 217, 236, 256, 289
Church fathers 65, 68; Ambrose 26, 67; Athanasius 32, 67, 101; Augustine 26, 67, 68, 103, 147, 181; Basil the Great 67, 105, 127, 195, 199, 270; Chrysostom, John xiii, 67, 101; Clement xiii, 66, 104, 105; Cyprian 26, 67; Hermas 66; Irenaeus 26, 65, 66, 102, 103; Justin Martyr 66, 88; Synesius of Cyrene 67, 177; Tertullian xiii, 66, 67, 99, 149
clairvoyant dreams 182
classifications (types) of dreams
    archetypal 172, 181, 201, 236-237
    balancing (compensatory) 177, 185-186
    big (prophetic) 126
    clear 5, 11, 175, 183
    counsel & instruction dreams 5, 10, 11, 61, 100. 115-117, 177, 285
    current events (every day) 57, 77, 79, 169, _178_, 179, 186
    death & dying xiii, 27, 28, 77, 119. 121, 122, 123. 164, 169, 182, 184-185, 198, 217, 229, 285-286
    divine encounter 19, 54, 67, 101, 181
    extrasensory perception (ESP) 125, 126, 178, 182, 186; anticipatory 182; precognitive 182; telepathic 182; clairvoyant 182; mutual 182; prophetic 55, 125, 126, 150, 164, 177, 182, 229, 231, 267; foretelling the future 125, 126, 150, 182
    gifts of grace (comfort) 122, 123
    growth & healing 30, 118, 120, 123-124, 143, 165, 169, 172, 177, 216, 238
    guidance & direction 56, 59, 69, 76, 79, 90, 114, 117, 220-221
    health 121, 122
    historic events 177, 180
    intentions of heart 78, 85, 88, 104, 119, 127, 128
    lucid 175, 183
    nightmares 74, 118, 119, 143, 166, 177, 183, 184, 231
    non-compensatory 186
    numinous (spectacular) 148, 164, 177, 181
    objective 161, 177, 186, 205, 217-218
    problem-solving 27, 74, 79, 109, 116, 127, 168, 178, 179
    routine maintenance 148, 177, 178, 229
    subjective 161, 217-219, 220
    trauma 30, 118-119, 130, 172, 177, 180, 184, 186
    warning 58, 59, 121, 182
clay pots 196
clear dreams (literal) 5, 11, 175, 183
Clement xiii, 66, 104, 105
Clift, Wallace & Jean 201, 237
cloak 230
clock 234
clothing 41, 139, 179, 196, 211, 212, 230, 233, 247, 275
collective unconscious 172, 173 (see spiritual layer)
color dreams 170-171
commitment, making 244
compensatory (balancing) dreams 177, 185-186
complexes, inferiority/mother 173, 209
composers' dreams 73-74
computer 127, 210, 223, 232
conclusion 174-175, 266, 268, 276, 294-295
concrete (uncured) 179
Constantine 65, 76
Construction/reconstruction 79, 173
contemporary dreams
    Come My Daughter 18-19, 181
    Dancing Skeleton 28-29, 34
    Who Is Dead In The White House 77
    Overturned Vatican 79, 81
    A Recurring Nightmare 119
    Truck Driving 121
    Fix The Waterworks 122
    A Baby Is Born 122
    I'm Your Wife 139
    Little Men 149
    Fighting A Dragon 150
context of dream 5, 229, 233, 260, 279, 295 (see current concerns, background, life situation)
counsel & instruction dreams 5, 10, 11, 61, 100. 115-117, 177, 285
counseling xiii, xiv, 30, 135 (see therapeutic function, healing)
cows 121, 126, 191, 196, 197
cowl 106
creating scripts for elements 269
Crisp, Anthony 163, 165, 184, 201
cross, of Christ 14, 45, 150, 153; dream symbol 75, 76, 172, 190
crying 120
culmination of plot 174, 294
cultivating dreams 244-245
cultural symbols 172, 176
current concerns (CC) 3, 5, 10, 58, 138, 154, 158, 248-249, 251, 260, 295 (see background, context, life situation)

Index

current events (every day) 57, 77, 79, 169, 178, 179, 186

curses 18

cup 196

Cyprian 26, 67

D

danger, of dreams 148-149, 154

dark sayings (*Chiydah*) 53, 61, 99, 105, 189, 190

dawn 196

death & dying dreams xiii, 27, 28, 77, 119, 121, 122, 123, 164, 169, 182, 184-185, 198, 217, 229, 285-286

decision making 141-142

details of dreams 134, 136, 145, 170, 187, 218, 221, 234

dialogue 38, 39, 68, 200, 240, 267, 269, 272-273 (see dream dialogue)

Dimnet, Ernest 166

direct & indirect voice 19, 115, 183 (see hearing voice of God, visual word of God)

discernment 7, 10, 20, 33, 97, 142, 147-157, 182, 261,

dispensationalism 39, 40

divination 38, 75, 87, 153

divine counsel 3, 5, 6, 8, 10, 22, 29, 33, 115-116, 151

divine encounter dreams 19, 54, 67, 101, 181

divine origin 100, 148, 230

divine purpose dreams 5, 19, 29, 30, 39, 42, 57, 69, 77, 90, 103, 110, 113, 149, 183, 200, 255

divine revelation 19, 26, 30, 33, 38, 43, 59, 65, 67, 87, 101, 102; see religious conversion 19, 75, 182

donkey 14

door 5, 15, 16, 41, 65, 89, 102, 135, 150, 165, 179, 180, 217, 252, 289

doves 196

dragon 150, 151, 159, 211, 229

draw-a-dream/image 4, 145, 230, 240, 248, 266-267, 271

drawer 41, 90

dream, nature of 164-165, 229; like a bucket 32-33; structure 174; typical themes 169

dream dialogue 38-39, 68, 200, 240-241, 269, 272-274

Dream Exploration Guide 255, 260, 289-296

dream interpretation 7, 28-29, 32, 34, 41, 54, 76, 83, 106-107, 114, 164, 170, 201, 227-228; guidelines/principles of 133-144, 186, 194, 227-241, 248, 296; techniques 263-265; testing validity 7, 150, 152-154, 260, 296

dream journal format 251-252

dream language 6, 19, 27, 97, 100, 105-106, 138, 165, 170, 189-202

dream sharing group 140, 141, 198, 265, 266

dream work 29, 31, 32, 33, 89, 101, 105, 130, 133, 136, 137-138, 139-141, 152, 153, 192, 228, 243; basic steps of 244-249

dreaming, science 148, 165-169, 192; history 163-164

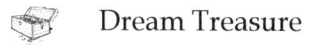

dreams & visions vi, xiii, 5, 14, 15-17, 21, 51- 55, 58-59, 61, 62; 66-67, 283

dresser 41

E

eagles 196

egg 103, 197

ego 5, 81, 88, 123, 141, 153-154, 167, 173, 212, 215, 228, 232, 235, 239, 264

ego figure 210, 232, 247; following ego figure 223, 267-268

Einstein, Albert 74, 292

element/s 95, 187, 196, 198, 201, 231, 247, 256-258, 257-258, 259, 266, 269, 271-272, 289-295

emotional feeling strategy 34-35, 250, 257, 264-265

energy, dream 30, 76, 95, 107-108, 120, 122, 124, 172, 191, 194, 200, 210, 235-236, 238, 240, 259, 261, 268, 270, 273 (see intensity)

enigmas 67, 105, 189, 190, 195

exploration, dream 174, 225, 255-261; 289

explore evoked questions 110, 267

extrasensory perception dreams (ESP) 125, 126, 177, 182, 186

eye 62, 140, 166, 208, 287

F

family members: husband/wife, brother/sister, son/daughter 55, 123, 135, 154, 182, 207, 217, 275

fear, dreams 147, 148, 156; Freud 40, 151; satan 148; unconscious 151; imagination 151; God 152; Holy Spirit 39-40

field 195

fig leaves 211

figures & characters, dream 209-214, 219, 256, 290; archetypal 236-237; devil 150
   ego figure 210, 232, 247
   extra-ordinary 171
   helper 41, 135, 179, 230, 232, 256, 290
   persona 211-212
   objective 217-218
   opposite-gender 213-215
   (the) Self 215-216
   same-sex 120, 212, 215
   shadow (same-sex) 90, 120, 212, 215
   subjective 217-220

figures of speech 170, 189, 195, 206-207

file cabinet 90

fire 171, 190

fish/fish dinner 142, 150, 192, 197, 247, 291

Dream Treasure

Index

Fisher, Charles 168
flood waters 41
flying 124, 142, 169, 257, 291
follow-the-dream ego figure 223, 267-268
food/hunger 118, 252, 257, 261, 267
foretelling the future dreams 125, 126, 150, 182
French & Fromm 169
Freud, Sigmund 40, 151, 164; Freudian 151, 259
Fromm, Erich 169, 172, 199

G

Gabriel, prince of dreams 57, 106, 124
garden pathway 93
General George Patton 76
Gerald Doctor's dreams
    Bluebird Of Happiness 4
    Flood Waters At My Doorstep 41
    House Foundation Is Sick 79
    Divine Hug From Pope 93
    Disparate Pieces Coming Together 108
    Last Of The Big Bruisers 120
    I Cry Out My Sorrow To God 120
    Transformed Basement 123
    Waif Unplugs Me 127
    Back Door Counselor 135-136
    Umbrellas Aren't Legal 168
    Wet Concrete 179
    This Dream Is Going Nowhere 183-184
    Helping Michael Jordan With Basketball 194
    Seize The Opportunity 210
    Naked On Route 211
    Sleeping Giant 230
    Office For A Writer 232
    I Can't Go Through With The Wedding 234
    Rhode Scholar 236
    People Are Hungry To Learn About Dreams 261
    Don't Sell Out My Pattern 275

Gerald Doctor's musings, "Jacob's Ladder" vi; "Musings on Joseph, the Dreamer" 9; "To Gerald's Sunday School Class" 91; "Wake Up, Wake Up" 44; "Butler's and Baker's Dreams" 198

Gestalt 109, 269
giant 215, 230, 240, 275
gift of God, dreams 6, 44, 51, 108-109, 122, 148, 213, 244
gift of grace (comfort) dreams 122, 123
Gilgamesh Epic 163
Godawa, Brian 17
Gordon, A. J. 13, 76
Grady, J. Lee 79

grape 198; grape vine 198
grasshoppers 196
group technique 265
growth & healing 30, 118, 120, 123-124, 143, 165, 169, 172, 177, 216, 238
guidance & direction 56, 59, 69, 76, 79, 90, 114, 117, 220-221

H

Hall, Calvin 169, 185
hallucination 167
healing xiv, 30, 123-124, 177, 184, (see counseling, therapeutic function)
health dreams 121, 122
hearing voice of God 1, 6, 14-21, 31, 41, 43, 57, 60, 66, 85, 87, 89, 101, 108, 153, 165, 245
heart 16, 20, 31-33, 55, 61-62, 103, 127-128, 137-139, 143, 190, 199, 270; issues 10; language of 138, 199 (see hidden man of the heart)
Hermas 66
Heschel, Abraham 287
hidden man of the heart 32, 85, 86, 193
hidden treasure 3, 31-33, 34, 105, 134
hill 174, 183-184, 238, 250
Hill, Clara 169, 265
historic events dreams 177, 180
historical testimony 73-80
holiness 103, 281
Holy Spirit 16, 20, 29, 41, 60, 78, 87, 104, 115, 134, 141, 56, 173, 281-282; dreams 27, 55, 62, 100, 115, 275; language of 6, 27, 100, 137, 189, 199; like a river of life 173; outpouring of xiii, 7, 41, 282; role of 27, 43, 45, 60, 106, 115, 152, 173, 231, 287-288; witness of 107, 142, 207, 217
honey 206
hospital 232
hotel 212
house 18, 28, 41, 77, 79, 102, 106, 122, 180-181, 190, 196, 217, 237, 252, 256, 289; basement 123; foundation 79

I

"if it were a play, a movie" 266
"if it were my dream" 81, 265
"if it were someone else's dream 81, 268
imagination 101, 138, 151, 166, 193, 194, 199-201, 230, 287-288
imaginative techniques 81, 130, 268-269
    creating scripts for elements 269
    imagine your dream belongs to someone else 81, 268
    listening prayer 130, 268
    meditational prayer 63, 268, 270

Index

  re-entering a dream 240, 268 (see turn and face it)
  what part of me is that (Gestalt) 269
  write a story 269
inferiority complex 173
inner dynamics 167, 191, 205, 219, 220, 232, 235
inner world 6, 32, 85-86, 88, 104-105, 127, 143, 153, 164-165, 167, 168, 182, 203, 213, 259, 269
intelligent intent 100
intentions of heart dreams 78, 85, 88, 104, 119, 127, 128
insects 196
intensity, dream 108, 120, 194, 235, 240, 270 (see energy, dream)
interpretation 7, 28-29, 32, 34, 54, 83, 106-107, 135, 137-138, 139, 142, 144, 228; art of 138
intuition 15, 20, 37, 87, 138, 157, 166, 193, 270, 287 (see knowings)
Irenaeus 26, 65, 66, 102, 103
"it is as though" 145, 265-266

J

Jacob's ladder dream vi, 56, 63, 81, 108, 114, 124, 143
Jeremiah 17, 51, 54, 55, 114, 134-135
Jerome 38, 68, 75
Jesus 14, 15, 16, 20, 27, 45, 54, 55, 58, 59, 60, 86, 88, 89, 92, 93, 102, 105, 130, 142, 150, 151, 154, 155, 157, 161, 184, 190, 195-196, 199, 215, 281; birth of 52, 55, 57; dreams of 13, 18, 43, 53, 76, 102, 181, 285; dream work technique 130, 268; words of 18, 43, 53, 86, 87, 103, 104, 134, 137, 140, 151, 152, 196, 205, 207, 208, 213, 266
Johnson, Robert 143, 167, 194, 220, 237, 270, 271
Joseph, earthly father of Jesus 9, 44, 59; dreams of 26, 51, 57, 58-59, 115, 117, 119, 121, 141
journey 28, 237
Judith Doctor's dreams
  Without A Degree 5
  Director Of Marketing 69
  Guidance From The Dream 89
  My New Bible 89
  Its Jesus! 102
  My Two Babies 106
  Until You Do What I Told You To Do 115
  Give Me Something From Your Purse 116
  Study Psychology 117
  Come, We're So Hungry 118
  Holding Our Deceased Son 123
  Three Embedded Lies 123-124
  Gabriel Teaches Me To Fly 124
  I Am In Rome 126
  No Fish Dinners For Me 142
  My Brother Calls Me 154
  River Held Back 173
  I Am An Inch Worm 180
  Phone Call 182
  I'm Not Going To Hire You 186
  Fig Leaves 211
  What Do I Wear? 212
  In Bed With My Male Friends 213
  Rotten Inside 215-216
  Most Alive Woman 216
  My Ill Brother Arrives 217
  Cut The Cord 221
  You Got A Good Thing Going Here 252
  Release The Anointing 275
Justin Martyr 66, 88

K

Kelsey, Morton 6, 26, 41, 52, 66, 67, 68, 78, 101, 107, 134, 138, 140, 143, 227, 270, 283
key statement 70, 249, 257, 293; example of 5, 69, 89, 106, 116, 142, 168, 234, 252
kingdom of God 3, 29, 53, 55, 86, 124, 152, 195, 199, 207
kings & queens 237
Kipling, Rudyard 74
knowing 117, 137, 143, 207, 238, 259; ways of 200
Kreider, Larry 16

L

ladder 56, 149
lamp stands 196
Larson, Will 215
Lechler, Walther 18
leopard 197
life situation 7, 186, 229, 249, 260, 279 (see background, context, current concerns)
light/s 69, 186, 196
lightning 237
Lincoln, Abraham 25, 26, 27, 77, 121
lion 196, 197, 256
listening prayer 130, 268
literal interpretation 5, 19, 21, 105, 135, 141, 155, 169, 170, 191, 235, 269; danger of 154, 170, 207
living word 8, 101
lucid dreams 175, 183
Luke, Helen 30
Luther, Martin 65

M

Magnifying glass 116
man/men, known/unknown 4, 41, 59, 69, 89, 106, 120, 135, 149, 186, 194, 213, 234, 236, 252, 283, 275, 290; wise man 18, 252
map 69, 126, 172

Dream Treasure   313

Index

marriage, wedding 191, 234, 237
Marshall, Catherine 41, 78, 141, 168, 182
Matthews, Boris 201
Mattoon, Mary Ann 165, 170, 185
meditate/meditation 16, 75, 134, 137-138, 199; techniques 63, 145, 240, 244-245, 265, 270
meditational prayer 63, 268, 270
Meier, Paul & Robert Wise 149, 150, 213, 273
mistakes, making 137, 150, 153, 167, 170, 207
monster 102, 128, 143, 150, 151, 174, 198
mood, dream 247, 248, 250, 257, 259, 293
Moody, D.L 39
mother complex 173
mother dream 150, 169, 182, 184, 221, 229, 238
Mother Theresa 76
mountain 172, 197, 208; climbing 78, 237
Mulder, Fox The X-Files 267
music 27, 73, 79, 193, 208
Musings on Joseph, the dreamer 9
Muslim/Islam xiii, 18, 43, 109, 114
mustard seed 195
mutual dreams 182

N

naked 211
nations 196
Native American Indians 79, 109
Nault, Ralph xvii, 20, 28, 78, 89, 90, 121, 190, 217, 275, 282
Nee, Watchman 20, 152, 157, 287
needle/thread 116
New Age xiii, 40, 43, 84, 99
Newton, Isaac 27, 74
Newton, John 75
nightmares 74, 118, 119, 143, 166, 177, 183, 184, 231 (see trauma dreams)
non-compensatory dreams 186
non-interpretation strategies
    consider emotional feelings 34-35, 94, 250, 257, 264-265
    consider it as a parable 63, 81, 207, 264
    draw-a- dream 4, 145, 230, 240, 248, 266-267, 271
    explore evoked questions 110, 267
    follow-the-dream ego figure 223, 267-268
    "if it were a play or movie" 266
    "if it were my dream" 265
    "if it were someone's else's dream" 81, 268
    "it is as though" 145, 266
    read dream aloud 63, 265
    share your dream 46, 140, 265

Nouwen, Henri J. M. 148
numinous (spectacular) dreams 148, 164, 177, 181
nun/s 79, 210
nurse 171, 232, 257

O

objective dreams 161, 177, 186, 205, 217-218, 260
O'Connell, Mark 256, 257
office 4, 41, 135, 179, 210, 217, 232
opposite-gender figure (anima/animus) 213, 214, 215

P

parable 63, 81, 86, 134, 189, 193, 195, 207, 209, 264
pastor, priest 234
pearls 195
people 135, 149, 194, 210, 230, 232, 252, 256, 261, 275, 290
persona figure 210-211, 212
personal symbols 171, 172 , 196, 200
personality 124, 127, 165, 167, 181, 185, 209, 212, 213, 215, 217, 219-220, 229, 230, 239; structure 104, 173; spiritual layer 173
personification 28, 128, 150, 195, 208, 214, 273
picture/s 17, 21, 56, 105, 107, 138, 155, 166, 170, 200, 259;
picture language 105, 190, 196, 199
plot development 174
Poe, Edgar Allan 74
poetry 189, 190, 192, 206, 208
Pope 93
prayer 8, 16, 19, 22, 28, 41, 59, 94, 123, 130, 140-141, 144, 153, 260, 268, 275
prayer group 141
precognitive dreams 182
pregnant 106, 122, 237, 285
priest, monk, nuns 79, 210, 230, 237
problem-solving dreams 27, 74, 79, 109, 116, 127, 168, 178, 179
problem-solving function 168
projection 153, 208-209, 212
prophetic 55, 125, 126, 150, 164, 177, 182, 229, 231, 267
psyche 104, 164, 165, 171, 185, 208, 236 (see soul)
psychology 32, 40, 67, 68, 85, 103, 117, 127, 140, 213; depth 31, 109, 181
public place 261
puns 142, 170, 189, 195, 207, 224, 236, 293
purse 116

Q

Index

question dream/God asks (Q) 46, 251
questions about dreams 8, 25, 60, 90, 148, 149, 150
questions evoked by dream 110, 141, 267
questions to ask 186, 208, 212, 214, 215, 217, 220, 222-224, 258, 259, 260, 272, 289-296

R

rainbow 237
rapid eye movement (REM) 166-167, 170
read aloud 63, 265
recall/remember 138, 140, 244, 245-246
record/log 4, 134-135, 246-248 (see dream journal format)
re-entering a dream 240, 268 (see turn & face it)
religious conversion 19, 75, 182
religious experience 30, 31, 37, 39, 44, 56, 75, 78, 85, 88, 102, 104
religious symbolic experience 29, 93, 191, 200
repetitive themes/dreams 133, 143, 231
Riffel, Herman xi, 5, 6, 25, 26, 30, 31, 40, 52, 73, 115, 137, 149, 153, 165, 219
rituals 143
river 173; Nile 191
river of life 172 (see Holy Spirit)
road/highway/ thoroughfare 74, 183, 211, 236, 275
rock 190, 196, 197; stones 196, 206
role play the symbol 272
root 196
rose 192
routine maintenance dreams 148, 177, 178, 229
Rush, Benjamin 77-78

S

sacraments 15, 140, 153
salt xi, 206, 216
Savary, Louis & Patrick Berne & Strephon Williams 140, 191, 237, 269, 270, 272, 273
scorpion 197
Scriptures, biblical basis of dreams 61-62; disputed 54
sea 196
seed/s 190, 196
(the) Self figure 123, 216
serpent/snake 196, 197
setting/scenery 174, 218, 247, 256, 289
sex/ sexual 40, 151, 155, 184, 234
shadow (same-sex) figure 90, 120, 212, 215
share your dream 46, 140, 265
sheaves 197
sheep 196
shepherd 196, 206

shoes 139, 171, 179, 191, 211
Signell, Karen 259, 271
Simpson, David 75
skeleton 28, 237
slipcovers 211
snake 74, 197, 237
sofa/slipcovers 211
Solomon 30, 32, 33, 51, 62, 101, 137, 190, 272
soul 18, 20, 30, 31, 32, 67, 79, 85, 86, 101, 104, 105, 107, 113, 121, 124, 128, 140, 143, 173, 200; and dreams 66, 109, 126, 165, 171, 172, 174, 213, 214 (also see psyche)
source of images 171-173, 232
Sperry 30, 123
spirit guide 272
spirit of man 9, 16, 20, 28, 85, 87, 88, 115, 122, 143, 151, 157, 166, 173, 207, 223
spiritual man 20, 28, 85, 157, 287
spiritual maturity 103, 104, 155-157, 220, 261
spiritual practice/s 16, 66, 101, 134, 152
spiritual reality xiii, 29, 32, 37, 66, 84, 86, 88, 91, 92, 94, 104, 199
spiritual senses 20, 21, 44, 92, 104, 142, 156, 157, 287
St. Thérèse of Lisieux 76
star 54, 55, 74, 125, 172, 256, 196, 230
Stevenson, Robert Louis 74
strategies, skills, techniques
    activity/action, dream 241, 247, 253, 254, 257, 289, 292
    actualize dream potential 141, 143, 144, 145, 146, 214
    affect, dream (A) 34, 35, 250, 251, 293
    (the) "Aha!" 94-95, 143, 154, 194, 200, 207, 221, 238, 255, 258, 259, 265, 271, 296
    amplification 194, 203, 204, 206, 212, 223, 225, 232, 235, 255, 258, 289-295, goal of 258
    association 191, 192, 193-194, 203, 224, 227, 232, 235, 248, 255, 258-259, 269, 271-272, 289
    background (dreamer's) 154, 158, 171, 186, 229, 260
    basic steps of dream work 244-249
    because factor 174, 175, 258, 268, 294
    biblical purpose 130, 260
    commitment, making 244
    conclusion 174-175, 266, 268, 276, 294-295
    context of dream 5, 229, 233, 260, 279, 295
    creating scripts for elements 269
    cultivating dreams 244-245
    culmination of plot 174, 294
    current concerns (CC) 3, 5, 10, 58, 138, 154, 158, 248-249, 251, 260, 295
    details of dreams 134, 136, 145, 170, 187, 218, 221, 234

Index

draw-a-dream 4, 145, 230, 240, 248, 266-267
draw-an-image 4, 271
element/s 95, 187, 196, 198, 201, 231, 247, 256-258, 257-258, 259, 266, 269, 271-272, 289-295
emotional feeling strategy 34-35, 250, 257, 264-265
explore evoked questions 110, 267
follow-the-dream ego figure 223, 267-268
"if it were a play, a movie" 266
"if it were my dream" 81, 265
"if it were someone else's dream 81, 268
"it is as though" 145, 265-266
key statement 70, 249, 257, 293
life situation 7, 186, 229, 249, 260, 279
listening prayer 130, 268
meditational prayer 63, 268, 270
objective or subjective 260, 295-296
prayer 22, 28, 130, 140-141, 144, 153, 260, 268
plot development 174
problem solved? 258, 294-295
puns 170, 195, 207, 224, 2363
question asked by God (Q) 46, 251
read aloud 63, 265
recall/remember 138, 140, 244, 245-246
record/log dream 4, 10, 134-135, 246-248
re-enter dream 240, 268
role play the symbol 272
setting/scenery 174, 218, 247, 256, 289
Your Life Situation 5, 7, 229, 260, 279
your reaction (R) 248, 251
your response 56, 63, 108, 143
share your dream 46, 140, 265
structure of dream 174
summarize 158, 255, 259-260, 292
TTAQ technique 47, 249-251
theme (T) 22, 250, 257, 264, 291
title (T) 10, 249-250
thank God 108, 144, 245, 253
turn and face it 110
"what area of my life" 46, 120, 186, 187, 221, 228, 256, 257, 265, 279, 295
"what is God trying to say" 22, 260, 296
"what part of me is that" (Gestalt) 269
words, spoken/unspoken 70, 257, 293-294
write a story 269

subjective dreams 161, 217-219, 220, 260
summarize 158, 255, 259-260, 292
sun 196
sunflower 196
supernatural phenomenon 26, 29, 38-40, 68, 69, 83-84, 97, 100, 152, 283
Survey of Attitudes & Beliefs about Dreams Appendix A, 277
symbolic action 143; awareness 66; experience 200; imagery 106, 196; thinking 170, 193-194
symbolic dreams 6, 11, 235
symbolic language xv, 6, 19, 105-106, 165, 170, 189-191, 194-200
symbolic techniques 235, 269-273
   draw-an-image 4, 271
   dream dialogue 272-274
   personal association 203, 235, 259, 271, 289-295
   personify object/place 28, 208, 273
   ponder/meditate 137-138, 270
   rate intensity of symbol 240, 270
   role play the symbol 271

symbolism 191-192; basis of 191; cardinal rules of 194
symbols 30, 95, 103, 105, 191-192, 199, 200; sources of 171-173, 232
Synesius of Cyrene 67, 177

T

Talmud 53, 57, 108, 263
telepathic dreams 182
telephone 154, 182
temple 196
Tertullian xiii, 66, 67, 99, 149
thanking God 108, 143, 144, 245, 253
theme (T) 22, 250, 257, 264, 291; typical 169
theory (Christian) of dreams 99, 109, 149
therapeutic function 30, 118-119, 123-124, 128 (see counseling, healing)
therapist 135, 163, 186
thoughts/intentions of heart dreams 78, 85, 88, 104, 119, 127, 128
Tillich, Paul 198, 200
tips 4, 5, 10, 11, 22, 56, 63, 79, 118, 120, 121, 127, 134, 13, 141, 142, 143, 148, 150, 155, 169, 174, 178, 180, 181, 182, 186, 194, 208, 210, 211, 212, 214, 221, 223, 231, 233, 236, 237, 239, 245, 247, 256, 258, 259, 261, 271
title (T) 10, 249-250
To Gerald's Sunday School Class 91-93
transformational symbols 172, 181 (see archetypal images)
trauma dreams 30, 118-119, 130, 169, 172, 177, 180, 184, 186 (see nightmares)
treasure, hidden 3, 31-33, 34, 105, 134
tree 18, 55, 180-181, 190, 195, 206, 208; branch 196
truck, flatbed, trailer 230
tsunami 79
TTAQ technique 47, 249-251
turn and face it 110
Tucson 207

U

Ullman, Montague 169, 265

umbilical cord 221

umbrella 168

unbelievers & dreams 44, 53, 110

unconscious 30, 31, 32, 67, 85-86, 104-105, 107, 122, 128, 151, 166, 167, 172-173, 182, 191-196, 201, 229, 235, 236, 271, 287 (see hidden man of the heart, spiritual layer)

(the) unseen place 6, 31-32, 33, 84, 104, 134, 185, 193

unicorn 237

universal symbols 172, 173

V

Vatican 45, 79

vehicle 187, 237, 247, 256, 292; flatbed, trailer 230

Virkler, Mark & Patti 62, 138, 165, 170, 199, 220

vision/s 8, 14-17, 19, 25-27, 37, 39, 41, 43, 52-62; 66-68; 73-77, 89, 100-101, 106, 283; auditory vision 5, 59, 60, 108

visual word of God 17, 195

voice of God hearing 14-21; direct & indirect 19, 115, 183

W

Wake Up, Wake Up 44

warning dreams 58, 59, 121, 182

Washington, George 77

water 32-33, 41, 85, 93, 104, 122, 172, 173, 190, 196, 206-207, 257, 289

wedding/marriage, bride 191, 234, 237

Wesley, John 75

"what area of my life" 46, 120, 186, 187, 221, 228, 256, 257, 265, 279, 295

"what is God trying to say" 22

"what part of me is that" (Gestalt) 269

whiteboard 261

wholeness xiii, xiv, 18, 30, 100, 103, 104, 172, 183, 185, 200, 210, 213, 215, 219, 281

Willow Creek Church 43

wind 190

window 4, 190, 232

wine 190, 198

wolf 196

woman, known/ unknown 41, 75, 127, 142, 210, 212, 216, 221, 234, 252, 275

Word of God 101; living word 8, 101 (see visual word of God)

words, spoken/unspoken 70, 257, 293-294

worldview, rationalistic 29, 39, 84, 100, 137; Christian 53, 83-85, 87-88; sources of knowledge 84, 200

write a story 269

writing dreams down 4, 60, 134-135, 170, 246-248, 251

X

Y

Your Life Situation 5, 7, 229, 260, 279

your reaction (R) 248, 251

your response 56, 63, 108, 143

Z

Zeiders, Charles 7

About The Authors

Seasoned spiritual adventurers, Gerald & Judith Doctor have wandered a long trail from their childhood evangelical heritage to their own transformative encounters with a personal God. On this journey they discovered that God still speaks through dreams in the night to ordinary people who have learned how to listen to the language of heaven. Between them they enjoy more than 60 years of benefiting from God's guidance, instruction and divine counsel in their dreams.

Christian author, teacher, and counselor, Judith A. Doctor, MSW, RN, received a Master of Social Work degree from Grand Valley State University (2005) and a Bachelor of Science degree in Community Development from Central Michigan University (1994). As a counselor and spiritual life mentor, Judith recognizes the value of dreams in helping people resolve life's conflicts, develop a closer relationship with God, and find meaning and purpose in life.

Gerald R. Doctor earned a MSEE degree from Purdue University (1966) and a BSEE degree from Michigan Technological University (1963). His career spans engineering, technical marketing, freelance writing, and ministry. Through the struggles of his mid-life depression and unsatisfactory career, Gerald experienced the love of Father God and learned to be led by the Holy Spirit. Having successfully navigated the long passage from head to heart, he knows the value of dreams to assist the journey.

Cofounders of Kairos Ministries, Inc., the Doctors minister both in the USA and Europe, nurturing spiritual growth, wholeness, and inner transformation through the Holy Spirit. They facilitate redemptive and restorative experiences for people who participate in their retreats, seminars and workshops. On her monthly program transmitted live from Radio Horeb in Germany, Judith shares out of her lived experiences with a loving God who brought her resurrection life in the illness and death of a son, battle-worn marriage, and troubled soul.

Since 1978, Gerald & Judith have been part of The New Life, Inc., a widespread community of both Catholics and Protestants. Married since 1959, they have two sons and daughters-in-law and four grandchildren. They currently reside in West Michigan.

Dream Resources

Dream seminars

Embedded in the message of Christianity is the belief that we can have direct, ongoing experiences with the living God. Led by His Spirit within us, we can be aware of what God is saying to us and understand His purpose for our lives. Believing that dreams offer a valuable resource for our spiritual journey, Gerald & Judith Doctor offer interactive seminars and workshops on understanding dreams.

Based on a biblical framework and established spiritual principles, valuable techniques are provided to help people find God's counsel and wisdom in dreams. A key goal is to help God's people become spiritually alive, find greater freedom and fulfillment, and discover their destiny in God.

To schedule a dream seminar for your church or group, contact Gerald & Judith Doctor:

dreams@kairosministries.us

For information on Kairos Ministries, Inc. and the ministry of Gerald & Judith Doctor, please visit the web site:

www.kairosministries.us

More information on dreams

Please visit www.dreamtreasure.us for additional resources on how to work with dreams from a Christian perspective.

How to order more copies of this book

Please visit www.dreamtreasure.us to order additional copies of *Dream Treasure*.

Made in the USA
Lexington, KY
15 October 2012